EIGHTEENTH-
CENTURY
PHILOSOPHY

READINGS IN THE HISTORY OF PHILOSOPHY

SERIES EDITORS:

PAUL EDWARDS, Brooklyn College

RICHARD H. POPKIN, University of California, San Diego

The Volumes and Their Editors:

GREEK PHILOSOPHY: THALES TO ARISTOTLE
Reginald E. Allen, Indiana University

GREEK AND ROMAN PHILOSOPHY AFTER ARISTOTLE
Jason L. Saunders, University of California, San Diego

MEDIEVAL PHILOSOPHY:
ST. AUGUSTINE TO OCKHAM
Father Allan B. Wolter, Catholic University of America

THE PHILOSOPHY OF THE SIXTEENTH AND
SEVENTEENTH CENTURIES
Richard H. Popkin, University of California, San Diego

EIGHTEENTH-CENTURY PHILOSOPHY
Lewis White Beck, The University of Rochester

NINETEENTH-CENTURY PHILOSOPHY:
HEGEL TO NIETZSCHE

TWENTIETH-CENTURY PHILOSOPHY:
THE SPECULATIVE TRADITION
Peter Koestenbaum, San Jose State College

TWENTIETH-CENTURY PHILOSOPHY:
THE ANALYTIC TRADITION
Morris Weitz, The Ohio State University

EIGHTEENTH-CENTURY PHILOSOPHY

Edited and with an Introduction by

Lewis White Beck

The Free Press, New York
Collier-Macmillan Limited, London

PHILOSOPHERS DEPICTED ON THE COVER ARE,
READING CLOCKWISE, HUME, LOCKE, KANT, VOLTAIRE.

Collier-Macmillan Canada, Ltd., Toronto, Ontario

Library of Congress Catalog Card Number: 66-10364

Second printing November 1967

CONTENTS

INTRODUCTION

THE PHILOSOPHY of the eighteenth century cannot be precisely defined as the philosophy written from 1700 to 1799. Or perhaps it would be better to say that such a definition suffers from a specious precision, for the life of the mind is not segmented and to be measured by the calendar. "Philosophy of the eighteenth century" names a state of mind, the state of mind best represented by the great thinkers who belonged, chronologically, to the century, who had much in common, and who differed clearly from thinkers who would be unequivocally assigned to the seventeenth or nineteenth centuries. So defined, eighteenth-century philosophy includes some books written toward the end of the 1600s; and in the 1700s we find out-of-date minds acting as if they were living in the century before, as well as others who are harbingers of the century to follow.

It is always so in the history of ideas. The eighteenth century, unique in so many wonderful ways, is not unique in having vague boundaries. But if, after all, one still wants some dates to mark the opening and closing of the career of the eighteenth-century mind, I may suggest two pairs, which are suggestively close together: 1688 to 1793—from the Glorious Revolution to the Reign of Terror; and 1687 to 1790—from Newton's *Principia* to the last of Kant's *Critiques*.

If the beginnings and ends are chronologically arbitrary—and I shall try to show that they are less arbitrary than they may at first seem—the middle is clear, definite, and indisputable. The state of mind I have referred to can be characterized in the way the people then characterized it: it was Enlightenment, *éclaircissement*, *Aufklärung*. Or, in Kant's apothegm, it was the "age of criticism": "Our age is, in especial degree, the age of criticism, and to criticism everything must submit. Religion through its sanctity, and law-giving through its majesty, may seek to exempt themselves from it. But they awaken just suspicion, and cannot claim the sincere respect which reason

1

accords only to that which has been able to sustain the test of free and open examination."[1]

Men in no other period in history before the twentieth century made so vigorous an effort to guide themselves by natural reason to natural ends, and for this reason the eighteenth century seems to many of us closer than the nineteenth. But at no other time did they feel so much at home in a hospitable nature, and for this reason the eighteenth century seems to many of us post-Darwinians almost immeasurably long ago. Never before or since has there been so enthusiastic a condemnation of enthusiasm, so passionate a denigration of passion, so insistent a demand for clarity, sobriety, utility, civility, and humanity. No other age has been so convinced that it had reached, or was about to reach, maturity, or that it had thrown off, or was about to throw off, the heavy-handed tutelage of church, tradition, and despotism.

But "of such crooked lumber as man is made of," Kant drily complained, "nothing perfectly straight can be builded." So unregenerate human nature did not tamely submit—and at the end it did not submit at all—to what the philosophers saw as the manifest destiny of their century. Kant called it an age of enlightenment, but he refused to call it an enlightened age. It was a time of spectacular debauchery. The slave trade was one of the largest industries, witchcraft still a crime. Exquisite tortures for blasphemy and *lèse majesté* were witnessed by delighted rabbles; filth was everywhere; there was hardly a year without war, and hardly a war which even hypocrisy could shroud with moral justification. If it was an age of reason, it was so in the sense that reason reigned, not in the sense that reason governed.

I mention the unseemly side of eighteenth-century life to keep us from thinking that it was in some way unusually easy then, as it is not now, to be reasonable, civil, and optimistic about human nature and institutions. True, the century saw fewer crimes against thought than earlier centuries, and our own, did; no Bruno was sent to the stake by Catholics and no Servetus by Protestants, no Campanella languished eighteen years in a dungeon, and Moses Mendelssohn died in his bed in Berlin. Still, though Berkeley was a bishop and Hume became rich on the earnings from his books, Diderot had to do much of his work in secret, Kant was forbidden to write or lecture on religion, Wolff had to leave Halle in twenty-four hours or be hanged, and Condorcet died just before the guillotine would have killed him. All honor then, to these men who proclaimed and practiced the free

---

1. *Critique of Pure Reason,* Preface to First Edition, trans. Norman Kemp Smith (London: Macmillan, 1933), 9n.

use of mind, and who through study of mind tried to perfect it for its work of guiding humanity without let or hindrance from state or church or private bigotry.

Their guiding thought was that human reason was adequate to human needs, that it was an instrument slowly developed by nature and history or given ready-made by God, perfectly fitted for the wise conduct of life. There is no paradox in the fact that there were skeptics, among them the greatest; for skepticism at that time was not concerned to point out insurmountable obstacles in the way of getting worthwhile knowledge, so much as it was concerned to show the illusoriness and worthlessness of what could not be got by reason and experience. There were few followers of Pascal, and one feels that Hamann really belonged to the next century. Skepticism was chiefly an instrument for the redirection of inquiry, not a blow to the pride of a sound mind. There was no skepticism of reason bent upon its proper work. There was nothing but confidence in reason doing its proper job; and if by reason we mean not the omnicompetent faculty of text-book rationalists but objective thought brought to bear upon the facts of experience, then never before had reason been accorded so great a responsibility and so big a task. When confidence in reason began to be lost about the time of the French Revolution, we can say that the eighteenth century, so far as philosophy was concerned, had finished its course. The romanticists condemned the reason of the eighteenth century in much the same way as the eighteenth century condemned the reason of the Schoolmen—as if "reason" meant the same in the thirteenth and in the eighteenth centuries.

If one takes this feature of intellectual self-confidence as the defining characteristic of eighteenth-century thought, one would have a strange chronology indeed. We should then have the eighteenth century as a state of mind extending as far back at least as Bacon. Now it is deeply significant that the eighteenth century did, as it were, rediscover Bacon, and typical eighteenth-century thinkers (men as different as Condillac and Kant) liberally quoted and perhaps extravagantly admired the Lord Chancellor. Diderot and d'Alembert made Bacon's classification of knowledge the pattern for their *Encyclopaedia*. Why, then, when we minimized the importance of the year 1700 in the history of the eighteenth-century mind, did we go back only to Newton and not to Bacon, who, in Lord Macauley's words, "blew the trumpet that called the wits together" to do the job that was finally assigned to the eighteenth century?

The difference between these two English giants, one at the beginning and the other at the end of the seventeenth century, is that between extravagant promise and solid performance. The confidence in reason we find in the seventeenth century seems daring when we remember how little really solid accomplishment the sixteenth had to pride itself on. Its most solid accomplishment, in the work of Copernicus, was not universally accepted; and in the next century Bacon's promise of a New Atlantis if men of reason would work together was only a promise. The Royal Society did solid work, but was laughed at; the most imposing accomplishments of Descartes and Spinoza were in metaphysics which baked no bread; the work of Hobbes was an attempt to hold up a political system which could not have been sustained no matter how much blood and brains had been devoted to it. But Newton—Newton, with a minimum of metaphysics and at least the appearance of humility—showed what the human mind could do, and in the best way possible: by doing it. Pope's words: "God said, 'Let Newton be,' and all was light," do not exaggerate the pride and self-confidence of the age in which Newtonian mathematics, mechanics, and optics triumphed over every rival in the academies and appeared in popular books for salon talk and milady's boudoir.[2]

What Newton accomplished was this: he took Kepler's laws of planetary motion and Galileo's laws of terrestrial motion and showed them to be special cases of a law which he called the law of *universal* gravitation. No longer was there a gap or hiatus in nature, between the earth and the cosmos. By showing that the same law described the motion of the moon and planets and the fall of the apple and the rising of the tides, nature became uniform, unified, and, it seemed, transparent in fact and not merely in hope and promise, as it had been for Galileo, Descartes, Kepler, Spinoza, and Hobbes. If it was not quite time yet to claim omnipotence—Bacon had said that knowledge is power—it was no longer madness to feel close to omniscience in everything that mattered.

Nobody, of course, claimed that we could know literally everything; the eighteenth century despised enthusiasm, and even the great Newton himself, in saying that he made no hypothesis to explain why nature behaved as she did, recognized that his methods did not apply to everything men might want to know. But humility was not one of the intellectual virtues of the century, either. What could not be handled by Newton's methods either ceased to be a matter of prime

---

2. Goldsmith, writing of French ladies in 1759, said: "The sprightly pedants are not to be caught by dumb show, by the squeeze of the hand, or the ogling of a broad eye; but must be pursued at once through all the labyrinths of the Newtonian system, or the metaphysics of Locke." (Quoted from Kenneth MacLean, *John Locke and English Literature of the Eighteenth Century* (New Haven: Yale University Press, 1936), 4.

concern to thinkers, or began to seem merely a refuge of superstition and ignorance, or—more positively—it was claimed that it could indeed be handled by his methods. Spinoza's professed purpose to deal with human actions as if they were lines, planes, and figures, was close to realization. Locke expressed himself content to be "employed as an under-labourer" in the work of "the incomparable Mr. Newton," and Hume subtitled his first work "An Attempt to Introduce the Experimental Method of Reasoning into Moral Subjects." Some used Newton to elaborate the law of nature as a moral law, while others used him in their efforts to deflate talk about the morality of nature. Some used him to prove the existence of God by a more detailed and persuasive argument from design, while others used him to prepare the way for La Place's reply to Napoleon: "Sire, we have no need for that hypothesis." "Nature" became a catchword of eighteenth-century thought in morals, politics, poetry, and religion, and almost everywhere (except in Germany) it was Newton's nature they were talking about.

With Newton's success in establishing, and not just in conjecturing, the uniformity and simplicity of the cosmos, it is no wonder that anyone challenging the competence of reason to answer important questions had an intolerable burden of proof on his shoulders, and that few, like Rousseau and Burke and Hamann, were willing to assume this burden. I do not wish to suggest that Newton's name was on everyone's lips, like Einstein's and Freud's in the present century; though it was on the lips of many, including many who understood him as little as many now understand Einstein. But I do say that the eighteenth century as a state of mind began in any country when the leaven of Newton was brought to it; for, depending upon the local ingredients with which it was mixed, it produced those characteristic doctrines of empiricism, deism, materialism, atheism, skepticism, utilitarianism, naturalism, and Kantian criticism which constitute the main body of thought of the century.

For the first time in our history since the decline of Aristotelianism, there was substantially unanimous agreement about the main features of the structure of the physical universe, features which had been ineffectually disputed about by philosophers who thought they were scientists. With this solid base, provided by science and accepted with little question, philosophy then became what we know it to be today: extrapolation from observed nature to the whole of reality, or adjudication of the claims for these new extrapolations and the claims of perennial human concerns in morals and politics and religion, or examination of the method of science and the warrants for these extrapolations. Science and philosophy became clearly differentiated; but more than ever before they became joined in fruitful union instead of being confused with each other and condemned to sterile opposition.

I must call attention to the fact—I believe it is a fact—that I am not exaggerating Newton's influence; I am not claiming him to be the sole initiator of the new way of looking at things. I might seem to do so, however, if I failed to explore the reasons I had. for suggesting another putative date for the beginning of our period. I referred to the Glorious Revolution, which was (of course quite fortuitously) almost simultaneous with Newton's greatest work. Intrinsically they had nothing in common and nothing to do with each other. One dealt with nature, the other with men. But the eighteenth century was at once both naturalistic and humanistic; Nature and Humanity were its most catholic symbols.

The Revolution, of which John Locke was the philosophical spokesman, prepared the stage in England for a peaceful development of the arts and sciences by ending the most baleful features of political absolutism and religious intolerance (or, perhaps more accurately, the fear of intolerance). Responsible self-government in the social and political spheres did not become a reality all at once, but it did cease to be a Utopian dream; it was something that could be worked for and written about openly, even enjoyed from time to time; and men could become Lockean men—safely propertied citizens of their own country and not mere subjects of arbitrary power that would not leave even their conscience and faith or lack of faith alone. Earlier, a line had been drawn between the things of reason and the things of faith, while the line between the things of faith and the things of power remained vague and wavering and subject to whim and accident. Now sharper lines were drawn between the things of faith and the things within the scope of political power, while the dividing line between reason and faith was progressively pushed farther and farther into the refuge of faith. Locke was the leader in both these shifts: his *Essay* narrowly confined revelation, and his *Letters on Toleration* narrowly confined the powers of government.

To cosmology were added, then, two more realms of perennial concern to philosophers, where free philosophizing could be carried on in comparative safety: man's relation to his fellows and his masters, and his relation to God. Thus not all the self-confidence of eighteenth-century thought came from Newton: much of it came from the English experiment of peaceful change of a government which threatened the religion and liberty of the people. While the fate of James II was monitory to the crowned heads of Europe, the Declaration of Rights was heartening to every thinker who wanted to live and think in freedom.

The history of philosophy in the eighteenth century, then, was largely the history of the expansion of the Newtonian universe to comprehend what Newton had omitted; of the Newtonian methods of analysis, synthesis, measurement, and experiment to all things under —and above—the sun; of Locke's ideas of the English revolution in matters of the rights of man, self-government, and toleration; and the history of the reactions of moral, religious, and political thinkers to these almost inevitable expansions.

It is natural that the eighteenth century should have been the century of great epistemologies, since the expansion of science required acute self-examination and inquiry into the methods, scope, and structure of knowledge; while the defenses against this expansion, in the name of piety and some conceptions of humanity, required even more fundamental examination of those who claimed to know that the world and man are Newtonian machines.

The selections from the great philosophers of the eighteenth century which make up the body of this book present manifold expansions of and responses to the Newtonian and Lockean theories of man and the world, and counter-responses to these responses, counter-responses which seem, if we do not trace the course of the debate, to have little to do with Newton's work and England's choice of a king. While much of Newton is now obsolete and few philosophers care much or think about the election of William and Mary, important philosophical thinking never remains restricted to the particular historical situation which occasions it. Philosophy has a life of its own, or at least great philosophy has. In selecting material for this book, I have tried, therefore, to keep before the reader two things: we are studying eighteenth-century thought, but also, we are studying thought on a level of abstractness and depth where dates and places are of only peripheral interest.

Because of the number and industry of philosophers still worthy of philosophical study today—a full list would have to include Shaftesbury, Clarke, Hutcheson, Price, Butler, Adam Smith, Burke, Lambert, Euler, Herder, Crusius, Hamann, Vico, d'Alembert, La Mettrie, Montesquieu, Helvetius, Thomasius, Edwards, Jefferson in addition to those we have chosen—we have had to be very selective both of men and their works. We have given most space to the problems of epistemology (how do we know?, how much can we know?) and metaphysics (what is there to know?) because it is these which were fundamental to their writings on other subjects. Their discussions of these problems are today the most important and instructive parts of their works. To read many of their works on other fields of philosophy requires an interest in the eighteenth century itself; but just an interest in epistemology and metaphysics, even in their present-day forms, is sufficient motive for reading what they wrote on knowledge and reality. We have, in addition, preserved a good bit of the religious debates which took place in their epistemological and metaphysical forums. We have had, regrettably, to omit writings of the kind that are favorites of historians of ideas who are less concerned with the permanent contributions of that century to philosophy;[3] the eighteenth century without *The Spectator* and *Candide,* Boswell and Lord Chesterfield, Frederick the Great and "the notorious Dr. Bahrdt," *Sturm und Drang* and the *ancien régime,* the Lisbon Earthquake, John Wesley, and Fanny Hill would not be the eighteenth century as we know it; but without Hume's analysis of causation, Berkeley's examination of abstract ideas, and Kant's treatment of space and time (to mention examples we *have* chosen), the *twentieth* century would not be what *it* is.

We shall proceed as follows. First we shall give selections from Newton's work to show his method, his cosmological presuppositions, and his metaphysical conjectures. Then we shall take in succession the three great British philosophers Locke, Berkeley, and Hume as classical representatives of empiricism and its development in realism, idealism, naturalism, and skepticism. We shall trace the gradual development of the problems of knowledge and metaphysics and theology from one theory (Locke's) which was perfectly fitted to Newton's world to another (Hume's) which was still Newtonian in spirit and inspiration but incompatible with it in most details and in outcome. Finally, we shall watch Thomas Reid attack these philosophers who, he thought, were bottled up in a *cul-de-sac,* and call them to come out into the common-sense world—a common-sense world that had, by this time, become pretty thoroughly Newtonian.

We shall turn next to France. Newton and Locke were made popular there by Voltaire's *Philosophical Letters,* and the French responded in manifold ways to the English triumph (as it seemed to them) of reason, experience, and liberty in science, religion, and polity. Had not the French been gifted with style, wit, and courage as well as industry, they would long since have been as forgotten as most of their German contemporaries who lacked the first three of these virtues and attempted to make up for their lack by the fourth. We may as well admit it: the Enlightenment in France was the work of highly gifted and courageous

---

3. There is a good collection of these in Crane Brinton's *The Age of Reason Reader* (New York: Viking Press, 1956).

writers who, with the exception of Rousseau, had no profound or original philosophical ideas. Had there been such names as "sociologist," "anthropologist" (in the modern sense), and "intellectual" these would have been the names they might have chosen for themselves. *Les philosophes*—the name under which they are known to history—is not quite correctly translated as "philosophers." The great French dictionary of philosophy defines *philosophes* in this way: "the group of writers who were partisans of reason, light, and tolerance, and more or less hostile to the existing religious institutions."[4] To see why the French had *philosophes* instead of philosophers in the English or German (and modern) sense, we should briefly compare the intellectual and social situation in France with that in England and Germany about 1750.

England had had her revolution; Germany was not to have hers for another century; France was moving towards hers. Germany had had her religious awakening in Pietism, and a Pietistic patina spread over almost all of German culture; England was beginning to have (in Methodism) a popular, emotional, and anti-intellectualist religious awakening; France had had hers, in Jansenism, but it was now a thing of the past. Put these two facts about each country together, and one can go far towards understanding the characteristics of the intellectual life of each country. In France, religious and political dissent was practiced and persecuted; in England, practiced but not persecuted; in Germany, not practiced and therefore not persecuted (except in rare instances).

The effect of these parameters in France was that philosophy was more social and religious criticism bent upon changing things than epistemological and metaphysical criticism bent upon understanding them. Hence the *philosophes* tended more to the ideological than to the philosophical; more to the belletristic than to the technical; more to epigram than to proof; more to appropriating and disseminating English ideas than to weighing them carefully; more to making fun of Leibniz than to understanding and correcting his ingenious system. The *philosophes* used whatever ideas they found at hand as weapons against church and state and each other; their ideas came from Gassendi, Bayle, Bacon, Hobbes, Leibniz, Locke, Hume, Newton, Shaftesbury, Bolingbroke, and even—*mirabile dictu!*—from the Latin works of Wolff. Yet all these ideas were given a new dimension that they had not had except in Bacon and Bayle: they were made militant. And they initiated a revolution in the French mind that was to lead to *the* Revolution.

---

4. *Vocabulaire technique et critique de la philosophie*, ed. A. Lalande (Paris: Presses Universitaires de France, 1960), 773.

The French writers chosen, therefore, have been chosen more because they are representative of *philosophie engagée* than because their works present original philosophical arguments with which a twentieth-century thinker has to come to terms as he does with, say, those of Berkeley or Kant. They represent the manifold and vigorous but essentially derivative intellectual life of France at that time. I have chosen d'Holbach for his atheism, Voltaire for his deism, Diderot for his materialism (and high spirits), and Condillac (the only epistemologist in our group) for his empiricism. Different selections from most of these men could have been made which would have permitted us to see each of them as a vehicle of some of the other ideas. Rousseau, however, stands alone: the foremost opponent of the leading ideas of his century, the enemy of its optimism, intellectualism, and enthusiasm for a specious progress.

Lastly we come to Germany. The Newtonian system was not accepted so early in Germany, and Germans lived with a modicum of satisfaction under social, political, economic, and intellectual conditions that would have been found intolerable in England (where far more benign conditions had in fact been found intolerable and had been changed). Many of the characteristics which the *philosophes* condemned in the Middle Ages, their *bête noir*, were to be seen in their own day, just across the Rhine. During the seventeenth century, when England and France were laying the philosophical, political, and scientific foundations of the modern world, Germany was being exhausted by the Thirty Years' War; philosophy in Germany meant scholasticism, occultism, mysticism, and heresy-hunting. Political thought was devoted to courtly intrigue in two hundred ridiculous principalities, or to natural law theory (borrowed from Holland) that was safe because it indicted little positive law and made little or no effort to criticize the boorish political life.

Towards the end of the seventeenth century, however, Germany at last produced a thinker of European stature. Leibniz, one of the greatest thinkers of his or any age, presented an alternative to Newton, Locke, and sterile Protestant scholasticism that had kept dangerous Cartesian thoughts out of the universities since the end of the Great War. But Leibniz was, in his lifetime, a prophet without honor in his own country. His peers were all in Holland, England, and France; and when his turn came to be accepted in his homeland, it was his fate to be presented to his fellow Germans by a systematic pedant. Leibniz supplied the matter and Wolff the form for the philosophy which was to reign in Germany for nearly fifty years. The Liebniz-Wolffian philosophy it was called then; but we might better call it, in spite of the oxymorons, scholastic rationalism, or enlightened scholasticism, or even pious enlightenment.[5] Our selections from Wolff well illustrate how anachronistic philosophy written in the eighteenth century seems when the English and French influence is studiedly resisted. (To give Wolff the justice due him, one has only to read other German philosophers of that time and see that he did move into the new century farther than his contemporaries; but these other philosophers have not been, and presumably never will be, translated into English.)

The German Enlightenment up to the middle of the century was a mixture of German pietism, French classicism, and Leibniz-Wolffian scholasticism. But all this was changed when Frederick the Great peopled the Berlin Academy (founded by Leibniz, but allowed to decay) with French freethinkers who preached, in a safety they did not enjoy in France, Lockean and Newtonian ideas, and who almost out-Englished the English in point of ostentatious toleration. The pedantry of Wolffianism disappeared from Berlin (though it continued in the universities), and Berlin for a while became "the Paris on the Spree"—stodgy, safe, not so amusing as Paris on the Seine and perhaps a shade too pious and certainly too deferential to the King who helped arrange its programs and read its minutes. But at last scholasticism was dead. Kant called his century "the century of Frederick," and its motto was *Sapere aude!*, Dare to know.[6]

Our examples of this stage of the German Enlightenment are Lessing and Kant. Lessing dealt historically with the problem of revelation in a time enthusiastic for reason and evidence. Kant, "the Prussian Hume," was the most thorough inquisitor of Newton's cosmology, Locke's empiricism, Berkeley's idealism, Hume's skepticism, Reid's common sense, Leibniz's rationalism, and the Frenchmen's eudaemonism, deism, atheism, materialism, and libertinism. Kant was the definer[7] of the Enlightenment and its spokesman who, it seemed to many, wrote its epitaph. Both Kant's disciples and opponents—men like Fichte, Goethe, Schelling, Hegel, Hamann, Jacobi, Schiller, even the old Herder —belong to the following century.

5. Some German historians of philosophy (e.g., J. E. Erdmann, *History of Philosophy* (New York: Macmillan, 1890, Vol. II) do not even date the beginning of the German Enlightenment until Wolff's influence waned.

6. *What is Enlightenment?* (1784), trans. L. W. Beck (New York: Library of Liberal Arts, 1959). These words, taken from Horace, were on the medallions of the Society of the Friends of Truth, a Wolffian society related to the Freemasons.

7. "Enlightenment is man's release from his self-incurred tutelage. Tutelage is man's inability to make use of his understanding without direction from another." *Ibid.*, first paragraph.

NEWTON

Sir Isaac Newton was born in 1642, the year of Galileo's death, and died in 1727. Most of his life was spent as a fellow of Trinity College, Cambridge, and in London, where he became Master of the Mint. Besides the work from which we have drawn our selections, his most important book was the *Opticks*, but he also wrote biblical studies. By 1666 he had invented the calculus, but, in keeping with the practices of the time, did not publish his invention. However he used it in his work on astronomy published, in Euclidean dress, in 1687 as *Philosophiae Naturalis Principia Mathematica*, commonly known as the *Principia*. It has often been said by qualified students in a judgment I would not wish to challenge, that the *Principia* is the most stupendous work ever accomplished by a scientific thinker.

We have made three selections from the nonmathematical parts of this masterpiece: (A) The Rules for Reasoning in Philosophy, which is the introduction to Book iii; (B) The Scholium to the Definitions, from Book i; (C) The General Scholium to the whole book.

In the first, Newton prescribes rules for the investigation of nature, rules that were regarded as canonical in the eighteenth century. In the second, he gives his account of absolute and relative space and time, which were matters of dispute throughout the eighteenth and nineteenth centuries and still are, sometimes, in our own day. Selections from Leibniz and Kant, later in this book, deal also with these issues. In the last, Newton describes the outcome of his work and delineates what we may call "the Newtonian world-view," relating it to theological and metaphysical questions while formulating his famous "I frame no hypotheses" and defining his conception of "mechanical philosophy."

All the selections are from the translation by Andrew Motte and are taken from the edition published by D. Adee in New York, 1846.

The Principia

A. Rules of Reasoning in Philosophy

RULE I

We are to admit no more causes of natural things than such as are both true and sufficient to explain their appearances.

To this purpose the philosophers say that Nature does nothing in vain, and more is in vain when less will serve; for Nature is pleased with simplicity, and affects not the pomp of superfluous causes.

RULE II

Therefore to the same natural effects we must, as far as possible, assign the same causes.

As to respiration in a man and in a beast; the descent of stones in *Europe* and in *America;* the light of our culinary fire and of the sun; the reflection of light in the earth, and in the planets.

RULE III

The qualities of bodies, which admit neither intension nor remission of degrees, and which are found to belong to all bodies within the reach of our experiments, are to be esteemed the universal qualities of all bodies whatsoever.

For since the qualities of bodies are only known to us by experiments, we are to hold for universal all such as universally agree with experiments; and such as are not liable to diminution can never be quite taken away. We are certainly not to relinquish the evidence of experiments for the sake of dreams and vain fictions of our own devising; nor are we to recede from the analogy of Nature, which uses to be simple, and always consonant to itself. We no other way know the extension of bodies than by our senses, nor do these reach it in all bodies; but because we perceive extension in all that are sensible,

13

therefore we ascribe it universally to all others also. That abundance of
bodies are hard, we learn by experience; and because the hardness of
the whole arises from the hardness of the parts, we therefore justly
infer the hardness of the undivided particles not only of the bodies we
feel but of all others. That all bodies are impenetrable, we gather not
from reason, but from sensation. The bodies which we handle we find
impenetrable, and thence conclude impenetrability to be an universal
property of all bodies whatsoever. That all bodies are moveable, and
endowed with certain powers (which we call the *vires inertiæ*) of
persevering in their motion, or in their rest, we only infer from the
like properties observed in the bodies which we have seen. The extension, hardness, impenetrability, mobility, and *vis inertiæ* of the whole,
result from the extension, hardness, impenetrability, mobility, and *vires
inertiæ* of the parts; and thence we conclude the least particles of all
bodies to be also all extended, and hard and impenetrable, and moveable, and endowed with their proper *vires inertiæ*. And this is the foundation of all philosophy. Moreover, that the divided but contiguous
particles of bodies may be separated from one another, is matter of
observation; and, in the particles that remain undivided, our minds are
able to distinguish yet lesser parts, as is mathematically demonstrated.
But whether the parts so distinguished, and not yet divided, may, by
the powers of Nature, be actually divided and separated from one
another, we cannot certainly determine. Yet, had we the proof of but
one experiment that any undivided particle, in breaking a hard and
solid body suffered a division, we might by virtue of this rule conclude
that the undivided as well as the divided particles may be divided and
actually separated to infinity.

Lastly, if it universally appears, by experiments and astronomical
observations, that all bodies about the earth gravitate towards the earth,
and that in proportion to the quantity of matter which they severally
contain: that the moon likewise, according to the quantity of its matter,
gravitates towards the earth; that, on the other hand, our sea gravitates
towards the moon; and all the planets mutually one towards another;
and the comets in like manner towards the sun; we must, in consequence of this rule, universally allow that all bodies whatsoever are
endowed with a principle of mutual gravitation. For the argument from
the appearances concludes with more force for the universal gravitation
of all bodies than for their impenetrability; of which, among those in
the celestial regions, we have no experiments, nor any manner of
observation. Not that I affirm gravity to be essential to bodies: by
their *vis insita* I mean nothing but their *vis inertiæ*. This is immutable.
Their gravity is diminished as they recede from the earth.

RULE IV

In experimental philosophy we are to look upon propositions collected by general induction from phænomena as accurately or very nearly true, notwithstanding any contrary hypotheses that may be imagined, till such time as other phænomena occur, by which they may either be made more accurate, or liable to exceptions.

This rule we must follow, that the argument of induction may not be evaded by hypotheses.

B. Scholium [to the Definitions]

Hitherto I have laid down the definitions of such words as are less known, and explained the sense in which I would have them to be understood in the following discourse. I do not define time, space, place and motion, as being well known to all. Only I must observe, that the vulgar conceive those quantities under no other notions but from the relation they bear to sensible objects. And thence arise certain prejudices, for the removing of which, it will be convenient to distinguish them into absolute and relative, true and apparent, mathematical and common.

I. Absolute, true, and mathematical time, of itself, and from its own nature flows equably without regard to anything external, and by another name is called duration: relative, apparent, and common time, is some sensible and external (whether accurate or unequable) measure of duration by the means of motion, which is commonly used instead of true time; such as an hour, a day, a month, a year.

II. Absolute space, in its own nature, without regard to anything external, remains always similar and immovable. Relative space is some movable dimension or measure of the absolute spaces; which our senses determine by its position to bodies; and which is vulgarly taken for immovable space; such is the dimension of a subterraneous, an aereal, or celestial space, determined by its position in respect of the earth. Absolute and relative space, are the same in figure and magnitude; but they do not remain always numerically the same. For if the earth, for instance, moves, a space of our air, which relatively and in respect of the earth remains always the same, will at one time be one part of the absolute space into which the air passes; at another time it will be another part of the same, and so absolutely understood, it will be perpetually mutable.

III. Place is a part of space which a body takes up, and is according to the space, either absolute or relative. I say, a part of space; not the situation, nor the external surface of the body. For the places of equal solids are always equal; but their superfices, by reason of their dissimilar figures, are often unequal. Positions properly have no quantity, nor are they so much the places themselves, as the properties of places. The motion of the whole is the same thing with the sum of the motions of the parts; that is, the translation of the whole, out of its place, is the same thing with the sum of the translations of the parts out of their places; and therefore the place of the whole is the same thing with the sum of the places of the parts, and for that reason, it is internal, and in the whole body.

IV. Absolute motion is the translation of a body from one absolute place into another; and relative motion, the translation from one relative place into another. Thus in a ship under sail, the relative place of a body is that part of the ship which the body possesses; or that part of its cavity which the body fills, and which therefore moves together with the ship: the relative rest is the continuance of the body in the same part of the ship, or of its cavity. But real, absolute rest, is the continuance of the body in the same part of that immovable space, in which the ship itself, its cavity, and all that it contains, is moved. Wherefore, if the earth is really at rest, the body, which relatively rests in the ship, will really and absolutely move with the same velocity which the ship has on the earth. But if the earth also moves, the true and absolute motion of the body will arise, partly from the true motion of the earth, in immovable space; partly from the relative motion of the ship on the earth; and if the body moves also relatively in the ship; its true motion will arise, partly from the true motion of the earth, in immovable space, and partly from the relative motions as well of the ship on the earth, as of the body in the ship; and from these relative motions will arise the relative motion of the body on the earth. As if that part of the earth, where the ship is, was truly moved toward the east, with a velocity of 10010 parts; while the ship itself, with a fresh gale, and full sails, is carried towards the west, with a velocity expressed by 10 of those parts; but a sailor walks in the ship towards the east, with 1 part of the said velocity; then the sailor will be moved truly in immovable space towards the east, with a velocity of 10001 parts, and relatively on the earth towards the west, with a velocity of 9 of those parts.

Absolute time, in astronomy, is distinguished from relative by the equation or correction of the vulgar time. For the natural days are truly unequal, though they are commonly considered as equal, and used for a measure of time; astronomers correct this inequality for their more accurate deducing of the celestial motions. It may be, that there is no such thing as an equable motion, whereby time may be accurately measured. All motions may be accelerated and retarded, but the true, or equable, progress of absolute time is liable to no change. The duration or perseverance of the existence of things remains the same, whether the motions are swift or slow, or none at all: and therefore it ought to be distinguished from what are only sensible measures thereof; and out of which we collect it, by means of the astronomical equation. The necessity of which equation, for determining the times of a phaenomenon, is evinced as well from the experiments of the pendulum clock, as by eclipses of the satellites of *Jupiter*.

As the order of the parts of time is immutable, so also is the order of the parts of space. Suppose those parts to be moved out of their places, and they will be moved (if the expression may be allowed) out of themselves. For times and spaces are, as it were, the places as well of themselves as of all other things. All things are placed in time as to order of succession; and in space as to order of situation. It is from their essence or nature that they are places; and that the primary places of things should be moveable, is absurd. These are therefore the absolute places; and translations out of those places, are the only absolute motions.

But because the parts of space cannot be seen, or distinguished from one another by our senses, therefore in their stead we use sensible measures of them. For from the positions and distances of things from any body considered as immovable, we define all places; and then with respect to such places, we estimate all motions, considering bodies as transferred from some of those places into others. And so, instead of absolute places and motions, we use relative ones; and that without any inconvenience in common affairs; but in philosophical disquisitions, we ought to abstract from our senses, and consider things themselves, distinct from what are only sensible measures of them. For it may be that there is no body really at rest, to which the places and motions of others may be referred.

But we may distinguish rest and motion, absolute and relative, one from the other by their properties, causes and effects. It is a property of rest, that bodies really at rest do rest in respect to one another. And therefore as it is possible, that in the remote regions of the fixed stars, or perhaps far beyond them, there may be some body absolutely at rest; but impossible to know, from the position of bodies to one another in our regions whether any of these do keep the same position to that remote body; it follows that absolute rest cannot be determined from the position of bodies in our regions.

C. [General] Scholium

The six primary planets are revolved about the sun in circles concentric with the sun, and with motions directed towards the same parts, and almost in the same plane. Ten moons are revolved about the earth, Jupiter and Saturn, in circles concentric with them, with the same direction of motion, and nearly in the planes of the orbits of those planets; but it is not to be conceived that mere mechanical causes could give birth to so many regular motions, since the comets range over all parts of the heavens in very eccentric orbits; for by that kind of motion they pass easily through the orbs of the planets, and with great rapidity; and in their aphelions, where they move the slowest, and are detained the longest, they recede to the greatest distances from each other, and thence suffer the least disturbance from their mutual attractions. This most beautiful system of the sun, planets, and comets, could only proceed from the counsel and dominion of an intelligent and powerful Being. And if the fixed stars are the centres of other like systems, these, being formed by the like wise counsel, must be all subject to the dominion of One; especially since the light of the fixed stars is of the same nature with the light of the sun, and from every system light passes into all the other systems: and lest the systems of the fixed stars should, by their gravity, fall on each other mutually, he hath placed those systems at immense distances one from another.

This Being governs all things, not as the soul of the world, but as Lord over all; and on account of his dominion he is wont to be called Lord God παντοκράτωρ, or Universal Ruler; for God is a relative word, and has a respect to servants; and Deity is the dominion of God not over his own body, as those imagine who fancy God to be the soul of the world, but over servants. The Supreme God is a Being eternal, infinite, absolutely perfect; but a being, however perfect, without dominion, cannot be said to be Lord God; for we say, my God, your God, the God of Israel, the God of Gods, and Lord of Lords; but we do not say, my Eternal, your Eternal, the Eternal of Israel, the Eternal of Gods; we do not say, my Infinite, or my Perfect: these are titles which have no respect to servants. The word God usually signifies Lord; but every lord is not a God. It is the dominion of a spiritual being which constitutes a God: a true, supreme, or imaginary dominion makes a true, supreme, or imaginary God. And from his true dominion it follows that the true God is a living, intelligent, and powerful Being; and, from his other perfections, that he is supreme, or most perfect. He is eternal and infinite, omnipotent and omniscient; that is, his duration reaches from eternity to eternity; his presence from infinity to infinity; he governs all things, and knows all things that are or can be done. He is not eternity or infinity, but eternal and infinite; he is not duration or space, but he endures and is present. He endures for ever, and is every where present; and by existing always and every where, he constitutes duration and space. Since every particle of space is *always*, and every indivisible moment of duration is *every where*, certainly the Maker and Lord of all things cannot be *never* and *no where*. Every soul that has perception is, though in different times and in different organs of sense and motion, still the same indivisible person. There are given successive parts in duration, co-existent parts in space, but neither the one nor the other in the person of a man, or his thinking principle; and much less can they be found in the thinking substance of God. Every man, so far as he is a thing that has perception, is one and the same man during his whole life, in all and each of his organs of sense. God is the same God, always and every where. He is omnipresent not *virtually* only, but also *substantially;* for virtue cannot subsist without substance. In him are all things contained and moved; yet neither affects the other: God suffers nothing from the motion of bodies; bodies find no resistance from the omnipresence of God. It is allowed by all that the Supreme God exists necessarily; and by the same necessity he exists *always* and *every where*. Whence also he is all similar, all eye, all ear, all brain, all arm, all power to perceive, to understand, and to act; but in a manner not at all human, in a manner not at all corporeal, in a manner utterly unknown to us. As a blind man has no idea of colours, so have we no idea of the manner by which the all-wise God perceives and understands all things. He is utterly void of all body and bodily figure, and can therefore neither be seen, nor heard, nor touched; not ought he to be worshipped under the representation of any corporeal thing. We have ideas of his attributes, but what the real substance of any thing is we know not. In bodies, we see only their figures and colours, we hear only the sounds, we touch only their outward surfaces, we smell only the smells, and taste the savours; but their inward substances are not to be known either by our senses, or by any reflex act of our minds: much less, then, have we any idea of the substance of God. We know him only by his most wise and excellent contrivances of things, and final causes; we admire him for his perfections; but we reverence and adore him on account of his dominion: for we adore him as his servants; and a god without dominion, providence, and final causes, is nothing else but Fate and Nature. Blind metaphysical necessity, which is certainly the same always and every where, could produce no variety of things. All that diversity of natural things which we find suited to different times and places could arise from nothing but the ideas and will of a Being necessarily existing. But, by way of allegory, God is said to see, to speak, to laugh, to love, to hate, to desire, to give, to receive, to rejoice, to be angry, to fight, to frame, to work, to build; for all our notions of God are taken from the ways of mankind by a certain similitude which, though not perfect, has some likeness, however. And thus much concerning God; to discourse of whom from the appearances of things, does certainly belong to Natural Philosophy.

Hitherto we have explained the phaenomena of the heavens and of our sea by the power of gravity, but have not yet assigned the cause of this power. This is certain, that it must proceed from a cause that penetrates to the very centres of the sun and planets, without suffering the least diminution of its force; that operates not according to the quantity of the surfaces of the particles upon which it acts (as mechanical causes use to do), but according to the quantity of the solid matter which they contain, and propagates its virtue on all sides to immense distances, decreasing always in the duplicate proportion of the distances. Gravitation towards the sun is made up out of the gravitations towards the several particles of which the body of the sun is composed; and in receding from the sun decreases accurately in the duplicate proportion of the distances as far as the orb of Saturn, as evidently appears from the quiescence of the aphelions of the planets; nay, and even to the remotest aphelions of the comets, if those aphelions are also quiescent. But hitherto I have not been able to discover the cause of those properties of gravity from phaenomena, and I frame no hypotheses; for whatever is not deduced from the phaenomena is to be called an hypothesis; and hypotheses, whether metaphysical or physical, whether of occult qualities or mechanical, have no place in experimental philosophy. In this philosophy particular propositions are inferred from the phaenomena, and afterwards rendered general by induction. Thus it was that the impenetrability, the mobility, and the impulsive force of bodies, and the laws of motion and of gravitation, were discovered. And to us it is enough that gravity does really exist, and act according to the laws which we have explained, and abundantly serves to account for all the motions of the celestial bodies, and of our sea.

And now we might add something concerning a certain most subtle Spirit which pervades and lies hid in all gross bodies; by the force and action of which Spirit the particles of bodies mutually attract one another at near distances, and cohere, if contiguous; and electric bodies operate to greater distances, as well repelling as attracting the neighbouring corpuscles; and light is emitted, reflected, refracted, inflected, and heats bodies; and all sensation is excited, and the members of animal bodies move at the command of the will, namely, by the vibrations of this Spirit, mutually propagated along the solid filaments of the nerves, from the outward organs of sense to the brain, and from the brain into the muscles. But these are things that cannot be explained in few words, nor are we furnished with that sufficiency of experiments which is required to an accurate determination and demonstration of the laws by which this electric and elastic Spirit operates.

LOCKE

JOHN LOCKE was born in 1632 and died in 1704. He was trained as a physician, but spent most of his life in government service. His most important works were the *Essay Concerning Human Understanding* (1690), *Some Thoughts Concerning Education* (1693), *The Reasonableness of Christianity* (1695), *Two Treatises on Government* (1690), and the *Letters on Toleration* (1689, 1690, 1692, 1704).

All the selections are from the *Essay*, the foundation-work of the philosophy known as British Empiricism. The *Essay* is composed of four Books: I, Of Innate Notions; II, Of Ideas; III, Of Words; IV, Of Knowledge and Opinion. The first book is a rejection of the theory of innate ideas, and the second teaches that all ideas come from experience. This was not an entirely new doctrine, but Locke's was the first and most successful attempt to apply the "plain, historical method" to the derivation of all our ideas, and it introduced what was called the "new way of ideas," which characterized most European philosophy for a century afterwards. Book IV discusses the nature, degrees, and limits of knowledge and ends with an examination of the claims of faith and revelation. But the whole *Essay* must be understood in connection with Locke's battle against religious and political intolerance.

Later in this book there are explicit criticisms of Locke by Berkeley (p. 66), Hume (p. 97), Reid (p. 136), and Leibniz (p. 208).

Our selections are drawn from Books II and IV, with the exception of the first selection, which is part of Book I, Chapter i, and is an introduction to the whole *Essay*. I have kept Locke's chapter and section numbers and most of his titles; occasionally, however, I have put into one chapter a section on the same subject from another chapter. I have indicated this by giving three numbers before a section title instead of the usual one. Thus, for example, on page 30 the number "II, xxiii, 11" means that this is Section 11 of Chapter 23 of Book II.

Essay Concerning Human Understanding

BOOK I—Of Innate Notions

Chapter I.—INTRODUCTION

1. Since it is the *understanding* that sets man above the rest of sensible beings, and gives him all the advantage and dominion which he has over them; it is certainly a subject, even for its nobleness, worth our labour to inquire into. The understanding, like the eye, whilst it makes us see and perceive all other things, takes no notice of itself; and it requires art and pains to set it at a distance and make it its own object. But whatever be the difficulties that lie in the way of this inquiry; whatever it be that keeps us so much in the dark to ourselves; sure I am that all the light we can let in upon our minds, all the acquaintance we can make with our own understandings, will not only be very pleasant, but bring us great advantage, in directing our thoughts in the search of other things.

2. This, therefore, being my purpose—to inquire into the original, certainty, and extent of *human knowledge,* together with the grounds and degrees of *belief, opinion,* and *assent;*—I shall not at present meddle with the physical consideration of the mind; or trouble myself to examine wherein its essence consists; or by what motions of our spirits or alterations of our bodies we come to have any *sensation* by our organs, or any *ideas* in our understandings; and whether those ideas do in their formation, any or all of them, depend on matter or not. These are speculations which, however curious and entertaining, I shall decline, as lying out of my way in the design I am now upon.

6. When we know our own strength, we shall better know what to undertake with hopes of success; and when we have well surveyed the powers of our own minds, and made some estimate of what we may expect from them, we shall not be inclined either to sit still and not set our thoughts on work at all, in despair of knowing anything, nor,

on the other side, question everything and disclaim all knowledge, because some things are not to be understood. . . . Our business here is not to know all things, but those which concern our conduct. If we can find out those measures whereby a rational creature, put in that state in which man is in this world, may and ought to govern his opinions and actions depending thereupon, we need not be troubled that some other things escape our knowledge. 7. . . . Were the capacities of our understandings well considered, the extent of our knowledge once discovered, and the horizon found which sets the bounds between the enlightened and the darkened part of things, between what is and what is not comprehensible by us, men would perhaps with less scruple acquiesce in the avowed ignorance of the one, and employ their thoughts and discourse with more advantage and satisfaction in the other.

BOOK II—Of Ideas

Chapter I.—OF IDEAS IN GENERAL, AND THEIR ORIGINAL

I, i, 8. I must here in the entrance beg pardon of my reader for the frequent use of the word *idea*, which he will find in the following treatise. It being that term which, I think, serves best to stand for whatsoever is the *object* of the understanding when a man thinks, I have used it to express whatever is meant by *phantasm, notion, species,* or *whatever it is which the mind can be employed about in thinking;* and I could not avoid frequently using it.

I presume it will be easily granted me, that there are such *ideas* in men's minds: every one is conscious of them in himself; and men's words and actions will satisfy him that they are in others.

1. *Idea is the Object of Thinking.* Every man being conscious to himself that he thinks; and that which his mind is applied about whilst thinking being the *ideas* that are there, it is past doubt that men have in their minds several ideas,—such as are those expressed by the words *whiteness, hardness, sweetness, thinking, motion, man, elephant, army, drunkenness,* and others: it is in the first place then to be inquired, *How he comes by them?*

I know it is a received doctrine, that men have native ideas, and original characters, stamped upon their minds in their very first being. This opinion I have at large examined already; and, I suppose what

I have said in the foregoing Book will be much more easily admitted, when I have shown whence the understanding may get all the ideas it has; and by what ways and degrees they may come into the mind; —for which I shall appeal to every one's own observation and experience.

2. *All Ideas come from Sensation or Reflection.* Let us then suppose the mind to be, as we say, white paper, void of all characters, without any ideas:—How comes it to be furnished? Whence comes it by that vast store which the busy and boundless fancy of man has painted on it with an almost endless variety? Whence has it all the *materials* of reason and knowledge? To this I answer, in one word, from EXPERIENCE. In that all our knowledge is founded; and from that it ultimately derives itself. Our observation employed either, about external sensible objects, or about the internal operations of our minds perceived and reflected on by ourselves, is that which supplies our understandings with all the *materials* of thinking. These two are the fountains of knowledge, from whence all the ideas we have, or can naturally have, do spring.

3. *The Objects of Sensation.* First, our Senses, conversant about particular sensible objects, do convey into the mind several distinct perceptions of things, according to those various ways wherein those objects do affect them. And thus we come by those *ideas* we have of *yellow, white, heat, cold, soft, hard, bitter, sweet,* and all those which we call sensible qualities; which when I say the senses convey into the mind, I mean, they from external objects convey into the mind what produces there those perceptions. This great source of most of the ideas we have, depending wholly upon our senses, and derived by them to the understanding, I call SENSATION.

4. *The Operations of our Minds, the other Source of them.* Secondly, the other fountain from which experience furnisheth the understanding with ideas is,—the perception of the operations of our own mind within us, as it is employed about the ideas it has got;—which operations, when the soul comes to reflect on and consider, do furnish the understanding with another set of ideas, which could not be had from things without. And such are *perception, thinking, doubting, believing, reasoning, knowing, willing,* and all the different actings of our own minds;—which we being conscious of, and observing in ourselves, do from these receive into our understandings as distinct ideas as we do from bodies affecting our senses. This source of ideas every man has wholly in himself; and though it be not sense, as having nothing to do with external objects, yet it is very like it, and might properly enough be called *internal sense.* But as I call the other Sensation, so I call this REFLECTION, the ideas it affords being such only as

the mind gets by reflecting on its own operations within itself. By reflection then, in the following part of this discourse, I would be understood to mean, that notice which the mind takes of its own operations, and the manner of them, by reason whereof there come to be ideas of these operations in the understanding. These two, I say, viz. external material things, as the objects of SENSATION, and the operations of our own minds within, as the objects of REFLECTION, are to me the only originals from whence all our ideas take their beginnings. The term *operations* here I use in a large sense, as comprehending not barely the actions of the mind about its ideas, but some sort of passions arising sometimes from them, such as is the satisfaction or uneasiness arising from any thought.

5. *All our Ideas are of the one or the other of these.* The understanding seems to me not to have the least glimmering of any ideas which it doth not receive from one of these two. *External objects* furnish the mind with the ideas of sensible qualities, which are all those different perceptions they produce in us; and *the mind* furnishes the understanding with ideas of its own operations.

These, when we have taken a full survey of them, and their several modes, combinations, and relations, we shall find to contain all our whole stock of ideas; and that we have nothing in our minds which did not come in one of these two ways. Let any one examine his own thoughts, and thoroughly search into his understanding; and then let him tell me, whether all the original ideas he has there, are any other than of the objects of his senses, or of the operations of his mind, considered as objects of his reflection. And how great a mass of knowledge soever he imagines to be lodged there, he will, upon taking a strict view, see that he has not any idea in his mind but what one of these two have imprinted;—though perhaps, with infinite variety compounded and enlarged by the understanding, as we shall see hereafter.

II, xi, 17. *Dark Room.* I pretend not to teach, but to inquire; and therefore cannot but confess here again,—that external and internal sensation are the only passages I can find of knowledge to the understanding. These alone, as far as I can discover, are the windows by which light is let into this *dark room*. For, methinks, the understanding is not much unlike a closet wholly shut from light, with only some little openings left, to let in external visible resemblances, or ideas of things without: would the pictures coming into such a dark room but stay there, and lie so orderly as to be found upon occasion, it would very much resemble the understanding of a man, in reference to all objects of sight, and the ideas of them.

These are my guesses concerning the means whereby the understanding comes to have and retain simple ideas, and the modes of them, with some other operations about them.

I proceed now to examine some of these simple ideas and their modes a little more particularly.

Chapter II.—OF SIMPLE IDEAS

1. *Uncompounded Appearances.* The better to understand the nature, manner, and extent of our knowledge, one thing is carefully to be observed concerning the ideas we have; and that is, that some of them are *simple* and some *complex.*

Though the qualities that affect our senses are, in the things themselves, so united and blended, that there is no separation, no distance between them; yet it is plain, the ideas they produce in the mind enter by the senses simple and unmixed. For, though the sight and touch often take in from the same object, at the same time, different ideas;—as a man sees at once motion and colour; the hand feels softness and warmth in the same piece of wax: yet the simple ideas thus united in the same subject, are as perfectly distinct as those that come in by different senses. The coldness and hardness which a man feels in a piece of ice being as distinct ideas in the mind as the smell and whiteness of a lily; or as the taste of sugar, and smell of a rose. And there is nothing can be plainer to a man than the clear and distinct perception he has of those simple ideas; which, being each in itself uncompounded, contains in it nothing but *one uniform appearance, or conception in the mind,* and is not distinguishable into different ideas.

2. *The Mind can neither make nor destroy them.* These simple ideas, the materials of all our knowledge, are suggested and furnished to the mind only by those two ways above mentioned, viz. sensation and reflection. When the understanding is once stored with these simple ideas, it has the power to repeat, compare, and unite them, even to an almost infinite variety, and so can make at pleasure new complex ideas. But it is not in the power of the most exalted wit, or enlarged understanding, by any quickness or variety of thought, to *invent* or *frame* one new simple idea in the mind, not taken in by the ways before mentioned: nor can any force of the understanding *destroy* those that are there. The dominion of man, in this little world of his own understanding being muchwhat the same as it is in the great world of visible things; wherein his power, however managed by art and skill,

reaches no farther than to compound and divide the materials that are made to his hand; but can do nothing towards the making the least particle of new matter, or destroying one atom of what is already in being. The same inability will every one find in himself, who shall go about to fashion in his understanding one simple idea, not received in by his senses from external objects, or by reflection from the operations of his own mind about them. I would have any one try to fancy any taste which had never affected his palate; or frame the idea of a scent he had never smelt: and when he can do this, I will also conclude that a blind man hath ideas of colours, and a deaf man true distinct notions of sounds.

Chapter VIII.—PRIMARY AND SECONDARY QUALITIES

8. *Our Ideas and the Qualities of Bodies.* Whatsoever the mind perceives *in itself,* or is the immediate object of perception, thought, or understanding, that I call *idea;* and the power to produce any idea in our mind, I call *quality* of the subject wherein that power is. Thus a snowball having the power to produce in us the ideas of white, cold, and round,—the power to produce those ideas in us, as they are in the snowball, I call qualities; and as they are sensations or perceptions in our understandings, I call them ideas; which *ideas,* if I speak of sometimes as in the things themselves, I would be understood to mean those qualities in the objects which produce them in us.

9. *Primary Qualities of Bodies.* Qualities thus considered in bodies are,

First, such as are utterly inseparable from the body, in what state soever it be; and such as in all the alterations and changes it suffers, all the force can be used upon it, it constantly keeps; and such as sense constantly finds in every particle of matter which has bulk enough to be perceived; and the mind finds inseparable from every particle of matter, though less than to make itself singly be perceived by our senses: v.g. Take a grain of wheat, divide it into two parts; each part has still solidity, extension, figure, and mobility: divide it again, and it retains still the same qualities; and so divide it on, till the parts become insensible; they must retain still each of them all those qualities. For division (which is all that a mill, or pestle, or any other body, does upon another, in reducing it to insensible parts) can never take away either solidity, extension, figure, or mobility from any body, but only makes two or more distinct separate masses of matter, of that which was but one before; all which distinct masses, reckoned as so many distinct bodies, after division, make a certain number. These I call *original* or *primary qualities* of body, which I think we may observe to produce simple ideas in us, viz. solidity, extension, figure, motion or rest, and number.

10. *Secondary Qualities of Bodies.* Secondly, such qualities which in truth are nothing in the objects themselves but powers to produce various sensations in us by their primary qualities, i.e. by the bulk, figure, texture, and motion of their insensible parts, as colours, sounds, tastes, &c. These I call *secondary qualities.* To these might be added a *third* sort, which are allowed to be barely powers; though they are as much real qualities in the subject as those which I, to comply with the common way of speaking, call qualities, but for distinction, secondary qualities. For the power in fire to produce a new colour, or consistency, in *wax* or *clay*,—by its primary qualities, is as much a quality in fire, as the power it has to produce in *me* a new idea or sensation of warmth or burning, which I felt not before,—by the same primary qualities, viz. the bulk, texture, and motion of its insensible parts.

11. *How Bodies produce Ideas in us.* The next thing to be considered is, how bodies produce ideas in us; and that is manifestly by impulse, the only way which we can conceive bodies to operate in.

12. *By motions, external, and in our organism.* If then external objects be not united to our minds when they produce ideas therein; and yet we perceive these *original* qualities in such of them as singly fall under our senses, it is evident that some motion must be thence continued by our nerves, or animal spirits, by some parts of our bodies, to the brains or the seat of sensation, there to produce in our minds the particular ideas we have of them. And since the extension, figure, number, and motion of bodies of an observable bigness, may be perceived at a distance by the sight, it is evident some singly imperceptible bodies must come from them to the eyes, and thereby convey to the brain some motion; which produces these ideas which we have of them in us.

13. *How secondary Qualities produce their ideas.* After the same manner that the ideas of these original qualities are produced in us, we may conceive that the ideas of *secondary* qualities are also produced, viz. by the operation of insensible particles on our senses. For, it being manifest that there are bodies and good store of bodies, each whereof are so small, that we cannot by any of our senses discover either their bulk, figure, or motion,—as is evident in the particles of the air and water, and others extremely smaller than those; perhaps as much smaller than the particles of air and water, as the particles of air and

water are smaller than peas or hail-stones;—let us suppose at present that the different motions and figures, bulk and number, of such particles, affecting the several organs of our senses, produce in us those different sensations which we have from the colours and smells of bodies; v.g. that a violet, by the impulse of such insensible particles of matter, of peculiar figures and bulks, and in different degrees and modifications of their motions, causes the ideas of the blue colour, and sweet scent of that flower to be produced in our minds. It being no more impossible to conceive that God should annex such ideas to such motions, with which they have no similitude, than that he should annex the idea of pain to the motion of a piece of steel dividing our flesh, with which that idea hath no resemblance.

14. *They depend on the primary Qualities.* What I have said concerning colours and smells may be understood also of tastes and sounds, and other the like sensible qualities; which, whatever reality we by mistake attribute to them, are in truth nothing in the objects themselves, but powers to produce various sensations in us; and depend on those primary qualities, viz. bulk, figure, texture, and motion of parts as I have said.

15. *Ideas of primary Qualities are Resemblances; of secondary, not.* From whence I think it easy to draw this observation,—that the ideas of primary qualities of bodies are resemblances of them, and their patterns do really exist in the bodies themselves, but the ideas produced in us by these secondary qualities have no resemblance of them at all. There is nothing like our ideas, existing in the bodies themselves. They are, in the bodies we denominate from them, only a power to produce those sensations in us: and what is sweet, blue, or warm in idea, is but the certain bulk, figure, and motion of the insensible parts, in the bodies themselves, which we call so.

II, xxiii, 11. *The now secondary Qualities of Bodies would disappear, if we could discover the primary ones of their minute Parts.* Had we senses acute enough to discern the minute particles of bodies, and the real constitution on which their sensible qualities depend, I doubt not but they would produce quite different ideas in us: and that which is now the yellow colour of gold, would then disappear, and instead of it we should see an admirable texture of parts, of a certain size and figure. This microscopes plainly discover to us; for what to our naked eyes produces a certain colour, is, by thus augmenting the acuteness of our senses, discovered to be quite a different thing; and the thus altering, as it were, the proportion of the bulk of the minute parts of a coloured object to our usual sight, produces different ideas from what it did before. Thus, sand or pounded glass, which is opaque, and white to the naked eye, is pellucid in a microscope; and a hair seen in this way, loses its former colour, and is, in a great measure, pellucid, with a mixture of some bright sparkling colours, such as appear from the refraction of diamonds, and other pellucid bodies. Blood, to the naked eye, appears all red; but by a good microscope, wherein its lesser parts appear, shows only some few globules of red, swimming in a pellucid liquor, and how these red globules would appear, if glasses could be found that could yet magnify them a thousand or ten thousand times more, is uncertain.

Chapter IX.—OF PERCEPTION

1. *Perception the first simple Idea of Reflection.* PERCEPTION, as it is the first faculty of the mind exercised about our ideas; so it is the first and simplest idea we have from reflection, and is by some called thinking in general. Though thinking, in the propriety of the English tongue, signifies that sort of operation in the mind about its ideas, wherein the mind is active; where it, with some degree of voluntary attention, considers anything. For in bare naked perception, the mind is, for the most part, only passive; and what it perceives, it cannot avoid perceiving.

2. *Reflection alone can give us the idea of what perception is.* What perception is, every one will know better by reflecting on what he does himself, when he sees, hears, feels, &c., or thinks, than by any discourse of mine. Whoever reflects on what passes in his own mind cannot miss it. And if he does not reflect, all the words in the world cannot make him have any notion of it.

3. *Arises in sensation only when the mind notices the organic impression.* This is certain, that whatever alterations are made in the body, if they reach not the mind; whatever impressions are made on the outward parts, if they are not taken notice of within, there is no perception. Fire may burn our bodies with no other effect than it does a billet, unless the motion be continued to the brain, and there the sense of heat, or idea of pain, be produced in the mind; wherein consists actual perception.

Chapter XII.—OF COMPLEX IDEAS

1. *Made by the Mind out of simple Ones.* We have hitherto considered those ideas, in the reception whereof the mind is only passive, which are those simple ones received from sensation and reflection before

mentioned, whereof the mind cannot make one to itself, nor have any idea which does not wholly consist of them. But as the mind is wholly passive in the reception of all its simple ideas, so it exerts several acts of its own, whereby out of its simple ideas, as the materials and foundations of the rest, the others are framed. The acts of the mind, wherein it exerts its power over its simple ideas, are chiefly these three: (1) Combining several simple ideas into one compound one; and thus all *complex ideas* are made. (2) The second is bringing two ideas, whether simple or complex, together, and setting them by one another, so as to take a view of them at once, without uniting them into one; by which way it gets all its *ideas of relations*. (3) The third is separating them from all other ideas that accompany them in their real existence: this is called abstraction: and thus all its *general ideas* are made. This shows man's power, and its ways of operation, to be much the same in the material and intellectual world. For the materials in both being such as he has no power over, either to make or destroy, all that man can do is either to unite them together, or to set them by one another, or wholly separate them. As simple ideas are observed to exist in several combinations united together, so the mind has a power to consider several of them united together as one idea; and that not only as they are united in external objects, but as itself has joined them together. Ideas thus made up of several simple ones put together, I call *complex;* —such as are beauty, gratitude, a man, an army, the universe; which, though complicated of various simple ideas, or complex ideas made up of simple ones, yet are, when the mind pleases, considered each by itself, as one entire thing, and signified by one name.

3. *Complex ideas are either of Modes, Substances, or Relations.* *Complex ideas*, however compounded and decompounded, though their number be infinite, and the variety endless, wherewith they fill and entertain the thoughts of men; yet I think they may be all reduced under these three heads:

1. *Modes.*
2. *Substances.*
3. *Relations.*

4. *Ideas of Modes.* First, *Modes* I call such complex ideas which, however compounded, contain not in them the supposition of subsisting by themselves, but are considered as dependences on, or affections of substances;—such as are the ideas signified by the words triangle, gratitude, murder, &c. And if in this I use the word mode in somewhat a different sense from its ordinary signification, I beg pardon; it being unavoidable in discourses, differing from the ordinary received notions, either to make new words, or to use old words in somewhat a new

signification; the later whereof, in our present case, is perhaps the more tolerable of the two.

6. *Ideas of Substances, single or collective.* Secondly, the ideas of *substances* are such combinations of simple ideas as are taken to represent distinct *particular* things subsisting by themselves; in which the supposed or confused idea of substance, such as it is, is always the first and chief. Thus if to substance be joined the simple idea of a certain dull whitish colour, with certain degrees of weight, hardness, ductility, and fusibility, we have the idea of lead; and a combination of the ideas of a certain sort of figure, with the powers of motion, thought and reasoning, joined to substance, make the ordinary idea of a man. Now of substances also, there are two sorts of ideas:—one of *single* substances, as they exist separately, as of a man or a sheep; the other of several of those put together, as an army of men, or flock of sheep—which *collective* ideas of several substances thus put together are as much each of them one single idea as that of a man or an unit.

7. *Ideas of Relation.* Thirdly, the last sort of complex ideas is that we call *relation,* which consists in the consideration and comparing one idea with another.

Chapter XXI.—OF POWER[1]

1. *This Idea, how got.* The mind being every day informed, by the senses, of the alteration of those simple ideas it observes in things without; and taking notice how one comes to an end, and ceases to be, and another begins to exist which was not before; reflecting also on what passes within itself, and observing a constant change of its ideas, sometimes by the impression of outward objects on the senses, and sometimes by the determination of its own choice; and concluding from what it has so constantly observed to have been, that the like changes will for the future be made in the same things, by like agents, and by the like ways,—considers in one thing the possibility of having any of its simple ideas changed, and in another the possibility of making that change; and so comes by that idea which we call *power*. Thus we say, Fire has a power to melt gold, i.e. to destroy the consistency of its insensible parts, and consequently its hardness, and make it fluid;

---

1. Power is here treated of as a complex idea, more specifically as a mode (defined above, p. 32); but Locke has previously (Book II, Chapter VII, Section 8) described power as a simple idea received from both sensation and reflection. "Of Cause and Effect," the last section in this chapter, is taken from Locke's later discussion of complex ideas of relation. L.W.B.

and gold has a power to be melted; that the sun has a power to blanch wax, and wax a power to be blanched by the sun, whereby the yellowness is destroyed, and whiteness made to exist in its room. In which, and the like cases, the power we consider is in reference to the change of perceivable ideas. For we cannot observe any alteration to be made in, or operation upon anything, but by the observable change of its sensible ideas; nor conceive any alteration to be made, but by conceiving a change of some of its ideas.

2. *Power, active and passive.* Power thus considered is two-fold, viz. as able to make, or able to receive any change. The one may be called *active,* and the other *passive* power. Whether matter be not wholly destitute of active power, as its author, God, is truly above all passive power; and whether the intermediate state of created spirits be not that alone which is capable of both active and passive power, may be worth consideration. I shall not now enter into that inquiry, my present business being not to search into the original of power, but how we come by the *idea* of it. But since active powers make so great a part of our complex ideas of natural substances, (as we shall see hereafter,) and I mention them as such, according to common apprehension; yet they being not, perhaps, so truly *active* powers as our hasty thoughts are apt to represent them, I judge it not amiss, by this intimation, to direct our minds to the consideration of God and spirits, for the clearest idea of *active* power.

4. *The clearest Idea of active Power had from Spirit.* We are abundantly furnished with the idea of *passive* power by almost all sorts of sensible things. In most of them we cannot avoid observing their sensible qualities, nay, their very substances, to be in a continual flux. And therefore with reason we look on them as liable still to the same change. Nor have we of *active* power (which is the more proper signification of the word power) fewer instances. Since whatever change is observed, the mind must collect a power somewhere able to make that change, as well as a possibility in the thing itself to receive it. But yet, if we will consider it attentively, bodies, by our senses, do not afford us so clear and distinct an idea of active power, as we have from reflection on the operations of our minds. For all power relating to action, and there being but two sorts of action whereof we have an idea, viz. thinking and motion, let us consider whence we have the clearest ideas of the powers which produce these actions. (1) Of thinking, body affords us no idea at all; it is only from reflection that we have that. (2) Neither have we from body any idea of the beginning of motion. A body at rest affords us no idea of any active power to move; and when it is set in motion itself, that motion is rather a passion

than an action in it. For, when the ball obeys the motion of a billiard-stick, it is not any action of the ball, but bare passion. Also when by impulse it sets another ball in motion that lay in its way, it only communicates the motion it had received from another, and loses in itself so much as the other received: which gives us but a very obscure idea of an *active* power of moving in body, whilst we observe it only to *transfer*, but not *produce* any motion. For it is but a very obscure idea of power which reaches not the production of the action, but the continuation of the passion. For so is motion in a body impelled by another; the continuation of the alteration made in it from rest to motion being little more an action, than the continuation of the altera-tion of its figure by the same blow is an action. The idea of the *beginning* of motion we have only from reflection on what passes in ourselves; where we find by experience, that, barely by willing it, barely by a thought of the mind, we can move the parts of our bodies, which were before at rest. So that it seems to me, we have, from the observa-tion of the operation of bodies by our senses, but a very imperfect obscure idea of *active* power; since they afford us not any idea in themselves of the power to begin any action, either motion or thought.

5. *Will and Understanding two Powers in Mind or Spirit.* This, at least, I think evident,—That we find in ourselves a power to begin or forbear, continue or end several actions of our minds, and motions of our bodies, barely by a thought of preference of the mind ordering, or as it were commanding, the doing or not doing such or such a particular action. This power which the mind has thus to order the consideration of any idea, or the forbearing to consider it; or to prefer the motion of any part of the body to its rest, and *vice versâ*, in any particular instance, is that which we call the *Will*. The actual exercise of that power, by directing any particular action, or its forbearance, is that which we call *volition* or *willing*. The forbearance of that action, consequent to such order or command of the mind, is called *voluntary*. And whatsoever action is performed without such a thought of the mind, is called *involuntary*. The power of perception is that which we call the *Understanding*. Perception, which we make the act of the understanding, is of three sorts:—1. The perception of ideas in our minds. 2. The perception of the signification of signs. 3. The perception of the connexion or repugnancy, agreement or disagreement, that there is between any of our ideas. All these are attributed to the understand-ing, or perceptive power, though it be the two latter only that use allows us to say we understand.

7. *Whence the idea of liberty and necessity.* Everyone, I think, finds in himself a power to begin or forbear, continue or put an end

to several actions in himself. From the consideration of the extent of this power of the mind over the actions of the man, which everyone finds in himself, arise the ideas of liberty and necessity.

II, xxvi, 1. *Of cause and effect.* In the notice that our senses take of the constant vicissitude of things, we cannot but observe that several particular, both qualities and substances, begin to exist, and that they receive this their existence from the due application and operation of some other being. From this operation we get our idea of cause and effect. That which produces any simple or complex idea we denote by the general name, *cause,* and that which is produced, *effect....*

Chapter XXIII.—OF OUR COMPLEX IDEAS OF SUBSTANCES

1. *Ideas of particular Substances, how made.* The mind being, as I have declared, furnished with a great number of the simple ideas, conveyed in by the senses as they are found in exterior things, or by reflection on its own operations, takes notice also that a certain number of these simple ideas go constantly together; which being presumed to belong to one thing, and words being suited to common apprehensions, and made use of for quick dispatch, are called, so united in one subject, by one name; which, by inadvertency, we are apt afterward to talk of and consider as one simple idea, which indeed is a complication of many ideas together: because, as I have said, not imagining how these simple ideas *can* subsist by themselves, we accustom ourselves to suppose some *substratum* wherein they do subsist, and from which they do result, which therefore we call *substance.*

2. *Our obscure Idea of Substance in general.* So that if any one will examine himself concerning his notion of pure substance in general, he will find he has no other idea of it at all, but only a supposition of he knows not what *support* of such qualities which are capable of producing simple ideas in us; which qualities are commonly called accidents. If any one should be asked, what is the subject wherein colour or weight inheres, he would have nothing to say, but the solid extended parts; and if he were demanded, what is it that solidity and extension adhere in, he would not be in a much better case than the Indian before mentioned who, saying that the world was supported by a great elephant, we asked what the elephant rested on; to which his answer was—a great tortoise: but being again pressed to know what gave support to the broad-backed tortoise, replied—*something, he knew not what.* And thus here, as in all other cases where we use

words without having clear and distinct ideas, we talk like children: who, being questioned what such a thing is, which they know not, readily give this satisfactory answer, that it is *something:* which in truth signifies no more, when so used, either by children or men, but that they know not what; and that the thing they pretend to know, and talk of, is what they have no distinct idea of at all, and so are perfectly ignorant of it, and in the dark. The idea then we have, to which we give the *general* name substance, being nothing but the supposed, but unknown, support of those qualities we find existing, which we imagine cannot subsist *sine re substante,* without something to support them, we call that support *substantia;* which, according to the true import of the word, is, in plain English, standing under or upholding.

4. *No clear or distinct idea of Substance in general.* Hence, when we talk or think of any particular sort of corporeal substances, as horse, stone, &c., though the idea we have of either of them be but the complication or collection of those several simple ideas of sensible qualities, which we used to find united in the thing called horse or stone; yet, *because we cannot conceive how they should subsist alone, nor one in another,* we suppose them existing in and supported by some common subject; which support we denote by the name substance, though it be certain we have no clear or distinct idea of that thing we suppose a support.

7. *Their active and passive Powers a great part of our complex Ideas of Substances.* For he has the perfectest idea of any of the particular sorts of substances, who has gathered, and put together, most of those simple ideas which do exist in it; among which are to be reckoned its active powers, and passive capacities, which, though not simple ideas, yet in this respect, for brevity's sake, may conveniently enough be reckoned amongst them. Thus, the power of drawing iron is one of the ideas of the complex one of that substance we call a loadstone; and a power to be so drawn is a part of the complex one we call iron: which powers pass for inherent qualities in those subjects. Because every substance, being as apt, by the powers we observe in it, to change some sensible qualities in other subjects, as it is to produce in us those simple ideas which we receive immediately from it, does, by those new sensible qualities introduced into other subjects, discover to us those powers which do thereby mediately affect our senses, as regularly as its sensible qualities do it immediately: v.g. we immediately by our senses perceive in fire its heat and colour; which are, if rightly considered, nothing but powers in it to produce those ideas in *us:* we also by our senses perceive the colour and brittleness of

charcoal, whereby we come by the knowledge of another power in fire, which it has to change the colour and consistency of *wood*. . . .

8. *And why.* Nor are we to wonder that powers make a great part of our complex ideas of substances; since their secondary qualities are those which in most of them serve principally to distinguish substances one from another, and commonly make a considerable part of the complex idea of the several sorts of them. For, our senses failing us in the discovery of the bulk, texture, and figure of the minute parts of bodies, on which their real constitutions and differences depend, we are fain to make use of their secondary qualities as the characteristical notes and marks whereby to frame ideas of them in our minds, and distinguish them one from another: all which secondary qualities, as has been shown, are nothing but bare powers. For the colour and taste of opium are, as well as its soporific or anodyne virtues, mere powers, depending on its primary qualities, whereby it is fitted to produce different operations on different parts of our bodies.

II, xxxi, 6. *Our ideas of substance are inadequate.* Ideas [of substance] have in the mind a double reference: (1) Sometimes they are referred to a supposed real essence of each species of things. (2) Sometimes they are only designed to be pictures and representations in the mind of things that do exist, by ideas of those qualities which are discoverable in them. In both which ways these copies of those originals and archetypes are imperfect and inadequate.

First, It is usual for men to make the names of substances stand for things as supposed to have certain real essences, whereby they are of this or that species; and names standing for nothing but the ideas that are in men's minds, they must consequently refer their ideas to such real essences, as to their archetypes. That men (especially such as have been bred up in the learning taught in this part of the world) do suppose certain specific essences of substances, which each individual in its several kinds is made conformable to and partakes of, is so far from needing proof that it will be thought strange if anyone should do otherwise. . . . Who is there almost, who would not take it amiss if it should be doubted whether he called himself man with any other meaning than as having the real essence of a man? And yet if you demand what those real essences are, it is plain men are ignorant and know them not. From whence it follows that the ideas they have in their minds, being referred to real essences, as to archetypes which are unknown, must be so far from being adequate that they cannot be supposed to be any representation of them at all. . . . And yet, though we know nothing of these real essences, there is nothing more ordinary than that men should attribute the sorts of things to such essences.

The particular parcel of matter which makes the ring I have on my finger is forwardly by most men supposed to have a real essence whereby it is *gold*, and from whence those qualities flow which I find in it. . . . This essence, from which all these properties flow, when I inquire into it and search after it, I plainly perceive I cannot discover. . . . I can have no idea of its essence, which is the cause that it has that particular shining yellowness, a greater weight than anything I know of the same bulk, and a fitness to have its colour changed by the touch of quicksilver.

xxxi, 8. Secondly, Those who, neglecting that useless supposition of unknown real essences . . . endeavour to copy the substances that exist in the world by putting together the ideas of those sensible qualities which are found co-existing in them, though they come much nearer a likeness of them than those who imagine they know not what real specific essences, yet they arrive not at perfectly adequate ideas of those substances they would thus copy into their minds; nor do those copies exactly and fully contain all that is to be found in their archetypes. Because those qualities and powers of substances, whereof we make their complex ideas, are so many and various that no man's complex idea contains them all. . . . 13. If we could have and actually had in our complex idea an exact collection of all the secondary qualities or powers of any substance, we should not yet thereby have an *idea* of the essence of that thing. For, since the powers or qualities that are observable by us are not the real essence of that substance but depend on it and flow from it, any collection whatsoever of these qualities cannot be the real essence of that thing. Whereby it is plain that our ideas of substance are not adequate, are not what the mind intends them to be. Besides, a man has no *idea* of substance in general, nor knows what substance is in itself.

BOOK IV—Of Knowledge and Opinion

Chapter I.—OF KNOWLEDGE IN GENERAL

1. *Our Knowledge conversant about our Ideas only.* Since the mind, in all its thoughts and reasonings, hath no other immediate object but its own ideas, which it alone does or can contemplate, it is evident that our knowledge is only conversant about them.

2. *Knowledge is the Perception of the Agreement or Disagreement*

of two Ideas. Knowledge then seems to me to be nothing but *the perception of the connexion of and agreement, or disagreement and repugnancy of any of our ideas.* In this alone it consists. Where this perception is, there is knowledge, and where it is not, there, though we may fancy, guess, or believe, yet we always come short of knowledge. For when we know that white is not black, what do we else but perceive, that these two ideas do not agree? When we possess ourselves with the utmost security of the demonstration, that the three angles of a triangle are equal to two right ones, what do we more but perceive, that equality to two right ones does necessarily agree to, and is inseparable from, the three angles of a triangle?

3. *This Agreement or Disagreement may be any of four sorts.* But to understand a little more distinctly wherein this agreement or disagreement consists, I think we may reduce it all to these four sorts:

    I. *Identity,* or *diversity.*

   II. *Relation.*

  III. *Co-existence,* or *necessary connexion.*

   IV. *Real existence.*

4. *First, Of Identity, or Diversity in ideas.* As to the first sort of agreement or disagreement, viz. *identity* or *diversity.* It is the first act of the mind, when it has any sentiments or ideas at all, to perceive its ideas; and so far as it perceives them, to know each what it is, and thereby also to perceive their difference, and that one is not another. This is so absolutely necessary, that without it there could be no knowledge, no reasoning, no imagination, no distinct thoughts at all. By this the mind clearly and infallibly perceives each idea to agree with itself, and to be what it is; and all distinct ideas to disagree, i.e. the one not to be the other: and this it does without pains, labour, or deduction; but at first view, by its natural power of perception and distinction. And though men of art have reduced this into those general rules, *What is, is,* and *It is impossible for the same thing to be and not to be,* for ready application in all cases, wherein there may be occasion to reflect on it: yet it is certain that the first exercise of this faculty is about particular ideas. A man infallibly knows, as soon as ever he has them in his mind, that the ideas he calls *white* and *round* are the very ideas they are; and that they are not other ideas which he calls *red* or *square.* Nor can any maxim or proposition in the world make him know it clearer or surer than he did before, and without any such general rule. This then is the first agreement or disagreement which the mind perceives in its ideas; which it always perceives at first sight: and if there ever happen any doubt about it, it will always

be found to be about the names, and not the ideas themselves, whose identity and diversity will always be perceived, as soon and clearly as the ideas themselves are; nor can it possibly be otherwise.

5. *Secondly, Of abstract Relations between ideas.* The next sort of agreement or disagreement the mind perceives in any of its ideas may, I think, be called *relative,* and is nothing but the perception of the *relation* between any two ideas, of what kind soever, whether substances, modes, or any other. For, since all distinct ideas must eternally be known not to be the same, and so be universally and constantly denied one of another, there could be no room for any positive knowledge at all, if we could not perceive any relation between our ideas, and find out the agreement or disagreement they have one with another, in several ways the mind takes of comparing them.

6. *Thirdly, Of their necessary Co-existence in Substances.* The third sort of agreement or disagreement to be found in our ideas, which the perception of the mind is employed about, is *co-existence* or *non-co-existence* in the *same subject;* and this belongs particularly to substances. Thus when we pronounce concerning gold, that it is fixed, our knowledge of this truth amounts to no more but this, that fixedness, or a power to remain in the fire unconsumed, is an idea that always accompanies and is joined with that particular sort of yellowness, weight, fusibility, malleableness, and solubility in *aqua regia,* which make our complex idea signified by the word gold.

7. *Fourthly, Of real Existence agreeing to any idea.* The fourth and last sort is that of *actual real existence* agreeing to any idea.

Within these four sorts of agreement or disagreement is, I suppose, contained all the knowledge we have, or are capable of. For all the inquiries we can make concerning any of our ideas, all that we know or can affirm concerning any of them, is, That it is, or is not, the same with some other; that it does or does not always co-exist with some other idea in the same subject; that it has this or that relation with some other idea; or that it has a real existence without the mind. Thus, "blue is not yellow," is of identity. "Two triangles upon equal bases between two parallels are equal," is of relation. "Iron is susceptible of magnetical impressions," is of co-existence. "God is," is of real existence. Though identity and co-existence are truly nothing but relations, yet they are such peculiar ways of agreement or disagreement of our ideas, that they deserve well to be considered as distinct heads, and not under relation in general; since they are so different grounds of affirmation and negation, as will easily appear to any one, who will but reflect on what is said in several places of this *Essay.*

Chapter II.—OF THE DEGREES OF OUR KNOWLEDGE

1. *Of the degrees, or differences in clearness, of our Knowledge: I. Intuitive.* All our knowledge consisting, as I have said, in the view the mind has of its own ideas, which is the utmost light and greatest certainty we, with our faculties, and in our way of knowledge, are capable of, it may not be amiss to consider a little the degrees of its evidence. The different clearness of our knowledge seems to me to lie in the different way of perception the mind has of the agreement or disagreement of any of its ideas. For if we will reflect on our own ways of thinking, we will find, that sometimes the mind perceives the agreement or disagreement of two ideas *immediately by themselves,* without the intervention of any other: and this I think we may call *intuitive knowledge.* For in this the mind is at no pains of proving or examining, but perceives the truth as the eye doth light, only by being directed towards it. Thus the mind perceives that *white* is not *black,* that a *circle* is not a *triangle,* that *three* are more than *two* and equal to *one and two.* Such kinds of truths the mind perceives at the first sight of the ideas together, by bare intuition; without the intervention of any other idea: and this kind of knowledge is the clearest and most certain that human frailty is capable of. This part of knowledge is irresistible, and like bright sunshine, forces itself immediately to be perceived, as soon as ever the mind turns its view that way; and leaves no room for hesitation, doubt, or examination, but the mind is presently filled with the clear light of it. *It is on this intuition that depends all the certainty and evidence of all our knowledge;* which certainty every one finds to be so great, that he cannot imagine, and therefore not require a greater: for a man cannot conceive himself capable of a greater certainty than to know that any idea in his mind is such as he perceives it to be; and that two ideas, wherein he perceives a difference, are different and not precisely the same. He that demands a greater certainty than this, demands he knows not what, and shows only that he has a mind to be a sceptic, without being able to be so. Certainty depends so wholly on this intuition, that, in the next degree of knowledge which I call demonstrative, this intuition is necessary in all the connexions of the intermediate ideas, without which we cannot attain knowledge and certainty.

2. *II. Demonstrative.* The next degree of knowledge is, where the mind perceives the agreement or disagreement of any ideas, but not immediately. Though wherever the mind perceives the agreement or disagreement of any of its ideas, there be certain knowledge; yet it does not always happen, that the mind sees that agreement or disagreement,

which there is between them, even where it is discoverable; and in that case remains in ignorance, and at most gets no further than a probable conjecture. The reason why the mind cannot always perceive presently the agreement or disagreement of two ideas, is, because those ideas, concerning whose agreement or disagreement the inquiry is made, cannot by the mind be so put together as to show it. In this case then, when the mind cannot so bring its ideas together as by their immediate comparison, and as it were juxta-position or application one to another, to perceive their agreement or disagreement, it is fain, *by the intervention of other ideas* (one or more, as it happens) to discover the agreement or disagreement which it searches; and this is that which we call *reasoning*. Thus, the mind being willing to know the agreement or disagreement in bigness between the three angles of a triangle and two right ones, cannot by an immediate view and comparing them do it: because the three angles of a triangle cannot be brought at once, and be compared with any other one, or two, angles; and so of this the mind has no immediate, no intuitive knowledge. In this case the mind is fain to find out some other angles, to which the three angles of a triangle have an equality; and, finding those equal to two right ones, comes to know their equality to two right ones.

4. *As certain, but not so easy and ready as Intuitive Knowledge.* This knowledge, by intervening proofs, though it be certain, yet the evidence of it is not altogether so clear and bright, nor the assent so ready, as in intuitive knowledge. For, though in demonstration the mind does at last perceive the agreement or disagreement of the ideas it considers; yet it is not without pains and attention: there must be more than one transient view to find it. A steady application and pursuit are required to this discovery: and there must be a progression by steps and degrees, before the mind can in this way arrive at certainty, and come to perceive the agreement or repugnancy between two ideas that need proofs and the use of reason to show it.

7. *Each Step in Demonstrated knowledge must have Intuitive Evidence.* Now, in every step reason makes in demonstrative knowledge, there is an intuitive knowledge of that agreement or disagreement it seeks with the next intermediate idea which it uses as a proof: for if it were not so, that yet would need a proof; since without the perception of such agreement or disagreement, there is no knowledge produced: if it be perceived by itself, it is intuitive knowledge: if it cannot be perceived by itself, there is need of some intervening idea, as a common measure, to show their agreement or disagreement. By which it is plain, that every step in reasoning that produces knowledge, has intuitive certainty; which when the mind perceives, there is no

more required but to remember it, to make the agreement or disagreement of the ideas concerning which we inquire visible and certain. So that to make anything a demonstration, it is necessary to perceive the immediate agreement of the intervening ideas, whereby the agreement or disagreement of the two ideas under examination (whereof the one is always the first, and the other the last in the account) is found. This intuitive perception of the agreement or disagreement of the intermediate ideas, in each step and progression of the demonstration, must also be carried exactly in the mind, and a man must be sure that no part is left out: which, because in long deductions, and the use of many proofs, the memory does not always so readily and exactly retain; therefore it comes to pass, that this is more imperfect than intuitive knowledge, and men embrace often falsehood for demonstrations.

9. It has been generally taken for granted that mathematics alone are capable of demonstrative certainty; but to have such an agreement or disagreement as may intuitively be perceived being, as I imagine, not the privilege of ideas of number, extension, and figure alone, it may possibly be the want of due method and application in us, and not of sufficient evidence in things, that demonstration has been thought to have so little to do in other parts of knowledge, and been scarce so much as aimed at by any but mathematicians. For whatever ideas we have wherein the mind can perceive the immediate agreement or disagreement that is between them, there the mind is capable of intuitive knowledge; and where it can perceive the agreement or disagreement of any two ideas, by an intuitive perception of the agreement or disagreement they have with any intermediate ideas, there the mind is capable of demonstration, which is not limited to ideas of extension, figure, number, and their modes.

14. *Sensitive Knowledge of the particular Existence of finite beings without us.* These two, viz. intuition and demonstration, are the degrees of our *knowledge;* whatever comes short of one of these, with what assurance soever embraced, is but *faith* or *opinion,* but not knowledge, at least in all general truths. There is, indeed, another perception of the mind, employed about *the particular existence of finite beings without us,* which, going beyond bare probability, and yet not reaching perfectly to either of the foregoing degrees of certainty, passes under the name of *knowledge.* There can be nothing more certain than that the idea we receive from an external object is in our minds: this is intuitive knowledge. But whether there be anything more than barely that idea in our minds; whether we can thence certainly infer the existence of anything without us, which corresponds to that idea, is that whereof some men think there may be a question made; be-

cause men may have such ideas in their minds, when no such thing
exists, no such object affects their senses. But yet here I think we are
provided with an evidence that puts us past doubting. For I ask any
one, Whether he be not invincibly conscious to himself of a different
perception, when he looks on the sun by day, and thinks on it by
night; when he actually tastes wormwood, or smells a rose, or only
thinks on that savour or odour? We as plainly find the difference
there is between any idea revived in our minds by our own memory,
and actually coming into our minds by our senses, as we do between
any two distinct ideas. If any one say, a dream may do the same
thing, and all these ideas may be produced in us without any external
objects; he may please to dream that I make him this answer:—1. That
it is no great matter, whether I remove his scruple or no: where all is
but dream, reasoning and arguments are of no use, truth and knowledge nothing. 2. That I believe he will allow a very manifest difference
between dreaming of being in the fire, and being actually in it. But yet
if he be resolved to appear so sceptical as to maintain, that what I call
being actually in the fire is nothing but a dream; and that we cannot
thereby certainly know, that any such thing as fire actually exists
without us: I answer, That we certainly finding that pleasure or pain
follows upon the application of certain objects to us, whose existence
we perceive, or dream that we perceive, by our senses; this certainty
is as great as our happiness or misery, beyond which we have no concernment to know or to be. So that, I think, we may add to the two
former sorts of knowledge this also, of the existence of particular external objects, by that perception and consciousness we have of the
actual entrance of ideas from them, and allow these three degrees of
knowledge, viz., *intuitive, demonstrative,* and *sensitive:* in each of
which there are different degrees and ways of evidence and certainty.

Chapter III.—OF THE EXTENT OF HUMAN KNOWLEDGE

1. *First, it extends no further than we have Ideas.* Knowledge, as
has been said, lying in the perception of the agreement or disagreement
of any of our ideas, it follows from hence, That,
First, we can have knowledge no further than we have *ideas.*
2. *It extends no further than we can perceive their Agreement or
Disagreement.* Secondly, That we can have no knowledge further than
we can have *perception* of that agreement or disagreement. Which perception being: 1. Either by *intuition,* or the immediate comparing any

two ideas; or, 2. By *reason*, examining the agreement or disagreement of two ideas, by the intervention of some others; or, 3. By *sensation*, perceiving the existence of particular things: hence it also follows:

3. *Intuitive Knowledge extends itself not to all the relations of all our Ideas.* Thirdly, That we cannot have an *intuitive knowledge* that shall extend itself to all our ideas, and all that we would know about them; because we cannot examine and perceive all the relations they have one to another, by juxta-position, or an immediate comparison one with another. Thus, having the ideas of an obtuse and an acute angled triangle, both drawn from equal bases, and between parallels, I can, by intuitive knowledge, perceive the one not to be the other, but cannot that way know whether they be equal or no; because their agreement or disagreement in equality can never be perceived by an immediate comparing them: the difference of figure makes their parts incapable of an exact immediate application; and therefore there is need of some intervening qualities to measure them by, which is demonstration, or rational knowledge.

4. *Nor does Demonstrative Knowledge.* Fourthly, It follows, also, from what is above observed, that our *rational knowledge* cannot reach to the whole extent of our ideas: because between two different ideas we would examine, we cannot always find such mediums as we can connect one to another with an intuitive knowledge in all the parts of the deduction; and wherever that fails, we come short of knowledge and demonstration.

5. *Sensitive Knowledge narrower than either.* Fifthly, *Sensitive knowledge* reaching no further than the existence of things actually present to our senses, is yet much narrower than either of the former.

6. *Our Knowledge, therefore, narrower than our Ideas.* Sixthly, From all which it is evident, that the *extent of our knowledge* comes not only short of the reality of things, but even of the extent of our own ideas. Though our knowledge be limited to our ideas, and cannot exceed them either in extent or perfection; and though these be very narrow bounds, in respect of the extent of All-being, and far short of what we may justly imagine to be in some even created understandings, not tied down to the dull and narrow information that is to be received from some few, and not very acute, ways of perception, such as are our senses; yet it would be well with us if our knowledge were but as large as our ideas, and there were not many doubts and inquiries *concerning the ideas we have,* whereof we are not, nor I believe ever shall be in this world resolved. Nevertheless, I do not question but that human knowledge, under the present circumstances of our beings and constitutions, may be carried much further than it has hitherto been, if men

would sincerely, and with freedom of mind, employ all that industry and labour of thought, in improving the means of discovering truth, which they do for the colouring or support of falsehood, to maintain a system, interest, or party they are once engaged in. But yet after all, I think I may, without injury to human perfection, be confident, that our knowledge would never reach to all we might desire to know concerning those ideas we have; nor be able to surmount all the difficulties, and resolve all the questions that might arise concerning any of them.

We have ideas of a square, a circle, and equality, and yet, perhaps, shall never be able to find a circle equal to a square, and certainly know that it is so. We have the ideas of matter and thinking, but possibly shall never be able to know whether any mere material being thinks or no . . . for I see no contradiction in it that the first eternal thinking Being should, if he pleased, give to certain systems of created senseless matter, put together as he thinks fit, some degree of sense, perception, and thought. . . .

Chapter IV.—ON MATHEMATICAL AND MORAL KNOWLEDGE

5. *All Complex Ideas, except ideas of Substances, are their own archetypes.*[2] *Secondly,* All our complex ideas, *except those of substances,* being archetypes of the mind's own making, not intended to be the copies of anything, nor referred to the existence of anything, as to their originals, cannot want any conformity necessary to real knowledge. For that which is not designed to represent anything but itself, can never be capable of a wrong representation, nor mislead us from the true apprehension of anything, by its dislikeness to it: and such, excepting those of substances, are all our complex ideas. Which, as I have showed in another place, are combinations of ideas, which the mind, by its free choice, puts together, without considering any connexion they have in nature. And hence it is, that in all these sorts the ideas themselves are considered as the archetypes, and things no otherwise regarded, but as they are conformable to them. So that we cannot but be infallibly certain, that all the knowledge we attain concerning these ideas is real, and reaches things themselves. Because in all our thoughts, reasonings, and discourses of this kind, we intend things no further than as they

2. Locke has previously argued (IV, iv, 4 and II, xxxi, 12-14) that simple ideas and our ideas of modes do not "copy" anything real, and are therefore "adequate," i.e., they have the "conformity necessary to real knowledge," whereas in II, xxxi, 6 (above, p. 38) he has shown that our ideas of substances are ectypal, not archetypal, and inadequate.

are conformable to our ideas. So that in these we cannot miss of a certain and undoubted reality.

6. *Hence the reality of Mathematical Knowledge.* I doubt not but it will be easily granted, that the knowledge we have of mathematical truths is not only certain, but real knowledge; and not the bare empty vision of vain, insignificant chimeras of the brain: and yet, if we will consider, we shall find that it is only of our own ideas. The mathematician considers the truth and properties belonging to a rectangle or circle only as they are in idea in his own mind. For it is possible he never found either of them existing mathematically, i.e. precisely true, in his life. But yet the knowledge he has of any truths or properties belonging to a circle, or any other mathematical figure, are nevertheless true and certain, even of real things existing: because real things are no further concerned, nor intended to be meant by any such propositions, than as things really agree to those archetypes in his mind. Is it true of the *idea* of a triangle, that its three angles are equal to two right ones? It is true also of a triangle, wherever it *really exists.* Whatever other figure exists, that it is not exactly answerable to that idea of a triangle in his mind, is not at all concerned in that proposition. And therefore he is certain all his knowledge concerning such ideas is real knowledge: because, intending things no further than they agree with those his ideas, he is sure what he knows concerning those figures, when they have *barely an ideal existence* in his mind, will hold true of them also when they have *a real existence* in matter: his consideration being barely of those figures, which are the same wherever or however they exist.

7. *And of Moral.* And hence it follows that moral knowledge is as capable of real certainty as mathematics. For certainty being but the perception of the agreement or disagreement of our ideas, and demonstration nothing but the perception of such agreement, by the intervention of other ideas or mediums; our moral ideas, as well as mathematical, being archetypes themselves, and so adequate and complete ideas; all the agreement or disagreement which we shall find in them will produce real knowledge, as well as in mathematical figures.

8. *Existence not required to make Abstract Knowledge real.* For the attaining of knowledge and certainty, it is requisite that we have determined ideas: and, to make our knowledge real, it is requisite that the ideas answer their archetypes. Nor let it be wondered, that I place the certainty of our knowledge in the consideration of our ideas, with so little care and regard (as it may seem) to the real existence of things: since most of those discourses which take up the thoughts and engage the disputes of those who pretend to make it their business to inquire after truth and certainty, will, I presume, upon examination,

be found to be general propositions, and notions in which existence is not at all concerned. All the discourses of the mathematicians about the squaring of a circle, conic sections, or any other part of mathematics, concern not the existence of any of those figures: but their demonstrations, which depend on their ideas, are the same, whether there be any square or circle existing in the world or no. In the same manner, the truth and certainty of moral discourses abstracts from the lives of men, and the existence of those virtues in the world whereof they treat: nor are Tully's Offices less true, because there is nobody in the world that exactly practises his rules, and lives up to that pattern of a virtuous man which he has given us, and which existed nowhere when he writ but in idea. If it be true in speculation, i.e. in idea, that murder deserves death, it will also be true in reality of any action that exists conformable to that idea of murder. As for other actions, the truth of that proposition concerns them not. And thus it is of all other species of things, which have no other essences but those ideas which are in the minds of men.

9. *Nor will it be less true or certain, because Moral Ideas are of our own making and naming.* But it will here be said, that if moral knowledge be placed in the contemplation of our own moral ideas, and those, as other modes, be of our own making, What strange notions will there be of justice and temperance? What confusion of virtues and vices, if every one may make what ideas of them he pleases? No confusion or disorder in the things themselves, nor the reasonings about them; no more than (in mathematics) there would be a disturbance in the demonstration, or a change in the properties of figures, and their relations one to another, if a man should make a triangle with four corners, or a trapezium with four right angles: that is, in plain English, change the names of the figures, and call that by one name, which mathematicians call ordinarily by another. For, let a man make to himself the idea of a figure with three angles, whereof one is a right one, and call it, if he please, *equilaterum* or *trapezium*, or anything else; the properties of, and demonstrations about that idea will be the same as if he called it a rectangular triangle. I confess the change of the name, by the impropriety of speech, will at first disturb him who knows not what idea it stands for: but as soon as the figure is drawn, the consequences and demonstrations are plain and clear. Just the same is it in moral knowledge: let a man have the idea of taking from others, without their consent, what their honest industry has possessed them of, and call this *justice* if he please. He that takes the name here without the idea put to it will be mistaken, by joining another idea of his own to that name: but strip the idea of that name, or take it

such as it is in the speaker's mind, and the same things will agree to it, as if you called it *injustice*. Indeed, wrong names in moral discourses breed usually more disorder, because they are not so easily rectified as in mathematics, where the figure, once drawn and seen, makes the name useless and of no force. For what need of a sign, when the thing signified is present and in view? But in moral names, that cannot be so easily and shortly done, because of the many decompositions that go to the making up the complex ideas of those modes. But yet for all this, the miscalling of any of those ideas, contrary to the usual signification of the words of that language, hinders not but that we may have certain and demonstrative knowledge of their several agreements and disagreements, if we will carefully, as in mathematics, keep to the same precise ideas, and trace *them* in their several relations one to another, without being led away by their names. If we but separate the idea under consideration from the sign that stands for it, our knowledge goes equally on in the discovery of real truth and certainty, whatever sounds we make use of.

Chapter X.—OF OUR KNOWLEDGE OF
THE EXISTENCE OF A GOD

1. *We are capable of knowing certainly that there is a God.* Though God has given us no innate ideas of himself; though he has stamped no original characters on our minds, wherein we may read his being; yet having furnished us with those faculties our minds are endowed with, he hath not left himself without witness: since we have sense, perception, and reason, and cannot want a clear proof of him, as long as we carry *ourselves* about us. Nor can we justly complain of our ignorance in this great point; since he has so plentifully provided us with the means to discover and know him; so far as is necessary to the end of our being, and the great concernment of our happiness. But, though this be the most obvious truth that reason discovers, and though its evidence be (if I mistake not) equal to mathematical certainty: yet it requires thought and attention; and the mind must apply itself to a regular deduction of it from some part of our intuitive knowledge, or else we shall be as uncertain and ignorant of this as of other propositions, which are in themselves capable of clear demonstration. To show, therefore, that we are capable of *knowing,* i.e. *being certain* that there is a God, and *how we may come by* this certainty, I think we need go no further than *ourselves,* and that undoubted knowledge we have of our own existence.

2. *For Man knows that he himself exists.* I think it is beyond question, that man has a clear idea of his own being; he knows certainly he exists, and that he is something. He that can doubt whether he be anything or no, I speak not to: no more than I would argue with pure nothing, or endeavour to convince nonentity that it were something. If any one pretends to be so sceptical as to deny his own existence, (for really to doubt of it is manifestly impossible,) let him for me enjoy his beloved happiness of being nothing, until hunger or some other pain convince him of the contrary. This, then, I think I may take for a truth, which every one's certain knowledge assures him of, beyond the liberty of doubting, viz. that he is *something that actually exists.*

3. *He knows also that Nothing cannot produce a Being; therefore Something must have existed from Eternity.* In the next place, man knows, by an intuitive certainty, that bare *nothing can no more produce any real being, than it can be equal to two right angles.* If a man knows not that nonentity, or the absence of all being, cannot be equal to two right angles, it is impossible he should know any demonstration in Euclid. If, therefore, we know there is some real being, and that nonentity cannot produce any real being, it is an evident demonstration, that *from eternity there has been something;* since what was not from eternity had a beginning; and what had a beginning must be produced by something else.

4. *And that eternal Being must be most powerful.* Next, it is evident, that what had its being and beginning from another, must also have all that which is in and belongs to its being from another too. All the powers it has must be owing to and received from the same source. This eternal source, then, of all being must also be the source and original of all power; and so *this eternal Being must be also the most powerful.*

5. *And most knowing.* Again, a man finds in *himself* perception and knowledge. We have then got one step further; and we are certain now that there is not only some being, but some knowing, intelligent being in the world. There was a time, then, when there was no knowing being, and when · knowledge began to be; or else there has been also *a knowing being from eternity.* If it be said, there was a time when no being had any knowledge, when that eternal being was void of all understanding; I reply, that then it was impossible there should ever have been any knowledge: it being as impossible that things wholly void of knowledge, and operating blindly, and without any perception, should produce a knowing being, as it is impossible that a triangle should make itself three angles bigger than two right ones. For it is as repugnant to the idea of senseless matter, that it should put into itself

sense, perception, and knowledge, as it is repugnant to the idea of a triangle, that it should put into itself greater angles than two right ones.

6. *And therefore God.* Thus, from the consideration of ourselves, and what we infallibly find in our own constitutions, our reason leads us to the knowledge of this certain and evident truth,—*That there is an eternal, most powerful, and most knowing Being;* which whether any one will please to call God, it matters not. The thing is evident; and from this idea duly considered, will easily be deduced all those other attributes, which we ought to ascribe to this eternal Being. If, nevertheless, any one should be found so senselessly arrogant, as to suppose man alone knowing and wise, but yet the product of mere ignorance and chance; and that all the rest of the universe acted only by that blind haphazard; I shall leave with him that very rational and emphatical rebuke of Tully (l. ii. De Leg.), to be considered at his leisure: 'What can be more sillily arrogant and misbecoming, than for a man to think that he has a mind and understanding in him, but yet in all the universe beside there is no such thing? Or that those things, which with the utmost stretch of his reason he can scarce comprehend, should be moved and managed without any reason at all?'

From what has been said, it is plain to me we have a more certain knowledge of the existence of a God, than of anything our senses have not immediately discovered to us. Nay, I presume I may say, that we more certainly know that there is a God, than that there is anything else without us. When I say we *know,* I mean there is such a knowledge within our reach which we cannot miss, if we will but apply our minds to that, as we do to several other inquiries.

Chapter XI.—OF OUR KNOWLEDGE OF THE EXISTENCE OF OTHER THINGS

1. *Knowledge of the existence of other Finite Beings is to be had only by actual Sensation.* The knowledge of our own being we have by intuition. The existence of a God, reason clearly makes known to us, as has been shown.

The knowledge of the existence of *any other thing* we can have only by *sensation:* for there being no necessary connexion of real existence with any *idea* a man hath in his memory; nor of any other existence but that of God with the existence of any particular man: no particular man can know the existence of any other being, but only when, by actual operating upon him, it makes itself perceived by him. For, the having the idea of anything in our mind, no more proves the existence of that thing, than the picture of a man evidences his being in the world, or the visions of a dream make thereby a true history.

2. *Instance: Whiteness of this Paper.* It is therefore the *actual receiving* of ideas from without that gives us notice of the existence of other things, and makes us know, that something doth exist at that time without us, which causes that idea in us; though perhaps we neither know nor consider how it does it. For it takes not from the certainty of our senses, and the ideas we receive by them, that we know not the manner wherein they are produced: v.g. whilst I write this, I have, by the paper affecting my eyes, that idea produced in my mind, which, whatever object causes, I call *white;* by which I know that that quality or accident (i.e. whose appearance before my eyes always causes that idea) doth really exist, and hath a being without me. And of this, the greatest assurance I can possibly have, and to which my faculties can attain, is the testimony of my eyes, which are the proper and sole judges of this thing; whose testimony I have reason to rely on as so certain, that I can no more doubt, whilst I write this, that I see white and black, and that something really exists that causes that sensation in me, than that I write or move my hand; which is a certainty as great as human nature is capable of, concerning the existence of anything, but a man's self alone, and of God.

3. *This notice by our Senses, though not so certain as Demonstration, yet may be called Knowledge, and proves the Existence of Things without us.* The notice we have by our senses of the existing of things without us, though it be not altogether so certain as our intuitive knowledge, or the deductions of our reason employed about the clear abstract ideas of our own minds; yet it is an assurance that deserves the name of *knowledge.* If we persuade ourselves that our faculties act and inform us right concerning the existence of those objects that affect them, it cannot pass for an ill-grounded confidence: for I think nobody can, in earnest, be so sceptical as to be uncertain of the existence of those things which he sees and feels. At least, he that can doubt so far, (whatever he may have with his own thoughts,) will never have any controversy with me; since he can never be sure I say anything contrary to his own opinion. As to myself, I think God has given me assurance enough of the existence of things without me: since, by their different application, I can produce in myself both pleasure and pain, which is one great concernment of my present state. This is certain: the confidence that our faculties do not herein deceive us, is the greatest assurance we are capable of concerning the existence of material beings. For we cannot act anything but by our faculties; nor talk of

knowledge itself, but by the help of those faculties which are fitted to apprehend even what knowledge is.

9. *But reaches no further than actual Sensation.* In fine, then, when our senses do actually convey into our understandings any idea, we cannot but be satisfied that there doth something *at that time* really exist without us, which doth affect our senses, and by them give notice of itself to our apprehensive faculties, and actually produce that idea which we then perceive: and we cannot so far distrust their testimony, as to doubt that such *collections* of simple ideas as we have observed by our senses to be united together, do really exist together. But this knowledge extends as far as the present testimony of our senses, employed about particular objects that do then affect them, and no further. For if I saw such a collection of simple ideas as is wont to be called *man,* existing together one minute since, and am now alone, I cannot be certain that the same man exists now, since there is no *necessary connexion* of his existence a minute since with his existence now: by a thousand ways he may cease to be, since I had the testimony of my senses for his existence. And if I cannot be certain that the man I saw last to-day is now in being, I can less be certain that he is so who hath been longer removed from my senses, and I have not seen since yesterday, or since the last year: and much less can I be certain of the existence of men that I never saw. And, therefore, though it be highly probable that millions of men do now exist, yet, whilst I am alone, writing this, I have not that certainty of it which we strictly call knowledge; though the great likelihood of it puts me past doubt, and it be reasonable for me to do several things upon the confidence that there are men (and men also of my acquaintance, with whom I have to do) now in the world: but this is but probability, not knowledge.

10. *Folly to expect Demonstration in everything.* Whereby yet we may observe how foolish and vain a thing it is for a man of a narrow knowledge, who having reason given him to judge of the different evidence and probability of things, and to be swayed accordingly; how vain, I say, it is to expect demonstration and certainty in things not capable of it; and refuse assent to very rational propositions, and act contrary to very plain and clear truths, because they cannot be made out so evident, as to surmount every the least (I will not say reason, but) pretence of doubting. He that, in the ordinary affairs of life, would admit of nothing but direct plain demonstration, would be sure of nothing in this world, but of perishing quickly. The wholesomeness of his meat or drink would not give him reason to venture on it: and I would fain know what it is he could do upon such grounds as are capable of no doubt, no objection.

Chapter XVIII.—OF FAITH AND REASON, AND THEIR DISTINCT PROVINCES

1. *Necessary to know their boundaries.* It has been above shown, 1. That we are of necessity ignorant, and want knowledge of all sorts, where we wánt ideas. 2. That we are ignorant, and want rational knowledge, where we want proofs. 3. That we want certain knowledge and certainly, as far as we want clear and determined specific ideas. 4. That we want probability to direct our assent in matters where we have neither knowledge of our own nor testimony of other men to bottom our reason upon.

From these things thus premised, I think we may come to lay down *the measures and boundaries between faith and reason:* the want whereof may possibly have been the cause, if not of great disorders, yet at least of great disputes, and perhaps mistakes in the world. For till it be resolved how far we are to be guided by reason, and how far by faith, we shall in vain dispute, and endeavour to convince one another in matters of religion.

2. *Faith and Reason, what, as contradistinguished.* I find every sect, as far as reason will help them, make use of it gladly: and where it fails them, they cry out, It is matter of faith, and above reason. And I do not see how they can argue with any one, or ever convince a gainsayer who makes use of the same plea, without setting down strict boundaries between faith and reason; which ought to be the first point established in all questions where faith has anything to do.

Reason, therefore, here, as contradistinguished to *faith,* I take to be the discovery of the certainty or probability of such propositions or truths, which the mind arrives at by deduction made from such ideas, which it has got by the use of its natural faculties; viz. by sensation or reflection.

Faith, on the other side, is the assent to any proposition, not thus made out by the deductions of reason, but upon the credit of the proposer, as coming from God, in some extraordinary way of communication. This way of discovering truths to men, we call *revelation.*

3. *First, No new simple Idea can be conveyed by traditional Revelation. First,* Then I say, that *no man inspired by God can by any revelation communicate to others any new simple ideas which they had not before from sensation of reflection.* For, whatsoever impressions he himself may have from the immediate hand of God, this revelation, if it be of new simple ideas, cannot be conveyed to another, either by words or any other signs. Because words, by their immediate operation on us, cause no other ideas but of their natural sounds: and it is by the custom of using them for signs, that they excite and revive in our

minds latent ideas; but yet only such ideas as were there before. For words, seen or heard, recall to our thoughts those ideas only which to us they have been wont to be signs of, but cannot introduce any perfectly new, and formerly unknown simple ideas. The same holds in all other signs; which cannot signify to us things of which we have before never had any idea at all.

Thus whatever things were discovered to St. Paul, when he was rapt up into the third heaven; whatever new ideas his mind there received, all the description he can make to others of that place, is only this, That there are such things, 'as eye hath not seen, nor ear heard, nor hath it entered into the heart of man to conceive.' And supposing God should discover to any one, supernaturally, a species of creatures inhabiting, for example, Jupiter or Saturn, (for that it is possible there may be such, nobody can deny,) which had six senses; and imprint on his mind the ideas conveyed to theirs by that sixth sense: he could no more, by words, produce in the minds of other men those ideas imprinted by that sixth sense, than one of us could convey the idea of any colour, by the sound of words, into a man who, having the other four senses perfect, had always totally wanted the fifth, of seeing. For our simple ideas, then, which are the foundation, and sole matter of all our notions and knowledge, we must depend wholly on our reason, I mean our natural faculties; and can by no means receive them, or any of them, from traditional revelation. I say, *traditional revelation*, in distinction to *original revelation*. By the one, I mean that first impression which is made immediately by God on the mind of any man, to which we cannot set any bounds; and by the other, those impressions delivered over to others in words, and the ordinary ways of conveying our conceptions one to another.

4. *Secondly, Traditional Revelation may make us know Propositions knowable also by Reason, but not with the same Certainty that Reason doth. Secondly,* I say that *the same truths may be discovered, and conveyed down from revelation, which are discoverable to us by reason, and by those ideas we naturally may have.* So God might, by revelation, discover the truth of any proposition in Euclid; as well as men, by the natural use of their faculties, come to make the discovery themselves. In all things of this kind there is little need or use of revelation, God having furnished us with natural and surer means to arrive at the knowledge of them. For whatsoever truth we come to the clear discovery of, from the knowledge and contemplation of our own ideas, will always be certainer to us than those which are conveyed to us by *traditional revelation*. For the knowledge we have that this revelation came at first from God, can never be so sure as the knowledge we have

from the clear and distinct perception of the agreement or disagreement of our own ideas: v.g. if it were revealed some ages since, that
the three angles of a triangle were equal to two right ones, I might
assent to the truth of that proposition, upon the credit of the tradition,
that it was revealed: but that would never amount to so great a certainty as the knowledge of it, upon the comparing and measuring my
own ideas of two right angles, and the three angles of a triangle. The
like holds in matter of fact knowable by our senses; v.g. the history
of the deluge is conveyed to us by writings which had their original
from revelation: and yet nobody, I think, will say he has as certain
and clear a knowledge of the flood as Noah, that saw it; or that he
himself would have had, had he then been alive and seen it. For he
has no greater an assurance than that of his senses, that it is writ in
the book supposed writ by Moses inspired: but he has not so great
an assurance that Moses wrote that book as if he had seen Moses write
it. So that the assurance of its being a revelation is less still than the
assurance of his senses.

5. *Even Original Revelation cannot be admitted against the clear
Evidence of Reason.* In propositions, then, whose certainty is built upon
clear perception of the agreement or disagreement of our ideas, attained
either by immediate intuition, as in self-evident propositions, or by
evident deduction of reason in demonstrations we need not the assistance of revelation, as necessary to gain our assent, and introduce them
into our minds. Because the natural ways of knowledge could settle
them there, or had done it already; which is the greatest assurance we
can possibly have of anything, unless where God immediately reveals
it to us: and there too our assurance can be no greater than our knowledge is, that it *is* a revelation from God. But yet nothing, I think, can,
under that title, shake or overrule plain knowledge; or rationally prevail with any man to admit it for true, in a direct contradiction to
the clear evidence of his own understanding. For, since no evidence of
our faculties, by which we receive such revelations, can exceed, if equal,
the certainty of our intuitive knowledge, we can never receive for a
truth anything that is directly contrary to our clear and distinct knowledge; v.g. the ideas of one body and one place do so clearly agree,
and the mind has so evident a perception of their agreement, that we
can never assent to a proposition that affirms the same body to be in
two distant places at once, however it should pretend to the authority
of a divine revelation: since the evidence, first, that we deceive not
ourselves, in ascribing it to God; secondly, that we understand it right;
can never be so great as the evidence of our own intuitive knowledge,
whereby we discern it impossible for the same body to be in two places

at once. And therefore *no proposition can be received for divine revelation, or obtain the assent due to all such, if it be contradictory to our clear intuitive knowledge.* Because this would be to subvert the principles and foundations of all knowledge, evidence, and assent whatsoever: and there would be left no difference between truth and falsehood, no measures of credible and incredible in the world, if doubtful propositions shall take place before self-evident; and what we certainly know give way to what we may possibly be mistaken in. In propositions therefore contrary to the clear perception of the agreement or disagreement of any of our ideas, it will be in vain to urge them as matters of faith. They cannot move our assent under that or any other title whatsoever. For faith can never convince us of anything that contradicts our knowledge. Because, though faith be founded on the testimony of God (who cannot lie) revealing any proposition to us: yet we cannot have an assurance of the truth of its being a divine revelation greater than our own knowledge. Since the whole strength of the certainty depends upon our knowledge that God revealed it; which, in this case, where the proposition supposed revealed contradicts our knowledge or reason, will always have this objection hanging to it, viz. that we cannot tell how to conceive that to come from God, the bountiful Author of our being, which, if received for true, must overturn all the principles and foundations of knowledge he has given us; render all our faculties useless; wholly destroy the most excellent part of his workmanship, our understandings; and put a man in a condition wherein he will have less light, less conduct than the beast that perisheth. For if the mind of man can never have a clearer (and perhaps not so clear) evidence of anything to be a divine revelation, as it has of the principles of its own reason, it can never have a ground to quit the clear evidence of its reason, to give a place to a proposition, whose revelation has not a greater evidence than those principles have.

6. *Traditional Revelation much less.* Thus far a man has use of reason, and ought to hearken to it, even in immediate and original revelation, where it is supposed to be made to himself. But to all those who pretend not to immediate revelation, but are required to pay obedience, and to receive the truths revealed to others, which, by the tradition of writings, or word of mouth, are conveyed down to them, reason has a great deal more to do, and is that only which can induce us to receive them. For matter of faith being only divine revelation, and nothing else, faith, as we use the word, (called commonly *divine faith*), has to do with no propositions, but those which are supposed to be divinely revealed. So that I do not see how those who make revelation alone the sole object of faith can say, That it is a matter

of faith, and not of reason, to believe that such or such a proposition, to be found in such or such a book, is of divine inspiration; unless it be revealed that that proposition, or all in that book, was communicated by divine inspiration. Without such a revelation, the believing, or not believing, that proposition, or book, to be of divine authority, can never be matter of faith, but matter of reason; and such as I must come to an assent to only by the use of my reason, which can never require or enable me to believe that which is contrary to itself: it being impossible for reason ever to procure any assent to that which to itself appears unreasonable.

In all things, therefore, where we have clear evidence from our ideas, and those principles of knowledge I have above mentioned, reason is the proper judge; and revelation, though it may, in consenting with it, confirm its dictates, yet cannot in such cases invalidate its decrees: nor can we be obliged, where we have the clear and evident sentence of reason, to quit it for the contrary opinion, under a pretence that it is matter of faith: which can have no authority against the plain and clear dictates of reason.

7. *Thirdly, Things above Reason are, when revealed, the proper matter of faith.* But, *Thirdly,* There being many things wherein we have very imperfect notions, or none at all; and other things, of whose past, present, or future existence, by the natural use of our faculties, we can have no knowledge at all; these, as being beyond the discovery of our natural faculties, and *above reason,* are, when revealed, *the proper matter of faith.* Thus, that part of the angels rebelled against God, and thereby lost their first happy state: and that the dead shall rise, and live again: these and the like, being beyond the discovery of reason, are purely matters of faith, with which reason has directly nothing to do.

8. *Or not contrary to Reason, if revealed, are Matter of Faith; and must carry it against probable conjectures of Reason.* But since God, in giving us the light of reason, has not thereby tied up his own hands from affording us, when he thinks fit, the light of revelation in any of those matters wherein our natural faculties are able to give a probable determination; *revelation,* where God has been pleased to give it, *must carry it against the probable conjectures of reason.* Because the mind not being certain of the truth of that it does not evidently know, but only yielding to the probability that appears in it, is bound to give up its assent to such a testimony which, it is satisfied, comes from one who cannot err, and will not deceive. But yet, it still belongs to reason to judge of the truth of its being a revelation, and of the signification of the words wherein it is delivered.

Indeed, if anything shall be thought revelation which is contrary to the plain principles of reason, and the evident knowledge the mind has of its own clear and distinct ideas; there reason must be hearkened to, as to a matter within its province. Since a man can never have so certain a knowledge, that a proposition which contradicts the clear principles and evidence of his own knowledge was divinely revealed, or that he understands the words rightly wherein it is delivered, as he has that the contrary is true, and so is bound to consider and judge of it as a matter of reason, and not swallow it, without examination, as a matter of faith.

9. *Revelation in Matters where Reason cannot judge, or but probably, ought to be hearkened to.* First, Whatever proposition is revealed, of whose truth our mind, by its natural faculties and notions, cannot judge, that is purely matter of faith, and above reason.

Secondly, All propositions whereof the mind, by the use of its natural faculties, can come to determine and judge, from naturally acquired ideas, are matter of reason; with this difference still, that, in those concerning which it has but an uncertain evidence, and so is persuaded of their truth only upon probable grounds, which still admit a possibility of the contrary to be true, without doing violence to the certain evidence of its own knowledge, and overturning the principles of all reason; in such probable propositions, I say, an evident revelation ought to determine our assent, even against probability. For where the principles of reason have not evidenced a proposition to be certainly true or false, there clear revelation, as another principle of truth and ground of assent, may determine; and so it may be matter of faith, and be also above reason. Because reason, in that particular matter, being able to reach no higher than probability, faith gave the determination where reason came short; and revelation discovered on which side the truth lay.

10. *In Matters where Reason can afford certain Knowledge, that is to be hearkened to.* Thus far the dominion of faith reaches, and that without any violence or hindrance to reason; which is not injured or disturbed, but assisted and improved by new discoveries of truth, coming from the eternal fountain of all knowledge. Whatever God hath revealed is certainly true: no doubt can be made of it. This is the proper object of faith: but whether it be a *divine* revelation or no, reason must judge; which can never permit the mind to reject a greater evidence to embrace what is less evident, nor allow it to entertain probability in opposition to knowledge and certainty. There can be no evidence that any traditional revelation is of divine original, in the words we receive it, and in the sense we understand it, so clear and

so certain as that of the principles of reason: and therefore *Nothing that is contrary to, and inconsistent with, the clear and self-evident dictates of reason, has a right to be urged or assented to as a matter of faith, wherein reason hath nothing to do.* Whatsoever is divine revelation, ought to overrule all our opinions, prejudices, and interest, and hath a right to be received with full assent. Such a submission as this, of our reason to faith, takes not away the landmarks of knowledge: this shakes not the foundations of reason, but leaves us that use of our faculties for which they were given us.

11. *If the Boundaries be not set between Faith and Reason, no Enthusiasm or Extravagancy in Religion can be contradicted.* If the provinces of faith and reason are not kept distinct by these boundaries, there will, in matter of religion, be no room for reason at all; and those extravagant opinions and ceremonies that are to be found in the several religions of the world will not deserve to be blamed. For, to this crying up of faith in *opposition* to reason, we may, I think, in good measure ascribe those absurdities that fill almost all the religions which possess and divide mankind. For men having been principled with an opinion, that they must not consult reason in the things of religion, however apparently contradictory to common sense and the very principles of all their knowledge, have let loose their fancies and natural superstition; and have been by them led into so strange opinions, and extravagant practices in religion, that a considerate man cannot but stand amazed at their follies, and judge them so far from being acceptable to the great and wise God, that he cannot avoid thinking them ridiculous and offensive to a sober good man. So that, in effect, religion, which should most distinguish us from beasts, and ought most peculiarly to elevate us, as rational creatures, above brutes, is that wherein men often appear most irrational, and more senseless than beasts themselves. *Credo, quia impossibile est:* I believe, because it is impossible, might, in a good man, pass for a sally of zeal; but would prove a very ill rule for men to choose their opinions or religion by.

III

BERKELEY

GEORGE BERKELEY was born in Ireland in 1685. From 1729 to 1731 he was in America attempting to establish a missionary college, and in 1734 he was made Bishop of Cloyne (Ireland). He died in Oxford in 1753. His most important writings were *Essay Towards a New Theory of Vision* (1709), *Treatise Concerning the Principles of Human Knowledge,* Part I (1710)—Part II was never published—*Three Dialogues between Hylas and Philonous* (1713), *Alciphron, or The Minute Philosopher* (1737), and *Siris* (1744). All of Berkeley's works are marked by great clarity and a limpid style.

Our selections are drawn from the *Principles,* "wherein the Chief Causes of Error and Difficulty in the Sciences, with the Grounds of Skepticism, Atheism, and Irreligion are Inquired into." This subtitle explains Berkeley's purpose: he thought he saw in Newton's and Locke's theories the germs of atheism and skepticism, which he would eradicate by making a direct argument for the existence of God without the weak (and, he thought, missing) link of a material world, which Locke had believed required God for its cause. The paradoxical sound of Berkeley's teaching led to attacks by Hume, Reid, Samuel Johnson, and Kant; but his philosophy remains instructive to the present time as a classical statement of the theory of idealism or phenomenalism. Many contemporary thinkers who regard sense data as the proper objects of perception and who think of physical objects as constructions from sense data, owe much to Berkeley and his criticism of the theory of representative realism, i.e., Locke's view that we know ideas directly and that we know external objects only insofar as they are represented by ideas in the mind. But most modern phenomenalists and many idealists reject the theological conclusions Berkeley drew from his theory of knowledge.

Our selections cover the first seventy-nine articles of the *Principles,* with two small omissions. The section titles are my own, not Berkeley's.

Treatise Concerning the Principles of Human Knowledge

¶ A. No Unperceived Ideas

It is evident to anyone who takes a survey of the objects of human knowledge, that they are either ideas (1) actually imprinted on the senses, or else such as are (2) perceived by attending to the passions and operations of the mind, or lastly (3) ideas formed by help of memory and imagination, either compounding, dividing, or barely representing those originally perceived in the aforesaid ways. By sight I have the ideas of lights and colors, with their several degrees and variations. By touch I perceive hard and soft, heat and cold, motion and resistance, and of all these more and less either as to quantity or degree. Smelling furnishes me with odors, the palate with tastes, and hearing conveys sounds to the mind in all their variety of tone and composition. And as several of these are observed to accompany each other, they come to be marked by one name, and so to be reputed as one thing. Thus, for example, a certain color, taste, smell, figure, and consistence, having been observed to go together, are accounted one distinct thing, signified by the name "apple." Other collections of ideas constitute a stone, a tree, a book, and the like sensible things; which, as they are pleasing or disagreeable, excite the passions of love, hatred, joy, grief, and so forth.

2. But besides all that endless variety of ideas or objects of knowledge, there is likewise something which knows or perceives them, and exercises divers operations, as willing, imagining, remembering, about them. This perceiving, active being is what I call *mind, spirit, soul,* or *myself.* By which words I do not denote any one of my ideas, but a thing entirely distinct from them wherein they exist, or, which is the same thing, whereby they are perceived; for the existence of an idea consists in being perceived.

3. That neither our thoughts, nor passions, nor ideas formed by the imagination, exist without the mind, is what everybody will allow. And

it seems no less evident that the various sensations or ideas imprinted on the sense, however blended or combined together (that is, whatever objects they compose), cannot exist otherwise than in a mind perceiving them. I think an intuitive knowledge may be obtained of this by anyone that shall attend to what is meant by the term 'exist' when applied to sensible things. The table I write on I say exists—that is, I see and feel it; and if I were out of my study I should say it existed—meaning thereby that if I was in my study I might perceive it, or that some other spirit actually does perceive it. There was an odor, that is, it was smelt; there was a sound, that is, it was heard; a color or figure, and it was perceived by sight or touch. This is all that I can understand by these and the like expressions. For as to what is said of the absolute existence of unthinking things without any relation to their being perceived, that seems perfectly unintelligible. Their *esse* is *percipi,* nor is it possible they should have any existence out of the minds or thinking things which perceive them.

4. It is indeed an opinion strangely prevailing amongst men, that houses, mountains, rivers, and in a word all sensible objects, have an existence, natural or real, distinct from their being perceived by the understanding. But with how great an assurance and acquiescence soever this principle may be entertained in the world, yet whoever shall find in his heart to call it in question may, if I mistake not, perceive it involve a manifest contradiction. For what are the forementioned objects but the things we perceive by sense? and what do we perceive *besides our own ideas or sensations?* and is it not plainly repugnant that any one of these, or any combination of them, should exist unperceived?

¶ B. Abstract Ideas

5. If we thoroughly examine this tenet it will perhaps be found at bottom to depend on the doctrine of *abstract ideas.* For can there be a nicer strain of abstraction than to distinguish the existence of sensible objects from their being perceived, so as to conceive them existing unperceived? Light and colors, heat and cold, extension and figures—in a word the things we see and feel—what are they but so many sensations, notions, ideas, or impressions on the sense? And is it possible to separate, even in thought, any of these from perception? For my part, I might as easily divide a thing from itself. I may, indeed, divide in my thoughts, or conceive apart from each other, those things which perhaps I never perceived by sense so divided. Thus I imagine the trunk of a human body without the limbs, or conceive

the smell of a rose without thinking on the rose itself. So far, I will not deny, I can abstract, if that may properly be called abstraction which extends only to the conceiving separately such objects as it is possible may really exist or be actually perceived asunder. But my conceiving or imagining power does not extend beyond the possibility of real existence or perception. Hence, as it is impossible for me to see or feel anything without an actual sensation of that thing, so it is impossible for me to conceive in my thoughts any sensible thing or object distinct from the sensation or perception of it.

¶ C. Spirit

6. Some truths there are so near and obvious to the mind that a man need only open his eyes to see them. Such I take this important one to be, to wit, that all the choir of heaven and furniture of the earth, in a word all those bodies which compose the mighty frame of the world, have not any subsistence without a mind, that their *being* is to be perceived or known; that consequently so long as they are not actually perceived by me, or do not exist in my mind or that of any other created spirit, they must either have no existence at all, or else subsist in the mind of some Eternal Spirit; it being perfectly unintelligible, and involving all the absurdity of abstraction, to attribute to any single part of them an existence independent of a spirit. To be convinced of which, the reader need only reflect and try to separate in his own thoughts the *being* of a sensible thing from its *being perceived*.

7. From what has been said it follows there is not any other substance than *spirit*, or that which perceives. But for the fuller proof of this point, let it be considered the sensible qualities are color, figure, motion, smell, taste, etc.—that is, the ideas perceived by sense. Now, for an idea to exist in an unperceiving thing is a manifest contradiction, for to have an idea is all one as to perceive; that therefore wherein color, figure, and the like qualities exist must perceive them; hence it is clear there can be no unthinking substance or *substratum* of those ideas.

¶ D. Ideas Not Copies

8. But, say you, though the ideas themselves do not exist without the mind, yet there may be things *like* them, whereof they are copies or resemblances, which things exist without the mind in an unthinking substance. I answer, an idea can be like nothing but an idea; a color

or figure can be like nothing but another color or figure. If we look but never so little into our thoughts, we shall find it impossible for us to conceive a likeness except only between our ideas. Again, I ask whether those supposed originals or external things, of which our ideas are the pictures or representations, be themselves perceivable or no? If they are, then they are ideas and we have gained our point; but if you say they are not, I appeal to anyone whether it be sense to assert a color is like something which is invisible; hard or soft, like something which is intangible; and so of the rest.

¶ E. PRIMARY AND SECONDARY QUALITIES

9. Some there are who make a distinction betwixt *primary* and *secondary* qualities. By the former they mean extension, figure, motion, rest, solidity or impenetrability, and number; by the latter they denote all other sensible qualities, as colors, sounds, tastes, and so forth. The ideas we have of these they acknowledge not to be the resemblances of anything existing without the mind, or unperceived, but they will have our ideas of the primary qualities to be patterns or images of things which exist without the mind, in an unthinking substance which they call *matter*. By *matter,* therefore, we are to understand an inert, senseless substance, in which extension, figure, and motion do actually subsist. But it is evident from what we have already shown, that extension, figure, and motion are only ideas existing in the mind, and that an idea can be like nothing but another idea, and that consequently neither they nor their archetypes can exist in an unperceiving substance. Hence, it is plain that the very notion of what is called *matter,* or *corporeal substance,* involves a contradiction in it.

10. They who assert that figure, motion, and the rest of the primary or original qualities do exist without the mind in unthinking substances, do at the same time acknowledge that color, sounds, heat, cold, and suchlike secondary qualities, do not; which they tell us are sensations existing in the mind alone, that depend on and are occasioned by the different size, texture, and motion of the minute particles of matter. This they take for an undoubted truth, which they can demonstrate beyond all exception. Now, if it be certain that those original qualities are inseparably united with the other sensible qualities, and not, even in thought, capable of being abstracted from them, it plainly follows that they exist only in the mind. But I desire anyone to reflect and try whether he can, by any abstraction of thought, conceive the extension and motion of a body without all other sensible qualities. For my own part, I see evidently that it is not in my power to frame an idea

of a body extended and moving, but I must withal give it some color or other sensible quality which is acknowledged to exist only in the mind. In short, extension, figure, and motion, abstracted from all other qualities, are inconceivable. Where therefore the other sensible qualities are, there must these be also, to wit, in the mind and nowhere else.

11. Again, *great* and *small, swift* and *slow,* are allowed to exist nowhere without the mind, being entirely relative, and changing as the frame or position of the organs of sense varies. The extension therefore which exists without the mind is neither great nor small, the motion neither swift nor slow, that is, they are nothing at all. But, say you, they are extension in general, and motion in general: thus we see how much the tenet of extended movable substances existing without the mind depends on the strange doctrine of *abstract ideas.* And here I cannot but remark how nearly the vague and indeterminate description of matter or corporeal substance, which the modern philosophers are run into by their own principles, resembles that antiquated and so much ridiculed notion of *materia prima,* to be met with in Aristotle and his followers. Without extension solidity cannot be conceived; since therefore it has been shewn that extension exists not in an unthinking substance, the same must also be true of solidity.

12. That *number* is entirely the creature of the mind, even though the other qualities be allowed to exist without, will be evident to whoever considers that the same thing bears a different denomination of number as the mind views it with different respects. Thus, the same extension is one, or three, or thirty-six, according as the mind considers it with reference to a yard, a foot, or an inch. Number is so visibly relative, and dependent on men's understanding, that it is strange to think how anyone should give it an absolute existence without the mind. We say one book, one page, one line; all these are equally units, though some contain several of the others. And in each instance, it is plain, the unit relates to some particular combination of ideas arbitrarily put together by the mind.

13. *Unity,* I know, some will have to be a simple or uncompounded idea, accompanying all other ideas into the mind. That I have any such idea answering the word "unity" I do not find; and if I had, methinks I could not miss finding it: on the contrary, it should be the most familiar to my understanding, since it is said to accompany all other ideas, and to be perceived by all the ways of sensation and reflection. To say no more, it is an *abstract idea.*

14. It shall farther add that, after the same manner as modern philosophers prove certain sensible qualities to have no existence in matter, or without the mind, the same thing may be likewise proved

of all other sensible qualities whatsoever. Thus, for instance, it is said that heat and cold are affections only of the mind, and not at all patterns of real beings, existing in the corporeal substances which excite them, for that the same body which appears cold to one hand seems warm to another. Now, why may we not as well argue that figure and extension are not patterns or resemblances of qualities existing in matter, because to the same eye at different stations, or eyes of a different texture at the same station, they appear various, and cannot therefore be the images of anything settled and determinate without the mind? Again, it is proved that sweetness is not really in the sapid thing, because the thing remaining unaltered the sweetness is changed into bitter, as in case of a fever or otherwise vitiated palate. Is it not as reasonable to say that motion is not without the mind, since if the succession of ideas in the mind become swifter, the motion, it is acknowledged, shall appear slower without any alteration in any external object?

¶ F. No Material Substance

15. In short, let anyone consider those arguments which are thought manifestly to prove that colors and tastes exist only in the mind, and he shall find they may with equal force be brought to prove the same thing of extension, figure, and motion—though it must be confessed this method of arguing does not so much prove that there is no extension or color in an outward object, as that we do not know by sense which is the true extension or color of the object. But the arguments foregoing plainly show it to be impossible that any color or extension at all, or other sensible quality whatsoever, should exist in an unthinking subject without the mind, or in truth, that there should be any such thing as an outward object.

16. But let us examine a little the received opinion. It is said extension is a mode or accident of matter, and that matter is the *substratum* that supports it. Now I desire that you would explain to me what is meant by matter's *supporting* extension. Say you, I have no idea of matter and therefore cannot explain it. I answer, though you have no positive, yet, if you have any meaning at all, you must at least have a relative idea of matter; though you know not what it is, yet you must be supposed to know what relation it bears to accidents, and what is meant by its supporting them. It is evident "support" cannot here be taken in its usual or literal sense—as when we say that pillars support a building; in what sense therefore must it be taken?

17. If we inquire into what the most accurate philosophers declare

themselves to mean by *material substance,* we shall find them acknowledge they have no other meaning annexed to those sounds but the idea of *Being in general,* together with the relative notion of its supporting accidents. The general idea of Being appeareth to me the most abstract and incomprehensible of all other; and as for its supporting accidents, this, as we have just now observed, cannot be understood in the common sense of those words; it must therefore be taken in some other sense, but what that is they do not explain. So that when I consider the two parts or branches which make the signification of the words *material substance,* I am convinced there is no distinct meaning annexed to them. But why should we trouble ourselves any farther, in discussing this material *substratum* or support of figure and motion, and other sensible qualities? Does it not suppose they have an existence without the mind? And is not this a direct repugnancy, and altogether inconceivable?

18. But though it were possible that solid, figured, movable substances may exist without the mind, corresponding to the ideas we have of bodies, yet how is it possible for us to know this? Either we must know it by sense or by reason. As for our senses, by them we have the knowledge only of our sensations, ideas, or those things that are immediately perceived by sense, call them what you will; but they do not inform us that things exist without the mind, or unperceived, like to those which are perceived. This the materialists themselves acknowledge. It remains therefore that if we have any knowledge at all of external things, it must be by reason, inferring their existence from what is immediately perceived by sense. But what reason can induce us to believe the existence of bodies without the mind, from what we perceive, since the very patrons of matter themselves do not pretend there is any necessary connection betwixt them and our ideas? I say it is granted on all hands (and what happens in dreams, frenzies, and the like, puts it beyond dispute) that *it is possible we might be affected with all the ideas we have now, though there were no bodies existing without, resembling them.* Hence, it is evident the supposition of external bodies is not necessary for the producing our ideas; since it is granted they are produced sometimes, and might possibly be produced always in the same order we see them in at present, without their concurrence.

19. But, though we might possibly have all our sensations without them, yet perhaps it may be thought easier to conceive and explain the manner of their production by supposing external bodies in their likeness rather than otherwise; and so it might be at least probable there are such things as bodies that excite their ideas in our minds. But neither can this be said; for though we give the materialists their ex-

ternal bodies, they by their own confession are never the nearer knowing how our ideas are produced, since they own themselves unable to
comprehend in what manner body can act upon spirit, or how it is
possible it should imprint any idea in the mind. Hence it is evident
the production of ideas or sensations in our minds can be no reason
why we should suppose matter or corporeal substances, since that is
acknowledged to remain equally inexplicable with or without this supposition. If therefore it were possible for bodies to exist without the
mind, yet to hold they do so, must needs be a very precarious opinion;
since it is to suppose, without any reason at all, that God has created
innumerable beings that are entirely useless, and serve to no manner
of purpose.

20. In short, if there were external bodies, it is impossible we should
ever come to know it; and if there were not, we might have the very
same reasons to think there were that we have now. Suppose (what no
one can deny possible) an intelligence without the help of external
bodies, to be affected with the same train of sensations or ideas that
you are, imprinted in the same order and with like vividness in his
mind. I ask whether that intelligence hath not all the reason to believe
the existence of corporeal substances, represented by his ideas, and
exciting them in his mind, that you can possibly have for believing the
same thing? Of this there can be no question; which one consideration
were enough to make any reasonable person suspect the strength of
whatever arguments he may think himself to have for the existence of
bodies without the mind.

22. I am afraid I have given cause to think I am needlessly prolix
in handling this subject. For, to what purpose is it to dilate on that
which may be demonstrated with the utmost evidence in a line or two,
to anyone that is capable of the least reflection? It is but looking into
your own thoughts, and so trying whether you can conceive it possible
for a sound, or figure, or motion, or color to exist without the mind or
unperceived. This easy trial may perhaps make you see that what you
contend for is a downright contradiction. Insomuch that I am content
to put the whole upon this issue: if you can but conceive it possible
for one extended movable substance, or, in general, for any one idea,
or anything like an idea, to exist otherwise than in a mind perceiving it,
I shall readily give up the cause; and, as for all that compages of
external bodies you contend for, I shall grant you its existence, though
you cannot either give me any reason why you believe it exists, or
assign any use to it when it is supposed to exist. I say, the bare possibility of your opinion's being true shall pass for an argument that it
is so.

23. But, say you, surely there is nothing easier than for me to imagine trees, for instance, in a park, or books existing in a closet, and nobody by to perceive them. I answer, you may so, there is no difficulty in it; but what is all this, I beseech you, more than framing in your mind certain ideas which you call books and trees, and the same time omitting to frame the idea of anyone that may perceive them? But do not you yourself perceive or think of them all the while? This therefore is nothing to the purpose; it only shews you have the power of imagining or forming ideas in your mind: but it doth not shew that you can conceive it possible the objects of your thought may exist without the mind. To make out this, it is necessary that you conceive them existing unconceived or unthought of, what is a manifest repugnancy. When we do our utmost to conceive the existence of external bodies, we are all the while only contemplating our own ideas. But the mind taking no notice of itself, is deluded to think it can and doth conceive bodies existing unthought of or without the mind, though at the same time they are apprehended by or exist in itself. A little attention will discover to anyone the truth and evidence of what is here said, and make it unnecessary to insist on any other proofs against the existence of *material substance*.

24. It is very obvious, upon the least inquiry into our thoughts, to know whether it is possible for us to understand what is meant by the *absolute existence of sensible objects in themselves, or without the mind*. To me it is evident those words mark out either a direct contradiction, or else nothing at all. And to conceive others of this, I know no readier or fairer way than to entreat they would calmly attend to their own thoughts; and if by this attention the emptiness or repugnancy of those expressions doth appear, surely nothing more is requisite for the conviction. It is on this therefore that I insist, to wit, that the absolute existence of unthinking things are words without a meaning, or which include a contradiction. This is what I repeat and inculcate, and earnestly recommend to the attentive thoughts of the reader.

¶ G. IDEAS INACTIVE; SPIRIT ACTIVE

25. All our ideas, sensations, notions, or the things which we perceive, by whatsoever names they may be distinguished, are visibly inactive: there is nothing of power or agency included in them. So that one idea or object of thought cannot produce or make any alteration in another. To be satisfied of the truth of this, there is nothing else requisite but a bare observation of our ideas. For, since they and every part of them exist only in the mind, it follows that there is nothing in

them but what is perceived: but whoever shall attend to his ideas, whether of sense or reflection, will not perceive in them any power or activity; there is, therefore, no such thing contained in them. A little attention will discover to us that the very being of an idea implies passiveness and inertness in it, insomuch that it is impossible for an idea to do anything, or, strictly speaking, to be the cause of anything: neither can it be the resemblance or pattern of any active being, as is evident from Sec. 8. Whence it plainly follows that extension, figure, and motion cannot be the cause of our sensations. To say, therefore, that these are the effects of powers resulting from the configuration, number, motion, and size of corpuscles, must certainly be false.

26. We perceive a continual succession of ideas, some are anew excited, others are changed or totally disappear. There is therefore some cause of these ideas, whereon they depend, and which produces and changes them. That this cause cannot be any quality or idea or combination of ideas, is clear from the preceding section. It must therefore be a substance; but it has been shewn that there is no corporeal or material substance: it remains therefore that the cause of ideas is an incorporeal active substance or Spirit.

27. A spirit is one simple, undivided, active being: as it perceives ideas it is called the *understanding,* and as it produces or otherwise operates about them it is called the *will.* Hence there can be no *idea* formed of a soul or spirit; for all ideas whatever, being passive and inert (*vide* Sec. 25), they cannot represent unto us, by way of image or likeness, that which acts. A little attention will make it plain to anyone, that to have an idea which shall be like that active principle of motion and change of ideas is absolutely impossible. Such is the nature of *spirit,* or that which acts, that it cannot be of itself perceived, but only by the effects which it produceth. If any man shall doubt of the truth of what is here delivered, let him but reflect and try if he can frame the idea of any power or active being, and whether he hath ideas of two principal powers, marked by the names *will* and *understanding,* distinct from each other as well as from a third idea of substance or being in general, with a relative notion of its supporting or being the subject of the aforesaid powers—which is signified by the name *soul* or *spirit.* This is what some hold; but, so far as I can see, the words *will, soul, spirit,* do not stand for different ideas, or, in truth, for any idea at all, but for something which is very different from ideas, and which, being an agent, cannot be like unto, or represented by, any idea whatsoever. Though it must be owned at the same time that we have some *notion* of soul, spirit, and the operations of the mind such as willing, loving, hating; inasmuch as we know or under-

stand the meaning of these words.

28. I find I can excite ideas in my mind at pleasure, and vary and shift the scene as oft as I think fit. It is no more than willing, and straightway this or that idea arises in my fancy; and by the same power it is obliterated and makes way for another. This making and unmaking of ideas doth very properly denominate the mind active. Thus much is certain and grounded on experience; but when we think of unthinking agents or of exciting ideas exclusive of volition, we only amuse ourselves with words.

¶ H. The Existence of Real Things

29. But, whatever power I may have over my own thoughts, I find the ideas actually perceived by sense have not a like dependence on my will. When in broad daylight I open my eyes, it is not in my power to choose whether I shall see or no, or to determine what particular objects shall present themselves to my view; and so likewise as to the hearing and other senses, the ideas imprinted on them are not creatures of my will. There is therefore some other will or spirit that produces them.

30. The ideas of sense are more strong, lively, and distinct than those of the imagination; they have likewise a steadiness, order, and coherence, and are not excited at random, as those which are the effects of human wills often are, but in a regular train or series, the admirable connection whereof sufficiently testifies the wisdom and benevolence of its Author. Now the set rules or established methods wherein the mind we depend on excites in us the ideas of sense, are called the *laws of nature;* and these we learn by experience, which teaches us that such and such ideas are attended with such and such other ideas, in the ordinary course of things.

31. This gives us a sort of foresight which enables us to regulate our actions for the benefit of life. And without this we should be eternally at a loss: we could not know how to act anything that might procure us the least pleasure, or remove the least pain of sense. That food nourishes, sleep refreshes, and fire warms us; that to sow in the seed-time is the way to reap in the harvest; and, in general, that to obtain such or such ends, such or such means are conducive—all this we know, not by discovering any necessary connection between our ideas, but only by the observation of the settled laws of nature, without which we should be all in uncertainty and confusion, and a grown man no more know how to manage himself in the affairs of life than an infant just born.

32. And yet this insistent uniform working, which so evidently dis-

plays the goodness and wisdom of that governing Spirit whose will constitutes the laws of nature, is so far from leading our thoughts to Him, that it rather sends them wandering after second causes. For, when we perceive certain ideas of sense constantly followed by other ideas and we know this is not of our own doing, we forthwith attribute power and agency to the ideas themselves, and make one the cause of another, than which nothing can be more absurd and unintelligible. Thus, for example, having observed that when we perceive by sight a certain round luminous figure we at the same time perceive by touch the idea or sensation called heat, we do from thence conclude the sun to be the cause of heat. And in like manner perceiving the motion and collision of bodies to be attended with sound, we are inclined to think the latter the effect of the former.

33. The ideas imprinted on the senses by the Author of nature are called *real things;* and those excited in the imagination, being less regular, vivid, and constant, are more properly termed *ideas,* or *images* of *things,* which they copy and represent. But then our sensations, be they never so vivid and distinct, are nevertheless ideas, that is, they exist in the mind, or are perceived by it, as truly as the ideas of its own framing. The ideas of sense are allowed to have more reality in them, that is, to be more strong, orderly, and coherent than the creatures of the mind; but this is no argument that they exist without the mind. They are also less dependent on the spirit, or thinking substance which perceives them, in that they are excited by the will of another and more powerful spirit; yet still they are *ideas,* and certainly no idea, whether faint or strong, can exist otherwise than in a mind perceiving it.

¶ I. REPLIES TO OBJECTIONS

34. Before we proceed any farther it is necessary we spend some time in answering objections which may probably be made against the principles we have hitherto laid down. In doing of which, if I seem too prolix to those of quick apprehensions, I hope it may be pardoned, since all men do not equally apprehend things of this nature, and I am willing to be understood by everyone.

First, then, it will be objected that by the foregoing principles all that is real and substantial in nature is banished out of the world, and instead thereof a chimerical scheme of *ideas* takes place. All things that exist, exist only in the mind, that is, they are purely notional. What therefore becomes of the sun, moon, and stars? What must we think of houses, rivers, mountains, trees, stones; nay, even of our own bodies? Are all these but so many chimeras and illusions on the fancy? To all

which, and whatever else of the same sort may be objected, I answer
that by the principles premised we are not deprived of any one thing
in nature. Whatever we see, feel, hear, or anywise conceive or understand remains as secure as ever, and is as real as ever. There is a *rerum
natura,* and the distinction between realities and chimeras retains its
full force. This is evident from Sec. 29, 30, and 33, where we have
shewn what is meant by *real things* in opposition to *chimeras* or ideas of
our own framing; but then they both equally exist in the mind, and
in that sense they are alike *ideas.*

35. I do not argue against the existence of any one thing that we
can apprehend either by sense or reflection. That the things I see with
my eyes and touch with my hands do exist, really exist, I make not the
least question. The only thing whose existence we deny is that which
philosophers call matter or corporeal substance. And in doing of this
there is no damage done to the rest of mankind, who, I dare say, will
never miss it. The atheist indeed will want the color of an empty name
to support his impiety; and the philosophers may possibly find they
have lost a great handle for trifling and disputation.

36. If any man thinks this detracts from the existence or reality of
things, he is very far from understanding what hath been premised in
the plainest terms I could think of. Take here an abstract of what has
been said. There are spiritual substances, minds, or human souls, which
will or excite ideas in themselves at pleasure; but these are faint, weak,
and unsteady in respect of others they perceive by sense—which, being
impressed upon them according to certain rules or laws of nature, speak
themselves the effects of a mind more powerful and wise than human
spirits. These latter are said to have more *reality* in them than the
former; by which is meant that they are more affecting, orderly, and
distinct, and that they are not fictions of the mind perceiving them.
And in this sense the sun that I see by day is the real sun, and that
which I imagine by night is the idea of the former. In the sense here
given of "reality" it is evident that every vegetable, star, mineral, and
in general each part of the mundane system, is as much as a real being
by our principles as by any other. Whether others mean anything by
the term "reality" different from what I do, I entreat them to look into
their own thoughts and see.

37. It will be urged that thus much at least is true, to wit, that we
take away all corporeal substances. To this my answer is that if the
word "substance" be taken in the vulgar sense—for a combination of
sensible qualities, such as extension, solidity, weight, and the like—this
we cannot be accused of taking away. But if it be taken in a philosophic
sense—for the support of accidents or qualities without the mind—then

indeed I acknowledge that we take it away, if one may be said to take away that which never had any existence, not even in the imagination.

38. But after all, say you, it sounds very harsh to say we eat and drink ideas, and are clothed with ideas. I acknowledge it does so; the word "idea" not being used in common discourse to signify the several combinations of sensible qualities which are called "things"; and it is certain that any expression which varies from the familiar use of language will seem harsh and ridiculous. But this doth not concern the truth of the proposition, which in other words is no more than to say, we are fed and clothed with those things which we perceive immediately by our senses. The hardness or softness, the color, taste, warmth, figure, or suchlike qualities, which combined together constitute the several sorts of victuals and apparel, have been shewn to exist only in the mind that perceives them; and this is all that is meant by calling them "ideas"; which word if it was as ordinarily used as "things," would sound no harsher nor more ridiculous than it. I am not for disputing about the propriety, but the truth of the expression. If therefore you agree with me that we eat and drink and are clad with the immediate objects of sense, which cannot exist unperceived or without the mind, I shall readily grant it is more proper or conformable to custom that they should be called things rather than ideas.

39. If it be demanded why I make use of the word "idea," and do not rather in compliance with custom call them "thing"; I answer, I do it for two reasons:—first, because the term "thing" in contradistinction to "idea," is generally supposed to denote somewhat existing without the mind; secondly, because "thing" hath a more comprehensive signification than "idea," including spirit or thinking things as well as ideas. Since therefore the objects of sense exist only in the mind, and are withal thoughtless and inactive, I chose to mark them by the word "idea," which implies those properties.

40. But, say what we can, someone perhaps may be apt to reply, he will still believe his senses, and never suffer any arguments, how plausible soever, to prevail over the certainty of them. Be it so; assert the evidence of sense as high as you please, we are willing to do the same. That what I see, hear, and feel doth exist, that is to say, is perceived by me, I no more doubt than I do of my own being. But I do not see how the testimony of sense can be alleged as a proof for the existence of anything which is not perceived by sense. We are not for having any man turn sceptic and disbelieve his senses; on the contrary, we give them all the stress and assurance imaginable; nor are there any principles more opposite to scepticism than those we have laid down, as shall be hereafter clearly shewn.

41. *Secondly,* it will be objected that there is a great difference betwixt real fire for instance, and the idea of fire, betwixt dreaming or imagining oneself burnt, and actually being so: if you suspect it to be only the idea of fire which you see, do but put your hand into it and you will be convinced with a witness. This and the like may be urged in opposition to our tenets. To all which the answer is evident from what hath been already said; and I shall only add in this place, that if real fire be very different from the idea of fire, so also is the real pain that it occasions very different from the idea of the same pain, and yet nobody will pretend that real pain either is, or can possibly be, in an unperceiving thing, or without the mind, any more than its idea.

42. *Thirdly,* it will be objected that we see things actually without or at distance from us, and which consequently do not exist in the mind; it being absurd that those things which are seen at the distance of several miles should be as near to us as our own thoughts. In answer to this, I desire it may be considered that in a dream we do oft perceive things as existing at a great distance off, and yet for all that, those things are acknowledged to have their existence only in the mind.

43. But, for the fuller clearing of this point, it may be worth while to consider how it is that we perceive distance and things placed at a distance by sight. For, that we should in truth see external space, and bodies actually existing in it, some nearer, others farther off, seems to carry with it some opposition to what hath been said of their existing nowhere without the mind. The consideration of this difficulty it was that gave birth to my *Essay towards a New Theory of Vision,* which was published not long since, wherein it is shewn that distance or outness is neither immediately of itself perceived by sight, nor yet apprehended or judged of by lines and angles, or anything that hath a necessary connection with it; but that it is only suggested to our thoughts by certain visible ideas and sensations attending vision, which in their own nature have no manner of similitude or relation either with distance or things placed at a distance; but, by a connection taught us by experience, they come to signify and suggest them to us, after the same manner that words of any language suggest the ideas they are made to stand for; insomuch that a man born blind and afterwards made to see, would not, at first sight, think the things he saw to be without his mind, or at any distance from him. (See Sec. 41 of the forementioned treatise.)

44. The ideas of sight and touch make two species entirely distinct and heterogeneous. *The former are marks and prognostics of the latter.* That the proper objects of sight neither exist without mind, nor are the images of external things, was shewn even in that treatise; though

throughout the same the contrary be supposed true of tangible objects—
not that to suppose that vulgar error was necessary for establishing the
notion therein laid down, but because it was beside my purpose to
examine and refute it in a discourse concerning *vision*. So that in strict
truth the ideas of sight, when we apprehend by them distance and
things placed at a distance, do not suggest or mark out to us things
actually existing at a distance, but only admonish us what ideas of
touch will be imprinted in our minds at such and such distances of time,
and in consequence of such or such actions. It is, I say, evident from
what has been said in the foregoing parts of this treatise, and in Sec.
147 and elsewhere of the essay concerning vision, that visible ideas are
the language whereby the governing Spirit on whom we depend informs
us what tangible ideas he is about to imprint upon us, in case we excite
this or that motion in our own bodies. But for a fuller information in
this point I refer to the essay itself.

45. *Fourthly*, it will be objected that from the foregoing principles
it follows things are every moment annihilated and created anew. The
objects of sense exist only when they are perceived; the trees therefore
are in the garden, or the chairs in the parlor, no longer than while
there is somebody by to perceive them. Upon shutting my eyes all the
furniture in the room is reduced to nothing, and barely upon opening
them it is again created. In answer to all which, I refer the reader to
what has been said in Sec. 3, 4, etc., and desire he will consider whether
he means anything by the actual existence of an idea distinct from its
being perceived. For my part, after the nicest inquiry I could make, I
am not able to discover that anything else is meant by those words;
and I once more entreat the reader to sound his own thoughts, and not
suffer himself to be imposed on by words. If he can conceive it possible
either for his ideas or their archetypes to exist without being perceived,
then I give up the cause; but if he cannot, he will acknowledge it is
unreasonable for him to stand up in defense of he knows not what,
and pretend to charge on me as an absurdity the not assenting to those
propositions which at bottom have no meaning in them.

49. *Fifthly*, it may perhaps be objected that if extension and figure
exist only in the mind, it follows that the mind is extended and
figured; since extension is a mode or attribute which (to speak with
the schools) is predicated of the subject in which it exists. I answer,
those qualities are in the mind only as they are perceived by it—that is,
not by way of *mode* or *attribute*, but only by way of *idea;* and it no
more follows the soul or mind is extended, because extension exists in
it alone, than it does that it is red or blue, because those colors are on
all hands acknowledged to exist in it, and nowhere else. As to what

philosophers say of subject and mode, that seems very groundless and unintelligible. For instance, in this proposition, "a die is hard, extended, and square," they will have it that the word "die" denotes a subject or substance, distinct from the hardness, extension, and figure which are predicated of it, and in which they exist. This I cannot comprehend: to me a die seems to be nothing distinct from those things which are termed its modes or accidents. And, to say a die is hard, extended, and square is not to attribute those qualities to a subject distinct from and supporting them, but only an explication of the meaning of the word "die."

50. *Sixthly*, you will say there have been a great many things explained by matter and motion; take away these and you destroy the whole corpuscular philosophy, and undermine those mechanical principles which have been applied with so much success to account for the phenomena. In short, whatever advances have been made, either by accident or modern philosophers, in the study of nature do all proceed on the supposition that corporeal substance or matter doth really exist. To this I answer that there is not any one phenomenon explained on that supposition which may not as well be explained without it, as might easily be made appear by an induction of particulars. To explain the phenomena, is all one as to shew why, upon such and such occasions, we are affected with such and such ideas. But how matter should operate on a spirit, or produce any idea in it, is what no philosopher will pretend to explain; it is therefore evident there can be no use of matter in natural philosophy. Besides, they who attempt to account for things do it not by corporeal substance, but by figure, motion, and other qualities, which are in truth no more than mere ideas, and, therefore, cannot be the cause of anything, as hath been already shewn. (See Sec. 25.)

51. *Seventhly*, it will upon this be demanded whether it does not seem absurd to take away natural causes, and ascribe everything to the immediate operation of spirits? We must no longer say upon these principles that fire heats, or water cools, but that a spirit heats, and so forth. Would not a man be deservedly laughed at, who should talk after this manner? I answer, he would so; in such things we ought to "think with the learned, and speak with the vulgar." They who to demonstration are convinced of the truth of the Copernican system do nevertheless say, "The sun rises," "The sun sets," or "comes to the meridian"; and if they affected a contrary style in common talk it would without doubt appear very ridiculous. A little reflection on what is here said will make it manifest that the common use of language would receive no manner of alteration or disturbance from the admission of our tenets.

52. In the ordinary affairs of life, any phrases may be retained, so long as they excite in us proper sentiments, or dispositions to act in such a manner as is necessary for our well-being, how false soever they may be if taken in a strict and speculative sense. Nay, this is unavoidable, since, propriety being regulated by custom, language is suited to the received opinions, which are not always the truest. Hence it is impossible, even in the most rigid, philosophic reasonings, so far to alter the bent and genius of the tongue we speak, as never to give a handle for cavilers to pretend difficulties and inconsistencies. But, a fair and ingenuous reader will collect the sense from the scope and tenor and connection of a discourse, making allowances for those inaccurate modes of speech which use has made inevitable.

53. As to the opinion that there are no corporeal causes, this has been heretofore maintained by some of the schoolmen, as it is of late by others among the modern philosophers, who though they allow matter to exist, yet will have God alone to be the immediate efficient cause of all things. These men saw that amongst all the objects of sense there was none which had any power or activity included in it; and that by consequence this was likewise true of whatever bodies they supposed to exist without the mind, like unto the immediate objects of sense. But then, that they should suppose an innumerable multitude of created beings, which they acknowledge are not capable of producing any one effect in nature, and which therefore are made to no manner of purpose, since God might have done everything as well without them: this I say, though we should allow it possible, must yet be a very unaccountable and extravagant supposition.

54. In the *eighth* place, the universal concurrent assent of mankind may be thought by some an invincible argument in behalf of matter, or the existence of external things. Must we suppose the whole world to be mistaken? And if so, what cause can be assigned of so widespread and predominant an error? I answer, first, that, upon a narrow inquiry, it will not perhaps be found so many as is imagined do really believe the existence of matter or things without the mind. Strictly speaking, to believe that which involves a contradiction, or has no meaning in it, is impossible; and whether the foregoing expressions are not of that sort, I refer it to the impartial examination of the reader. In one sense, indeed, men may be said to believe that matter exists, that is, they *act* as if the immediate cause of their sensations, which affects them every moment, and is so nearly present to them, were some senseless unthinking being. But, that they should clearly apprehend any meaning marked by those words, and form thereof a settled speculative opinion, is what I am not able to conceive. This is

not the only instance wherein men impose upon themselves, by imagining they believe those propositions which they have often heard, though at bottom they have no meaning in them.

55. But secondly, though we should grant a notion to be never so universally and steadfastly adhered to, yet this is weak argument of its truth to whoever considers what a vast number of prejudices and false opinions are everywhere embraced with the utmost tenaciousness, by the unreflecting (which are the far greater) part of mankind. There was a time when the antipodes and motion of the earth were looked upon as monstrous absurdities even by men of learning: and if it be considered what a small proportion they bear to the rest of mankind, we shall find that at this day those notions have gained but a very inconsiderable footing in the world.

56. But it is demanded that we assign a cause of this prejudice, and account for its obtaining in the world. To this I answer, that men knowing they perceived several ideas, whereof they themselves were not the authors (as not being excited from within nor depending on the operation of their wills) this made them maintain those ideas, or objects of perception had an existence independent of and without the mind, without ever dreaming that contradiction was involved in those words. But philosophers having plainly seen that the immediate objects of perception do not exist without the mind, they in some degree corrected the mistake of the vulgar; but at the same time run into another which seems no less absurd, to wit, that there are certain objects really existing without the mind, or having a subsistence distinct from being perceived, of which our ideas are only images or resemblances, imprinted by those objects on the mind. And this notion of the philosophers owes its origin to the same cause with the former, namely, their being conscious that they were not the authors of their own sensations, which they evidently knew were imprinted from without, and which therefore must have some cause distinct from the minds on which they are imprinted.

57. But why they should suppose the ideas of sense to be excited in us by things in their likeness, and not rather have recourse to *spirit*, which alone can act, may be accounted for, first, because they were not aware of the repugnancy there is, as well in supposing things like unto our ideas existing without, as in attributing to them power or activity. Secondly, because the Supreme Spirit, which excites those ideas in our minds, is not marked out and limited to our view by any particular finite collection of sensible ideas, as human agents are by their size, complexion, limbs, and motions. And thirdly, because His operations are regular and uniform. Whenever the course of nature is interrupted by a

miracle, men are ready to own the presence of a superior agent. But, when we see things go on in the ordinary course they do not excite in us any reflection; their order and concatenation, though it be an argument of the greatest wisdom, power, and goodness in their creator, is yet so constant and familiar to us that we do not think them the immediate effects of a free spirit; especially since inconsistency and mutability in acting, thought it be an imperfection, is looked on as a mark of freedom.

58. *Tenthly,* it will be objected that the notions we advance are inconsistent with several sound truths in philosophy and mathematics. For example, the motion of the earth is now universally admitted by astronomers as a truth grounded on the clearest and most convincing reasons. But, on the foregoing principles, there can be no such thing. For, motion being only an idea, it follows that if it be not perceived it exists not; but the motion of the earth is not perceived by sense. I answer, that tenet, if rightly understood, will be found to agree with the principles we have premised; for, the question whether the earth moves or no amounts in reality to no more than this, to wit, whether we have reason to conclude, from what has been observed by astronomers, that if we were placed in such and such circumstances, and such or such a position and distance both from the earth and sun, we should perceive the former to move among the choir of the planets, and appearing in all respects like one of them; and this, by the established rules of nature which we have no reason to mistrust, is reasonably collected from the phenomena.

59. We may, from the experience we have had of the train and succession of ideas in our minds, often make, I will not say uncertain conjectures, but sure and well-grounded predictions concerning the ideas we shall be affected with pursuant to a great train of actions, and be enabled to pass a right judgment of what would have appeared to us, in case we were placed in circumstances very different from those we are in at present. Herein consists the knowledge of nature, which may preserve its use and certainty very consistently with what hath been said. It will be easy to apply this to whatever objections of the like sort may be drawn from the magnitude of the stars, or any other discoveries in astronomy or nature.

60. In the *eleventh* place, it will be demanded to what purpose serves that curious organization of plants, and the animal mechanism in the parts of animals: might not vegetables grow, and shoot forth leaves of blossoms, and animals perform all their motions as well without as with all that variety of internal parts so elegantly contrived

and put together, which, being ideas, have nothing powerful or operative in them, nor have any necessary connection with the effects ascribed to them? If it be a Spirit that immediately produces every effect by a *fiat* or act of His will, we must think all that is fine and artificial in the works, whether of man or nature, to be made in vain. By this doctrine, though an artist hath made the spring and wheels, and every movement of a watch, and adjusted them in such a manner as he knew would produce the motions he designed, yet he must think all this done to no purpose, and that it is an Intelligence which directs the index, and points to the hour of the day. If so, why may not the Intelligence do it, without his being at the pains of making the movements and putting them together? Why does not an empty case serve as well as another? And how comes it to pass that whenever there is any fault in the going of a watch, there is some corresponding disorder to be found in the movements, which being mended by a skillful hand all is right again? The like may be said of all the clock-work of nature, great part whereof is so wonderfully fine and subtle as scarce to be discerned by the best microscope. In short, it will be asked, how, upon our principles, any tolerable account can be given, or any final cause assigned of an innumerable multitude of bodies and machines, framed with the most exquisite art, which in the common philosophy have very apposite uses assigned them, and serve to explain abundance of phenomena?

61. To all which I answer, *first,* that though there were some difficulties relating to the administration of Providence, and the uses by it assigned to the several parts of nature, which I could not solve by the foregoing principles, yet this objection could be of small weight against the truth and certainty of those things which may be proved *a priori,* with the utmost evidence and rigor of demonstration. *Secondly,* but neither are the received principles free from the like difficulties; for, it may still be demanded to what end God should take those roundabout methods of effecting things by instruments and machines, which no one can deny might have been effected by the mere command of His will without all that apparatus; nay, if we narrowly consider it, we shall find the objection may be retorted with greater force on those who hold the existence of those machines without of mind; for it has been made evident that solidity, bulk, figure, motion, and the like have no *activity* or *efficacy* in them, so as to be capable of producing any one effect in nature. (See Sec. 25.) Whoever therefore supposes them to exist (allowing the supposition possible) when they are not perceived does it manifestly to no purpose; since the only use that is

assigned to them, as they exist unperceived, is that they produce those perceivable effects which in truth cannot be ascribed to anything but Spirit.

62. But, to come nigher the difficulty, it must be observed that though the fabrication of all those parts and organs be not absolutely necessary to the producing any effect, yet it is necessary to the producing of things in a constant regular way according to the laws of nature. There are certain general laws that run through the whole chain of natural effects; these are learned by the observation and study of nature, and are by men applied as well to the framing artificial things for the use and ornament of life as to the explaining various phenomena —which explication consists only in shewing the conformity any particular phenomenon hath to the general laws of nature, or, which is the same thing, in discovering the *uniformity* there is in the production of natural effects; as will be evident to whoever shall attend to the several instances wherein philosophers pretend to account for appearances. That there is a great and conspicuous use in these regular constant methods of working observed by the Supreme Agent hath been shewn in Sec. 31. And it is no less visible that a particular size, figure, motion, and disposition or parts are necessary, though not absolutely to the producing any effect, yet to the producing it according to the standing mechanical laws of nature. Thus, for instance, it cannot be denied that God, or the Intelligence that sustains and rules the ordinary course of things, might if He were minded to produce a miracle, cause all the motions on the dial-plate of a watch, though nobody had ever made the movements and put them in it: but yet, if He will act agreeably to the rules of the mechanism, by Him for wise ends established and maintained in the creation, it is necessary that those actions of the watchmaker, whereby he makes the movements and rightly adjusts them, precede the production of the aforesaid motions; as also that any disorder in them be attended with the perception of some corresponding disorder in the movements, which being once corrected all is right again.

63. It may indeed on some occasions be necessary that the Author of nature display His overruling power in producing some appearance out of the ordinary series of things. Such exceptions from the general rules of nature are proper to surprise and awe men into an acknowledgment of the Divine Being; but then they are to be used but seldom, otherwise there is a plain reason why they should fail of that effect. Besides, God seems to choose the convincing our reason of His attributes by the works of nature, which discover so much harmony and contrivance in their make, and are such plain indications of wisdom

and beneficence in their Author, rather than to astonish us into a belief of His Being by anomalous and surprising events.

64. To set this matter in a yet clearer light, I shall observe that what has been objected in Sec. 60 amounts in reality to no more than this:—ideas are not anyhow and at random produced, there being a certain order and connection between them, like to that of cause and effect; there are also several combinations of them made in a very regular and artificial manner, which seem like so many instruments in the hand of nature that, being hid as it were behind the scenes, have a secret operation in producing those appearances which are seen on the theater of the world, being themselves discernible only to the curious eye of the philosopher. But, since one idea cannot be the cause of another, to what purpose is that connection? And, since those instruments, being barely *inefficacious perceptions* in the mind, are not subservient to the production of natural effects, it is demanded why they are made; or, in other words, what reason can be assigned why God should make us, upon a close inspection into His works, behold so great variety of ideas so artfully laid together, and so much according to rule; it not being credible that He would be at the expense (if one may so speak) of all that art and regularity to no purpose.

65. To all which my answer is, first, that the connection of ideas does not imply the relation of *cause and effect,* but only of a mark or *sign* with the thing *signified.* The fire which I see is not the cause of the pain I suffer upon my approaching it, but the mark that forewarns me of it. In like manner the noise that I hear is not the effect of this or that motion or collision of the ambient bodies, but the sign thereof. Secondly, the reason why ideas are formed into machines, that is, artificial and regular combinations, is the same with that for combining letters into words. That a few original ideas may be made to signify a great number of effects and actions, it is necessary they be variously combined together. And, to the end their use be permanent and universal, these combinations must be made by *rule,* and with *wise contrivance.* By this means abundance of information is conveyed unto us, concerning what we are to expect from such and such actions, and what methods are proper to be taken for the exciting such and such ideas; which in effect is all that I conceive to be distinctly meant when it is said that, by discerning a figure, texture, and mechanism of the inward parts of bodies, whether natural or artificial, we may attain to know the several uses and properties depending thereon, or the nature of the thing.

66. Hence, it is evident that those things which, under the notion of a cause co-operating or concurring to the production of effects, are

altogether inexplicable, and run us into great absurdities, may be very naturally explained, and have a proper and obvious use assigned to them, when they are considered only as marks or signs for our information. And it is the searching after and endeavoring to understand those signs instituted by the Author of Nature, that ought to be the employment of the natural philosopher; and not the pretending to explain things by corporeal causes, which doctrine seems to have too much estranged the minds of men from that active principle, that supreme and wise Spirit "in whom we live, move, and have our being."

67. In the *twelfth* place, it may perhaps be objected that—though it be clear from what has been said that there can be no such thing as an inert, senseless, extended, solid, figured, movable substance existing without the mind, such as philosophers describe matter—yet, if any man shall leave out of his idea of matter the positive ideas of extension, figure, solidity and motion, and say that he means only by that word an inert, senseless substance, that exists without the mind or unperceived, which is the *occasion of our ideas,* or at the presence whereof God is pleased to excite ideas in us: it doth not appear but that matter taken in this sense may possibly exist. In answer to which I say, first, that it seems no less absurd to suppose a substance without accidents, than it is to suppose accidents without a substance. But secondly, though we should grant this unknown substance may possibly exist, yet where can it be supposed to be? That it exists not in the mind is agreed; and that it exists not in place is no less certain —since all place or extension exists only in the mind, as hath been already proved. It remains therefore that it exists nowhere at all.

68. Let us examine a little the description that is here given us of *matter*. It neither acts, nor perceives, nor is perceived; for this is all that is meant by saying it is an inert, senseless, unknown substance: which is a definition entirely made up of negatives, excepting only the relative notion of its standing under or supporting. But then it must be observed that it supports nothing at all, and how nearly this comes to the description of a *nonentity* I desire may be considered. But, say you, it is the *unknown occasion,* at the presence of which ideas are excited in us by the will of God. Now, I would fain know how anything can be present to us, which is neither perceivable by sense nor reflection, nor capable of producing any idea in our minds, nor is at all extended, nor hath any form, nor exists in any place. The words "to be present," when thus applied, must needs be taken in some abstract and strange meaning, and which I am not able to comprehend.

69. Again, let us examine what is meant by *occasion*. So far as

I can gather from the common use of language, that word signifies either the agent which produces any effect, or else something that is observed to accompany or go before it in the ordinary course of things. But when it is applied to matter as above described, it can be taken in neither of those senses; for matter is said to be passive and inert, and so cannot be an agent or efficient cause. It is also unperceivable, as being devoid of all sensible qualities, and so cannot be the occasion of our perceptions in the latter sense: as when the burning my finger is said to be the occasion of the pain that attends it. What therefore can be meant by calling matter an *occasion?* The term is either used in no sense at all, or else in some very distant from its received signification.

70. You will perhaps say that matter, though it be not perceived by us, is nevertheless perceived by God, to whom it is the occasion of exciting ideas in our minds. For, say you, since we observe our sensations to be imprinted in an orderly and constant manner, it is but reasonable to suppose there are certain constant and regular occasions of their being produced. That is to say, that there are certain permanent and distinct parcels of matter, corresponding to our ideas, which, though they do not excite them in our minds, or anywise immediately affect us, as being altogether passive and unperceivable to us, they are nevertheless to God, by whom they are perceived, as it were so many occasions to remind Him when and what ideas to imprint on our minds; that so things may go on in a constant uniform manner.

71. In answer to this, I observe that, as the notion of matter is here stated, the question is no longer concerning the existence of a thing distinct from *spirit* and *idea,* from perceiving and being perceived; but whether there are not certain ideas of I know not what sort, in the mind of God which are so many marks or notes that direct Him how to produce sensations in our minds in a constant and regular method— much after the same manner as a musician is directed by the notes of music to produce that harmonious train and composition of sound which is called a tune, though they who hear the music do not perceive the notes, and may be entirely ignorant of them. But, this notion of matter seems too extravagant to deserve a confutation. Besides, it is in effect no objection against what we have advanced, to wit, that there is no senseless unperceived substance.

72. If we follow the light of reason, we shall, from the constant uniform method of our sensations, collect the goodness and wisdom of the Spirit who excites them in our minds; but this is all that I can see reasonably concluded from thence. To me, I say, it is evident that the being of a spirit infinitely wise, good, and powerful is abundantly suffi-

cient to explain all the appearances of nature. But as for *inert, senseless matter,* nothing that I perceive has any the least connection with it, or leads to the thoughts of it. And I would fain see any one explain any the meanest phenomenon in nature by it, or shew any manner of reason, though in the lowest rank of probability, that he can have for its existence, or even make any tolerable sense or meaning of that supposition. For, as to its being an occasion, we have, I think, evidently shewn that with regard to us it is no occasion. It remains therefore that it must be, if at all, the occasion to God of exciting ideas in us; and what this amounts to we have just now seen.

73. It is worth while to reflect a little on the motives which induced men to suppose the existence of *material substance;* that so having observed the gradual ceasing and expiration of those motives or reasons, we may proportionably withdraw the assent that was grounded on them. First, therefore, it was thought that color, figure, motion, and the rest of the sensible qualities or accidents, did really exist without the mind; and for this reason it seemed needful to suppose some unthinking *substratum* or substance wherein they did exist, since they could not be conceived to exist by themselves. Afterwards, in process of time, men being convinced that colors, sounds, and the rest of the sensible, secondary qualities had no existence without the mind, they stripped this *substratum* or material substance of those qualities, leaving only the primary ones, figure, motion, and suchlike, which they still conceived to exist without the mind, and consequently to stand in need of a material support. But, it having been shewn that none even of these can possibly exist otherwise than in a spirit or mind which perceives them, it follows that we have no longer any reason to suppose the being of matter; nay, that it is utterly impossible there should be any such thing, so long as that word is taken to denote an *unthinking substratum* of qualities or accidents wherein they exist without the mind.

74. But though it be allowed by the materialists themselves that matter was thought of only for the sake of supporting accidents, and, the reason entirely ceasing, one might expect the mind should naturally, and without any reluctance at all, quit the belief of what was solely grounded thereon; yet the prejudice is riveted so deeply in our thoughts, that we can scarce tell how to part with it, and are therefore inclined, since the *thing* itself is indefensible, at least to retain the *name,* which we apply to I know not what abstracted and indefinite notions of being, or occasion, though without any show of reason, at least so far as I can see. For, what is there on our part, or what do we perceive, amongst all the ideas, sensations, notions which are imprinted on our minds, either by sense or reflection, from whence may be inferred the

existence of an inert, thoughtless, unperceived occasion? And, on the other hand, on the part of an all-sufficient Spirit, what can there be that should make us believe or even suspect He is directed by an inert occasion to excite ideas in our minds?

75. It is a very extraordinary instance of the force of prejudice, and much to be lamented, that the mind of man retains so great a fondness, against all the evidence of reason, for a stupid thoughtless *somewhat,* by the interposition whereof it would as it were screen itself from the providence of God, and remove it farther off from the affairs of the world. But, though we do the utmost we can to secure the belief of *matter,* though, when reason forsakes us, we endeavor to support our opinion on the bare possibility of the thing, and though we indulge ourselves in the full scope of an imagination not regulated by reason to make out that poor possibility, yet the upshot of all is, that there are certain *unknown ideas* in the mind of God; for this, if anything, is all that I conceive to be meant by *occasion* with regard to God. And this at the bottom is no longer contending for the thing, but for the name.

76. Whether therefore there are such ideas in the mind of God, and whether they may be called by the name "matter," I shall not dispute. But, if you stick to the notion of an unthinking substance or support of extension, motion, and other sensible qualities, then to me it is most evidently impossible there should be any such thing; since it is a plain repugnancy that those qualities should exist in or be supported by an unperceiving substance.

77. But, say you, though it be granted that there is no thoughtless support of extension and the other qualities or accidents which we perceive, yet there may perhaps be some inert, unperceiving substance or *substratum* of some other qualities, as incomprehensible to us as colors are to a man born blind, because we have not a sense adapted to them. But, if we had a new sense, we should possibly no more doubt of their existence than a blind man made to see does of the existence of light and colors. I answer, first, if what you mean by the word "matter" be only the unknown support of unknown qualities, it is no matter whether there is such a thing or no, since it no way concerns us; and I do not see the advantage there is in disputing about what we know not *what,* and we know not *why.*

78. But, secondly, if we had a new sense it could only furnish us with new ideas or sensations; and then we should have the same reason against their existing in an unperceiving substance that has been already offered with relation to figure, motion, color, and the like. Qualities, as hath been shewn, are nothing else but *sensations* or *ideas,* which exist only in a *mind* perceiving them; and this is true not only of

the ideas we are acquainted with at present, but likewise of all possible ideas whatsoever.

79. But, you will insist, what if I have no reason to believe the existence of matter? what if I cannot assign any use to it or explain anything by it, or even conceive what is meant by that word? yet still it is no contradiction to say that matter exists, and that this matter is in general a *substance*, or *occasion of ideas*; though indeed to go about to unfold the meaning or adhere to any particular explication of those words may be attended with great difficulties. I answer, when words are used without a meaning, you may put them together as you please without danger of running into a contradiction. You may say, for example, that twice two is equal to seven, so long as you declare you do not take the words of that proposition in their usual acceptation but for marks of you know not what. And, by the same reason, you may say there is an inert thoughtless substance without accidents which is the occasion of our ideas. And we shall understand just as much by one proposition as the other.

80. In the *last* place, you will say, what if we give up the cause of material substance, and stand to it that matter is an unknown *somewhat* —neither substance nor accident, spirit nor idea, inert, thoughtless, indivisible, immovable, unextended, existing in no place. For, say you, whatever may be urged against *substance* or *occasion*, or any other positive or relative notion of matter, hath no place at all, so long as this *negative* definition of matter is adhered to. I answer, you may, if so it shall seem good, use the word "matter" in the same sense as other men use "nothing," and so make those terms convertible in your style. For, after all, this is what appears to me to be the result of that definition, the parts whereof when I consider with attention, either collectively or separate from each other, I do not find that there is any kind of effect or impression made on my mind different from what is excited by the term "nothing."

HUME

DAVID HUME, the Scotch philosopher, was born in 1711 and died in 1776. He tells us in his delightful autobiography that his main ambition in life was to gain fame as a writer; he was disappointed that his *Treatise of Human Nature* (1739) fell "deadborn from the press." But he did gain fame and wealth as an essayist and historian, and later he revised and rewrote much of the teaching of the *Treatise* and published his *Enquiry Concerning Human Understanding* (1748) and *Enquiry Concerning the Principles of Morals* (1751). His *Dialogues Concerning Natural Religion* were published posthumously. Hume's friend Adam Smith described him as "approaching as nearly to the idea of a perfectly wise and virtuous man as perhaps the nature of human frailty will permit."

Hume has been seen in many lights by historians. To most of his contemporaries, he was a dangerous infidel; Johnson seldom tired of abusing him. To Reid, and to most professional historians of philosophy, he has seemed to be the denouement of English empiricism. They see him as the last of the great triumvirate of British empiricists; they delight in showing how Locke's innocent-looking theory, when consistently developed, led first to Berkeley's paradoxes and then to Hume's skepticism, which awoke Kant from his dogmatic slumber and thus started philosophy on a new path. Later historians, not thinking that the history of philosophy lends itself to quite such dramatic treatment, have emphasized Hume's naturalism over his skepticism; that is, they see him as drawing pragmatistic consequences concerning the proper function of reason from his study of the nonintellectual features of human experience and the nonrational factors in knowledge. His skepticism seems to them to be not a confession of the bankruptcy of empiricism but an effort to direct thought away from futile metaphysics and theology. Hume has thus become something of a hero to modern naturalists, pragmatists, and positivists. All agree that as a philosophic analyst he has few peers, and his analyses of the concept of causation, as well as his distinction between "relations of ideas" and "matters of fact" have become the starting point of most modern discussions of these topics.

All our selections have been taken from the *Enquiry Concerning Human Understanding*. They are taken in order, with the exception of the last. This is a part of Section XI, which Hume entitled, "Of a Particular Providence and of a Future State." This section pretends to be a report of a conversation Hume had with a friend, in the course of which his friend composed a speech he attributed to Epicurus, on trial in Athens for having denied "divine existence, and consequently a providence and future state" and for thus having "loosened in a great measure the ties of morality." We have presented the "speech of Epicurus" in its entirety, because it is Hume's defense against identical charges often brought against him.

Enquiry Concerning Human Understanding

SECTION II—Of the Origin of Ideas

Everyone will readily allow that there is a considerable difference between the perceptions of the mind, when a man feels the pain of excessive heat, or the pleasure of moderate warmth, and when he afterwards recalls to his memory this sensation, or anticipates it by his imagination. These faculties may mimic or copy the perceptions of the senses; but they never can entirely reach the force and vivacity of the original sentiment. The utmost we say of them, even when they operate with greatest vigor, is, that they represent their object in so lively a manner, that we could *almost* say we feel or see it: But, except the mind be disordered by disease or madness, they never can arrive at such a pitch of vivacity, as to render these perceptions altogether undistinguishable. All the colors of poetry, however splendid, can never paint natural objects in such a manner as to make the description be taken for a real landscape. The most lively thought is still inferior to the dullest sensation.

We may observe a like distinction to run through all the other perceptions of the mind. A man in a fit of anger, is actuated in a very different manner from one who only thinks of that emotion. If you tell me, that any person is in love, I easily understand your meaning, and form a just conception of his situation; but never can mistake that conception for the real disorders and agitations of the passion. When we reflect on our past sentiments and affections, our thought is a faithful mirror, and copies its objects truly; but the colors which it employs are faint and dull, in comparison of those in which our original perceptions were clothed. It requires no nice discernment or metaphysical head to mark the distinction between them.

Here therefore we may divide all the perceptions of the mind into two classes or species, which are distinguished by their different degrees of force and vivacity. The less forcible and lively are commonly denominated *thoughts* or *ideas*. The other species want a name in our language, and in most others; I suppose, because it was not requisite for any, but philosophical purposes, to rank them under a general term or appellation. Let us, therefore, use a little freedom, and call them *impressions;* employing that word in a sense somewhat different from the usual. By the term *impression*, then, I mean all our more lively perceptions, when we hear, or see, or feel, or love, or hate, or desire, or will. And impressions are distinguished from ideas, which are the less lively perceptions, of which we are conscious, when we reflect on any of those sensations or movements above mentioned.

Nothing, at first view, may seem more unbounded than the thought of man, which not only escapes all human power and authority, but is not even restrained within the limits of nature and reality. To form monsters, and join incongruous shapes and appearances, costs the imagination no more trouble than to conceive the most natural and familiar objects. And while the body is confined to one planet, along which it creeps with pain and difficulty; the thought can in an instant transport us into the most distant regions of the universe; or even beyond the universe, into the unbounded chaos, where nature is supposed to lie in total confusion. What never was seen, or heard of, may yet be conceived; nor is anything beyond the power of thought, except what implies an absolute contradiction.

But though our thought seems to possess this unbounded liberty, we shall find, upon a nearer examination, that it is really confined within very narrow limits, and that all this creative power of the mind amounts to no more than the faculty of compounding, transposing, augmenting, or diminishing the materials afforded us by the senses and experience. When we think of a golden mountain, we only join two consistent ideas, *gold,* and *mountain,* with which we were formerly acquainted. A virtuous horse we can conceive, because, from our own feeling, we can conceive virtue; and this we may unite to the figure and shape of a horse, which is an animal familiar to us. In short, all the materials of thinking are derived either from our outward or inward sentiment: the mixture and composition of these belongs alone to the mind and will. Or, to express myself in philosophical language, all our ideas or more feeble perceptions are copies of our impressions or more lively ones.

To prove this, the two following arguments will, I hope, be sufficient. First, when we analyze our thoughts or ideas, however compounded or sublime, we always find that they resolve themselves into such simple ideas as were copied from a precedent feeling or sentiment. Even those ideas, which, at first view, seem the most wide of this origin, are found, upon a nearer scrutiny, to be derived from it. The idea of God, as meaning an infinitely intelligent, wise, and good Being, arises from reflecting on the operations of our own mind, and augmenting, without limit, those qualities of goodness and wisdom. We may prosecute this inquiry to what length we please; where we shall always find, that every idea which we examine is copied from a similar impression. Those who would assert that this position is not universally true nor without exception, have only one, and that an easy method of refuting it; by producing that idea, which, in their opinion, is not derived from this source. It will then be incumbent on us, if we would maintain our doctrine, to produce the impression, or lively perception, which corresponds to it.

Secondly. If it happen, from a defect of the organ, that a man is not susceptible of any species of sensation, we always find that he is as little susceptible of the correspondent ideas. A blind man can form no notion of colors; a deaf man of sounds. Restore either of them that sense in which he is deficient; by opening this new inlet for his sensations, you also open an inlet for the ideas; and he finds no difficulty in conceiving these objects. The case is the same, if the object, proper for exciting any sensation, has never been applied to the organ. A Laplander or Negro has no notion of the relish of wine. And though there are few or no instances of a like deficiency in the mind, where a person has never felt or is wholly incapable of a sentiment or passion that belongs to his species; yet we find the same observation to take place in a less degree. A man of mild manners can form no idea of inveterate revenge or cruelty; nor can a selfish heart easily conceive the heights of friendship and generosity. It is readily allowed, that other beings may possess many senses of which we can have no conception; because the ideas of them have never been introduced to us in the only manner by which an idea can have access to the mind, to wit, by the actual feeling and sensation.

There is, however, one contradictory phenomenon, which may prove that it is not absolutely impossible for ideas to arise, independent of their correspondent impressions. I believe it will readily be allowed, that the several distinct ideas of color, which enter by the eye, or those of sound, which are conveyed by the ear, are really different from each other; though, at the same time, resembling. Now if this be true of different colors, it must be no less so of the different shades of the same color; and each shade produces a distinct idea, independent of the rest. For if this should be denied, it is possible, by the continual gradation of shades, to run a color insensibly into what is most remote from it;

and if you will not allow any of the means to be different, you cannot, without absurdity, deny the extremes to be the same. Suppose, therefore, a person to have enjoyed his sight for thirty years, and to have become perfectly acquainted with colors of all kinds except one particular shade of blue, for instance, which it never has been his fortune to meet with. Let all the different shades of that color, except that single one, be placed before him, descending gradually from the deepest to the lightest; it is plain that he will perceive a blank, where that shade is wanting, and will be sensible that there is a greater distance in that place between the contiguous colors than in any other. Now I ask, whether it be possible for him, from his own imagination, to supply this deficiency, and raise up to himself the idea of that particular shade, though it had never been conveyed to him by his senses? I believe there are few but will be of opinion that he can: and this may serve as a proof that the simple ideas are not always, in every instance, derived from the correspondent impressions; though this instance is so singular, that it is scarcely worth our observing, and does not merit that for it alone we should alter our general maxim.

Here, therefore, is a proposition, which not only seems, in itself, simple and intelligible; but, if a proper use were made of it, might render every dispute equally intelligible, and banish all that jargon, which has so long taken possession of metaphysical reasonings, and drawn disgrace upon them. All ideas, especially abstract ones, are naturally faint and obscure: the mind has but a slender hold of them: they are apt to be confounded with other resembling ideas; and when we have often employed any term, though without a distinct meaning, we are apt to imagine it has a determinable idea annexed to it. On the contrary, all impressions, that is, all sensations, either outward or inward, are strong and vivid: the limits between them are more exactly determined: nor is it easy to fall into any error or mistake with regard to them. When we entertain, therefore, any suspicion that a philosophical term is employed without any meaning or idea (as is but too frequent), we need but inquire, *from what impression is that supposed idea derived?* And if it be impossible to assign any, this will serve to confirm our suspicion.[1] By bringing ideas into so clear a light we may reasonably hope to remove all dispute, which may arise, concerning their nature and reality.

---

1. It is probable that no more was meant by those, who denied innate ideas, than that all ideas were copies of our impressions; though it must be confessed, that the terms, which they employed, were not chosen with such caution, nor so exactly defined, as to prevent all mistakes about their doctrine. For what is meant by *innate?* If innate be equivalent to natural, then all the perceptions and ideas of the mind must be allowed to be innate or natural, in whatever sense we take the latter word,

SECTION III—Of the Association of Ideas

It is evident that there is a principle of connection between the different thoughts or ideas of the mind, and that, in their appearance to the memory or imagination, they introduce each other with a certain degree of method and regularity. In our more serious thinking or discourse this is so observable that any particular thought, which breaks in upon the regular tract or chain of ideas, is immediately remarked and rejected. And even in our wildest and most wandering reveries, nay in our very dreams, we shall find, if we reflect, that the imagination ran not altogether at adventures, but that there was still a connection upheld among the different ideas, which succeeded each other. Were the loosest and freest conversation to be transcribed, there would immediately be observed something which connected it in all its transitions. Or where this is wanting, the person who broke the thread of discourse might still inform you, that there had secretly revolved in his mind a succession of thought, which had gradually led him from the subject of conversation. Among different languages, even where we cannot suspect the least connection or communication, it is found, that the words, expressive of ideas, the most compounded, do yet nearly correspond to each other: a certain proof that the simple ideas, comprehended in the compound ones, were bound together by some universal principle, which had an equal influence on all mankind.

Though it be too obvious to escape observation, that different ideas are connected together; I do not find that any philosopher has attempted to enumerate or class all the principles of association; a subject, however, that seems worthy of curiosity. To me, there appear to be only three principles of connection among ideas, namely, *resemblance, contiguity* in time or place, and *cause* or *effect*.

---

whether in opposition to what is uncommon, artificial, or miraculous. If by innate be meant, contemporary to our birth, the dispute seems to be frivolous; nor is it worth while to inquire at what time thinking begins, whether before, at, or after our birth. Again, the word *idea*, seems to be commonly taken in a very loose sense, by Locke and others; as standing for any of our perceptions, our sensations and passions, as well as thoughts. Now in this sense, I should desire to know, what can be meant by asserting, that self-love, or resentment of injuries, or the passion between the sexes is not innate?

But admitting these terms, *impressions* and *ideas,* in the sense above explained, and understanding by *innate*, what is original or copied from no precedent perception, then may we assert that all our impressions are innate and our ideas not innate.

To be ingenuous, I must own it to be my opinion, that Locke was betrayed into this question by the schoolmen, who, making use of undefined terms, draw out their disputes to a tedious length, without ever touching the point in question. A like ambiguity and circumlocution seem to run through that philosopher's reasonings on this as well as most other subjects.

That these principles serve to connect ideas will not, I believe, be much doubted. A picture naturally leads our thoughts to the original:[2] the mention of one apartment in a building naturally introduces an inquiry or discourse concerning the others:[3] and if we think of a wound, we can scarcely forbear reflecting on the pain which follows it.[4] But that this enumeration is complete, and that there are no other principles of association except these, may be difficult to prove to the satisfaction of the reader, or even to a man's own satisfaction. All we can do, in such cases, is to run over several instances, and examine carefully the principle which binds the different thoughts to each other, never stopping till we render the principle as general as possible.[5] The more instances we examine, and the more care we employ, the more assurance shall we acquire, that the enumeration, which we form from the whole, is complete and entire.

SECTION IV—Sceptical Doubts Concerning the Operations of the Understanding

PART I

All the objects of human reason or inquiry may naturally be divided into two kinds, to wit, *relations of ideas*, and *matters of fact*. Of the first kind are the sciences of geometry, algebra, and arithmetic; and in short, every affirmation which is either intuitively or demonstratively certain. *That the square of the hypothenuse is equal to the squares of the two sides*, is a proposition which expresses a relation between these figures. *That three times five is equal to the half of thirty*, expresses a relation between these numbers. Propositions of this kind are discoverable by the mere operation of thought, without dependence on what is anywhere existent in the universe. Though there never was a circle or triangle in nature, the truths demonstrated by Euclid would for ever retain their certainty and evidence.

---

2. Resemblance.
3. Contiguity.
4. Cause and effect.
5. For instance, *contrast* or *contrariety* is also a connection among ideas but it may, perhaps, be considered as a mixture of *causation* and *resemblance*. Where two objects are contrary, the one destroys the other; that is, the cause of its annihilation and the idea of the annihilation of an object implies the idea of its former existence.

Matters of fact, which are the second objects of human reason, are not ascertained in the same manner; nor is our evidence of their truth, however great, of a like nature with the foregoing. The contrary of every matter of fact is still possible; because it can never imply a contradiction, and is conceived by the mind with the same facility and distinctness, as if ever so comformable to reality. *That the sun will not rise tomorrow* is no less intelligible a proposition, and implies no more contradiction than the affirmation, *that it will rise*. We should in vain, therefore, attempt to demonstrate its falsehood. Were it demonstratively false, it would imply a contradiction, and could never be distinctly conceived by the mind.

It may, therefore, be a subject worthy of curiosity, to inquire what is the nature of that evidence which assures us of any real existence and matter of fact, beyond the present testimony of our senses, or the records of our memory. This part of philosophy, it is observable, has been little cultivated, either by the ancients or moderns; and therefore our doubts and errors, in the prosecution of so important an inquiry, may be the more excusable; while we march through such difficult paths without any guide or direction. They may even prove useful, by exciting curiosity, and destroying that implicit faith and security, which is the bane of all reasoning and free inquiry. The discovery of defects in the common philosophy, if any such there be, will not, I presume, be a discouragement, but rather an incitement, as is usual, to attempt something more full and satisfactory than has yet been proposed to the public.

All reasonings concerning matter of fact seem to be founded on the relation of *cause and effect*. By means of that relation alone we can go beyond the evidence of our memory and senses. If you were to ask a man, why he believes any matter of fact, which is absent; for instance, that his friend is in the country, or in France; he would give you a reason; and this reason would be some other fact; as a letter received from him, or the knowledge of his former resolutions and promises. A man finding a watch or any other machine in a desert island, would conclude that there had once been men in that island. All our reasonings concerning fact are of the same nature. And here it is constantly supposed that there is a connection between the present fact and that which is inferred from it. Were there nothing to bind them together, the inference would be entirely precarious. The hearing of an articulate voice and rational discourse in the dark assures us of the presence of some person: Why? because these are the effects of the human make and fabric, and closely connected with it. If we anatomize all the other reasonings of this nature, we shall find that they are founded on the relation of cause and effect, and that this relation is either near or remote, direct or collateral. Heat and light are collateral effects of fire, and the one effect may justly be inferred from the other.

If we would satisfy ourselves, therefore, concerning the nature of that evidence, which assures us of matters of fact, we must inquire how we arrive at the knowledge of cause and effect.

I shall venture to affirm, as a general proposition, which admits of no exception, that the knowledge of this relation is not, in any instance, attained by reasonings *a priori;* but arises entirely from experience, when we find that any particular objects are constantly conjoined with each other. Let an object be presented to a man of ever so strong natural reason and abilities; if that object be entirely new to him, he will not be able, by the most accurate examination of its sensible qualities, to discover any of its causes or effects. Adam, though his rational faculties be supposed, at the very first, entirely perfect, could not have inferred from the fluidity and transparency of water that it would suffocate him, or from the light and warmth of fire that it would consume him. No object ever discovers, by the qualities which appear to the senses, either the causes which produced it, or the effects which will arise from it; nor can our reason, unassisted by experience, ever draw any inference concerning real existence and matter of fact.

This proposition, *that causes and effects are discoverable, not by reason but by experience,* will readily be admitted with regard to such objects, as we remember to have once been altogether unknown to us; since we must be conscious of the utter inability, which we then lay under, of foretelling what would arise from them. Present two smooth pieces of marble to a man who has no tincture of natural philosophy; he will never discover that they will adhere together in such a manner as to require great force to separate them in a direct line, while they make so small a resistance to a lateral pressure. Such events, as bear little analogy to the common course of nature, are also readily confessed to be known only by experience; nor does any man imagine that the explosion of gunpowder, or the attraction of a loadstone, could ever be discovered by arguments *a priori.* In like manner, when an effect is supposed to depend upon an intricate machinery or secret structure of parts, we make no difficulty in attributing all our knowledge of it to experience. Who will assert that he can give the ultimate reason, why milk or bread is proper nourishment for a man, not for a lion or a tiger?

But the same truth may not appear, at first sight, to have the same evidence with regard to events, which have become familiar to us from our first appearance in the world, which bear a close analogy to the whole course of nature, and which are supposed to depend on the simple qualities of objects, without any secret structure of parts. We are apt to imagine that we could discover these effects by the mere operation of our reason, without experience. We fancy, that were we brought on a sudden into this world, we could at first have inferred that one billiard ball would communicate motion to another upon impulse; and that we needed not to have waited for the event, in order to pronounce with certainty concerning it. Such is the influence of custom, that, where it is strongest, it not only covers our natural ignorance, but even conceals itself, and seems not to take place, merely because it is found in the highest degree.

But to convince us that all the laws of nature, and all the operations of bodies without exception, are known only by experience, the following reflections may, perhaps, suffice. Were any object presented to us, and were we required to pronounce concerning the effect, which will result from it, without consulting past observation; after what manner, I beseech you, must the mind proceed in this operation? It must invent or imagine some event, which it ascribes to the object as its effect; and it is plain that this invention must be entirely arbitrary. The mind can never possibly find the effect in the supposed cause, by the most accurate scrutiny and examination. For the effect is totally different from the cause, and consequently can never be discovered in it. Motion in the second billiard ball is a quite distinct event from motion in the first: nor is there anything in the one to suggest the smallest hint of the other. A stone or piece of metal raised into the air, and left without any support, immediately falls: but to consider the matter *a priori*, is there anything we discover in this situation which can beget the idea of a downward, rather than an upward, or any other motion, in the stone or metal?

And as the first imagination or invention of a particular effect, in all natural operations, is arbitrary, where we consult not experience; so must we also esteem the supposed tie or connection between the cause and effect, which binds them together, and renders it impossible that any other effect could result from the operation of that cause. When I see, for instance, a billiard ball moving in a straight line towards another; even suppose motion in the second ball should by accident be suggested to me, as the result of their contact or impulse; may I not conceive, that a hundred different events might as well follow from that cause? May not both these balls remain at absolute rest? May not the first ball return in a straight line, or leap off from the second in any line or direction? All these suppositions are consistent and conceivable. Why then should we give the preference to one, which is no more consistent or conceivable than the rest? All our reasonings *a priori* will never be able to show us any foundation for this preference.

In a word, then, every effect is a distinct event from its cause. It could not, therefore, be discovered in the cause, and the first invention or conception of it, *a priori*, must be entirely arbitrary. And even after it is suggested, the conjunction of it with the cause must appear equally arbitrary; since there are always many other effects, which, to reason, must seem fully as consistent and natural. In vain, therefore, should we pretend to determine any single event, or infer any cause or effect, without the assistance of observation and experience.

Hence we may discover the reason why no philosopher, who is rational and modest, has ever pretended to assign the ultimate cause of any natural operation, or to show distinctly the action of that power, which produces any single effect in the universe. It is confessed, that the utmost effort of human reason is to reduce the principles, productive of natural phenomena, to a greater simplicity, and to resolve the many particular effects into a few general causes, by means of reasonings from analogy, experience, and observation. But as to the causes of these general causes, we should in vain attempt their discovery; nor shall we ever be able to satisfy ourselves, by any particular explication of them. These ultimate springs and principles are totally shut up from human curiosity and inquiry. Elasticity, gravity, cohesion of parts, communication of motion by impulse; these are probably the ultimate causes and principles which we ever discover in nature; and we may esteem ourselves sufficiently happy, if, by accurate inquiry and reasoning, we can trace up the particular phenomena to, or near to, these general principles. The most perfect philosophy of the natural kind only staves off our ignorance a little longer: as perhaps the most perfect philosophy of the moral or metaphysical kind serves only to discover larger portions of it. Thus the observation of human blindness and weakness is the result of all philosophy, and meets us at every turn, in spite of our endeavors to elude or avoid it.

Nor is geometry, when taken into the assistance of natural philosophy, ever able to remedy this defect, or lead us into the knowledge of ultimate causes, by all that accuracy of reasoning for which it is so justly celebrated. Every part of mixed mathematics proceeds upon the supposition that certain laws are established by nature in her operations; and abstract reasonings are employed, either to assist experience in the discovery of these laws, or to determine their influence in particular instances, where it depends upon any precise degree of distance and quantity. Thus, it is a law of motion, discovered by experience, that the moment or force of any body in motion is in the compound ratio or proportion of its solid contents and its velocity; and consequently, that a small force may remove the greatest obstacle or raise the greatest weight, if, by any contrivance or machinery, we can increase the velocity of that force, so as to make it an overmatch for its antagonist. Geometry assists us in the application of this law, by giving us the just dimensions of all the parts and figures which can enter into any species of machine; but still the discovery of the law itself is owing merely to experience, and all the abstract reasonings in the world could never lead us one step towards the knowledge of it. When we reason *a priori,* and consider merely any object or cause, as it appears to the mind, independent of all observation, it never could suggest to us the notion of any distinct object, such as its effect; much less, show us the inseparable and inviolable connection between them. A man must be very sagacious who could discover by reasoning that crystal is the effect of heat, and ice of cold, without being previously acquainted with the operation of these qualities.

PART II

But we have not yet attained any tolerable satisfaction with regard to the question first proposed. Each solution still gives rise to a new question as difficult as the foregoing, and leads us on to farther inquiries. When it is asked, *What is the nature of all our reasonings concerning matter of fact?* the proper answer seems to be, that they are founded on the relation of cause and effect. When again it is asked, *What is the foundation of all our reasonings and conclusions concerning that relation?* it may be replied in one word, *experience.* But if we still carry on our sifting humor, and ask, *What is the foundation of all conclusions from experience?* this implies a new question, which may be of more difficult solution and explication. Philosophers, that give themselves airs of superior wisdom and sufficiency, have a hard task when they encounter persons of inquisitive dispositions, who push them from every corner to which they retreat, and who are sure at last to bring them to some dangerous dilemma. The best expedient to prevent this confusion, is to be modest in our pretensions; and even to discover the difficulty ourselves before it is objected to us. By this means, we may make a kind of merit of our very ignorance.

I shall content myself, in this section, with an easy task, and shall pretend only to give a negative answer to the question here proposed. I say then, that, even after we have experience of the operations of cause and effect, our conclusions from that experience are *not* founded on reasoning, or any process of the understanding. This answer we must endeavor both to explain and to defend.

It must certainly be allowed, that nature has kept us at a great distance from all her secrets, and has afforded us only the knowledge of a few superficial qualities of objects; while she conceals from us those powers and principles on which the influence of those objects entirely depends. Our senses inform us of the color, weight, and consistence of bread; but neither sense nor reason can ever inform us of those qualities which fit it for the nourishment and support of a human body. Sight or feeling conveys an idea of the actual motion of bodies; but as to that wonderful force or power, which would carry on a moving body for ever in a continued change of place, and which bodies never lose but by communicating it to others; of this we cannot form the most distant conception. But notwithstanding this ignorance of natural powers[6] and principles, we always presume, when we see like sensible qualities, that they have like secret powers, and expect that effects, similar to those which we have experienced, will follow from them. If a body of like color and consistence with that bread, which we have formerly eat, be presented to us, we make no scruple of repeating the experiment, and foresee, with certainty, like nourishment and support. Now this is a process of the mind or thought, of which I would willingly know the foundation. It is allowed on all hands that there is no known connection between the sensible qualities and the secret powers; and consequently, that the mind is not led to form such a conclusion concerning their constant and regular conjunction, by anything which it knows of their nature. As to past *experience,* it can be allowed to give *direct* and *certain* information of those precise objects only, and that precise period of time, which fell under its cognizance: but why this experience should be extended to future times, and to other objects, which, for aught we know, may be only in appearance similar; this is the main question on which I would insist. The bread, which I formerly eat, nourished me; that is, a body of such sensible qualities was, at that time, endued with such secret powers: but does it follow, that other bread must also nourish me at another time, and that like sensible qualities must always be attended with like secret powers? The consequence seems no wise necessary. At least, it must be acknowledged that there is here a consequence

6. The word, *power,* is here used in a loose and popular sense. The more accurate explication of it would give additional evidence to this argument. See Sect. 7.

drawn by the mind; that there is a certain step taken; a process of thought, and an inference, which wants to be explained. These two propositions are far from being the same, *I have found that such an object has always been attended with such an effect,* and *I forsee, that other objects, which are, in appearance, similar, will be attended with similar effects.* I shall allow, if you please, that the one proposition may justly be inferred from the other; I know, in fact, that it always is inferred. But if you insist that the inference is made by a chain of reasoning, I desire you to produce that reasoning. The connection between these propositions is not intuitive. There is required a medium, which may enable the mind to draw such an inference, if indeed it be drawn by reasoning and argument. What that medium is, I must confess, passes my comprehension; and it is incumbent on those to produce it, who assert that it really exists, and is the origin of all our conclusions concerning matter of fact.

This negative argument must certainly, in process of time, become altogether convincing, if many penetrating and able philosophers shall turn their inquiries this way and no one be ever able to discover any connecting proposition or intermediate step, which supports the understanding in this conclusion. But as the question is yet new, every reader may not trust so far to his own penetration, as to conclude, because an argument escapes his inquiry, that therefore it does not really exist. For this reason it may be requisite to venture upon a more difficult task; and enumerating all the branches of human knowledge, endeavor to show that none of them can afford such an argument.

All reasonings may be divided into two kinds, namely demonstrative reasoning, or that concerning relations of ideas, and moral reasoning, or that concerning matter of fact and existence. That there are no demonstrative arguments in the case seems evident; since it implies no contradiction that the course of nature may change, and that an object, seemingly like those which we have experienced, may be attended with different or contrary effects. May I not clearly and distinctly conceive that a body, falling from the clouds, and which, in all other respects, resembles snow, has yet the taste of salt or feeling of fire? Is there any more intelligible proposition than to affirm, that all the trees will flourish in December and January, and decay in May and June? Now whatever is intelligible, and can be distinctly conceived, implies no contradiction, and can never be proved false by any demonstrative argument or abstract reasoning *a priori.*

If we be, therefore, engaged by arguments to put trust in past experience, and make it the standard of our future judgment, these arguments must be probable only, or such as regard matter of fact and real existence, according to the division above mentioned. But that there is no argument of this kind, must appear, if our explication of that species of reasoning be admitted as solid and satisfactory. We have said that all arguments concerning existence are founded on the relation of cause and effect; that our knowledge of that relation is derived entirely from experience; and that all our experimental conclusions proceed upon the supposition that the future will be conformable to the past. To endeavor, therefore, the proof of this last supposition by probable arguments, or arguments regarding existence, must be evidently going in a circle, and taking that for granted, which is the very point in question.

In reality, all arguments from experience are founded on the similarity which we discover among natural objects, and by which we are induced to expect effects similar to those which we have found to follow from such objects. And though none but a fool or madman will ever pretend to dispute the authority of experience, or to reject that great guide of human life, it may surely be allowed a philosopher to have so much curiosity at least as to examine the principle of human nature, which gives this mighty authority to experience, and makes us draw advantage from that similarity which nature has placed among different objects. From causes which appear *similar* we expect similar effects. This is the sum of all our experimental conclusions. Now it seems evident that, if this conclusion were formed by reason, it would be as perfect at first, and upon one instance, as after ever so long a course of experience. But the case is far otherwise. Nothing so like as eggs; yet no one, on account of this appearing similarity, expects the same taste and relish in all of them. It is only after a long course of uniform experiments in any kind, that we attain a firm reliance and security with regard to a particular event. Now where is that process of reasoning which, from one instance, draws a conclusion, so different from that which it infers from a hundred instances that are nowise different from that single one? This question I propose as much for the sake of information, as with an intention of raising difficulties. I cannot find, I cannot imagine any such reasoning. But I keep my mind still open to instruction, if anyone will vouchsafe to bestow it on me.

Should it be said that, from a number of uniform experiments, we *infer* a connection between the sensible qualities and the secret powers; this, I must confess, seems the same difficulty, couched in different terms. The question still recurs, on what process of argument this *inference* is founded? Where is the medium, the interposing ideas, which join propositions so very wide of each other? It is confessed that the color, consistence, and other sensible qualities of bread appear not, of themselves, to have any connection with the secret powers of nourishment and support. For otherwise we could infer these secret powers from the first appearance of these sensible qualities, without the aid of experience; contrary to the sentiment of all philosophers, and contrary to plain matter of fact. Here, then, is our natural state of ignorance with regard to the powers and influence of all objects. How is this remedied by experience? It only shows us a number of uniform effects, resulting from certain objects, and teaches us that those particular objects, at that particular time, were endowed with such powers and forces. When a new object, endowed with similar sensible qualities, is produced, we expect similar powers and forces, and look for a like effect. From a body of like color and consistence with bread we expect like nourishment and support. But this surely is a step or progress of the mind, which wants to be explained. When a man says, *I have found, in all past instances, such sensible qualities conjoined with such secret powers:* And when he says, *Similar sensible qualities will always be conjoined with similar secret powers,* he is not guilty of a tautology, nor are these propositions in any respect the same. You say that the one proposition is an inference from the other. But you must confess that the inference is not intuitive; neither is it demonstrative: Of what nature is it, then? To say it is experimental, is begging the question. For all inferences from experience suppose, as their foundation, that the future will resemble the past, and that similar powers will be conjoined with similar sensible qualities. If there be any suspicion that the course of nature may change, and that the past may be no rule for the future, all experience becomes useless, and can give rise to no inference or conclusion. It is impossible, therefore, that any arguments from experience can prove this resemblance of the past to the future; since all these arguments are founded on the supposition of that resemblance. Let the course of things be allowed hitherto ever so regular; that alone, without some new argument or inference, proves not that, for the future, it will continue so. In vain do you pretend to have learned the nature of bodies from your past experience. Their secret nature, and consequently all their effects and influence, may change, without any change in their sensible qualities. This happens sometimes, and with regard to some objects: Why may it not happen always, and with regard to all objects? What logic, what process of argument secures you against this supposition? My practice, you say, refutes my doubts. But you mistake the purport of my question. As an agent, I am quite satisfied in the point; but as a philosopher, who has some share of curiosity, I will not say scepticism, I want to learn the foundation of this inference. No reading, no inquiry has yet been able to remove my difficulty, or give me satisfaction in a matter of such importance. Can I do better than propose the difficulty to the public, even though, perhaps, I have small hopes of obtaining a solution? We shall, at least, by this means, be sensible of our ignorance, if we do not augment our knowledge.

I must confess that a man is guilty of unpardonable arrogance who concludes, because an argument has escaped his own investigation, that therefore it does not really exist. I must also confess that, though all the learned, for several ages, should have employed themselves in fruitless search upon any subject, it may still, perhaps, be rash to conclude positively that the subject must, therefore, pass all human comprehension. Even though we examine all the sources of our knowledge, and conclude them unfit for such a subject, there may still remain a suspicion, that the enumeration is not complete, or the examination not accurate. But with regard to the present subject, there are some considerations which seem to remove all this accusation of arrogance or suspicion of mistake.

It is certain that the most ignorant and stupid peasants—nay infants, nay even brute beasts—improve by experience, and learn the qualities of natural objects, by observing the effects which result from them. When a child has felt the sensation of pain from touching the flame of a candle, he will be careful not to put his hand near any candle; but will expect a similar effect from a cause which is similar in its sensible qualities and appearance. If you assert, therefore, that the understanding of the child is led into this conclusion by any process of argument or ratiocination, I may justly require you to produce that argument; nor have you any pretense to refuse so equitable a demand. You cannot say that the argument is abstruse, and may possibly escape your inquiry; since you confess that it is obvious to the capacity of a mere infant. If you hesitate, therefore, a moment, or if, after reflection, you produce any intricate or profound argument, you, in a manner, give up the question, and confess that it is not reasoning which engages us to suppose the past resembling the future, and to expect similar effects from causes which are, to appearance, similar. This is the proposition which I intended to enforce in the present section. If I be right, I pretend not to have made any mighty discovery. And if I be wrong, I must acknowledge myself to be indeed a very backward scholar; since I cannot now discover an argument which, it seems, was perfectly familiar to me long before I was out of my cradle.

SECTION V—Sceptical Solution of These Doubts

PART I

The passion for philosophy, like that for religion, seems liable to this inconvenience, that, though it aims at the correction of our manners, and extirpation of our vices, it may only serve, by imprudent management, to foster a predominant inclination, and push the mind, with more determined resolution, towards that side which already *draws* too much, by the bias and propensity of the natural temper. It is certain that, while we aspire to the magnanimous firmness of the philosophic sage, and endeavor to confine our pleasures altogether within our own minds, we may, at last, render our philosophy like that of Epictetus, and other *stoics,* only a more refined system of selfishness, and reason ourselves out of all virtue as well as social enjoyment. While we study with attention the vanity of human life, and turn all our thoughts towards the empty and transitory nature of riches and honors, we are, perhaps, all the while flattering our natural indolence, which, hating the bustle of the world, and drudgery of business, seeks a pretense of reason to give itself a full and uncontrolled indulgence. There is, however, one species of philosophy which seems little liable to this inconvenience, and that because it strikes in with no disorderly passion of the human mind, nor can mingle itself with any natural affection or propensity; and that is the *academic* or *sceptical* philosophy. The academics always talk of doubt and suspense of judgment, of danger in hasty determinations, of confining to very narrow bounds the inquiries of the understanding, and of renouncing all speculations which lie not within the limits of common life and practice. Nothing, therefore, can be more contrary than such a philosophy to the supine indolence of the mind, its rash arrogance, its lofty pretensions, and its superstitious credulity. Every passion is mortified by it, except the love of truth; and that passion never is, nor can be, carried to too high a degree. It is surprising, therefore, that this philosophy, which, in almost every instance, must be harmless and innocent, should be the subject of so much groundless reproach and obloquy. But, perhaps, the very circumstance which renders it so innocent is what chiefly exposes it to the public hatred and resentment. By flattering no irregular passion, it gains few partisans: By opposing so many vices and follies, it raises to itself abundance of enemies, who stigmatize it as libertine, profane, and irreligious.

Nor need we fear that this philosophy, while it endeavors to limit our inquiries to common life, should ever undermine the reasonings of common life, and carry its doubts so far as to destroy all action, as well as speculation. Nature will always maintain her rights, and prevail in the end over any abstract reasoning whatsoever. Though we should conclude, for instance, as in the foregoing section, that, in all reasonings from experience, there is a step taken by the mind which is not supported by any argument or process of the understanding; there is no danger that these reasonings, on which almost all knowledge depends, will ever be affected by such a discovery. If the mind be not engaged by argument to make this step, it must be induced by some other principle of equal weight and authority; and that principle will preserve its influence as long as human nature remains the same. What that principle is may well be worth the pains of inquiry.

Suppose a person, though endowed with the strongest faculties of reason and reflection, to be brought on a sudden into this world; he would, indeed, immediately observe a continual succession of objects, and one event following another; but he would not be able to discover anything farther. He would not, at first, by any reasoning, be able to reach the idea of cause and effect; since the particular powers, by which all natural operations are performed, never appear to the senses; nor is it reasonable to conclude, merely because one event, in one instance, precedes another, that therefore the one is the cause, the other the effect. Their conjunction may be arbitrary and casual. There may be no reason to infer the existence of one from the appearance of the other. And in a word, such a person, without more experience, could never employ his conjecture or reasoning concerning any matter of fact, or be assured of anything beyond what was immediately present to his memory and senses.

Suppose, again, that he has acquired more experience, and has lived so long in the world as to have observed familiar objects or events to be constantly conjoined together; what is the consequence of this experience? He immediately infers the existence of one object from the appearance of the other. Yet he has not, by all his experience, acquired any idea or knowledge of the secret power by which the one object produces the other; nor is it, by any process of reasoning, he is engaged to draw this inference. But still he finds himself determined to draw it: And though he should be convinced that his understanding has no part in the operation, he would nevertheless continue in the same course of thinking. There is some other principle which determines him to form such a conclusion.

This principle is *custom* or *habit*. For wherever the repetition of any particular act or operation produces a propensity to renew the same act or operation, without being impelled by any reasoning or process of the understanding, we always say, that this propensity is the effect of *custom*. By employing that word, we pretend not to have given the ultimate reason of such a propensity. We only point out a principle of human nature, which is universally acknowledged, and which is well known by its effects. Perhaps we can push our inquiries no farther, or pretend to give the cause of this cause; but must rest contented with it as the ultimate principle, which we can assign, of all our conclusions from experience. It is sufficient satisfaction, that we can go so far, without repining at the narrowness of our faculties because they will carry us no farther. And it is certain we here advance a very intelligible proposition at least, if not a true one, when we assert that, after the constant conjunction of two objects—heat and flame, for instance, weight and solidity—we are determined by custom alone to expect the one from the appearance of the other. This hypothesis seems even the only one which explains the difficulty, why we draw, from a thousand instances, an inference which we are not able to draw from one instance, that is, in no respect, different from them. Reason is incapable of any such variation. The conclusions which it draws from considering one circle are the same which it would form upon surveying all the circles in the universe. But no man, having seen only one body move after being impelled by another, could infer that every other body will move after a like impulse. All inferences from experience, therefore, are effects of custom, not of reasoning.[7]

---

7. Nothing is more useful than for writers, even, on *moral, political,* or *physical* subjects, to distinguish between *reason* and *experience,* and to suppose, that these species of argumentation are entirely different from each other. The former are taken for the mere result of our intellectual faculties, which, by considering *a priori* the nature of things, and examining the effects, that must follow from their operation, establish particular principles of science and philosophy. The latter are supposed to be derived entirely from sense and observation, by which we learn what has actually resulted from the operation of particular objects, and are thence able to infer, what will, for the future, result from them. Thus, for instance, the limitations and restraints of civil government, and a legal constitution, may be defended, either from *reason*, which reflecting on the great frailty and corruption of human nature, teaches, that no man can safely be trusted with unlimited authority; or from *experience* and history, which inform us of the enormous abuses, that ambition, in every age and country, has been found to make of so imprudent a confidence.

The same distinction between reason and experience is maintained in all our deliberations concerning the conduct of life; while the experienced statesman, general, physician, or merchant is trusted and followed; and the unpracticed novice,

Custom, then, is the great guide of human life. It is that principle alone which renders our experience useful to us, and makes us expect, for the future, a similar train of events with those which have appeared in the past. Without the influence of custom, we should be entirely ignorant of every matter of fact beyond what is immediately present to the memory and senses. We should never know how to adjust means to ends, or to employ our natural powers in the production of any effect. There would be an end at once of all action, as well as of the chief part of speculation.

---

with whatever natural talents endowed, neglected and despised. Though it be allowed, that reason may form very plausible conjectures with regard to the consequences of such a particular conduct in such particular circumstances; it is still supposed imperfect, without the assistance of experience, which is alone able to give stability and certainty to the maxims, derived from study and reflection.

But notwithstanding that this distinction be thus universally received, both in the active and speculative scenes of life, I shall not scruple to pronounce, that it is, at bottom, erroneous, at least, superficial.

If we examine those arguments, which, in any of the sciences above mentioned, are supposed to be the mere effects of reasoning and reflection, they will be found to terminate, at last, in some general principle or conclusion, for which we can assign no reason but observation and experience. The only difference between them and those maxims, which are vulgarly esteemed the result of pure experience, is, that the former cannot be established without some process of thought, and some reflection on what we have observed, in order to distinguish its circumstances, and trace its consequences: Whereas in the latter, the experienced event is exactly and fully familiar to that which we infer as the result of any particular situation. The history of a Tiberius or a Nero makes us dread a like tyranny, were our monarchs freed from the restraints of laws and senates. But the observation of any fraud or cruelty in private life is sufficient, with the aid of a little thought, to give us the same apprehension; while it serves as an instance of the general corruption of human nature, and shows us the danger which we must incur by reposing an entire confidence in mankind. In both cases, it is experience which is ultimately the foundation of our inference and conclusion.

There is no man so young and inexperienced, as not to have formed, from observation, many general and just maxims concerning human affairs and the conduct of life; but it must be confessed, that, when a man comes to put these in practice, he will be extremely liable to error, till time and farther experience both enlarge these maxims, and teach him their proper use and application. In every situation or incident, there are many particular and seemingly minute circumstances, which the man of greatest talent is, at first, apt to overlook, though on them the justness of his conclusions, and consequently the prudence of his conduct, entirely depend. Not to mention, that, to a young beginner, the general observations and maxims occur not always on the proper occasions, nor can be immediately applied with due calmness and distinction. The truth is, an unexperienced reasoner could be no reasoner at all, were he absolutely unexperienced; and when we assign that character to anyone, we mean it only in a comparative sense, and suppose him possessed of experience, in a smaller and more imperfect degree.

But here it may be proper to remark, that though our conclusions from experience carry us beyond our memory and senses, and assure us of matters of fact which happened in the most distant places and most remote ages, yet some fact must always be present to the senses or memory, from which we may first proceed in drawing these conclusions. A man, who should find in a desert country the remains of pompous buildings, would conclude that the country had, in ancient times, been cultivated by civilized inhabitants; but did nothing of this nature occur to him, he could never form such an inference. We learn the events of former ages from history; but then we must peruse the volumes in which this instruction is contained, and thence carry up our inferences from one testimony to another, till we arrive at the eyewitnesses and spectators of these distant events. In a word, if we proceed not upon some fact, present to the memory or senses, our reasonings would be merely hypothetical; and however the particular links might be connected with each other, the whole chain of inferences would have nothing to support it, nor could we ever, by its means, arrive at the knowledge of any real existence. If I ask why you believe any particular matter of fact, which you relate, you must tell me some reason; and this reason will be some other fact, connected with it. But as you cannot proceed after this manner, *in infinitum,* you must at last terminate in some fact, which is present to your memory or senses; or must allow that your belief is entirely without foundation.

What, then, is the conclusion of the whole matter? A simple one; though, it must be confessed, pretty remote from the common theories of philosophy. All belief of matter of fact or real existence is derived merely from some object, present to the memory or senses, and a customary conjunction between that and some other object. Or in other words; having found, in many instances, that any two kinds of objects —flame and heat, snow and cold—have always been conjoined together; if flame or snow be presented anew to the senses, the mind is carried by custom to expect heat or cold, and to *believe* that such a quality does exist, and will discover itself upon a nearer approach. This belief is the necessary result of placing the mind in such circumstances. It is an operation of the soul, when we are so situated, as unavoidable as to feel the passion of love, when we receive benefits; or hatred, when we meet with injuries. All these operations are a species of natural instincts, which no reasoning or process of the thought and understanding is able either to produce or to prevent.

SECTION XII—Of the Academical
or Sceptical Philosophy

PART I

There is not a greater number of philosophical reasonings, displayed upon any subject, than those, which prove the existence of a Deity, and refute the fallacies of *atheists;* and yet the most religious philosophers still dispute whether any man can be so blinded as to be a speculative atheist. How shall we reconcile these contradictions? The knights-errant, who wandered about to clear the world of dragons and giants, never entertained the least doubt with regard to the existence of these monsters.

The *sceptic* is another enemy of religion, who naturally provokes the indignation of all divines and graver philosophers; though it is certain, that no man ever met with any such absurd creature, or conversed with a man, who had no opinion or principle concerning any subject, either of action or speculation. This begets a very natural question; What is meant by a sceptic? And how far is it possible to push these philosophical principles of doubt and uncertainty?

There is a species of scepticism, *antecedent* to all study and philosophy, which is much inculcated by Descartes and others, as a sovereign preservative against error and precipitate judgment. It recommends an universal doubt, not only of all our former opinions and principles, but also of our very faculties; of whose veracity, say they, we must assure ourselves, by a chain of reasoning, deduced from some original principle, which cannot possibly be fallacious or deceitful. But neither is there any such original principle, which has a prerogative above others, that are self-evident and convincing: or if there were, could we advance a step beyond it, but by the use of those very faculties, of which we are supposed to be already diffident. The Cartesian doubt, therefore, were it ever possible to be attained by any human creature (as it plainly is not) would be entirely incurable; and no reasoning could every bring us to a state of assurance and conviction upon any subject.

It must, however, be confessed, that this species of scepticism, when more moderate, may be understood in a very reasonable sense, and is a necessary preparative to the study of philosophy, by preserving a proper impartiality in our judgments, and weaning our mind from all those prejudices, which we may have imbibed from education or rash opinion. To begin with clear and self-evident principles, to advance by timorous and sure steps, to review frequently our conclusions, and examine accurately all their consequences; though by these means we shall make both a slow and a short progress in our systems; are the only methods, by which we can ever hope to reach truth, and attain a proper stability and certainty in our determinations.

There is another species of scepticism, *consequent* to science and inquiry, when men are supposed to have discovered either the absolute fallaciousness of their mental faculties, or their unfitness to reach any fixed determination in all those curious subjects of speculation, about which they are commonly employed. Even our very senses are brought into dispute, by a certain species of philosophers; and the maxims of common life are subjected to the same doubt as the most profound ·principles or conclusions of metaphysics and theology. As these para-doxical tenets (if they may be called tenets) are to be met with in some philosophers, and the refutation of them in several, they naturally excite our curiosity, and make us inquire into the arguments, on which they may be founded.

I need not insist upon the more trite topics, employed by the sceptics in all ages, against the evidence of *sense;* such as those which are derived from the imperfection and fallaciousness of our organs, on numberless occasions; the crooked appearance of an oar in water; the various aspects of objects, according to their different distances; the double images which arise from the pressing one eye; with many other appearances of a like nature. These sceptical topics, indeed, are only sufficient to prove, that the senses alone are not implicitly to be depended on; but that we must correct their evidence by reason, and by considerations, derived from the nature of the medium, the distance of the object, and the disposition of the organ, in order to render them, within their sphere, the proper *criteria* of truth and falsehood. There are other more profound arguments against the senses, which admit not of so easy a solution.

It seems evident, that men are carried, by a natural instinct or pre-possession, to repose faith in their senses; and that, without any reasoning, or even almost before the use of reason, we always suppose an external universe, which depends not on our perception, but would exist, though we and every sensible creature were absent or annihilated. Even the animal creation are governed by a like opinion, and preserve this belief of external objects, in all their thoughts, designs, and actions.

It seems also evident, that, when men follow this blind and powerful instinct of nature, they always suppose the very images, presented by the senses, to be the external objects, and never entertain any suspicion, that the one are nothing but representations of the other. This very table, which we see white, and which we feel hard, is believed to exist, independent of our perception, and to be something external to our mind, which perceives it. Our presence bestows not being on it; our absence does not annihilate it. It preserves its existence uniform and entire, independent of the situation of intelligent beings, who perceive or contemplate it.

But this universal and primary opinion of all men is soon destroyed by the slightest philosophy, which teaches us, that nothing can ever be present to the mind but an image or perception, and that the senses are only the inlets, through which these images are conveyed, without being able to produce any immediate intercourse between the mind and the object. The table, which we see, seems to diminish, as we remove farther from it; but the real table, which exists independent of us, suffers no alteration: it was, therefore, nothing but its image, which was present to the mind. These are the obvious dictates of reason; and no man, who reflects, ever doubted, that the existences, which we consider, when we say, *this house* and *that tree,* are nothing but perceptions in the mind, and fleeting copies or representations of other existences, which remain uniform and independent.

So far, then, are we necessitated by reasoning to contradict or depart from the primary instincts of nature, and to embrace a new system with regard to the evidence of our senses. But here philosophy finds herself extremely embarrassed, when she would justify this new system, and obviate the cavils and objections of the sceptics. She can no longer plead the infallible and irresistible instinct of nature: for that led us to a quite different system, which is acknowledged fallible and even erroneous. And to justify this pretended philosophical system, by a chain of clear and convincing argument, or even any appearance of argument, exceeds the power of all human capacity.

By what argument can it be proved, that the perceptions of the mind must be caused by external objects, entirely different from them, though resembling them (if that be possible) and could not arise either from the energy of the mind itself, or from the suggestion of some invisible and unknown spirit, or from some other cause still more unknown to us? It is acknowledged, that, in fact, many of these perceptions arise not from anything external, as in dreams, madness, and other diseases. And nothing can be more inexplicable than the manner, in which body should so operate upon mind as ever to convey an image of itself to a substance, supposed of so different, and even contrary a nature.

It is a question of fact, whether the perceptions of the senses be produced by external objects, resembling them: how shall this question be determined? By experience surely; as all other questions of a like nature. But here experience is, and must be entirely silent. The mind has never anything present to it but the perceptions, and cannot possibly reach any experience of their connection with objects. The supposition of such a connection is, therefore, without any foundation in reasoning.

To have recourse to the veracity of the supreme Being, in order to prove the veracity of our senses, is surely making a very unexpected circuit. If this veracity were at all concerned in this matter, our senses would be entirely infallible; because it is not possible that he can ever deceive. Not to mention, that, if the external world be once called in question, we shall be at a loss to find arguments, by which we may prove the existence of that Being or any of his attributes.

This is a topic, therefore, in which the profounder and more philosophical sceptics will always triumph, when they endeavor to introduce an universal doubt into all subjects of human knowledge and inquiry. Do you follow the instincts and propensities of nature, may they say, in assenting to the veracity of sense? But these lead you to believe that the very perception or sensible image is the external object. Do you disclaim this principle, in order to embrace a more rational opinion, that the perceptions are only representations of something external? You here depart from your natural propensities and more obvious sentiments; and yet are not able to satisfy your reason, which can never find any convincing argument from experience to prove, that the perceptions are connected with any external objects.

There is another sceptical topic of a like nature, derived from the most profound philosophy; which might merit our attention, were it requisite to dive so deep, in order to discover arguments and reasonings, which can so little serve to any serious purpose. It is universally allowed by modern inquirers, that all the sensible qualities of objects, such as hard, soft, hot, cold, white, black, etc. are merely secondary, and exist not in the objects themselves, but are perceptions of the mind, without any external archetype or model, which they represent. If this be allowed, with regard to secondary qualities, it must also follow, with regard to the supposed primary qualities of extension and solidity; nor can the latter be any more entitled to that denomination than the former. The idea of extension is entirely acquired from the senses of sight and feeling; and if all the qualities, perceived by the senses, be in the mind, not in the object, the same conclusion must reach the idea of extension, which is wholly dependent on the sensible ideas or the ideas of secondary qualities. Nothing can save us from this conclusion, but the asserting, that the ideas of those primary qualities are attained by *abstraction,* an opinion, which, if we examine it accurately, we shall find to be unintelligible, and even absurd. An extension, that is neither tangible nor visible, cannot possibly be conceived; and a tangible or visible extension, which is neither hard nor soft, black or white, is equally beyond the reach of human conception. Let any man try to conceive a triangle in general, which is neither *isosceles* nor *scalenum,* nor has any particular length or proportion of sides; and he will soon perceive the absurdity of all the scholastic notions with regard to abstraction and general ideas.[8]

Thus the first philosophical objection to the evidence of sense or to the opinion of external existence consists in this, that such an opinion, if rested on natural instinct, is contrary to reason, and if referred to reason, is contrary to natural instinct, and at the same time carries no rational evidence with it, to convince an impartial inquirer. The second objection goes farther, and represents this opinion as contrary to reason, at least, if it be a principle of reason, that all sensible qualities are in the mind, not in the object. Bereave matter of all its intelligible qualities, both primary and secondary, you in a manner annihilate it, and leave only a certain unknown, inexplicable *something,* as the cause of our perceptions; a notion so imperfect, that no sceptic will think it worth while to contend against it.

PART II

It may seem a very extravagant attempt of the sceptics to destroy *reason* by argument and ratiocination; yet is this the grand scope of all their inquiries and disputes. They endeavor to find objections, both to our abstract reasonings, and to those which regard matter of fact and existence.

The chief objection against all *abstract* reasonings is derived from the ideas of space and time; ideas, which, in common life and to a

---

8. This argument is drawn from Dr. Berkeley; and indeed most of the writings of that very ingenious author form the best lessons of scepticism, which are to be found either among the ancient or modern philosophers, Bayle not excepted. He professes, however, in his title-page (and undoubtedly with great truth) to have composed his book against the sceptics as well as against the atheists and free-thinkers. But that all his arguments, though otherwise intended, are, in reality, merely sceptical, appears from this, *that they admit of no answer and produce no conviction.* Their only effect is to cause that momentary amazement and irresolution and confusion, which is the result of scepticism.

careless view, are very clear and intelligible, but when they pass through the scrutiny of the profound sciences (and they are the chief object of these sciences) afford principles, which seem full of absurdity and contradiction. No priestly *dogmas*, invented on purpose to tame and subdue the rebellious reason of mankind, ever shocked common sense more than the doctrine of the infinite divisibility of extension, with its consequences; as they are pompously displayed by all geometricians and metaphysicians, with a kind of triumph and exultation. A real quantity, infinitely less than any finite quantity, containing quantities infinitely less than itself, and so on *in infinitum;* this is an edifice so bold and prodigious, that it is too weighty for any pretended demonstration to support, because it shocks the clearest and most natural principles of human reason.[9] But what renders the matter more extraordinary, is, that these seemingly absurd opinions are supported by a chain of reasoning, the clearest and most natural; nor is it possible for us to allow the premises without admitting the consequences. Nothing can be more convincing and satisfactory than all the conclusions concerning the properties of circles and triangles; and yet, when these are once received, how can we deny, that the angle of contact between a circle and its tangent is infinitely less than any rectilineal angle, that as you may increase the diameter of the circle *in infinitum,* this angle of contact becomes still less, even *in infinitum,* and that the angle of contact between other curves and their tangents may be infinitely less than those between any circle and its tangent, and so on, *in infinitum?* The demonstration of these principles seems as unexceptionable as that which proves the three angles of a triangle to be equal to two right ones, though the latter opinion be natural and easy, and the former big with contradiction and absurdity. Reason here seems to be thrown into a kind of amazement and suspense, which, without the suggestions of any sceptic, gives her a diffidence of herself, and of the ground on which she treads. She sees a full light, which illuminates certain places; but that light borders upon the most profound darkness. And between these she is so dazzled and confounded, that she scarcely can pronounce with certainty and assurance concerning any one object.

---

9. Whatever disputes there may be about mathematical points, we must allow that there are physical points; that is, parts of extension, which cannot be divided or lessened, either by the eye or imagination. These images, then, which are present to the fancy or senses, are absolutely indivisible, and consequently must be allowed by mathematicians to be infinitely less than any real part of extension; and yet nothing appears more certain to reason, than that an infinite number of them composes an infinite extension. How much more an infinite number of those infinitely small parts of extension, which are still supposed infinitely divisible.

The absurdity of these bold determinations of the abstract sciences seems to become, if possible, still more palpable with regard to time than extension. An infinite number of real parts of time, passing in succession, and exhausted one after another, appears so evident a contradiction, that no man, one should think, whose judgment is not corrupted, instead of being improved, by the sciences, would ever be able to admit of it.

Yet still reason must remain restless, and unquiet, even with regard to that scepticism, to which she is driven by these seeming absurdities and contradictions. How any clear, distinct idea can contain circumstances, contradictory to itself, or to any other clear, distinct idea, is absolutely incomprehensible; and is, perhaps, as absurd as any proposition, which can be formed. So that nothing can be more sceptical, or more full of doubt and hesitation, than this scepticism itself, which arises from some of the paradoxical conclusions of geometry or the science of quantity.[10]

The sceptical objections to *moral* evidence, or to the reasonings concerning matter of fact, are either *popular* or *philosophical*. The popular objections are derived from the natural weakness of human understanding; the contradictory opinions, which have been entertained in different ages and nations; the variations of our judgment in sickness and health, youth and old age, prosperity and adversity; the perpetual contradiction of each particular man's opinions and sentiments; with many other topics of that kind. It is needless to insist farther on this head. These objections are but weak. For as, in common life, we reason every moment concerning fact and existence, and cannot possibly subsist, without continually employing this species of argument, any popular objections, derived from thence, must be insufficient to destroy

10. It seems to me not impossible to avoid these absurdities and contradictions, if it be admitted, that there is no such thing as abstract or general ideas, properly speaking; but that all general ideas are, in reality, particular ones, attached to a general term, which recalls, upon occasion, other particular ones, that resemble, in certain circumstances, the idea, present to the mind. Thus when the term *horse* is pronounced, we immediately figure to ourselves the idea of a black or a white animal, of a particular size or figure: but as that term is also usually applied to animals of other colors, figures and sizes, these ideas, though not actually present to the imagination, are easily recalled; and our reasoning and conclusion proceed in the same way, as if they were actually present. If this be admitted (as seems reasonable) it follows that all the ideas of quantity, upon which mathematicians reason, are nothing but particular, and such as are suggested by the senses and imagination, and consequently, cannot be infinitely divisible. It is sufficient to have dropped this hint at present, without prosecuting it any farther. It certainly concerns all lovers of science not to expose themselves to the ridicule and contempt of the ignorant by their conclusions; and this seems the readiest solution of these difficulties.

that evidence. The great subverter of *Pyrrhonism* or the excessive principles of scepticism is action, and employment, and the occupations of common life. These principles may flourish and triumph in the schools; where it is, indeed, difficult, if not impossible, to refute them. But as soon as they leave the shade, and by the presence of the real objects, which actuate our passions and sentiments, are put in opposition to the more powerful principles of our nature, they vanish like smoke, and leave the most determined sceptic in the same condition as other mortals.

The sceptic, therefore, had better keep within his proper sphere, and display those *philosophical* objections, which arise from more profound researches. Here he seems to have ample matter of triumph; while he justly insists, that all our evidence for any matter of fact, which lies beyond the testimony of sense or memory, is derived entirely from the relation of cause and effect; that we have no other idea of this relation than that of two objects, which have been frequently *conjoined* together; that we have no argument to convince us, that objects, which have, in our experience, been frequently conjoined, will likewise, in other instances, be conjoined in the same manner; and that nothing leads us to this inference but custom or a certain instinct of our nature; which it is indeed difficult to resist, but which, like other instincts, may be fallacious and deceitful. While the sceptic insists upon these topics, he shows his force, or rather, indeed, his own and our weakness; and seems, for the time at least, to destroy all assurance and conviction. These arguments might be displayed at greater length, if any durable good or benefit to society could ever be expected to result from them.

For here is the chief and most confounding objection to *excessive* scepticism, that no durable good can ever result from it; while it remains in its full force and vigor. We need only ask such a sceptic, *What his meaning is? And what he proposes by all these curious researches?* He is immediately at a loss, and knows not what to answer. A Copernican or Ptolemaic, who supports each his different system of astronomy, may hope to produce a conviction, which will remain constant and durable, with his audience. A Stoic or Epicurean displays principles, which may not be durable, but which have an effect on conduct and behavior. But a Pyrrhonian cannot expect, that his philosophy will have any constant influence on the mind: or if it had, that its influence would be beneficial to society. On the contrary, he must acknowledge, if he will acknowledge anything, that all human life must perish, were his principles universally and steadily to prevail. All discourse, all action would immediately cease; and men remain in a total lethargy, till the necessities of nature, unsatisfied, put an end to their miserable existence. It is true; so fatal an event is very little to be dreaded. Nature is always too strong for principle. And though a Pyrrhonian may throw himself or others into a momentary amazement and confusion by his profound reasonings; the first and most trivial event in life will put to flight all his doubts and scruples, and leave him the same, in every point of action and speculation, with the philosophers of every other sect, or with those who never concerned themselves in any philosophical researches. When he awakes from his dream, he will be the first to join in the laugh against himself, and to confess, that all his objections are mere amusement, and can have no other tendency than to show the whimsical condition of mankind, who must act and reason and believe; though they are not able, by their most diligent inquiry, to satisfy themselves concerning the foundation of these operations, or to remove the objections, which may be raised against them.

PART III

There is, indeed, a more *mitigated* scepticism or *academical* philosophy, which may be both durable and useful, and which may, in part, be the result of this Pyrrhonism, or *excessive* scepticism, when its undistinguished doubts are, in some measure, corrected by common sense and reflection. The greater part of mankind are naturally apt to be affirmative and dogmatical in their opinions; and while they see objects only on one side, and have no idea of any counterpoising argument, they throw themselves precipitately into the principles, to which they are inclined; nor have they any indulgence for those who entertain opposite sentiments. To hesitate or balance perplexes their understanding, checks their passion, and suspends their action. They are, therefore, impatient till they escape from a state, which to them is so uneasy: and they think, that they could never remove themselves far enough from it, by the violence of their affirmations and obstinacy of their belief. But could such dogmatical reasoners become sensible of the strange infirmities of human understanding, even in its most perfect state, and when most accurate and cautious in its determinations; such a reflection would naturally inspire them with more modesty and reserve, and diminish their fond opinion of themselves, and their prejudice against antagonists. The illiterate may reflect on the disposition of the learned, who, amidst all the advantages of study and reflection, are commonly still diffident in their determinations: and if any of the learned be inclined, from their natural temper, to haughtiness and obstinacy, a small tincture of Pyrrhonism might abate their pride, by showing them, that the few advantages, which they may have attained over their fellows, are but inconsiderable, if compared with the universal perplexity and confusion, which is inherent in human nature. In general, there is a degree of doubt, and caution, and modesty, which, in all kinds of scrutiny and decision, ought forever to accompany a just reasoner.

Another species of *mitigated* scepticism which may be of advantage to mankind, and which may be the natural result of the Pyrrhonian doubts and scruples, is the limitation of our inquiries to such subjects as are best adapted to the narrow capacity of human understanding. The *imagination* of man is naturally sublime, delighted with whatever is remote and extraordinary, and running, without control, into the most distant parts of space and time in order to avoid the objects, which custom has rendered too familiar to it. A correct *judgment* observes a contrary method, and avoiding all distant and high inquiries, confines itself to common life, and to such subjects as fall under daily practice and experience; leaving the more sublime topics to the embellishment of poets and orators, or to the arts of priests and politicians. To bring us to so salutary a determination, nothing can be more serviceable, than to be once thoroughly convinced of the force of the Pyrrhonian doubt, and of the impossibility, that anything, but the strong power of natural instinct, could free us from it. Those who have a propensity to philosophy, will still continue their researches; because they reflect, that, besides the immediate pleasure, attending such an occupation, philosophical decisions are nothing but the reflections of common life, methodized and corrected. But they will never be tempted to go beyond common life, so long as they consider the imperfection of those faculties which they employ, their narrow reach, and their inaccurate operations. While we cannot give a satisfactory reason, why we believe, after a thousand experiments, that a stone will fall, or fire burn; can we ever satisfy ourselves concerning any determination, which we may form, with regard to the origin of worlds, and the situation of nature, from, and to eternity?

This narrow limitation, indeed, of our inquiries, is, in every respect, so reasonable, that it suffices to make the slightest examination into the natural powers of the human mind and to compare them with their objects, in order to recommend it to us. We shall then find what are the proper subjects of science and inquiry.

It seems to me, that the only objects of the abstract science or of demonstration are quantity and number, and that all attempts to extend this more perfect species of knowledge beyond these bounds are mere sophistry and illusion. As the component parts of quantity and number are entirely similar, their relations become intricate and involved; and nothing can be more curious, as well as useful, than to trace, by a variety of mediums, their equality or inequality, through their different appearances. But as all other ideas are clearly distinct and different from each other, we can never advance farther, by our utmost scrutiny, than to observe this diversity, and, by an obvious reflection, pronounce one thing not to be another. Or if there be any difficulty in these decisions, it proceeds entirely from the undeterminate meaning of words, which is corrected by juster definitions. That *the square of the hypothenuse is equal to the squares of the other two sides,* cannot be known, let the terms be ever so exactly defined, without a train of reasoning and inquiry. But to convince us of this proposition, *that where there is no property, there can be no injustice,* it is only necessary to define the terms, and explain injustice to be a violation of property. This proposition is, indeed, nothing but a more imperfect definition. It is the same case with all those pretended syllogistical reasonings, which may be found in every other branch of learning, except the sciences of quantity and number; and these may safely, I think, be pronounced the only proper objects of knowledge and demonstration.

All other inquiries of men regard only matter of fact and existence; and these are evidently incapable of demonstration. Whatever *is* may *not be.* No negation of a fact can involve a contradiction. The nonexistence of any being, without exception, is as clear and distinct an idea as its existence. The proposition, which affirms it not to be, however false, is no less conceivable and intelligible, than that which affirms it to be. The case is different with the sciences, properly so called. Every proposition, which is not true, is there confused and unintelligible. That the cube root of 64 is equal to the half of 10, is a false proposition, and can never be distinctly conceived. But that Caesar, or the angel Gabriel, or any being never existed, may be a false proposition, but still is perfectly conceivable, and implies no contradiction.

The existence, therefore, of any being can only be proved by arguments from its cause or its effect; and these arguments are founded entirely on experience. If we reason *a priori,* anything may appear able to produce anything. The falling of a pebble may, for aught we know, extinguish the sun; or the wish of a man control the planets in their orbits. It is only experience, which teaches us the nature and bounds of cause and effect, and enables us to infer the existence of one object from that of another.[11] Such is the foundation of moral reasoning, which forms the greater part of human knowledge, and is the source of all human action and behavior.

Moral reasonings are either concerning particular or general facts. All deliberations in life regard the former; as also all disquisitions in history, chronology, geography, and astronomy.

The sciences, which treat of general facts, are politics, natural philosophy, physics, chemistry, etc., where the qualities, causes and effects of a whole species of objects are inquired into.

Divinity or Theology, as it proves the existence of a Deity, and the immortality of souls, is composed partly of reasonings concerning particular, partly concerning general facts. It has a foundation in *reason,* so far as it is supported by experience. But its best and most solid foundation is *faith* and divine revelation.

Morals and criticism are not so properly objects of the understanding as of taste and sentiment. Beauty, whether moral or natural, is felt, more properly than perceived. Or if we reason concerning it, and endeavor to fix its standard, we regard a new fact, to wit, the general tastes of mankind, or some such fact, which may be the object of reasoning and inquiry.

When we run over libraries, persuaded of these principles, what havoc must we make? If we take in our hand any volume; of divinity or school metaphysics, for instance; let us ask, *Does it contain any abstract reasoning concerning quantity or number?* No. *Does it contain any experimental reasoning concerning matter of fact and existence?* No. Commit it then to the flames: for it can contain nothing but sophistry and illusion.

The Speech of Epicurus[12]

I come hither, O ye Athenians, to justify in your assembly what I maintained in my school, and I find myself impeached by furious antagonists, instead of reasoning with calm and dispassionate inquirers.

---

11. That impious maxim of the ancient philosophy, *Ex nihilo, nihil fit,* by which the creation of matter was excluded, ceases to be a maxim, according to this philosophy. Not only the will of the supreme Being may create matter; but, for aught we know *a priori,* the will of any other being might create it, or any other cause, that the most whimsical imagination can assign.

12. From *Enquiry Concerning Human Understanding,* Section xi. Cf. introductory note, p. 92.

Your deliberations, which of right should be directed to questions of public good, and the interest of the commonwealth, are diverted to the disquisitions of speculative philosophy; and these magnificent, but perhaps fruitless inquiries, take place of your more familiar but more useful occupations. But so far as in me lies, I will prevent this abuse. We shall not here dispute concerning the origin and government of worlds. We shall only inquire how far such questions concern the public interest. And if I can persuade you, that they are entirely indifferent to the peace of society and security of government, I hope that you will presently send us back to our schools, there to examine, at leisure, the question the most sublime, but at the same time, the most speculative of all philosophy.

The religious philosophers, not satisfied with the tradition of your forefathers, and doctrine of your priests (in which I willingly acquiesce), indulge a rash curiosity, in trying how far they can establish religion upon the principles of reason; and they thereby excite, instead of satisfying, the doubts, which naturally arise from a diligent and scrutinous inquiry. They paint, in the most magnificent colors, the order, beauty, and wise arrangement of the universe; and then ask, if such a glorious display of intelligence could proceed from the fortuitous concourse of atoms, or if chance could produce what the greatest genius can never sufficiently admire. I shall not examine the justness of this argument. I shall allow it to be as solid as my antagonists and accusers can desire. It is sufficient, if I can prove, from this very reasoning, that the question is entirely speculative, and that, when, in my philosophical disquisitions, I deny a providence and a future state, I undermine not the foundations of society, but advance principles, which they themselves, upon their own topics, if they argue consistently, must allow to be solid and satisfactory.

You then, who are my accusers, have acknowledged, that the chief or sole argument for a divine existence (which I never questioned) is derived from the order of nature; where there appear such marks of intelligence and design, that you think it extravagant to assign for its cause, either chance, or the blind and unguided force of matter. You allow, that this is an argument drawn from effects to causes. From the order of the work, you infer, that there must have been project and forethought in the workman. If you cannot make out this point, you allow, that your conclusion fails; and you pretend not to establish the conclusion in a greater latitude than the phenomena of nature will justify. These are your concessions. I desire you to mark the consequences.

When we infer any particular cause from an effect, we must proportion the one to the other, and can never be allowed to ascribe to the cause any qualities, but what are exactly sufficient to produce the effect. A body of ten ounces raised in any scale may serve as a proof, that the counterbalancing weight exceeds ten ounces; but can never afford a reason that it exceeds a hundred. If the cause, assigned for any effect, be not sufficient to produce it, we must either reject that cause, or add to it such qualities as will give it a just proportion to the effect. But if we ascribe to it further qualities, or affirm it capable of producing other effects, we can only indulge the license of conjecture, and arbitrarily suppose the existence of qualities and energies, without reason or authority.

The same rule holds, whether the cause assigned be brute unconscious matter, or a rational intelligent being. If the cause be known only by the effect, we never ought to ascribe to it any qualities, beyond what are precisely requisite to produce the effect; nor can we, by any rules of just reasoning, return back from the cause, and infer other effects from it, beyond those by which alone it is known to us. No one, merely from the sight of one of Zeuxis's pictures, could know, that he was also a statuary or architect, and was an artist no less skillful in stone and marble than in colors. The talents and taste, displayed in the particular work before us; these we may safely conclude the workman to be possessed of. The cause must be proportioned to the effect; and if we exactly and precisely proportion it, we shall never find in it any qualities, that point farther, or afford an inference concerning any other design or performance. Such qualities must be somewhat beyond what is merely requisite for producing the effect, which we examine.

Allowing, therefore, the gods to be the authors of the existence or order of the universe; it follows, that they possess that precise degree of power, intelligence, and benevolence, which appears in their workmanship; but nothing farther can ever be proved, except we call in the assistance of exaggeration and flattery to supply the defects of argument and reasoning. So far as the traces of any attributes, at present, appear, so far may we conclude these attributes to exist. The supposition of farther attributes is mere hypothesis; much more the supposition, that, in distant regions of space or periods of time, there has been, or will be, a more magnificent display of these attributes, and a scheme of administration more suitable to such imaginary virtues. We can never be allowed to mount up from the universe, the effect, to Jupiter, the cause; and then descend downwards, to infer any new effect from that cause; as if the present effects alone were not entirely worthy of the glorious attributes, which we ascribe to that deity. The knowledge of the cause being derived solely from the effect, they must be exactly adjusted to each other; and the one can never refer to anything farther, or be the foundation of any new inference and conclusion.

You find certain phenomena in nature. You seek a cause or author. You imagine that you have found him. You afterwards become so enamored of this offspring of your brain, that you imagine it impossible, but he must produce something greater and more perfect than the present scene of things, which is so full of ill and disorder. You forget, that this superlative intelligence and benevolence are entirely imaginary, or, at least, without any foundation in reason; and that you have no ground to ascribe to him any qualities, but what you see he has actually exerted and displayed in his productions. Let your gods, therefore, O philosophers, be suited to the present appearances of nature: and presume not to alter these appearances by arbitrary suppositions, in order to suit them to the attributes, which you so fondly ascribe to your deities.

When priests and poets, supported by your authority, O Athenians, talk of a golden or silver age, which preceded the present state of vice and misery, I hear them with attention and with reverence. But when philosophers, who pretend to neglect authority, and to cultivate reason, hold the same discourse, I pay them not, I own, the same obsequious submission and pious deference. I ask, who carried them into the celestial regions, who admitted them into the councils of the gods, who opened to them the book of fate, that they thus rashly affirm, that their deities have executed, or will execute, any purpose beyond what has actually appeared? If they tell me, that they have mounted on the steps or by the gradual ascent of reason, and by drawing inferences from effects to causes, I still insist, that they have aided the ascent of reason by the wings of imagination; otherwise they could not thus change their manner of inference, and argue from causes to effects; presuming, that a more perfect production than the present world would be more suitable to such perfect beings as the gods, and forgetting that they have no reason to ascribe to these celestial beings any perfection or any attribute, but what can be found in the present world.

Hence all the fruitless industry to account for the ill appearances of nature, and save the honor of the gods; while we must acknowledge the reality of that evil and disorder, with which the world so much abounds. The obstinate and intractable qualities of matter, we are told, or the observance of general laws, or some such reason, is the sole cause, which controlled the power and benevolence of Jupiter, and obliged him to create mankind and every sensible creature so imperfect and so unhappy. These attributes then, are, it seems, beforehand, taken for granted, in their greatest latitude. And upon that supposition, I own that such conjectures may, perhaps, be admitted as plausible solutions of the ill phenomena. But still I ask, Why take these attributes for granted, or why ascribe to the cause any qualities but what actually appear in the effect? Why torture your brain to justify the course of nature upon suppositions, which, for aught you know, may be entirely imaginary, and of which there are to be found no traces in the course of nature?

The religious hypothesis, therefore, must be considered only as a particular method of accounting for the visible phenomena of the universe: but no just reasoner will ever presume to infer from it any single fact, and alter or add to the phenomena, in any single particular. If you think, that the appearances of things prove such causes, it is allowable for you to draw an inference concerning the existence of these causes. In such complicated and sublime subjects, everyone should be indulged in the liberty of conjecture and argument. But here you ought to rest. If you come backward, and arguing from your inferred causes, conclude, that any other fact has existed, or will exist, in the course of nature, which may serve as a fuller display of particular attributes; I must admonish you, that you have departed from the method of reasoning, attached to the present subject, and have certainly added something to the attributes of the cause, beyond what appears in the effect; otherwise you could never, with tolerable sense or propriety, add anything to the effect, in order to render it more worthy of the cause.

Where, then, is the odiousness of that doctrine, which I teach in my school, or rather, which I examine in my gardens? Or what do you find in this whole question, wherein the security of good morals, or the peace and order of society, is in the least concerned?

I deny a providence, you say, and supreme governor of the world, who guides the course of events, and punishes the vicious with infamy and disappointment, and rewards the virtuous with honor and success, in all their undertakings. But surely, I deny not the course itself of events, which lies open to everyone's inquiry and examination. I acknowledge, that, in the present order of things, virtue is attended with more peace of mind than vice, and meets with a more favorable reception from the world. I am sensible, that, according to the past experience of mankind, friendship is the chief joy of human life, and moderation the only source of tranquillity and happiness. I never balance between the virtuous and the vicious course of life; but am sensible, that, to a well-disposed mind, every advantage is on the side of the former. And what can you say more, allowing all your suppositions and reasonings? You tell me, indeed, that this disposition of things proceeds from intelligence and design. But whatever it proceeds from, the disposition itself, on which depends our happiness or misery, and consequently our conduct and deportment in life, is still the same. It is still open for me, as well as you, to regulate my behavior, by my experience of past events. And if you affirm, that, while a divine providence is allowed, and a supreme distributive justice in the universe, I ought to expect some more particular reward of the good, and punishment of the bad, beyond the ordinary course of events; I here find the same fallacy, which I have before endeavored to detect. You persist in imagining, that, if we grant that divine existence, for which you so earnestly contend, you may safely infer consequences from it, and add something to the experienced order of nature, by arguing from the attributes which you ascribe to your gods. You seem not to remember, that all your reasonings on this subject can only be drawn from effects to causes; and that every argument, deduced from causes to effects, must of necessity be a gross sophism; since it is impossible for you to know anything of the cause, but what you have antecedently, not inferred, but discovered to the full, in the effect.

But what must a philosopher think of those vain reasoners, who, instead of regarding the present scene of things as the sole object of their contemplation, so far reverse the whole course of nature, as to render this life merely a passage to something farther; a porch, which leads to a greater, and vastly different building; a prologue, which serves only to introduce the piece, and give it more grace and propriety? Whence, do you think, can such philosophers derive their idea of the gods? From their own conceit and imagination surely. For if they derived it from the present phenomena, it would never point to anything farther, but must be exactly adjusted to them. That the divinity may *possibly* be endowed with attributes, which we have never seen exerted; may be governed by principles of action, which we cannot discover to be satisfied: all this will freely be allowed. But still this is mere *possibility* and hypothesis. We never can have reason to *infer* any attributes, or any principles of action in him, but so far as we know them to have been exerted and satisfied.

Are there any marks of a distributive justice in the world? If you answer in the affirmative, I conclude, that, since justice here exerts itself, it is satisfied. If you reply in the negative, I conclude, that you have then no reason to ascribe justice, in our sense of it, to the gods. If you hold a medium between affirmation and negation, by saying, that the justice of the gods, at present, exerts itself in part, but not in its full extent; I answer, that you have no reason to give it any particular extent, but only so far as you see it, *at present,* exert itself.

Thus I bring the dispute, O Athenians, to a short issue with my antagonists. The course of nature lies open to my contemplation as well as to theirs. The experienced train of events is the great standard, by which we all regulate our conduct. Nothing else can be appealed to in the field, or in the senate. Nothing else ought ever to be heard of in the school, or in the closet. In vain would our limited understanding break through those boundaries, which are too narrow for our fond imagination. While we argue from the course of nature, and infer a particular intelligent cause, which first bestowed, and still preserves order in the universe, we embrace a principle, which is both uncertain and useless. It is uncertain; because the subject lies entirely beyond the reach of human experience. It is useless; because our knowledge of this cause being derived entirely from the course of nature, we can never, according to the rules of just reasoning, return back from the cause with any new inference, or making additions to the common and experienced course of nature, establish any new principles of conduct and behavior.

V

REID

THOMAS REID (1710-1796) was the founder of the Scotch Philosophy of Common Sense, sometimes called simply the Scottish School. Unlike all the philosophers represented in this volume except Wolff and Kant, Reid was a professor of philosophy (professor of moral philosophy in the University of Glasgow). It is interesting to note (though it is not at all surprising) that professors of philosophy have opportunities to establish "schools of philosophy" which carry their influence from generation to generation, while the influence of the "freelance philosophers" may be deeper and longer-lasting, but more various and intermittent. Reid and his successors, especially Sir William Hamilton, influenced generations of Scottish thinkers and Presbyterian divines and teachers in both Scotland and America.

There has recently been a marked revival of interest in Reid's philosophy, since his analysis of knowledge has much in common with analyses made by some contemporary British and American philosophers. Common Sense Philosophy reappeared in the twentieth century in theories of direct or naive realism (we directly perceive objects, not ideas or sensa or sense data), and in G. E. Moore's rejection of philosophies that would not permit him to make, in a straightforward and literal sense, statements he *knew* to be true even if he could not give a correct analysis of them or explain *how* he knew them.

Reid's argument is very simple. Berkeley and Hume, he held, drew necessary consequences from Locke's assumption that ideas are the proper object of knowledge. These conclusions conflict with common sense, and hence are to be rejected. Therefore their premise in the works of Locke must be rejected; objects, not ideas, must be immediately given to the mind. What, then, of Locke's argument? Reid says flatly: There is no argument. Locke says it and repeats it, but never proves or tries to prove it.

Kant sarcastically attacks Reid "for missing the point of the problem; for for while [he] was ever taking for granted that which Hume doubted, and demonstrating with zeal and often with impudence that which Hume never thought of doubting, [he] so misconstrued Hume's valuable suggestion that everything remained in its old condition, as if nothing had happened."[1] But one may now well question whether Reid or Kant had the better answer to Hume.

All our selections are taken from *Essays on the Intellectual Powers of Man* (1785). The divisions do not follow Reid's, nor do the titles always correspond to his chapter headings; but the sources of each passage are given in footnotes.

---

1. Kant, *Prolegomena to any Future Metaphysics,* Introduction. Ed. L. W. Beck (New York: Liberal Arts Press, 1950), 6.

Essays on the Intellectual Powers of Man

A. Of Principles Taken for Granted[1]

As there are words common to philosophers and to the vulgar, which need no explication, so there are principles common to both, which need no proof, and which do not admit of direct proof.

One who applies to any branch of science, must be come to years of understanding, and, consequently, must have exercised his reason, and the other powers of his mind, in various ways. He must have formed various opinions and principles, by which he conducts himself in the affairs of life. Of those principles, some are common to all men, being evident in themselves, and so necessary in the conduct of life that a man cannot live and act according to the rules of common prudence without them. . . . There are, therefore, common principles, which are the foundation of all reasoning and of all science. Such common principles seldom admit of direct proof, nor do they need it. Men need not be taught them; for they are such as all men of common understanding know; or such, at least, as they give a ready assent to, as soon as they are proposed and understood. Such principles, when we have occasion to use them in science, are called *axioms*. . . .

It may, however, be observed, that the first principles of natural philosophy are of a quite different nature from mathematical axioms; they have not the same kind of evidence, nor are they necessary truths, as mathematical axioms are. . . . Their evidence is not demonstrative, but intuitive. They require not proof, but to be placed in a proper point of view. . . .

[For example] I take it for granted, that, in most operations of the mind, there must be an object distinct from the operation itself. I cannot see, without seeing something. To see without having any

---

1. From Essay I, Chapter ii.

object of sight is absurd. I cannot remember, without remembering something. The thing remembered is past, while the remembrance of it is present; and, therefore, the operation and the object of it must be distinct things. The operations of our mind are denoted, in all languages, by active transitive verbs, which, from their construction in grammar, require not only a person or agent, but likewise an object of the operation. Thus the verb know, denotes an operation of mind. From the general structure of language, this verb requires a person —I know, you know, or he knows; but it requires no less a noun in the accusative case, denoting the thing known; for he that knows must know something; and, to know, without having any object of knowledge, is an absurdity too gross to admit of reasoning.

We ought likewise to take for granted, as first principles, things wherein we find an universal agreement, among the learned and unlearned, in the different nations and ages of the world. A consent of ages and nations, of the learned and vulgar, ought, at least, to have great authority, unless we can shew some prejudice as universal as that consent is, which might be the cause of it. Truth is one, but error is infinite. There are many truths so obvious to the human faculties, that it may be expected that men should universally agree in them. And this is actually found to be the case with regard to many truths, against which we find no dissent, unless perhaps that of a few sceptical philosophers, who may be justly suspected, in such cases, to differ from the rest of mankind, through pride, obstinacy, or some favourite passion. . . .

I need hardly say that I shall also take for granted such facts as are attested to the conviction of all sober and reasonable men, either by our senses, by memory, or by human testimony. Although some writers on this subject have disputed the authority of the senses, of memory, and of every human faculty, yet we find that such persons, in the conduct of life, in pursuing their ends, or in avoiding dangers, pay the same regard to the authority of their senses and other faculties, as the rest of mankind. By this they give us just grounds to doubt of their candour in their professions of scepticism.

This, indeed, has always been the fate of the few that have professed scepticism, that, when they have done what they can to discredit their senses, they find themselves, after all, under a necessity of trusting to them. Mr. Hume has been so candid as to acknowledge this; and it is no less true of those who have not shewn the same candour; for I never heard that any sceptic runs his head against a post, or stepped into a kennel, because he did not believe his eyes.

B. On the Theory of Ideas[2]

... It is very natural to ask, Whether it was Mr Locke's opinion, that ideas are the only objects of thought? or, Whether it is not possible for men to think of things, which are not ideas in the mind? To this question it is not easy to give a direct answer. On the one hand, he says often, in distinct and studied expressions, that the term *idea* stands for whatever is the object of the understanding when a man thinks, or whatever it is which the mind can be employed about in thinking: that the mind perceives nothing but its own ideas: that all knowledge consists in the perception of the agreement or disagreement of our ideas: that we can have no knowledge farther than we have ideas. These, and many other expressions of the like import, evidently imply that every object of thought must be an idea, and can be nothing else.

On the other hand, I am persuaded that Mr Locke would have acknowledged that I may think of Alexander the Great, or of the planet Jupiter, and of numberless other things which he would have owned are not ideas in the mind, but objects which exist independent of the mind that thinks them.

How shall we reconcile the two parts of this apparent contradiction? All I am able to say, upon Mr Locke's principles, to reconcile them, is this, That we cannot think of Alexander, or of the planet Jupiter, unless we have in our minds an idea—that is, an image or picture of these objects. The idea of Alexander is an image, or picture, or representation of that hero in my mind; and this idea is the immediate object of my thought when I think of Alexander. That this was Locke's opinion, and that it has been generally the opinion of philosophers, there can be no doubt.

But, instead of giving light to the question proposed, it seems to involve it in greater darkness. When I think of Alexander, I am told there is an image or idea of Alexander in my mind, which is the immediate object of this thought. The necessary consequence of this seems to be, that there are two objects of this thought—the idea, which is in the mind, and the person represented by that idea; the first, the immediate object of the thought, the last, the object of the same thought, but not an immediate object. This is a hard saying; for it makes every thought of things external to have a double object. Every man is conscious of his thoughts, and yet, upon attentive reflection, he perceives no such duplicity in the object he thinks about. Sometimes

---

2. From Essay II, Chapters ix, x, xiv, and xv.

men see objects double, but they always know when they do so: and I know of no philosopher who has expressly owned this duplicity in the object of thought, though it follows necessarily from maintaining that, in the same thought, there is one object that is immediate and in the mind itself, and another object which is not immediate, and which is not in the mind.

Besides this, it seems very hard, or rather impossible, to understand what is meant by an object of thought that is not an immediate object of thought. A body in motion may move another that was at rest, by the medium of a third body that is interposed. This is easily understood; but we are unable to conceive any medium interposed between a mind and the thought of that mind; and, to think of any object by a medium, seems to be words without meaning. There is a sense in which a thing may be said to be perceived by a medium. Thus any kind of sign may be said to be the medium by which I perceive or understand the thing signified. The sign by custom, or compact, or perhaps by nature, introduces the thought of the thing signified. But here the thing signified, when it is introduced to the thought, is an object of thought no less immediate than the sign was before. And there are here two objects of thought, one succeeding another, which we have shewn is not the case with respect to an idea, and the object it represents.

I apprehend, therefore, that, if philosophers will maintain that ideas in the mind are the only immediate objects of thought, they will be forced to grant that they are the sole objects of thought, and that it is impossible for men to think of anything else. Yet, surely, Mr Locke believed that we can think of many things that are not ideas in the mind; but he seems not to have perceived, that the maintaining that ideas in the mind are the only immediate objects of thought, must necessarily draw this consequence along with it. The consequence, however, was seen by Bishop Berkeley and Mr Hume, who rather chose to admit the consequence than to give up the principle from which it follows. . . .

. . . In the new [i.e., Locke's] philosophy, the pillars by which the existence of a material world was supported, were so feeble that it did not require the force of a Sampson to bring them down; and in this we have not so much reason to admire the strength of Berkeley's genius, as his boldness in publishing to the world an opinion which the unlearned would be apt to interpret as the sign of a crazy intellect. . . . The foundation on which such a fabric [i.e., Berkeley's philosophy] rests ought to be very solid and well established; yet Berkeley says nothing more for it than that it is evident. If he means that it is self-evident, this indeed might be a good reason for not offering any direct argument in proof of it. But I apprehend this cannot justly be said. Self-evident propositions are those which appear evident to every man of sound understanding who apprehends the meaning of them distinctly, and attends to them without prejudice. Can this be said of this proposition, That all the objects of our understanding are ideas in our own minds? I believe that, to any man uninstructed in philosophy, this proposition will appear very improbable, if not absurd. However scanty his knowledge may be, he considers the sun and moon, the earth and sea, as objects of it; and it will be difficult to persuade him that those objects of his knowledge are ideas in his own mind, and have no existence when he does not think of them. If I may presume to speak my own sentiments, I once believed this doctrine of ideas so firmly as to embrace the whole of Berkeley's system in consequence of it; till, finding other consequences to follow from it, which gave me more uneasiness than the want of a material world, it came to my mind, more than forty years ago, to put the question, What evidence have I for this doctrine, that all the objects of my knowledge are ideas in my own mind? From that time to the present I have been candidly and impartially, as I think, seeking for the evidence of this principle, but can find none, excepting the authority of philosophers. . . .

But, supposing this principle to be true, Berkeley's system is impregnable. No demonstration can be more evident than his reasoning from it. Whatever is perceived is an idea, and an idea can only exist in a mind. It has no existence when it is not perceived; nor can there be anything like an idea, but an idea.

Berkeley has employed much pains and ingenuity to shew that his system, if received and believed, would not be attended with those bad consequences in the conduct of life, which superficial thinkers may be apt to impute to it. His system does not take away or make any alteration upon our pleasures or our pains; our sensations, whether agreeable or disagreeable, are the same upon his system as upon any other. These are real things, and the only things that interest us. They are produced in us according to certain laws of nature, by which our conduct will be directed in attaining the one, and avoiding the other; and it is of no moment to us, whether they are produced immediately by the operation of some powerful intelligent being upon our minds; or by the mediation of some inanimate being which we call *matter*.

The evidence of an all-governing mind, so far from being weakened, seems to appear in an even more striking light upon his hypothesis, than upon the common one. The powers which inanimate matter is supposed to possess, have always been the stronghold of atheists, to which they had recourse in defence of their system. This fortress of atheism must be most effectually overturned, if there is no such thing as matter in the universe. In all this the Bishop reasons justly and acutely. But there is one uncomfortable consequence of his system, which he seems not to have attended to, and from which it will be found difficult, if at all possible, to guard it.

The consequence I mean is this—that, although it leaves us sufficient evidence of a supreme intelligent mind, it seems to take away all the evidence we have of other intelligent beings like ourselves. What I call a father, a brother, or a friend, is only a parcel of ideas in my own mind; and, being ideas in my mind, they cannot possibly have that relation to another mind which they have to mine, any more than the pain felt by me can be the individual pain felt by another. I can find no principle in Berkeley's system, which affords me even probable ground to conclude that there are other intelligent beings, like myself, in the relations of father, brother, friend, or fellow-citizen. I am left alone, as the only creature of God in the universe, in that forlorn state of *egoism* into which it said some disciples of Des Cartes were brought by his philosophy.

After so long a detail of the sentiments of philosophers, ancient and modern, concerning ideas, it may seem presumptuous to call in question their existence. But no philosophical opinion, however ancient, however generally received, ought to rest upon authority. There is no presumption in requiring evidence for it, or in regulating our belief by the evidence we can find.

To prevent mistakes, the reader must again be reminded, that if by ideas are meant only the acts or operations of our minds in perceiving, remembering, or imagining objects, I am far from calling in question the existence of those acts; we are conscious of them every day and every hour of life; and I believe no man of a sound mind ever doubted of the real existence of the operations of mind, of which he is conscious. Nor is it to be doubted that, by the faculties which God has given us, we can conceive things that are absent, as well as perceive those that are within the reach of our senses; and that such conceptions may be more or less distinct, and more or less lively and strong. We have reason to ascribe to the all-knowing and all-perfect Being distinct conceptions of all things existent and possible, and of all their relations; and if these conceptions are called his eternal ideas, there ought to be no dispute among philosophers about a word.

The ideas, of whose existence I require the proof, are not operations of any mind, but supposed objects of those operations. They are not perception, remembrance, or conception, but things that are said to be perceived, or remembered, or imagined.

Nor do I dispute the existence of what the vulgar call the objects of perception. These, by all who acknowledge their existence, are called real things, not ideas. But philosophers maintain that, besides these, there are immediate objects of perception in the mind itself: that, for instance, we do not see the sun immediately, but an idea; or, as Mr Hume calls it, an impression in our own minds. This idea is said to be the image, the resemblance, the representative of the sun, if there be a sun. It is from the existence of the idea that we must infer the existence of the sun. But the idea, being immediately perceived, there can be no doubt, as philosophers think, of its existence.

... The *first* reflection I would make on this philosophical opinion is, that it is directly contrary to the universal sense of men who have not been instructed in philosophy. When we see the sun or moon, we have no doubt that the very objects which we immediately see are very far distant from us, and from one another. We have not the least doubt that this is the sun and moon which God created some thousands of years ago, and which have continued to perform their revolutions in the heavens every since. But how are we astonished when the philosopher informs us that we are mistaken in all this; that the sun and moon which we see are not, as we imagine, many miles distant from us, and from each other, but that they are in our own mind; that they had no existence before we saw them, and will have none when we cease to perceive and think of them; because the objects we perceive are only ideas in our minds, which can have no existence a moment longer than we think of them! If a plain man, uninstructed in philosophy, has faith to receive these mysteries, how great must be his astonishment! He is brought into a new world, where everything he sees, tastes, or touches, is an idea—a fleeting kind of being which he can conjure into existence, or can annihilate in the twinkling of an eye.

After his mind is somewhat composed, it will be natural for him to ask his philosophical instructor, Pray, sir, are there then no substantial and permanent things called the sun and moon, which continue to exist whether we think of them or not?

Here the philosophers differ. Mr Locke, and those that were before him, will answer to this question, that it is very true there are substantial and permanent beings called the sun and moon; but they never appear to us in their own person, but by their representatives, the ideas in our own minds, and we know nothing of them but what we can gather from those ideas. Bishop Berkeley and Mr Hume would give a different answer to the question proposed. They would assure the querist that it is a vulgar error, a mere prejudice of the ignorant and unlearned, to think that there are any permanent and substantial beings called the sun and moon; that the heavenly bodies, our own bodies, and all bodies whatsoever, are nothing but ideas in our minds; and that there can be nothing like the ideas of one mind, but the ideas of another mind. There is nothing in nature but minds and ideas, says the Bishop;—nay, says Mr Hume, there is nothing in nature but ideas only; for what we call a mind is nothing but a train of ideas connected by certain relations between themselves. . . .

A *second* reflection upon this subject is—that the authors who have treated of ideas, have generally taken their existence for granted, as a thing that could not be called in question; and such arguments as they have mentioned incidentally, seem too weak to support the conclusion. . . .

A *third* reflection I would make upon this subject is, that philosophers, notwithstanding their unanimity as to the existence of ideas, hardly agree in any one thing else concerning them. If ideas be not a mere fiction, they must be, of all objects of human knowledge, the things we have best access to know, and to be acquainted with; yet there is nothing about which men differ so much. . . .

A *fourth* reflection is, that ideas do not make any of the operations of the mind to be better understood, although it was probably with that view that they have been first invented, and afterwards so generally received. . . .

The *last* reflection I shall make upon this theory, is—that the natural and necessary consequences of it furnish a just prejudice against it to every man who pays a due respect to the common sense of mankind. . . .

Every man feels that perception gives him an invincible belief of the existence of that which he perceives; and that this belief is not the effect of reasoning, but the immediate consequence of perception. When philosophers have wearied themselves and their readers with their speculations upon this subject, they can neither strengthen this belief, nor weaken it; nor can they shew how it is produced. It puts the philosopher and the peasant upon a level; and neither of them can give any other reason for believing his senses, than that he finds it impossible for him to do otherwise.

C. On Sensation and Primary and Secondary Qualities[3]

When I smell a rose, there is in this operation both sensation and perception. The agreeable odour I feel, considered by itself, without relation to any external object, is merely a sensation. If affects the mind in a certain way; and this affection of the mind may be conceived, without a thought of the rose, or any other object. This sensation can be nothing else than it is felt to be. Its very essence consists in being felt; and, when it is not felt, it is not. There is no difference between the sensation and the feeling of it—they are one and the same thing. It is for this reason that we before observed that, in sensation, there is no object distinct from that act of the mind by which it is felt,—and this holds true with regard to all sensations.

Let us next attend to the perception which we have in smelling a rose. Perception has always an external object; and the object of my perception, in this case, is that quality in the rose which I discern by the sense of smell. Observing that the agreeable sensation is raised when the rose is near, and ceases when it is removed, I am led, by my nature, to conclude some quality to be in the rose, which is the cause of this sensation. This quality in the rose is the object perceived; and that act of my mind by which I have the conviction and belief of this quality, is what in this case I call perception.

But it is here to be observed, that the sensation I feel, and the quality in the rose which I perceive, are both called by the same name. The smell of a rose is the name given to both: so that this name hath two meanings; and the distinguishing its different meanings removes all perplexity, and enables us to give clear and distinct answers to questions about which philosophers have held much dispute.

Thus, if it is asked, whether the smell be in the rose, or in the mind that feels it, the answer is obvious: That there are two different things signified by the smell of a rose; one of which is in the mind, and can be in nothing but a sentient being; the other is truly and properly in the rose. . . . [The sensation] in my mind is occasioned by a certain quality in the rose, which is called by the same name with the sensation, not on account of any similitude, but because of their constant concomitancy. . . .

. . . There appears to me to be a real foundation for the distinction [between primary and secondary qualities]; and it is this—that our

_____
3. From Essay II, Chapters xvi and xvii.

senses give us a direct and distinct notion of the primary qualities, and inform us what they are in themselves. But of the secondary qualities, our senses give us only a relative and obscure notion. They inform us only, that they are qualities that affect us in a certain manner—that is, produce in us a certain sensation; but as to what they are in themselves, our senses leave us in the dark. . . . If you ask me, what is that quality or modification in a rose which I call its smell, I am at a loss to answer directly. Upon reflection, I find, that I have a distinct notion of the sensation which it produces in my mind. But there can be nothing like to this sensation in the rose, because it is insentient. The quality in the rose is something which occasions the sensation in me, but what that something is, I know not. . . . [I] proceed to make some reflections on this subject.

1. The primary qualities are neither sensations, nor are they resemblances to sensations. . . . Sensation is the act or the feeling (I dispute not which) of a sentient being. Figure, divisibility, solidity, are neither acts nor feelings. Sensation supposes a sentient being as its subject; for a sensation that is not felt by some sentient being is an absurdity. Figure and divisibility supposes a subject that is figured and divisible, but not a subject that is sentient.

2. We have no reason to think that any of the secondary qualities resemble any sensation. This absurdity of this notion has been clearly shewn by Des Cartes, Locke, and many modern philosophers. . . .

3. The distinctness of our notions of primary qualities prevents all questions and disputes about their nature. . . . Their nature is manifest to our senses, and cannot be unknown to any man, or be mistaken by him, though their causes may admit of dispute.

The primary qualities are the object of the mathematical sciences; and the distinctness of our notions of them enables us to reason demonstratively about them to a great extent. Their various modifications are precisely defined in the imagination, and thereby capable of being compared, and their relations determined with precision and certainty.

It is not so with secondary qualities. Their nature not being manifest to the sense, may be a subject of dispute. Our feeling informs us that fire is hot; but it does not inform us what that heat of fire is. But does it not appear a contradiction, to say we know that the fire is hot, but we know not what that heat is? I answer, there is the same appearance of contradiction in many things that must be granted. We know that wine has an inebriating quality; but we know not what that quality is. It is true, indeed, that, if we had not some notion of what is meant by the heat of fire, and by an inebriating quality, we

could affirm nothing of either with understanding. We have a notion
of both; but it is only a relative notion.[4] We know that they are the
causes of certain known effects.

4. The nature of secondary qualities is a proper subject of philosophical disquisition; and in this philosophy has made some progress.
It has been discovered, that the sensation of smell is occasioned by the
effluvia of bodies; that of sound by their vibration. The disposition
of bodies to reflect a particular kind of light, occasions the sensations
of color. Very curious discoveries have been made of the nature of
heat, and an ample field of discovery in these subjects remains.

5. We may see why the sensations belonging to the secondary qualities are an object of our attention, while those which belong to the
primary are not. The first are not only signs of the object perceived,
but they bear a capital part in the notion we form of it. We conceive
it only as that which occasions such a sensation, and therefore cannot
reflect upon it without thinking of the sensation it occasions: we have
no other mark whereby to distinguish it. The thought of a secondary
quality, therefore, always carries us back to the sensation which it
produces. We give the same name to both, and are apt to confound
them together. But, having a clear and distinct conception of primary
qualities, we have no need, when we think of them, to recall their
sensations. When a primary quality is perceived, the sensation immediately leads our thought to the quality signified by it, and is itself
forgot. We have no occasion afterwards to reflect upon it; and so we
come to be as little acquainted with it as if we had never felt it.
This is the case with the sensations of all primary qualities, when
they are not so painful or pleasant as to draw our attention. . . .

D. Of Perception[5]

. . . The operations of our minds are known, not by sense, but by
consciousness, the authority of which is as certain and irresistible
as that of sense.

In order, however, to our having a distinct notion of any of the
operations of our own minds, it is not enough that we be conscious
of them; for all men have this consciousness. It is farther necessary

4. Reid has previously defined relative notion as "strictly speaking, no notion
of the thing at all, but only of some relation which it bears to something else." Thus
an "unknown cause" is a "relative notion." L.W.B.
5. From Essay II, Chapter v.

that we attend to them while they are exerted, and reflect upon them with care, while they are recent and fresh in our memory. . . . For the proof of facts which I shall have occasion to mention upon this subject, I can only appeal to the reader's own thoughts, whether such facts are not agreeable to what he is conscious of in his own mind.

If, therefore, we attend to that act of our mind which we call the perception of an external object of sense, we shall find in it these three things:—*First*, Some conception or notion of the object perceived; *Secondly*, A strong and irresistible conviction and belief of its present existence; and, *Thirdly*, That this conviction and belief are immediate, and not the effect of reasoning.

First, It is impossible to perceive an object without having some notion or conception of that which we perceive. We may, indeed, conceive an object which we do not perceive; but, when we perceive the object, we must have some conception of it at the same time; and we have commonly a more clear and steady notion of the object while we perceive it, than we have from memory or imagination when it is not perceived. Yet, even in perception, the notion which our senses give of the object may be more or less clear, more or less distinct, in all possible degrees. . . . In a matter so obvious to every person capable of reflection, it is necessary only farther to observe, that the notion which we get of an object, merely by our external sense, ought not to be confounded with that more scientific notion which a man, come to the years of understanding, may have of the same object, by attending to its various attributes, or to its various parts, and to their relations to each other, and to the whole. . . .

Secondly, In perception we not only have a notion more or less distinct of the object perceived, but also an irresistible conviction and belief of its existence. This is always the case when we are certain that we perceive it. There may be a perception so faint and indistinct as to leave us in doubt whether we perceive the object or not; . . . but when the perception is in any degree clear and steady, there remains no doubt of its reality; and when the reality of the perception is ascertained, the existence of the object perceived can no longer be doubted.

. . . I observed, *thirdly*, That this conviction is not only irresistible, but it is immediate; that is, it is not by a train of reasoning and argumentation that we come to be convinced of the existence of what we perceive; we ask no argument for the existence of the object, but that we perceive it; perception commands our belief upon its own authority, and disdains to rest its authority upon any reasoning whatsoever.

The conviction of a truth may be irresistible, and yet not immediate. Thus, my conviction that the three angles of every plain triangle are equal to two right angles, is irresistible, but it is not immediate; I am convinced of it by demonstrative reasoning. There are other truths in mathematics of which we have not only an irresistible but an immediate conviction. Such are the axioms. Our belief of the axioms in mathematics is not grounded upon argument—arguments are grounded upon them; but their evidence is discerned immediately by the human understanding.

It is, no doubt, one thing to have an immediate conviction of a self-evident axiom; it is another thing to have an immediate conviction of the existence of what we see; but the conviction is equally immediate and equally irresistable in both cases. No man thinks of seeking a reason to believe what he sees; and, before we are capable of reasoning, we put no less confidence in our senses than after. The rudest savage is as fully convinced of what he sees, and hears, and feels, as the most expert logician. The constitution of our understanding determines us to hold the truth of a mathematical axiom as a first principle, from which other truths may be deduced, but it is deduced from none; and the constitution of our power of perception determines us to hold the existence of what we distinctly perceive as a first principle, from which other truths may be deduced; but it is deduced from none. . . .

The account I have given of our perception of external objects, is intended as a faithful delineation of what every man, come to years of understanding, and capable of giving attention to what passes in his own mind, may feel in himself. In what manner the notion of external objects, and the immediate belief of their existence, is produced by means of our senses, I am not able to shew, and I do not pretend to shew. If the power of perceiving external objects in certain circumstances, be a part of the original constitution of the human mind, all attempts to account for it will be vain. No other account can be given of the constitution of things, but the will of Him that made them. . . . The Supreme Being intended that we should have such knowledge of the material objects that surround us, as is necessary in order to our supplying the wants of nature, and avoiding the dangers to which we are constantly exposed; and he has admirably fitted our powers of perception to this purpose. If the intelligence we have of external objects were to be got by reasoning only, the greatest part of men would be destitute of it; for the greatest part of men hardly ever learn to reason; and in infancy and childhood no man can reason: Therefore, as this intelligence of the objects that surround us, and from which we receive so much benefit or harm, is equally necessary to children and to men, to the ignorant and to the learned, God in his wisdom conveys it to us in a way that puts all upon a level. The information of the senses is as perfect, and gives as full conviction to the most ignorant as to the most learned.

E. Of the Evidence of Sense, and of Belief in General[6]

Belief must have an object. For he that believes must believe something; and that which he believes, is called the object of his belief. Of this object of his belief, he must have some conception, clear or obscure; for although there may be the most clear and distinct conception of an object without any belief of its existence, there can be no belief without conception.

Belief is always expressed in language by a proposition, wherein something is affirmed or denied. This is the form of speech which in all languages is appropriated to that purpose, and without belief there could be neither affirmation nor denial, nor should we have any form of words to express either. Belief admits of all degrees, from the slightest suspicion to the fullest assurance. . . .

I proceed to observe that there are many operations of the mind in which, when we analyze them as far as we are able, we find belief to be an essential ingredient. A man cannot be conscious of his own thoughts, without believing that he thinks. He cannot perceive an object of sense, without believing that it exists. He cannot distinctly remember a past event, without believing that it did exist. Belief therefore is an ingredient in consciousness, in perception, and in remembrance.

Not only in most of our intellectual operations, but in many of the active principles of the human mind, belief enters as an ingredient. Joy and sorrow, hope and fear, imply a belief of good or ill, either present or in expectation. Esteem, gratitude, pity, and resentment, imply a belief of certain qualities in their objects. In every action that is done for an end, there must be a belief of its tendency to that end. So large a share has belief in our intellectual operations, in our active principles, and in our actions themselves, that, as faith in things divine is represented as the main spring in the life of a Christian, so belief in general is the main spring in the life of a man. . . .

We give the name of evidence to whatever is a ground of belief.

---

6. From Essay II, Chapter xx.

To believe without evidence is a weakness which every man is concerned to avoid, and which every man wishes to avoid. Nor is it in a man's power to believe anything longer than he thinks he has evidence. What this evidence is, is more easily felt than described. Those who never reflected upon its nature, feel its influence in governing their belief. It is the business of the logician to explain its nature, and to distinguish its various kinds and degrees; but every man of understanding can judge of it, and commonly judges right, when the evidence is fairly laid before him, and his mind is free from prejudice. A man who knows nothing of the theory of vision may have a good eye; and a man who never speculated about evidence in the abstract may have a good judgment.

The common occasions of life lead us to distinguish evidence into different kinds, to which we give names that are well understood; such as the evidence of sense, the evidence of memory, the evidence of consciousness, the evidence of testimony, the evidence of axioms, the evidence of reasoning. All men of common understanding agree that each of these kinds of evidence may afford just ground of belief, and they agree very generally in the circumstances that strengthen or weaken them.

Philosophers have endeavoured, by analysing the different sorts of evidence, to find out some common nature wherein they all agree, and thereby reduce them all to one. This was the aim of the schoolmen in their intricate disputes about the criterion of truth. Des Cartes placed this criterion of truth in clear and distinct perception, and laid it down as a maxim, that whatever we clearly and distinctly perceive to be true, is true; but it is difficult to know what he understands by clear and distinct perception in this maxim. Mr Locke placed it in a perception of the agreement or disagreement of our ideas, which perception is immediate in intuitive knowledge, and by the intervention of other ideas in reasoning.

I confess that, although I have, as I think, a distinct notion of the different kinds of evidence above-mentioned, and, perhaps, of some others, which it is unnecessary here to enumerate, yet I am not able to find any common nature to which they may all be reduced. They seem to me to agree only in this, that they are all fitted by Nature to produce belief in the human mind, some of them in the highest degree, which we call certainty, others in various degrees according to circumstances.

I shall take it for granted that the evidence of sense, when proper circumstances concur, is good evidence, and a just ground of belief. My intention in this place is only to compare it with the other kinds that have been mentioned, that we may judge whether it be reducible to any of them, or of a nature peculiar to itself.

First, it seems to be quite different from the evidence of reasoning. All good evidence is commonly called reasonable evidence, and very justly, because it ought to govern our belief as reasonable creatures. And, according to this meaning, I think the evidence of sense no less reasonable than that of demonstration. If Nature give us information of things that concern us, by other means than by reasoning, reason itself will direct us to receive that information with thankfulness, and to make the best use of it. But when we speak of the evidence of reasoning as a particular kind of evidence, it means the evidence of propositions that are inferred by reasoning, from propositions already known and believed. Thus, the evidence of the fifth proposition of the first book of Euclid's Elements consists in this, That it is shewn to be the necessary consequence of the axioms, and of the preceding propositions. In all reasoning, there must be one or more premises, and a conclusion drawn from them. And the premises are called the reason why we must believe the conclusion which we see to follow from them.

That the evidence of sense is of a different kind, needs little proof. No man seeks a reason for believing what he sees or feels; and, if he did, it would be difficult to find one. But, though he can give no reason for believing his senses, his belief remains as firm as if it were grounded on demonstration.

Many eminent philosophers, thinking it unreasonable to believe when they could not shew a reason, have laboured to furnish us with reasons for believing our senses; but their reasons are very insufficient, and will not bear examination. Other philosophers have shewn very clearly the fallacy of these reasons, and have, as they imagine, discovered invincible reasons against this belief; but they have never been able either it shake it in themselves, or to convince others. The statesman continues to plod, the soldier to fight, and the merchant to export and import, without being in the least moved by the demonstrations that have been offered of the non-existence of those things about which they are so seriously employed. And a man may as soon, by reasoning, pull the moon out of her orbit, as destroy the belief of the objects of the senses.

Shall we say, then, that the evidence of sense is the same with that of axioms, or self-evident truths? I answer, *First*, That, all modern philosophers seem to agree that the existence of the objects of sense is not self-evident, because some of them have endeavoured to prove it by subtle reasoning, others to refute it. Neither of these can consider it as self-evident. *Secondly*, I would observe that the word *axiom* is taken by philosophers in such a sense that the existence of the objects of sense cannot, with propriety, be called an axiom. They give the name of axiom only to self-evident truths, that are necessary, and are not limited to time and place, but must be true at all times and in all places. The truths attested by our senses are not of this kind; they are contingent, and limited to time and place. Thus, that one is the half of two, is an axiom. It is equally true at all times and in all places. We perceive, by attending to the proposition itself, that it cannot but be true; and, therefore, it is called an eternal, necessary, and immutable truth. That there is at present a chair on my right hand, and another on my left, is a truth attested by my senses; but it is not necessary, nor eternal, nor immutable. It may not be true next minute; and, therefore, to call it an axiom would, I apprehend, be to deviate from the common use of the word. *Thirdly,* If the word axiom be put to signify every truth which is known immediately, without being deduced from any antecedent truth, then the existence of the objects of sense may be called an axiom; for my senses give me as immediate conviction of what they testify, as my understanding gives of what is commonly called an axiom.

There is, no doubt, an analogy between the evidence of sense and the evidence of testimony. Hence, we find, in all languages, the analogical expressions of the *testimony of sense,* of giving *credit* to our senses, and the like. But there is a real difference between the two, as well as a similitude. In believing upon testimony, we rely upon the authority of a person who testifies; but we have no such authority for believing our senses.

Shall we say, then, that this belief is the inspiration of the Almighty? I think this may be said in good sense; for I take it to be the immediate effect of our constitution, which is the work of the Almighty. But, if inspiration be understood to imply a persuasion of its coming from God, our belief in the objects of sense is not inspiration; for a man would believe his senses though he had no notion of a Deity. He who is persuaded that he is the workmanship of God, and that it is a part of his constitution to believe his senses, may think that a good reason to confirm his belief. But he had the belief before he could give this or any other reason for it. . . .

It is no wonder that the pride of philosophy should lead some to invent vain theories in order to account for this knowledge [of the existence of objects of sense]; and others, who see this to be impracticable, to spurn at a knowledge they cannot account for, and vainly attempt to throw it off as a reproach to their understanding. But the wise and humble will receive it as the gift of Heaven, and endeavour to make the best use of it.

VI

ROUSSEAU

JEAN-JACQUES ROUSSEAU (1712-1788), "citizen of Geneva," was the worst enemy of many of the ideas of the *philosophes* (and surely his own worst enemy; Hume said of him that he was born without a skin). He stood with the *philosophes* against the tyranny of ignorance, church, and state, but he opposed both their ends and the means they wanted to use to achieve them. For to him the source of all the trouble was not that there was too little education and *éclaircissement,* but that there was too much, and of the wrong kind. Man was born free, yet everywhere he is in chains. These chains are not the products of a crafty priesthood (as most *philosophes* believed) but they are of a man's own forging. We cannot, then, throw them off by more "progress" in the same direction, but must "go back," in some sense (in just what sense has been debated for two centuries) to Nature. Amongst classic restraint and the artifices of a sophisticated society, Rousseau's pathologically disordered life and emotional thought and style fascinated his contemporaries and influenced the development of sentimentalism in England, *Sturm und Drang* in Germany, and romanticism everywhere. His influence on Kant's ethical and political thought was profound; and among all the *philosophes,* it was he who was thought of as *the* philosopher of the Revolution. His personal relations with Diderot, Voltaire, Walpole, d'Holbach, Hume, and Boswell were so intricate that they are still the subject of learned debate.

The work that made him famous, *Discourse on the Arts and Sciences,* was written in 1749 and gained the prize offered by the Dijon Academy for the best essay on the question: "Did the re-establishment of science and arts contribute to morals?" On his way to the Vincennes prison to visit Diderot (who was imprisoned there for his *Letters on the Blind*) Rousseau went through a wildly emotional experience when he saw that the answer was an emphatic No! (At least this is the way he describes the origin of this discourse in his

Confessions, Book viii; others are more inclined to credit Diderot with the central idea of the discourse.) Much of the rest of Rousseau's troubled life was devoted to developing an alternative to what he had so roundly condemned: he proposed a new theory of government in the *Social Contract* (1762), and a new theory of education in *Julie* and *Émile* (1760, 1762). His deism is eloquently expressed in the "Confession of Faith of a Savoyard Vicar" in Book IV of *Émile*.

The selections following are from the book *The Social Contract and Other Discourses* by Jean Jacques Rousseau. Translated by G. D. H. Cole. Everyman's Library. Reprinted by permission of E. P. Dutton & Co., Inc., and J. M. Dent & Sons, Ltd., London.

Discourse on the Arts and Sciences

THE SECOND PART

An ancient tradition passed out of Egypt into Greece, that some god, who was an enemy to the repose of mankind, was the inventor of the sciences. What must the Egyptians, among whom the sciences first arose, have thought of them? And they beheld, near at hand, the sources from which they sprang. In fact, whether we turn to the annals of the world, or eke out with philosophical investigations the uncertain chronicles of history, we shall not find for human knowledge an origin answering to the idea we are pleased to entertain of it at present. Astronomy was born of superstition, eloquence of ambition, hatred, falsehood, and flattery; geometry of avarice; physics of an idle curiosity; and even moral philosophy of human pride. Thus the arts and sciences owe their birth to our vices; we should be less doubtful of their advantages, if they had sprung from our virtues.

Their evil origin is, indeed, but too plainly reproduced in their objects. What would become of the arts, were they not cherished by luxury? If men were not unjust, of what use were jurisprudence? What would become of history, if there were no tyrants, wars, or conspiracies? In a word who would pass his life in barren speculations, if everybody, attentive only to the obligations of humanity and the necessities of nature, spent his whole life in serving his country, obliging his friends, and relieving the unhappy? Are we then made to live and die on the brink of that well at the bottom of which Truth lies hid? This reflection alone is, in my opinion, enough to discourage at first setting out every man who seriously endeavours to instruct himself by the study of philosophy.

What a variety of dangers surrounds us! What a number of wrong paths present themselves in the investigation of the sciences! Through how many errors, more perilous than truth itself is useful, must we not pass to arrive at it? The disadvantages we lie under are evident;

153

for falsehood is capable of an infinite variety of combinations; but the truth has only one manner of being. Besides, where is the man who sincerely desires to find it? Or even admitting his good will, by what characteristic marks is he sure of knowing it? Amid the infinite diversity of opinions where is the criterion[1] by which we may certainly judge of it? Again, what is still more difficult, should we even be fortunate enough to discover it, who among us will know how to make right use of it?

If our sciences are futile in the objects they propose, they are no less dangerous in the effects they produce. Being the effect of idleness, they generate idleness in their turn; and an irreparable loss of time is the first prejudice which they must necessarily cause to society. To live without doing some good is a great evil as well in the political as in the moral world; and hence every useless citizen should be regarded as a pernicious person. Tell me then, illustrious philosophers, of whom we learn the ratios in which attraction acts *in vacuo;* and in the revolution of the planets, the relations of spaces traversed in equal times; by whom we are taught what curves have conjugate points, points of inflexion, and cusps; how the soul and body correspond, like two clocks, without actual communication; what planets may be inhabited; and what insects reproduce in an extraordinary manner. Answer me, I say, you from whom we receive all this sublime information, whether we should have been less numerous, worse governed, less formidable, less flourishing, or more perverse, supposing you had taught us none of all these fine things.

Reconsider therefore the importance of your productions; and, since the labours of the most enlightened of our learned men and the best of our citizens are of so little utility, tell us what we ought to think of that numerous herd of obscure writers and useless *littérateurs,* who devour without any return the substance of the State.

Useless, do I say? Would God they were! Society would be more peaceful, and morals less corrupt. But these vain and futile declaimers go forth on all sides, armed with their fatal paradoxes, to sap the foundations of our faith, and nullify virtue. They smile contemptuously at such old names as patriotism and religion, and consecrate their talents and philosophy to the destruction and defamation of all that men hold sacred. Not that they bear any real hatred to virtue or

---

1. The less we know, the more we think we know. The Peripatetics doubted of nothing. Did not Descartes construct the universe with cubes and vortices? And is there in all Europe one single physicist who does not boldly explain the inexplicable mysteries of electricity, which will, perhaps, be for ever the despair of real philosophers?

dogma; they are the enemies of public opinion alone; to bring them
to the foot of the altar, it would be enough to banish them to a land
of atheists. What extravagancies will not the rage of singularity induce
men to commit!

The waste of time is certainly a great evil; but still greater evils
attend upon literature and the arts. One is luxury, produced like them
by indolence and vanity. Luxury is seldom unattended by the arts and
sciences; and they are always attended by luxury. I know that our
philosophy, fertile in paradoxes, pretends, in contradiction to the
experience of all ages, that luxury contributes to the splendour of
States. But, without insisting on the necessity of sumptuary laws, can
it be denied that rectitude of morals is essential to the duration of
empires, and that luxury is diametrically opposed to such rectitude?
Let it be admitted that luxury is a certain indication of wealth; that
it even serves, if you will, to increase such wealth; what conclusion
is to be drawn from this paradox, so worthy of the times? And what
will become of virtue if riches are to be acquired at any cost? The
politicians of the ancient world were always talking of morals and
virtue; ours speak of nothing but commerce and money. One of them
will tell you that in such a country a man is worth just as much as he
will sell for at Algiers: another, pursuing the same mode of calculation,
finds that in some countries a man is worth nothing, and in others
still less than nothing; they value men as they do droves of oxen.
According to them, a man is worth no more to the State than the
amount he consumes; and thus a Sybarite would be worth at least
thirty Lacedaemonians. Let these writers tell me, however, which of
the two republics, Sybaris or Sparta, was subdued by a handful of
peasants, and which became the terror of Asia.

The monarchy of Cyrus was conquered by thirty thousand men,
led by a prince poorer than the meanest of Persian Satraps: in like
manner the Scythians, the poorest of all nations, were able to resist the
most powerful monarchs of the universe. When two famous republics
contended for the empire of the world, the one rich and the other poor,
the former was subdued by the latter. The Roman empire in its turn,
after having engulfed all the riches of the universe, fell a prey to
peoples who knew not even what riches were. The Franks conquered
the Gauls, and the Saxons England, without any other treasures than
their bravery and their poverty. A band of poor mountaineers, whose
whole cupidity was confined to the possession of a few sheep-skins,
having first given a check to the arrogance of Austria, went on to
crush the opulent and formidable house of Burgundy, which at that
time made the potentates of Europe tremble. In short, all the power

and wisdom of the heir of Charles the Fifth, backed by all the treasures of the Indies, broke before a few herring-fishers. Let our politician
condescend to lay aside their calculations for a moment, to reflect o
these examples; let them learn for once that money, though it buy
everything else, cannot buy morals and citizens. What then is th
precise point in dispute about luxury? It is to know which is mos
advantageous to empires, that their existence should be brilliant an
momentary, or virtuous and lasting. I say brilliant, but with wha
lustre? A taste for ostentation never prevails in the same minds as
taste for honesty. No, it is impossible that understandings, degrade
by a multitude of futile cares, should ever rise to what is truly grea
and noble; even if they had the strength, they would want the courage

Every artist loves applause. The praise of his contemporaries is th
most valuable part of his recompense. What then will he do to obtai
it, if he have the misfortune to be born among a people, and at
time, when learning is in vogue, and the superficiality of youth i
in a position to lead the fashion; when men have sacrificed their tast
to those who tyrannize over their liberty, and one sex dare not approv
anything but what is proportionate to the pusillanimity of the other[2]
when the greatest masterpieces of dramatic poetry are condemnec
and the noblest of musical productions neglected? This is what h
will do. He will lower his genius to the level of the age, and will rathe
submit to compose mediocre works, that will be admired during hi
lifetime, than labour at sublime achievements which will not b
admired till long after he is dead. Let the famous Voltaire tell us hov
many nervous and masculine beauties he has sacrificed to our fals
delicacy, and how much that is great and noble, that spirit of gallantry
which delights in what is frivolous and petty, has cost him.

It is thus that the dissolution of morals, the necessary consequenc
of luxury, brings with it in its turn the corruption of taste. Furthei
if by chance there be found among men of average ability, an individua
with enough strength of mind to refuse to comply with the spirit o

---

2. I am far from thinking that the ascendancy which women have obtained ove
men is an evil in itself. It is a present which nature has made them for the goo
of mankind. If better directed, it might be productive of as much good, as it is nov
of evil. We are not sufficiently sensible of what advantage it would be to society
to give a better education to that half of our species which governs the other. Mei
will always be what women choose to make them. If you wish then that they shoul
be noble and virtuous, let women be taught what greatness of soul and virtue are
The reflections which this subject arouses, and which Plato formerly made, deserv
to be more fully developed by a pen worthy of following so great a master, an
defending so great a cause.

the age, and to debase himself by puerile productions, his lot will be hard. He will die in indigence and oblivion. This is not so much a prediction as a fact already confirmed by experience! Yes, Charles and Pierre Vanloo, the time is already come when your pencils, destined to increase the majesty of our temples by sublime and holy images, must fall from your hands, or else be prostituted to adorn the panels of a coach with lascivious paintings. And you, inimitable Pigalle, rival of Phidias and Praxiteles, whose chisel the ancients would have employed to carve them gods, whose images almost excuse their idolatry in our eyes; even your hand must condescend to fashion the belly of an ape, or else remain idle.

We cannot reflect on the morality of mankind without contemplating with pleasure the picture of the simplicity which prevailed in the earliest times. This image may be justly compared to a beautiful coast, adorned only by the hands of nature; towards which our eyes are constantly turned, and which we see receding with regret. While men were innocent and virtuous and loved to have the gods for witnesses of their actions, they dwelt together in the same huts; but when they became vicious, they grew tired of such inconvenient onlookers, and banished them to magnificent temples. Finally, they expelled their deities even from these, in order to dwell there themselves; or at least the temples of the gods were no longer more magnificent than the palaces of the citizens. This was the height of degeneracy; nor could vice ever be carried to greater lengths than when it was seen, supported, as it were, at the doors of the great, on columns of marble, and graven on Corinthian capitals.

As the conveniences of life increase, as the arts are brought to perfection, and luxury spreads, true courage flags, the virtues disappear; and all this is the effect of the sciences and of those acts which are exercised in the privacy of men's dwellings. When the Goths ravaged Greece, the libraries only escaped the flames owing to an opinion that was set on foot among them, that it was best to leave the enemy with a possession so calculated to divert their attention from military exercises, and keep them engaged in indolent and sedentary occupations.

Charles the Eighth found himself master of Tuscany and the kingdom of Naples, almost without drawing sword; and all his court attributed this unexpected success to the fact that the princes and nobles of Italy applied themselves with greater earnestness to the cultivation of their understandings than to active and martial pursuits. In fact, says the sensible person who records these characteristics, experience plainly tells us that in military matters and all that resemble them application to the sciences tends rather to make men effeminate and cowardly than resolute and vigorous.

The Romans confessed that military virtue was extinguished among them, in proportion as they became connoisseurs in the arts of the painter, the engraver, and the goldsmith, and began to cultivate the fine arts. Indeed, as if this famous country was to be for ever an example to other nations, the rise of the Medici and the revival of letters has once more destroyed, this time perhaps for ever, the martial reputation which Italy seemed a few centuries ago to have recovered.

The ancient republics of Greece, with that wisdom which was so conspicuous in most of their institutions, forbade their citizens to pursue all those inactive and sedentary occupations, which by enervating and corrupting the body diminish also the vigour of the mind. With what courage, in fact, can it be thought that hunger and thirst, fatigues, dangers, and death, can be faced by men whom the smallest want overwhelms and the slightest difficulty repels? With what resolution can soldiers support the excessive toils of war, when they are entirely unaccustomed to them? With what spirits can they make forced marches under officers who have not even the strength to travel on horseback? It is no answer to cite the reputed valour of all the modern warriors who are so scientifically trained. I hear much of their bravery in a day's battle; but I am told nothing of how they support excessive fatigue, how they stand the severity of the seasons and the inclemency of the weather. A little sunshine or snow, or the want of a few superfluities, is enough to cripple and destroy one of our finest armies in a few days. Intrepid warriors! permit me for once to tell you the truth, which you seldom hear. Of your bravery I am fully satisfied. I have no doubt that you would have triumphed with Hannibal at Cannae, and at Trasimene: that you would have passed the Rubicon with Caesar, and enabled him to enslave his country; but you never would have been able to cross the Alps with the former, or with the latter to subdue your own ancestors, the Gauls.

A war does not always depend on the events of battle: there is in generalship an art superior to that of gaining victories. A man may behave with great intrepidity under fire, and yet be a very bad officer. Even in the common soldier, a little more strength and vigour would perhaps be more useful than so much courage, which after all is no protection from death. And what does it matter to the State whether its troops perish by cold and fever, or by the sword of the enemy?

If the cultivation of the sciences is prejudicial to military qualities, it is still more so to moral qualities. Even from our infancy an absurd system of education serves to adorn our wit and corrupt our judgment.

We see, on every side, huge institutions, where our youth are educated at great expense, and instructed in everything but their duty. Your children will be ignorant of their own language, when they can talk others which are not spoken anywhere. They will be able to compose verses which they can hardly understand; and, without being capable of distinguishing truth from error, they will possess the art of making them unrecognizable by specious arguments. But magnanimity, equity, temperance, humanity, and courage will be words of which they know not the meaning. The dear name of country will never strike on their ears; and if they ever hear speak of God, it will be less to fear than to be frightened of Him. I would as soon, said a wise man, that my pupil had spent his time in the tennis court as in this manner; for there his body at least would have got exercise.

I well know that children ought to be kept employed, and that idleness is for them the danger most to be feared. But what should they be taught? This is undoubtedly an important question. Let them be taught what they are to practice when they come to be men; not what they ought to forget.

Our gardens are adorned with statues and our galleries with pictures. What would you imagine these masterpieces of art, thus exhibited to public admiration, represent? The great men who have defended their country, or the still greater men who have enriched it by their virtues? Far from it. They are the images of every perversion of heart and mind, carefully selected from ancient mythology, and presented to the early curiosity of our children, doubtless that they may have before their eyes the representations of vicious actions, even before they are able to read.

Whence arise all those abuses, unless it be from that fatal inequality introduced among men by the difference of talents and the cheapening of virtue? This is the most evident effect of all our studies, and the most dangerous of all their consequences. The question is no longer whether a man is honest, but whether he is clever. We do not ask whether a book is useful, but whether it is well written. Rewards are lavished on wit and ingenuity, while virtue is left unhonoured. There are a thousand prizes for fine discourses, and none for good actions. I should be glad, however, to know whether the honour attaching to the best discourse that ever wins the prize in this Academy is comparable with the merit of having founded the prize.

A wise man does not go in chase of fortune; but he is by no means insensible to glory, and when he sees it so ill distributed, his virtue, which might have been animated by a little emulation, and turned to the advantage of society, droops and dies away in obscurity and indigence. It is for this reason that the agreeable arts must in time everywhere be preferred to the useful; and this truth has been but too much confirmed since the revival of the arts and sciences. We have physicists, geometricians, chemists, astronomers, poets, musicians, and painters in plenty; but we have no longer a citizen among us; or if there be found a few scattered over our abandoned countryside, they are left to perish there unnoticed and neglected. Such is the condition to which we are reduced, and such are our feelings towards those who give us our daily bread, and our children milk.

I confess, however, that the evil is not so great as it might have become. The eternal providence, in placing salutary simples beside noxious plants, and making poisonous animals contain their own antidote, has taught the sovereigns of the earth, who are its ministers, to imitate its wisdom. It is by following this example that the truly great monarch, to whose glory every age will add new lustre, drew from the very bosom of the arts and sciences the very fountains of a thousand lapses from rectitude, those famous societies, which, while they are depositaries of the dangerous trust of human knowledge, are yet the sacred guardians of morals, by the attention they pay to their maintenance among themselves in all their purity, and by the demands which they make on every member whom they admit.

These wise institutions, confirmed by his august successor and imitated by all the kings of Europe, will serve at least to restrain men of letters, who, all aspiring to the honour of being admitted into these Academies, will keep watch over themselves, and endeavour to make themselves worthy of such honour by useful performances and irreproachable morals. Those Academies also, which, in proposing prizes for literary merit, make choice of such subjects as are calculated to arouse the love of virtue in the hearts of citizens, prove that it prevails in themselves, and must give men the rare and real pleasure of finding learned societies devoting themselves to the enlightenment of mankind, not only by agreeable exercises of the intellect, but also by useful instructions.

An objection which may be made is, in fact, only an additional proof of my argument. So much precaution proves but too evidently the need for it. We never seek remedies for evils that do not exist. Why, indeed, must these bear all the marks of ordinary remedies, on an account of our knowledge: it is to begin with the most general of the learned are only adapted to make men mistake the objects of the sciences, and turn men's attention to the cultivation of them. One would be inclined to think, from the precautions everywhere taken, that we are overstocked with husbandmen, and are afraid of a shortage of philosophers. I will not venture here to enter into a comparison between agriculture and philosophy, as they would not bear it. I shall only ask: What is philosophy? What is contained in the writings of the most celebrated philosophers? What are the lessons of these friends of wisdom. To hear them, should we not take them for so many mountebanks, exhibiting themselves in public, and crying out, *Here, Here, come to me, I am the only true doctor?* One of them teaches that there is no such thing as matter, but that everything exists only in representation. Another declares that there is no other substance than matter, and no other God than the world itself. A third tells you that there are no such things as virtue and vice, and that moral good and evil are chimeras; while a fourth informs you that men are only beasts of prey, and may conscientiously devour one another. Why, my great philosophers, do you not reserve these wise and profitable lessons for your friends and children? You would soon reap the benefit of them, nor should we be under the apprehension of our own becoming your disciples.

Such are the wonderful men, whom their contemporaries held in the highest esteem during their lives, and to whom immortality has been attributed since their decease. Such are the wise maxims we have received from them, and which are transmitted, from age to age, to our descendants. Paganism, though given over to all the extravagances of human reason, has left nothing to compare with the shameful monuments which have been prepared by the art of printing, during the reign of the gospel. The impious writings of Leucippus and Diagoras perished with their authors. The world, in their days, was ignorant of the art of immortalizing the errors and extravagances of the human mind. But thanks to the art of printing[3] and the use we make of it, the pernicious reflections of Hobbes and Spinoza will last for ever.

---

3. If we consider the frightful disorders which printing has already caused in Europe, and judge of the future by the progress of its evils from day to day, it is easy to forsee that sovereigns will hereafter take as much pains to banish this dreadful art from their dominions, as they ever took to encourage it. The Sultan Achmet, yielding to the importunities of certain pretenders to taste, consented to have a press erected at Constantinople; but it was hardly set to work before they were obliged to destroy it, and throw the plant into a well.

It is related that the Caliph Omar, being asked what should be done with the library at Alexandria, answered in these words: "If the books in the library contain anything contrary to the Alcoran, they are evil and ought to be burnt; if they contain only what the Alcoran teaches, they are superfluous." This reasoning has been cited by our men of letters as the height of absurdity; but if Gregory the Great had been in the place of Omar, and the Gospel in the place of the Alcoran, the library would still have been burnt, and it would have been perhaps the finest action of his life.

Go, famous writings, of which the ignorance and rusticity of our fore-fathers would have been incapable. Go to our descendants, along with those still more pernicious works which reek of the corrupted manners of the present age! Let them together convey to posterity a faithful history of the progress and advantages of our arts and sciences. If they are read, they will leave not a doubt about the question we are now discussing, and unless mankind should then be still more foolish than we, they will lift up their hands to Heaven and exclaim in bitterness of heart: "Almighty God! Thou who holdest in Thy hand the minds of men, deliver us from the fatal arts and sciences of our forefathers; give us back ignorance, innocence, and poverty, which alone can make us happy and are precious in Thy sight."

But if the progress of the arts and sciences had added nothing to our real happiness; if it has corrupted our morals, and if that corruption has vitiated our taste, what are we to think of the herd of text-book authors, who have removed those impediments which nature purposely laid in the way to the Temple of the Muses, in order to guard its approach and try the powers of those who might be tempted to seek knowledge? What are we to think of those compilers who have indiscreetly broken open the door of the sciences, and introduced into their sanctuary a populace unworthy to approach it, when it was greatly to be wished that all who should be found incapable of making a considerable progress in the career of learning should have been repulsed at the entrance, and thereby cast upon those arts which are useful to society. A man who will be all his life a bad versifier, or a third-rate geometrician, might have made nevertheless an excellent clothier. Those whom nature intended for her disciples have not needed masters. Bacon, Descartes, and Newton, those teachers of mankind, had themselves no teachers. What guide indeed could have taken them so far as their sublime genius directed them? Ordinary masters would only have cramped their intelligence, by confining it within the narrow limits of their own capacity. It was from the obstacles they met with at first that they learned to exert themselves, and bestirred themselves to traverse the vast field which they covered. If it be proper to allow some men to apply themselves to the study of the arts and sciences, it is only those who feel themselves able to walk alone in their footsteps and to outstrip them. It belongs only to these few to raise monuments to the glory of the human under-standing. But if we are desirous that nothing should be above their genius, nothing should be beyond their hopes. This is the only encouragement they require. The soul insensibly adapts itself to the objects on which it is employed, and thus it is that great occasions produce great men. The greatest orator in the world was Consul of Rome, and perhaps the greatest of philosophers Lord Chancellor of England. Can it be conceived that, if the former had only been a professor at some University, and the latter a pensioner of some Academy, their works would not have suffered from their situation. Let not princes disdain to admit into their councils those who are most capable of giving them good advice. Let them renounce the old prejudice, which was invented by the pride of the great, that the art of governing mankind is more difficult than that of instructing them; as if it was easier to induce men to do good voluntarily than to compel them to it by force. Let the learned of the first rank find an honourable refuge in their courts; let them there enjoy the only recompense worthy of them, that of promoting by their influence the happiness of the peoples they have enlightened by their wisdom. It is by this means only that we are likely to see what virtue, science and authority can do, when animated by the noblest emulation, and working unanimously for the happiness of mankind.

But so long as power alone is on one side, and knowledge and understanding alone on the other, the learned will seldom make great objects their study, princes will still more rarely do great actions, and the peoples will continue to be, as they are, mean, corrupt, and miserable.

As for us, ordinary men, on whom Heaven has not been pleased to bestow such great talents; as we are not destined to reap such glory, let us remain in our obscurity. Let us not covet a reputation we should never attain, and which, in the present state of things, would never make up to us for the trouble it would have cost us, even if we were fully qualified to obtain it. Why should we build our happiness on the opinions of others, when we can find it in our own hearts? Let us leave to others the task of instructing mankind in their duty, and confine ourselves to the discharge of our own. We have no occasion for greater knowledge than this.

Virtue! sublime science of simple minds, are such industry and preparation needed if we are to know you? Are not your principles graven on every heart? Need we do more, to learn your laws, than examine ourselves and listen to the voice of conscience, when the passions are silent?

This is the true philosophy, with which we must learn to be content, without envying the fame of those celebrated men, whose names are immortal in the republic of letters. Let us, instead of envying them, endeavour to make, between them and us, that honourable distinction which was formerly seen to exist between two great peoples, that the one knew how to speak, and the other how to act, aright.

CONDILLAC

ETIENNE BONNOT DE CONDILLAC (1715-1780) was the most systematic and "technical" of the *philosophes*; his style was that of the professional philosopher, and he was chiefly concerned with psychological and epistemological issues. Diderot called him *Locke perfecté* because of his almost ruthless carrying through of Locke's "plain, historical method."[1] In his famous *Treatise on Sensations* (1754) he imagined a marble statue given first the sense of smell and then one by one the other senses, until its "mind" was, as Locke would say, "furnished with ideas" just as the human mind is. This book reversed the procedure of Diderot's *Letters on the Blind* (1749), in which Diderot considered the effects on our consciousness and knowledge of the deprivation of one or more of the senses.

This tour de force by Condillac was and is so famous that its fame has obscured, at least outside France, his other works. But his studies of the logic of philosophical and scientific systems in his *Treatise on Systems* (1749) and his studies of language in his *Essay on the Origin of Human Knowledge* (1764) deserve to be better known. Our selection is from these latter works, which have not hitherto been translated into English.

---

1. His views on "maxims" and "hypotheses" in the selection which follows should be compared with Locke's treatment of them in *Essay Concerning Human Understanding*, Book IV, Chapter xii.

Treatise on Systems and Essay on the Origin of Human Knowledge

Rationalism, Hypotheses, and Empiricism[1]

A system is nothing but the arrangement of the different parts of an art or science in such a manner that they will mutually support each other, or so that the earlier parts will explain the later. The parts which give the reasons for the others are called principles, and a system is the more perfect the fewer principles it has. It is even to be hoped that the principles can be reduced to a single one.

In the works of philosophers there are three kinds of principles, from which three kinds of systems are formed. The principles in the first class, the most common one, are general or abstract maxims. Of such a principle it is required that it be so evident or so well demonstrated that it cannot be subject of any doubt. For if it were uncertain, we could have no assurance in the consequences drawn from it. The author[s] of *The Art of Thought*[2] are speaking of these principles when they say:

Everyone agrees that it is important to have in mind general axioms or principles which, being clear and indubitable, can serve as the foundation of knowledge of the most abstruse things. But those which are ordinarily cited are of such little utility that it is useless to know them. Now that which they call the first principle of knowledge—it is impossible that the same thing be and not be—is very clear and very certain; but I can see no place at all where it could ever serve to give us any knowledge. I believe that these can be more useful. . . .

And so they give us as the first principle this maxim: Everything which is implicit in the clear and distinct idea of a thing can be truly

---

1. The whole of Chapter i of *Treatise on Systems;* the last three paragraphs are from Book II, Part 2, Chapter iii: §35, 36, and 44 of *Essay on the Origin of Human Knowledge.* The translations are my own.
2. *The Port Royal Logic,* Book IV, Chapter vii.

affirmed of the thing itself. As the second: At least possible existence is implicit in the idea of any thing which we clearly and distinctly perceive. And the third: Nothing cannot be the cause of something. They imagine that there are eleven such rules; but it is useless to repeat the others—these suffice as examples.

The power these philosophers attribute to this sort of principle is so great that it is natural they should try to multiply their number. Metaphysicians do this more than any. Descartes, Malebranche, Leibniz, and others have deluged us with them, and we have only ourselves to blame if we do not penetrate to the most recondite things.

The principles of the second kind are hypotheses or suppositions for explaining things that one could not explain otherwise. If the suppositions do not seem impossible, if they give some explanation of known phenomena, the philosophers do not doubt that they have discovered the true springs of nature. Would it be possible, they ask, for a false supposition to have such fortunate consequences? From this comes the opinion that giving an explanation of phenomena is proof of the truth of a supposition, and that one cannot judge a system by its principles except with regard to the manner in which the principles give a reason for things. Suppositions, originally arbitrary, become incontestable through the success one has with them in explaining things.

Metaphysicians have been as inventive of the second species of principle as of the first, and by their efforts metaphysics has done nothing but run into what can be only mysteries for it. Whoever says "metaphysics" in their language says "the science of the primordial truths, the science of the first principles of things"—only it is necessary to remark that this science is not found in the works of these gentlemen.

Abstract notions are only ideas formed from what is common to several particular ideas. Such is the notion of animal; it is extracted from that which pertains equally to the idea of man, horse, monkey, and the like. Thus an abstract notion seems to provide a reason for that which we note in particular objects. If, for example, one asks why the horse walks, drinks, and eats, one will respond, very philosophically, that it is because the horse is an animal. This answer, upon closer analysis, seems to say that the horse walks, drinks, eats because in fact it walks, drinks, eats. But it is a rare man who is not content with the answer, "because it is an animal." One might say that men's curiosity leads them less to learn about one thing than to ask questions about many; the assured air of the philosopher impresses them, and they fear that they would seem stupid if they insisted on one point. It suffices that the oracle be given in familiar expressions; then they would be ashamed not to understand it. If they were not able to hide a certain puzzlement, a single look from the master would serve to dispel it. Can we doubt when one to whom we have given all our confidence has no doubt? There is nothing to astonish us in the fact that abstract principles become so greatly multiplied and have always been regarded as the source of our knowledge.

Abstract notions are absolutely necessary to bring order into our knowledge, for they put each idea into its class. That is their whole use. But to imagine that they are made to guide us to particular knowledge—this is blindness all the more profound, for they themselves are formed only after we have already got knowledge of particular things. When I condemn abstract principles, it is not right to say that I think we can get along without any abstract ideas; that would be absurd. I mean only that we should never take them to be the correct principles to lead us to new discoveries.

So much for suppositions: they are a great resource of ignorance; they are convenient; imagination spins them with pleasure and little pain; lying in one's bed, one can create them and govern the universe. But—it is all only a dream. And a philosopher dreams easily.

But it is not easy to consult experience and to collect facts with care and discernment. It is for this reason that we so rarely take only established facts as principles, even though perhaps we have many more of them than we think. But by lack of practice in making use of them, we do not know how to apply them. We truly have in our hands the explanation of many phenomena, but we look for it far beyond our reach. For example, the gravity of a body is a fact that has always been well established; but only in our own day has it been recognized as a principle in the explanation of nature.

It is on principles of this latter kind that true systems are built. These are the only ones that merit the name. For it is only by means of them that we can give reasons for the things whose causes we can discover. I would call systems abstract only if their principles are abstract; I would call them hypotheses if suppositions are their foundations. By the mixture of different sorts of principles, we get different kinds of systems, but they all resemble more or less the three sorts I have described; it is useless to make other classifications.

Established facts—these are the only principles of science. How has anyone been able to imagine that there are any others? I shall now examine this question.

Systems are older than philosophers. Nature is responsible for this, and its work is not bad. Men have nature only for their master. A system is and can only be the fruit of observation. One does not ask the reason for everything; one has needs, and looks only for means to satisfy them. Only observation can make these needs known, and one observes what one is forced to observe. Though ignorant of that which we have since called principles, one at least had the advantage of sparing oneself many errors, for one must have a beginning of knowledge even to make a mistake. And it seems that some philosophers have never got farther than the beginning.

Human beings observe; that is, they remark facts related to their needs. Since they have few needs, few observations need be made; and since needs were at the beginning imperious, it was rare that one was deceived. The errors made at the beginning, at least, were only fleeting, and one turned away from them since they did not satisfy the needs. Observation was only a groping; it was not possible to be sure of a fact as soon as one believed he had perceived it. One opined, or supposed it; and in the absence of better knowledge, supposition took the place of discovery, until a new observation confirmed or destroyed it.

Thus it was that nature guided and instructed men without their noticing that they went from one bit of knowledge to another by a series of observed facts. After they had made observations relevant to their needs, it was evident that to make discoveries of another sort they had only to follow the same practice. A first observation, which can be only tentative, gives them some surmises; these indicate other observations to be made; and these observations confirm or deny the supposed facts.

When we have facts in sufficiently large number to explain the phenomena for which we sought the reason, system is achieved in some manner simply by itself, because the facts arrange themselves in the order in which, one by one, they explain each other. Thus we see that in every system there is a first fact, a fact which is at the beginning of the system and which can properly be called a principle. (Principle and beginning are two words that ordinarily mean the same thing.)

Suppositions are, properly speaking, only surmises or guesses. And if we have to make them, it is because we are condemned to grope and fumble. Since they are only conjectures, they are not established facts; they cannot be the principles or beginnings of a system, for the system itself would then be only a conjecture. Though not the principle or beginning of a system, they are at least the principle or the beginning of the means we have of discovering a system. Since they are the principle of the means, some have believed that they are also the principle of the system, but they thereby confused two very different things.

As we acquire knowledge, we are obliged to distribute it into different classes; there is no other way to bring it into order. The least general classes comprise the individuals, and we name them species in relation to more general classes, which we call genera. The classes which are genera, compared to those to which they are subordinated, are in their turn species. Thus we go from classes through classes to a genus which comprehends them all.

When this distribution is made, we have a brief means of giving an account of our knowledge: it is to begin with the most general classes. For the supreme genus is really only an abbreviation comprehending all subordinate classes which can be embraced in a single glance. When I say "being," for example, I see substance and mode, body and mind, quality and property—in a word, I see all the divisions and subdivisions between being and individuals. For this reason I ought to begin with a general class when I want to represent quickly a multitude of things; hence we can say that the general class is the beginning, or the principle. But this has been only little understood, and therefore some wrongly say that general ideas, general maxims, are the principles of the sciences.

I therefore repeat: well-established facts can be the only true principles of the sciences; and if others took for the principle of a system some supposition or general maxim, it was because, not recognizing this truth, they saw that the supposition or the general maxim was the principle or the beginning of something.

According to Descartes, it is necessary to begin by defining things and to regard the definitions as the right principles for discovering the properties of things. I believe, on the other hand, that one must begin by searching out the properties; this is the reasonable way to proceed. If the [general] notions we are capable of acquiring are (as I have tried to show) collections of simple ideas which experience has made us assemble under certain names, it is far more natural to look for ideas in the order in which experience gave them to us than to begin with the definitions, in order subsequently to deduce the different properties of the things.

Thus one sees that we ought to follow in the search for truth the order I have already indicated in speaking of analysis. It consists in re-ascending to the origin of ideas, in tracing their genealogy, and in making different compositions and decompositions of them, in order to compare them on all sides and to show the relations between them.

These were my reflections on method when I read for the first time

Chancellor Bacon. I was so flattered to find myself in agreement with that great man that I was surprised that the Cartesians had not borrowed anything from him. No one knew better than he the causes of our errors; for he saw that ideas, the work of the mind, had been ill-made and that we must re-make them if we are to advance in the search for truth. That is counsel he often repeated. But did men hearken? Prevented by the jargon of the schools and by innate ideas, did not mankind treat as chimerical his project to renew human understanding? The method Bacon proposed was too perfect for him to be the author of a revolution; while the method of Descartes was to succeed because it left standing a good part of error. Add to this that the English philosopher had occupations which did not permit him to execute for himself what he counseled others to do, and was therefore obliged to limit himself to giving opinions, which could make only a light impression on minds incapable of sensing their solidity. Descartes, on the contrary, lived entirely for philosophy, and having a more lively and fecund mind he sometimes only substituted for the errors of others errors still more seductive—errors which contributed not a little to his reputation.

DIDEROT

DENIS DIDEROT (1713-1784) was an enormously prolific and gifted writer of novels, plays, tales, fables, and artistic and literary criticism which would have made him a leader of the *philosophes* even if he had not produced the greatest single work of the French Enlightenment. For it was Diderot who, with courage, imagination, and industry, edited—finally alone—this mammoth work in which the ideas and programs of the Enlightenment were made available to all. Besides the many philosophical articles he contributed to the *Encyclopaedia,* he wrote *Philosophical Thoughts on the Sciences* (1746) which is deistic, but perhaps with tongue-in-cheek; *Letters on the Blind* (1749) which is empiricistic and skeptical, and which earned him imprisonment, and, finally, his two fanciful dialogues with his friend and colleague, the mathematician d'Alembert. D'Alembert had been his co-editor on the *Encyclopaedia,* but withdrew in 1759 when the work was suppressed. The project had to be carried on by Diderot alone, clandestinely.

We print most of the first of these dialogues, "Conversation between d'Alembert and Diderot" (1769). To pass the time between reading good books for reviewing, he said to his mistress, he "made extracts from books not yet written." In this "extract," we see Diderot present a completely materialistic theory not just of physical nature but of the living organism. This theory, encouraged by Locke's suggestion that matter might be endowed with thought, was opposed, of course, to Descartes' dualism of mind and matter. Similar theories were developed and defended by La Mettrie in *Man a Machine* (1748) and d'Holbach in *System of Nature* (1770), but never so skillfully and amusingly as by Diderot.

Conversation between d'Alembert and Diderot[1]

d'Alembert: I confess that a Being who exists somewhere and yet corresponds to no point in space, a Being who, lacking extension, yet occupies space; who is present in his entirety in every part of that space, who is essentially different from matter and yet is one with matter, who follows its motion, and moves it, without himself being in motion, who acts on matter and yet is subject to all its vicissitudes, a Being about whom I can form no idea; a Being of so contradictory a nature, is an hypothesis difficult to accept. But other problems arise if we reject it; for if this faculty of sensation, which you propose as substitute, is a general and essential quality of matter, then stone must be sensitive.

Diderot: Why not?

d'Alembert: It's hard to believe.

Diderot: Yes, for him who cuts, chisels, and crushes it, and does not hear it cry out.

d'Alembert: I'd like you to tell me what difference there is, according to you, between a man and a statue, between marble and flesh.

Diderot: Not much. Flesh can be made from marble, and marble from flesh.

d'Alembert: But one is not the other.

Diderot: In the same way that what you call animate force is not the same as inanimate force.

d'Alembert: I don't follow you.

Diderot: I'll explain. The transference of a body from one place to another is not itself motion, it is the consequence of motion. Motion exists equally in the body displaced and in the body that remains stationary.

---

1. From Jean Stewart and Jonathan Kemp, trans., in *Diderot, Interpreter of Nature*, ed. Jonathan Kemp (New York: International Publishers, 1937). Reprinted by permission of International Publishers Co., Inc. None of the notes are by Diderot; the fourth originates with Mr. Kemp, the others with me.

d'Alembert: That's a new way of looking at things.

Diderot: True none the less. Take away the obstacle that prevents the displacement of a stationary body, and it will be transferred. Suddenly rarefy the air that surrounds the trunk of this huge oak, and the water contained in it, suddenly expanding, will burst it into a hundred thousand fragments. I say the same of your own body.

d'Alembert: That may be so. But what relation is there between motion and the faculty of sensation? Do you, by any chance, distinguish between an active and an inactive sensitiveness, as between animate and inanimate force? An animate force which is revealed by displacement, an inanimate force which manifests itself by pressure; an active sensitiveness which would be characterized by certain recognizable behaviour in the animal and perhaps in the plant, while your inactive sensitiveness only makes itself known when it changes over to the active state?

Diderot: Precisely; just as you say.

d'Alembert: So, then, the statue merely has inactive sensitiveness; and man, animals, perhaps even plants, are endowed with active sensitiveness.

Diderot: There is undoubtedly that difference between the marble block and living tissue; but you can well imagine that's not the only one.

d'Alembert: Of course. Whatever likeness there may be in outward form between a man and a statue, there is no similarity in their internal organization. The chisel of the cleverest sculptor cannot make even an epidermis. But there is a very simple way of transforming an inanimate force into an animate one—the experiment is repeated a hundred times a day before our eyes; whereas I don't quite see how a body can be made to pass from the state of inactive to that of active sensitiveness.

Diderot: Because you don't want to see it. It is just as common a phenomenon.

d'Alembert: And what is this common phenomenon, if you please?

Diderot: I'll tell you, since you want to be put to shame; it occurs every time you eat.

d'Alembert: Every time I eat!

Diderot: Yes, for what do you do when you eat? You remove obstacles that prevented the food from possessing active sensitiveness. You assimilate it, you turn it into flesh, you make it animal, you give it the faculty of sensation, and, what you do to this foodstuff, I can do, when I please, to marble.

d'Alembert: And how?

Diderot: How? I shall make it edible.

d'Alembert: Make marble edible? That doesn't seem easy to me.

Diderot: It's my business to show you the process. I take the statue you see there, I put it in a mortar, then with great blows from a pestle . . .

d'Alembert: Careful, please; that's Falconet's masterpiece! If it were only by Huez or some one like that—.

Diderot: Falconet won't mind; the statue is paid for, and Falconet cares little for present respect and not at all for that of posterity.

d'Alembert: Go on then, crush it to powder.

Diderot: When the block of marble is reduced to impalpable powder, I mix it with humus or leaf-mould; I knead them well together; I water the mixture, I let it decompose for a year or two or a hundred, time doesn't matter to me. When the whole has turned into a more or less homogeneous substance, into humus, do you know what I do?

d'Alembert: I'm sure you don't eat humus.

Diderot: No; but there is a means of connection, of assimilation, a link, between the humus and myself, a *latus* as the chemist would say.

d'Alembert: And that is plant life?

Diderot: Quite right, I sow peas, beans, cabbages, and other vegetables; these plants feed on the soil and I feed on the plants.

d'Alembert: Whether it's true or false, I like this passage from marble into humus, from humus to the vegetable kingdom, from the vegetable to the animal kingdom, to flesh.

Diderot: So, then, I make flesh, or soul as my daughter said, an actively sensitive substance; and if I do not thus solve the problem you set me, at any rate I get pretty near solving it; for you will admit that a piece of marble is much further removed from a being that can feel, than a being that can feel is from a being that can think.

d'Alembert: I agree. But nevertheless the feeling being is not yet the thinking being.

Diderot: Before going one step further let me tell you the history of one of the greatest geometricians[2] in Europe. What was this wonderful creature to begin with? Nothing.

d'Alembert: What, nothing? Nothing comes from nothing.

Diderot: You take my words too literally. I mean to say that, before his mother, the beautiful and wicked Madame de Tencin, had reached the age of puberty, and before the adolescence of the soldier La Touche, the molecules which were to form the first rudiments of our geometrician were scattered throughout the frail young bodies of these two, filtering through with the lymph, circulating with the blood,

---

2. Namely, d'Alembert himself.

till at last they reached the vessels whence they were destined to unite, the germ cells of his father and mother. The precious germ, then, is formed; now according to the common belief, it is brought through the Fallopian tubes to the womb, it is attached to the womb by a long cord; it grows gradually and develops into a foetus; now comes the moment for it to leave the dark prison; it is born, abandoned on the steps of Saint-Jean-le-Rond, whence it receives its name; now, taken from the foundlings' home it is put to the breast of good Madame Rousseau, the glazier's wife; it is given suck, it grows in body and mind, becomes a man of letters, an engineer, a geometrician. How was all this done? Just through eating and other purely mechanical operations. Here, in four words you have the general formula. Eat, digest, distil *in vasi licito, et fiat homo secundum artem*.[3] And to expound before the Academy the process of the formation of a man or an animal, one need employ only material agents, the successive results of which would be an inert being, a feeling being, a thinking being, a being solving the problem of the precession of the equinoxes, a sublime being, a marvelous being, a being growing old, fading away, dying, dissolved and given back to the soil.

. . . .

Diderot: Can you tell me what constitutes the existence of a perceiving being, for that being itself?

d'Alembert: The consciousness of continued identity from the first moment of reflection to the present.

Diderot: And on what is this consciousness based?

d'Alembert: On the memory of its actions.

Diderot: And without this memory?

d'Alembert: Without this memory it would have no identity, since, realizing its existence only at the instant of receiving an impression, it would have no life-story. Its life would be an interrupted series of sensations with nothing to connect them.

Diderot: Very good. And what is this memory? Whence does it spring?

d'Alembert: From a certain organization, which develops, grows weaker, and is sometimes lost entirely.

Diderot: Then, if a being that can feel, and that possesses this organization that gives rise to memory, connects up the impressions it receives, forms through this connection a story which is that of its life, and so acquires consciousness of its identity, it can then deny, affirm, conclude and think.

---

3. In a suitable vessel, let a man be made by art.

d'Alembert: So it appears to me; there is only one more difficulty.

Diderot: You are wrong; there are many more.

d'Alembert: But one chief one; that is, it seems to me that we can only think of one thing at a time, and that to form even a simple proposition, let alone those vast chains of reasoning that embrace in their course thousands of ideas, one would need to have at least two things present—the object, which seems to remain in the mind's eye while that mind considers the quality which it is to attribute or to deny to that object.

Diderot: I think that is so; that has made me sometimes compare the fibres of our organs to sensitive vibrating strings which vibrate and resound long after they have been plucked. It is this vibration, this kind of inevitable resonance, which holds the object present, while the mind is busied about the quality that belongs to that object. But vibrating strings have yet another property, that of making other strings vibrate; and that is how the first idea recalls a second, the two of them a third, these three a fourth and so on, so that there is no limit to the ideas awakened and interconnected in the mind of the philosopher, as he meditates and hearkens to himself amid silence and darkness. This instrument makes surprising leaps, and an idea once aroused may sometimes set vibrating an harmonic at an inconceivable distance. If this phenomenon may be observed between resonant strings that are lifeless and separate, why should it not occur between points that are alive and connected, between fibres that are continuous and sensitive?

d'Alembert: Even if it's not true, that is at least very ingenious. But I am inclined to think that you are, without realizing it, slipping into a difficulty that you wished to avoid.

Diderot: What is that?

d'Alembert: You are opposed to making a distinction between the two substances.

Diderot: I don't deny it.

d'Alembert: And if you look closer, you'll see that you are making of the philosopher's mind a being distinct from the instrument, a musician, as it were, who listens to the vibrating strings and decides as to their harmony or dissonance.[4]

Diderot: I may have laid myself open to this objection, but you might not have made it if you had considered the difference between the instrument philosopher and the instrument harpsichord. The philosopher is an instrument that has the faculty of sensation; he is, at

---

4. An allusion to Simmias' theory of the relation of mind to body in Plato's *Phaedo*, 86ff. (Simmias uses the metaphor of the lyre.)

the same time, both the musician and the instrument. As he can feel, he is immediately conscious of the sound he gives forth; as he is an animal, he retains the memory of it. This faculty of the organism, connecting up the sounds within him, produces and preserves the melody there. Just suppose that your harpsichord has the power to feel and to remember, and tell me if it will not know and repeat of its own accord the airs that you have played on its keys. We are instruments endowed with feeling and memory; our senses are so many keys that are struck by surrounding nature, and that often strike themselves. This is all, in my opinion, that happens in a harpsichord which is organized like you or me. An impression is created by some cause either within or outside the instrument, a sensation is aroused by this impression, a sensation that persists, since you cannot imagine it arising and dying instantaneously; another impression follows, which equally has its cause either within or outside the animal, a second sensation, and voices to indicate them by natural or conventional sounds.

d'Alembert: I understand. So then, if this harpsichord were not only sensitive and animate but were further endowed with the faculty of feeding and reproducing itself, it would live and breed of itself, or with its female, little harpsichords, also living and vibrating.

Diderot: Undoubtedly. In your opinion, what, other than this, is a chaffinch, a nightingale, a musician or a man? And what other difference do you find between a bird and a bird-organ?[5] Do you see this egg? With this you can overthrow all the schools of theology, all the churches of the earth. What is this egg? An unperceiving mass, before the germ is introduced into it; and after the germ is introduced, what is it then? still only an unperceiving mass, for this germ itself is only a crude inert fluid. How will this mass develop into a different organization, to sensitiveness, to life? By means of heat. And what will produce the heat? Motion. What will be the successive effects of this motion? Instead of answering me, sit down and let's watch them from moment to moment. First there's a dot that quivers, a little thread that grows longer and takes on colour; tissue is formed; a beak, tiny wings, eyes, feet appear; a yellowish material unwinds and produces intestines; it is an animal. This animal moves, struggles, cries out; I hear its cries through the shell; it becomes covered with down; it sees. The weight of its head, shaking about, brings its beak constantly up against the inner wall of its prison; now the wall is broken; it comes out, it walks about, flies, grows angry, runs away, comes near again, complains, suffers, loves, desires, enjoys; it has the same affections as

5. Mechanical musical-box to teach a canary tunes.

yourself, it performs the same actions. Are you going to assert with Descartes that it is a purely imitative machine? Little children will laugh at you, and philosophers will retort that if this be a machine then you, too, are a machine. If you admit that between the animal and yourself the difference is merely one of organization, you will be showing good sense and reason, you will be honest; but from this there will be drawn the conclusion that refutes you; namely that, from inert matter, organized in a certain way, and impregnated with other inert matter, and given heat and motion, there results the faculty of sensation, life, memory, consciousness, passion and thought. You have only two courses left to take: either to imagine within the inert mass of the egg a hidden element that awaited the egg's development before revealing its presence, or to assume that this invisible element crept in through the shell at a definite moment in the development. But what is this element? Did it occupy space or did it not? How did it come, or did it escape without moving? What was it doing there or elsewhere? Was it created at the instant it was needed? Was it already in existence? Was it waiting for a home? If it was homogeneous it was material; if heterogeneous, one cannot account for its previous inertia nor its activity in the developed animal. Just listen to yourself, and you will be sorry for yourself; you will perceive that, in order to avoid making a simple supposition that explains everything, namely the faculty of sensation as a general property of matter or a product of its organization, you are giving up common sense and plunging headlong into an abyss of mysteries, contradictions and absurdities.[6]

d'Alembert: A supposition! It pleases you to say so. But suppose this quality is in its essence incompatible with matter?

Diderot: And how do you know that the faculty of sensation is essentially incompatible with matter, you who do not know the essence of anything, either of matter or of sensation? Do you understand the nature of motion any better, how it comes to exist in a body, and its transmission from one to another?

d'Alembert: Without understanding the nature of sensation or that of matter, I can see that the faculty of sensation is a simple quality, entire, indivisible, and incompatible with a subject or substratum which is divisible.

Diderot: Metaphysico-theological nonsense! What! don't you see that all the qualities, all the forms by which nature becomes perceptible to our senses, are essentially indivisible? You cannot have more or less

---

6. Diderot's point here is that sensation as a faculty of matter, as conjectured by Locke, cf. above, p. 47, is more plausible than Cartesian dualism, which d'Alembert favors.

impenetrability. There is half a round body, but there is not a half of roundness; you can have motion to a greater or less degree, but either there is motion or there is not. You cannot have half, or a third, or a quarter of a head, an ear, a finger, any more than half, a third, or a quarter of a thought. If in the universe no one particle is like another, in a particle no one point like another, acknowledge that the atom itself possesses an indivisible quality or form; acknowledge that division is incompatible with the essence of forms, since it destroys them. Be a physicist, and acknowledge the produced character of an effect when you see it produced, even if you cannot explain all the steps that led from the cause to the effect. Be logical, and do not substitute for a cause which exists and which explains everything, another cause which cannot be comprehended, whose connection with the effect is even more difficult to grasp, which engenders an infinite number of difficulties and solves not one of them.

d'Alembert: But what if I give up this cause?

Diderot: There is only one substance in the universe, in man and in the animal. The bird-organ is made of wood, man of flesh. The bird is of flesh, the musician of flesh differently organized; but both of them have the same origin, the same formation, the same functions and the same end.

d'Alembert: And how is the convention of sounds established between your two harpsichords?

Diderot: Since an animal is a perceiving instrument, resembling any other in all respects, having the same structure, being strung with the same chords, stimulated in the same way by joy, pain, hunger, thirst, colic, wonder, terror, it is impossible that at the Pole and at the Equator it should utter different sounds. And so you will find that interjections are about the same in all languages, living and dead. The origin of conventional sounds must be ascribed to need and to proximity. The instrument endowed with the faculty of sensation, or the animal, has discovered by experience that when it uttered a certain sound a certain result followed outside it, feeling instruments like itself or other animals drew nearer, went away, asked or offered things, hurt or caressed it. All these consequences became connected in its memory and in that of others with the utterance of these sounds; and note that human intercourse consists only of sounds and actions. And, to appreciate the power of my system, notice further that it is subject to the same insurmountable difficulty that Berkeley brought against the existence of bodies. There came a moment of madness when the feeling harpsichord thought that it was the only harpsichord in the world, and that the whole harmony of the universe resided in it.

d'Alembert: There's a lot to be said on all that.

Diderot: True.

d'Alembert: For instance, your system doesn't make it clear how we form syllogisms or draw inferences.

Diderot: We don't draw them; they are all drawn by nature. We only state the existence of connected phenomena, which are known to us practically, by experience, whose existence may be either necessary or contingent; necessary in the case of mathematics, physics, and other exact sciences; contingent in ethics, politics and other conjectural sciences.

d'Alembert: Is the connection between phenomena less necessary in one case than in another?

Diderot: No, but the cause undergoes too many particular vicissitudes which escape our observation, for us to be able to count with certainty upon the result that will ensue. Our certainty that a violent-tempered man will grow angry at an insult is not the same as our certainty that one body striking a smaller body will set it in motion.

d'Alembert: What about analogy?

Diderot: Analogy, in the most complex cases, is only a rule of three working out in the feeling instrument. If a familiar natural phenomenon is followed by another familiar natural phenomenon, what will be the fourth phenomenon that will follow a third, either provided by nature or imagined in imitation of nature? If the lance of an ordinary warrior is ten feet long, how long will the lance of Ajax be? If I can throw a stone weighing four pounds, Diomedes must be able to shift a large block of rock. The strides of gods and the leaps of their horses will correspond to the imagined proportion between gods and men. You have here a fourth chord in harmony with and proportional to three others; and the animal awaits its resonance, which always occurs within itself, though not always in nature. The poet doesn't mind about that, it doesn't affect his kind of truth. But it is otherwise with the philosopher; he must proceed to examine nature which often shows him a phenomenon quite different from what he had supposed, and then he perceives that he had been seduced by an analogy.

d'Alembert: Farewell, my friend, good evening and good night to you.

D'HOLBACH

PAUL HEINRICH DIETRICH, Baron d'Holbach (1723-1789) was born in Germany but lived in Paris, where he was patron to many of the less fortunate *philosophes*, a contributor to and supporter of the *Encyclopaedia*, and host of a salon where Hume and all the *philosophes* with the exception of Voltaire saw each other frequently.

d'Holbach was a more thorough materialist than his friend Diderot and the most forthright and militant atheist of his time. Frederick the Great attacked him for being a mechanistic determinist and at the same time attempting to be a reformer, and Voltaire (cf. p. 187) rejected his atheism because of what he thought to be the moral consequences of atheism. When the reaction against the Enlightenment set in later in the century, it was d'Holbach who was regarded (e.g., by Goethe) as the epitome of all the "gray theory" to be rejected for "life's golden tree." Rousseau, however, who agreed with him on nothing and left his salon early in his career, gave a sympathetic portrait of him as "the virtuous atheist" in *Julie*.

His most famous book was *The System of Nature* (1770) but this was long and diffuse. Two years later he published a briefer account of his materialism and atheism in *Good* (or *Common*) *Sense, or Natural Ideas vs. Supernatural Ideas*. Our selections are from this book, in the translation by H. D. Robinson (Fourth edition, New York: G. W. and A. J. Matsell, 1836), slightly emended.

Good Sense

Refutation of Arguments for the
Existence of God

2. There is a science that has for its object only things incomprehensible. Contrary to all other sciences, it treats only of what cannot fall under our senses, Hobbes calls it the *kingdom of darkness*. It is a country, where every thing is governed by laws, contrary to those which mankind are permitted to know in the world they inhabit. In this marvellous region, light is only darkness; evidence is doubtful or false; imposibilities are credible: reason is a deceitful guide; and good sense becomes madness. This *science* is called *Theology*, and this theology is a continual insult to the reason of man.

4. The principles of every religion are founded upon the idea of a God. Now, it is impossible to have true ideas of a being, who acts upon none of our senses. All our ideas are representations of sensible objects. What then can represent to us the idea of God, which is evidently an idea without an object? Is not such an idea as impossible, as an effect without a cause? Can an idea without an archetype be any thing, but a chimera? There are however, divines, who assure us that the idea of God is innate; or that we have this in our mother's womb. Every principle is the result of reason; all reason is the result of experience; experience is acquired only by the exercise of our senses: therefore religious principles are not founded upon reason, and are not innate.

10. Ignorance and fear are the two hinges of all religion. The uncertainty in which man finds himself in relation to his God, is precisely the motive that attaches him to his religion. Man is fearful in the dark—in moral, as well as physical darkness. His fear becomes habitual, and habit makes it natural; he would think that he wanted something, if he had nothing to fear.

13. In point of religion, men are only great children. The more a

religion is absurd, and filled with wonders, the greater ascendancy it acquires over them. The devout man thinks himself obliged to place no bounds to his credulity; the more things are inconceivable, they appear to him divine; the more they are incredible, the greater merit he imagines, there is in believing them.

38. Nature, you say, is totally inexplicable without a God. That is to say, to explain what you understand very little, you have need of a cause which you understand not at all. You think to elucidate what is obscure, by doubling the obscurity; to solve difficulties, by doubling them. O enthusiastic philosophers! To prove the existence of a God, write complete treatises of botany; enter into a minute detail of the parts of the human body; launch forth into the sky, to contemplate the revolution of the stars; then return to the earth to admire the course of waters; behold with transport the butterflies, the insects, the polypi, and the organized atoms, in which you think you discern the greatness of your God. All these things will not prove the existence of that God; they will prove only, that you have not just ideas of the immense variety of matter, and of the effects, producible by its infinitely diversified combinations, that constitute the universe. They will prove only your ignorance of nature; that you have no idea of her powers, when you judge her incapable of producing a multitude of forms and beings, of which your eyes, even with the assistance of microscopes, never discern but the smallest part. In a word, they will prove, that, for want of knowing sensible agents, or those possible to know, you find it shorter to have recourse to a word, expressing an inconceivable agent.

39. We are gravely and repeatedly told, that *there is no effect without a cause;* that *the world did not make itself.* But the universe is a cause, it is not an effect; it is not a work; it has not been made because it is impossible that it should have been made. The world has always been; its existence is necessary; it is its own cause. Nature, whose essence is visibly to act and produce, requires not, to discharge her functions, an invisible mover, much more unknown than herself. Matter moves by its own energy, by a necessary consequence of its own heterogeneity.

43. "What!" you will say, "is intelligent man, is the universe, and all it contains, the effect of *chance?*" No; I repeat it, *the universe is not an effect;* it is the cause of all effects; every being it contains is the necessary effect of this cause, which sometimes shows us its manner of acting, but generally conceals its operations. Men use the word *chance* to hide their ignorance of true causes, which, though not understood, act not less according to certain laws. There is no effect without a cause. Nature is a word used to denote the immense assemblage

of beings, various matter, infinite combinations, and diversified motions, that we behold. All bodies, organized or unorganized, are necessary effects of certain causes. Nothing in nature can happen by chance. Every thing is subject to fixed laws. These laws are only the necessary connection of certain effects with their causes. One atom of matter cannot meet another *by chance;* this meeting is the effect of permanent laws, which cause every being necessarily to act as it does, and hinder it from acting otherwise, in given circumstances. To talk of the *fortuitous concourse of atoms,* or to attribute some effects to chance, is merely saying that we are ignorant of the laws, by which bodies act, meet, combine, or separate.

44. The worshippers of a God find, above all in the order of the universe, an invincible proof of the existence of an intelligent and wise being, who governs it. But this order is nothing but a series of movements necessarily produced by causes or circumstances, which are sometimes favourable, and sometimes hurtful to us: we approve of some, and complain of others.

Nature uniformly follows the same round; that is, the same causes produce the same effects, as long as their action is not disturbed by other causes, which force them to produce different effects. When the operation of causes, whose effects we experience, is interrupted by causes, which, though unknown, are not the less natural and necessary, we are confounded; we cry out, *a miracle!* and attribute it to a cause much more unknown than any of those acting before our eyes.

The universe is always in order. It cannot be in disorder, it is our machine alone, that suffers, when we complain of disorder. The bodies, causes, and beings, which this world contains, necessarily act in the manner in which we see them act, whether we approve or disapprove of the effects. Earthquakes, volcanos, inundations, pestilences, and famines are effects as necessary, or as much in the order of nature, as the fall of heavy bodies, the courses of rivers, the periodical motions of the seas, the blowing of the winds, the fruitful rains, and the favourable effects, for which men praise God, and thank him for his goodness.

To be astonished that a certain order reigns in the world, is to be surprised that the same causes constantly produce the same effects. To be shocked at disorder, is to forget, that when things change, or are interrupted in their actions, the effects can no longer be the same. To wonder at the order of nature, is to wonder that any thing can exist; it is to be surprised at one's own existence. What is order to one being, is disorder to another. All wicked beings find that every thing is in order, when they can with impunity put every thing in disorder.

They find, on the contrary, that every thing is in disorder, when they are disturbed in the exercise of their wickedness.

54. The logic of common sense teaches, that we cannot, and ought not, to judge of a cause, but by its effects. A cause, can be reputed constantly good, only when it constantly produces good, useful, and agreeable effects. A cause which produces both good and evil, is sometimes good, and sometimes evil. But the logic of theology destroys all this. According to that, the phenomena of nature, or the effects we behold in this world, prove to us the existence of a cause infinitely good; and this cause is God. Although this world is full of evils; although disorder often reigns in it; although men incessantly repine at their hard fate; we must be convinced, that these effects are owing to a beneficent and immutable cause; and many people believe it, or feign to believe it.

Every thing that passes in the world, proves to us, in the clearest manner, that it is not governed by an intelligent being. We can judge of the intelligence of a being only by the conformity of the means, which he employs to attain his proposed object. The object of God, is, it is said, the happiness of man. Yet, a like necessity governs the fate of all sensible beings, who are born only to suffer much, enjoy little, and die. The cup of man is filled with joy and bitterness; good is every where attended with evil; order gives place to disorder; generation is followed by destruction. If you tell me, that the designs of God are mysterious and that his ways are impenetrable; I answer, that, in this case, it is impossible for me to judge whether God be intelligent.

56. The universe can be only what it is; all sensible beings there enjoy and suffer, that is, are moved sometimes in an agreeable, and sometimes in a disagreeable manner. These effects are necessary; they result necessarily from causes, which act only according to their properties. These effects necessarily please, or displease me, by a consequence of my own nature. This same nature compels me to avoid, avert, and resist some things, and to seek, desire, and procure others. In a world, where every thing is necessary, a God, who remedies nothing, who leaves things to run in their necessary course,—is he any thing but destiny, or necessity personified? It is a deaf and useless God, who can effect no change in general laws, to which he is himself subject. Of what importance to me is the infinite power of a being, who will do very little in my favour? Where is the infinite goodness of a being, indifferent to my happiness? Of what service to me is the favour of a being, who, being able to do me an infinite good, does not do me even a finite one?

VOLTAIRE

FRANCOIS MARIE AROUET (1694-1778), who chose the name Voltaire, was perhaps even less a philosopher than the other *philosophes*. But what does that matter? He was a genius so dazzling that almost anything he said on any topic, including philosophical topics, was certain to be interesting. If what he said was not new at least it would be witty; and if superficial, at least it would stick in the mind of the reader longer than deeper stuff. And much of it has indeed stuck in the European mind; for every man who knows Leibniz's careful metaphysical argument that this must be (in spite of appearances) the best of of all possible worlds, a thousand know Voltaire's "refutation" of it, which does not come even near dealing with the intricate metaphysics of possibility and actuality on which Leibniz based his conclusion. As satirist, playwright, poet, historian, conversationalist, popularizer of science (of Newton and Locke), propagandist, and crusader against injustice, he was surpassed by no one in his time; and in the whole combination of his diverse literary gifts he is probably unique in history.

In 1765 he published his *Philosophical Dictionary*, which in some respects is reminiscent of Bayle's *Dictionary*. From 1765 to 1774 new material was added in four editions. We have chosen articles constructive in purpose, which argue for toleration and, against d'Holbach, for deism instead of atheism.

The text is drawn from the translation of the *Dictionary* by Abner Kneeland (Boston: J. P. Mendum, 1836); I have made a good many minor changes in it.

Philosophical Dictionary

A. Atheism and Deism[1]

The great, the interesting object, as it appears to me, is not to argue metaphysically but to consider whether, for the common good of us miserable and thinking animals, we should admit a rewarding, an avenging God, at once our restraint and consolation, or should reject this idea and so abandon ourselves to calamity without hope, and crime without remorse. . . . From Job down to us, a great many men have cursed their existence; we have, therefore, perpetual need of consolation and hope. Of these your [i.e., Holbach's] philosophy deprives us. The fable of Pandora was better; it left us hope—which you snatch from us. Philosophy, you say, furnishes no proof of happiness to come. No—but you have no demonstration of the contrary. There may be in us an indestructible monad which feels and thinks, without our knowing anything at all of how that monad is made. Reason is not absolutely opposed to this idea, though reason alone does not prove it. Has not this opinion a prodigious advantage over yours? Mine is useful to mankind, yours is baneful; say of it what you will, it may encourage a Nero, an Alexander VI, or a Cartouche; mine may restrain them. . . . In the state of doubt in which we both are, I do not say to you with Pascal, "choose the safest." There is no safety in uncertainty. We are here not to talk, but to examine; we must judge, and our judgment is not determined by our will. I do not propose to you to believe extravagant things, in order to escape embarrassment. I do not say to you, Go to Mecca and instruct yourself by kissing the black stone, take hold of a cow's tail, muffle yourself in a scapulary, or be imbecile and fanatical to acquire the favor of the Being of Beings. I say to you, Continue to cultivate virtue, to be beneficent, to regard all superstition with horror, or with pity; but adore, with me, the design which is manifested in all Nature, and

---

1. From the articles "God," "Atheism," "Deism" and "Deist."

consequently the Author of that design—the primordial and final Cause of all; hope with me that our monad, which reasons on the great Eternal Being may be happy through that Great Being. You can no more demonstrate its impossibility than I can demonstrate mathematically that it is so. In metaphysics we scarcely reason on anything but probabilities; we are all swimming in a sea of which we have never seen the shore. Woe be to those who fight while they swim! Land who can; but he who cries out to me, "you swim in vain, there is no land"—he disheartens me, and deprives me of all my strength.— What is the object of our dispute? To console our unhappy existence. Who consoles it—You, or I?

A word on the question in morals, agitated by Bayle: Whether a society of atheists can subsist? Here let us observe first the enormous self-contradictions of men in disputation. Those who have been most violent in opposing the opinion of Bayle, those who have denied with the greatest virulence the possibility of a society of atheists, are the very men who have since maintained with equal ardor that atheism is the religion of the Chinese government.

They have most assuredly been mistaken about the government of China; they had only to read the edicts of the Emperors of that vast land, and they would have seen that those edicts are sermons in which a Supreme Being, governing, avenging, and rewarding, is continually spoken of.

But at the same time they are no less deceived respecting the impossibility of a society of atheists; nor can I conceive how Bayle could forget a striking instance which might have rendered his cause victorious. For in what does the apparent impossibility of a society of atheists consist? In this: it is judged that men without some restraint could not live together; that laws have no power against secret crimes; and that it is necessary to have an avenging God, punishing in this world or the next, such crimes as escape human justice. . . . But among the Gentiles, various sects had no [such] restraint: the Skeptics doubted of everything; the Academics suspended their judgment on everything; the Epicureans were persuaded that the Divinity could not meddle in human affairs, and in their hearts they admitted no divinity. They were convinced that the soul is not a substance, but a faculty which is born and perishes with the body; consequently they had no restraint but that of morality and honor. The Roman senators and knights were in reality atheists; for to men who neither feared nor hoped anything from them, the gods could not exist. The Roman senate, then, in the time of Caesar and Cicero, was in fact an assembly of atheists. . . .

It appears, then, that Bayle should rather have examined whether atheism or fanaticism is the more dangerous to society. Fanaticism is certainly a thousand times the more to be dreaded; for atheism inspires no sanguinary passion but fanaticism does; atheism does not oppose crime but fanaticism prompts to its commission. . . . The massacres of St. Bartholomew were committed by fanatics; Hobbes passed for an atheist, yet he led a life of innocence and quiet while the fanatics of his time deluged England, Scotland, and Ireland with blood. Spinoza was not only an atheist, he taught atheism; but assuredly he had no part in the juridical assassination of Barneveldt, nor was it he who tore in pieces the brothers De Witt and ate them off the gridiron.

Atheists are for the most part men of learning, bold but bewildered, who reason ill, and, unable to comprehend the creation, the origin of evil, and other difficulties, have recourse to the hypothesis of the eternity of things and of necessity. The ambitious and voluptuous have but little time to reason. They have other occupations than that of comparing Lucretius with Socrates. Such is the case with us and our time. . . . [But] I should not wish to come in the way of an atheistical prince, whose interest it should be to have me pounded in a mortar —I am quite sure I should be so pounded. And were I a sovereign, I would not have to do with atheistical courtiers, whose interest it was to poison me: I should be under the necessity of taking an antidote every day. It is, then, absolutely necessary for princes and people that the idea of a Supreme Being, creating, governing, rewarding and punishing, be profoundly graven on their minds.

. . . If there be atheists, who are to blame?—Who but the mercenary tyrants of our souls, who, while disgusting us with their knavery, urge some weak spirits to deny the Gods whom such monsters dishonor. . . . Men who have fattened on our substance cry out to us: Be persuaded that an ass spoke; believe that a fish swallowed a man and threw him up after three days, safe and sound, on the shore; doubt not that the God of the universe ordered one Jewish prophet to eat excrement and another to buy two prostitutes and have bastards by them—such are the words put into the mouth of the God of purity and truth. Believe a hundred things either visibly abominable or mathematically impossible, otherwise the God of Mercy will burn you in hell-fire not only for millions of years but for all eternity—whether you have or have not a body.

These brutal absurdities are revolting to rash and weak minds as well as to firm and wise ones. They say: Our teachers represent God to us as the most insensate and barbarous of all beings, therefore there is no God. But they ought to say: Our teachers represent God as furious and ridiculous, therefore God is the reverse of what they describe Him to be; He is as wise and good as they say He is foolish and wicked.

The deist is a man firmly persuaded of the existence of a Supreme Being equally good and powerful, who has formed all extended, sentient, and reflective existences; who perpetuates their species, who punishes crimes without cruelty, and rewards virtue with kindness.

Many persons ask whether deism, considered abstractly and without any religious ceremony, is in fact a religion? The answer is easy: he who recognizes only a creating God, he who views in God only a being infinitely powerful, and who sees in his creatures only wonderful machines, is not religious towards him any more than an European, admiring the King of China, would profess allegiance to that prince. But he who thinks that God has deigned to place a relation between Himself and mankind; that He has made them free, capable of good and evil; that He has given all of them that good sense which is the instinct of man and on which the law of nature is founded—such a one undoubtedly has a religion, and a much better religion than all those sects which are beyond the pale of our church; for all those sects are false, and the law of nature true. Thus deism is good sense not yet instructed by revelation; and other religions are good sense perverted by superstition. All sects differ, because they come from men; morality is everywhere the same, because it comes from God.

B. Toleration[2]

If it were allowed to reason logically in matters of religion, it is clear we ought all to become Jews, since Jesus Christ our Savior was born a Jew, lived a Jew, and died a Jew and since he expressly said that he accomplished and fulfilled the Jewish religion. But it is still more clear that we ought mutually to tolerate one another, because we are all weak, irrational, and subject to change and error. A reed prostrated by the wind in the mire—ought it to say to a neighboring reed fallen in a different direction: Creep after my fashion, wretch! or I will present a request for you to be seized and burned? . . .

I would say to my brother the Turk: Let us eat together a good hen with rice, invoking Allah; your religion seems to me to be very

---

2. From the article, "Toleration."

respectable, you adore but one God; you are obliged to give the fortieth part of your revenue everyday in alms, and to be reconciled with your enemies on the day of the bairam. Our bigots, who calumniate the world, have said a hundred times that your religion succeeded only because it was wholly sensual. They have lied, poor fellows. Your religion is very austere; it commands prayer five times a day; it imposes the most rigorous fast; it denies you the wine and liquors which our spiritual directors encourage; and if it permits only four wives ... it condemns by this restriction Jewish incontinence, which allowed eighteen wives to the homicide David and seven hundred to Solomon, the assassin of his brother (without reckoning concubines).

I will say to my brother the Chinese: Let us sup together without ceremony, for I dislike grimaces; but I like your law, the wisest of all and perhaps the most ancient. I will say nearly as much to my brother the Indian.

But what shall I say to my brother the Jew? Shall I invite him to supper? Yes, on the condition that during the repast Baalam's ass does not take it into his head to bray; that Ezekiel does not mix his dinner with our supper; that a fish does not swallow one of the guests and keep him three days in his belly; that a serpent does not join in the conversation in order to seduce my wife; that a prophet does not think it proper to sleep with her, as the worthy man Hosea did for five francs and a bushel of barley; above all, that no Jew parades through my house to the sound of the trumpet, causes the walls to fall down, and cuts the throats of myself, my father, my mother, my wife, my children, my cat and my dog according to the ancient practice of the Jews.

Come, my friends, let us have peace and say our grace.

LEIBNIZ

GOTTFRIED WILHELM LEIBNIZ, the universal genius of his age, was born in Leipzig in 1646 and after a busy life devoted to philosophy, mathematics, physics, theology, politics, diplomacy, and travel, died in Hannover in 1716. The full richness of his work has not even yet been measured, since his vast literary remains have not been fully published. He invented the calculus and published his results before Newton did; it is now recognized that Newton made the discovery first, but that Leibniz's discovery was independent of Newton's.

Most of his philosophical work is to be found in his correspondence; he published only one philosophical book during his life, *Theodicy* (which was the object of Voltaire's ridicule in *Candide*). We have chosen three selections from his posthumous works: (A) The *Monadology,* perhaps his best known work, first published in 1720; (B) Part of the *New Essays Concerning Human Understanding*, which Leibniz wrote in criticism of Locke's *Essay* but withheld from publication when Locke died in 1704. It was first published in 1768; and (C) Part of his *Correspondence with Samuel Clarke*, which contains his criticism of Newton, for whom Clarke was the spokesman. This was first published in 1717.

Leibniz, though in his own eyes an opponent of Descartes and Spinoza, is generally named by historians of philosophy as the last of the triumvirate of Continental Rationalists, after these two. While in his epistemology he does belong to the rationalistic tradition with its emphasis on reason as contrasted with experience, the issues that divide him from Spinoza and Descartes in metaphysics are so important and fundamental that we do him an injustice if we call him just a rationalist. His anticipations of later developments in symbolic logic, his pluralistic spiritualism, and his "two-world theory" (as expounded towards the end of the *Monadology*) which influenced some of

Kant's views, were historically as important as his rationalism. His clear distinction between two kinds of truths (Monadology, 33), in which he anticipated Hume's distinction between relations of ideas and matters of fact (cf. p. 198) has an importance in the history of epistemology that cannot be overestimated.

The Monadology[1]

1. The Monad, of which we will speak here, is nothing else than a simple substance, which goes to make up composites; by simple, we mean without parts.

2. There must be simple substances because there are composites; for a composite is nothing else than a collection or *aggregatum* of simple substances.

3. Now, where there are no constituent parts there is possible neither extension, nor form, nor divisibility. These Monads are the true Atoms of nature, and, in fact, the Elements of things.

4. Their dissolution, therefore, is not to be feared and there is no way conceivable by which a simple substance can perish through natural means.

5. For the same reason there is no way conceivable by which a simple substance might, through natural means, come into existence, since it can not be formed by composition.

6. We may say then, that the existence of Monads can begin or end only all at once, that is to say, the Monad can begin only through creation and end only through annihilation. Composites, however, begin or end gradually.

7. There is also no way of explaining how a Monad can be altered or changed in its inner being by any other created thing, since there is no possibility of transposition within it, nor can we conceive of any internal movement which can be produced, directed, increased or diminished there within the substance, such as can take place in the case of composites where a change can occur among the parts. The Monads have no windows through which anything may come in or go out. The Attributes are not liable to detach themselves and make an excursion outside the substance, as could *sensible species* of the Schoolmen. In the same way neither substance nor attribute can enter from without into a Monad.

---

1. From Leibniz, *Discourse on Metaphysics,* trans. G. R. Montgomery (La Salle, Illinois: Open Court Publishing Co., 1927). Reprinted by permission.

8. Still Monads must needs have some qualities, otherwise they would not even be existences. And if simple substances did not differ at all in their qualities, there would be no means of perceiving any change in things. Whatever is in a composite can come into it only through its simple elements and the Monads, if they were without qualities, since they do not differ at all in quantity, would be indistinguishable one from another. For instance, if we imagine *a plenum* or completely filled space, where each part receives only the equivalent of its own previous motion, one state of things would not be distinguishable from another.

9. Each Monad, indeed, must be different from every other. For there are never in nature two beings which are exactly alike, and in which it is not possible to find a difference either internal or based on an intrinsic property.

10. I assume it as admitted that every created being, and consequently the created Monad, is subject to change, and indeed that this change is continuous in each.

11. It follows from what has just been said, that the natural changes of the Monad come from an internal principle, because an external cause can have no influence upon its inner being.

12. Now besides this principle of change there must also be in the Monad a manifoldness which changes. This manifoldness constitutes, so to speak, the specific nature and the variety of the simple substances.

13. This manifoldness must involve a multiplicity in the unity or in that which is simple. For since every natural change takes place by degrees, there must be something which changes and something which remains unchanged, and consequently there must be in the simple substance a plurality of conditions and relations, even though it has no parts.

14. The passing condition which involves and represents a multiplicity in the unity, or in the simple substance, is nothing else than what is called Perception. This should be carefully distinguished from Apperception or Consciousness, as will appear in what follows. In this matter the Cartesians have fallen into a serious error, in that they treat as nonexistent those perceptions of which we are not conscious. It is this also which has led them to believe that spirits alone are Monads and that there are no souls of animals or other Entelechies, and it has led them to make the common confusion between a protracted period of unconsciousness and actual death. They have thus adopted the Scholastic error that souls can exist entirely separated from bodies, and have even confirmed ill-balanced minds in the belief that souls are mortal.

15. The action of the internal principle which brings about the change or the passing from one perception to another may be called Appetition. It is true that the desire *(l'appetit)* is not always able to attain to the whole of the perception which it strives for, but it always attains a portion of it and reaches new perceptions.

16. We, ourselves, experience a multiplicity in a simple substance, when we find that the most trifling thought of which we are conscious involves a variety in the object. Therefore all those who acknowledge that the soul is a simple substance ought to grant this multiplicity in the Monad, and Monsieur Bayle should have found no difficulty in it, as he has done in his *Dictionary* article, "Rorarius."

17. It must be confessed, however, that Perception, and that which depends upon it, are inexplicable by mechanical causes, that is to say, by figures and motions. Supposing that there were a machine whose structure produced thought, sensation, and perception, we could conceive of it as increased in size with the same proportions until one was able to enter into its interior, as he would into a mill. Now, on going into it he would find only pieces working upon one another, but never would he find anything to explain Perception. It is accordingly in the simple substance, and not in the composite nor in a machine that the Perception is to be sought. Furthermore, there is nothing besides perceptions and their changes to be found in the simple substance. And it is in these alone that all the internal activities of the simple substance can consist.

18. All simple substances or created Monads may be called Entelechies, because they have in themselves a certain perfection (ἔχουσι τὸ ἐντελές). There is in them a sufficiency (αὐτάρκεια) which makes them the source of their internal activities, and renders them, so to speak, incorporeal Automatons.

19. If we wish to designate as soul everything which has perceptions and desires in the general sense that I have just explained, all simple substances or created Monads could be called souls. But since feeling is something more than a mere perception I think that the general name of Monad or Entelechy should suffice for simple substances which have only perception, while we may reserve the term Soul for those whose perception is more distinct and is accompanied by memory.

20. We experience in ourselves a state where we remember nothing and where we have no distinct perception, as in periods of fainting, or when we are overcome by a profound, dreamless sleep. In such a state the soul does not sensibly differ at all from a simple Monad. As this state, however, is not permanent and the soul can recover from it, the soul is something more.

21. Nevertheless it does not follow at all that the simple substance is in such a state without perception. This is so because of the reasons given above; for it cannot perish, nor on the other hand would it exist without some affection and the affection is nothing else than its perception. When, however, there are a great number of weak perceptions where nothing stands out distinctively, we are stunned; as when one turns around and around in the same direction, a dizziness comes on, which makes him swoon and makes him able to distinguish nothing. Among animals, death can occasion this state for quite a period.

22. Every present state of a simple substance is a natural consequence of its preceding state, in such a way that its present is big with its future.

23. Therefore, since on awakening after a period of unconsciousness we become conscious of our perceptions, we must, without having been conscious of them, have had perceptions immediately before; for one perception can come in a natural way only from another perception, just as a motion can come in a natural way only from a motion.

24. It is evident from this that if we were to have nothing distinctive, or so to speak prominent, and of a higher flavor in our perceptions, we should be in a continual state of stupor. This is the condition of Monads which are wholly bare.

25. We see that nature has given to animals heightened perceptions, having provided them with organs which collect numerous rays of light or numerous waves of air and thus make them more effective in their combination. Something similar to this takes place in the case of smell, in that of taste and of touch, and perhaps in many other senses which are unknown to us. I shall have occasion very soon to explain how that which occurs in the soul represents that which goes on in the sense-organs.

26. The memory furnishes a sort of consecutiveness which imitates reason but is to be distinguished from it. We see that animals when they have the perception of something which they notice and of which they have had a similar previous perception, are led by the representation of their memory to expect that which was associated in the preceding perception, and they come to have feelings like those which they had before. For instance, if a stick be shown to a dog, he remembers the pain which it has caused him and he whines or runs away.

27. The vividness of the picture, which comes to him or moves him, is derived either from the magnitude or from the number of the previous perceptions. For, oftentimes, a strong impression brings about, all at once, the same effect as a long-continued habit or as a great many re-iterated, moderate perceptions.

28. Men act in like manner as animals, in so far as the sequence of their perceptions is determined only by the law of memory, resembling the *empirical physicians* who practice simply, without any theory, and we are empiricists in three-fourths of our actions. For instance, when we expect that there will be day-light to-morrow, we do so empirically, because it has always happened so up to the present time. It is only the astronomer who uses his reason in making such an affirmation.

29. But the knowledge of eternal and necessary truths is that which distinguishes us from mere animals and gives us reason and the sciences, thus raising us to a knowledge of ourselves and of God. This is what is called in us the Rational Soul or the Mind.

30. It is also through the knowledge of necessary truths and through abstractions from them that we come to perform Reflective Acts, which cause us to think of what is called the I, and to decide that this or that is within us. It is thus, that in thinking upon ourselves we think of *being*, of *substance*, of the *simple* and *composite*, of a *material* thing and of *God* himself, conceiving that what is limited in us is in him without limits. These Reflective Acts furnish the principal objects of our reasonings.

31. Our reasoning is based upon two great principles: first, that of Contradiction, by means of which we decide that to be false which involves contradiction and that to be true which contradicts or is opposed to the false.

32. And second, the principle of Sufficient Reason, in virtue of which we believe that no fact can be real or existing and no statement true unless it has a sufficient reason why it should be thus and not otherwise. Most frequently, however, these reasons cannot be known by us.

33. There are also two kinds of Truths: those of Reasoning and those of Fact. The Truths of Reasoning are necessary, and their opposite is impossible. Those of Fact, however, are contingent, and their opposite is possible. When a truth is necessary, the reason can be found by analysis in resolving it into simpler ideas and into simpler truths until we reach those which are primary.

34. It is thus that with mathematicians the Speculative Theorems and the practical Canons are reduced by analysis to Definitions, Axioms, and Postulates.

35. There are finally simple ideas of which no definition can be given. There are also the Axioms and Postulates or, in a word, the primary principles which cannot be proved and, indeed, have no need of proof. These are identical propositions whose opposites involve express contradictions.

36. But there must be also a sufficient reason for contingent truths or truths of fact; that is to say, for the sequence of the things which extend throughout the universe of created beings, where the analysis into more particular reasons can be continued into greater detail without limit because of the immense variety of the things in nature and because of the infinite division of bodies. There is an infinity of figures and of movements, present and past, which enter into the efficient cause of my present writing, and in its final cause there are an infinity of slight tendencies and dispositions of my soul, present and past.

37. And as all this detail again involves other and more detailed contingencies, each of which again has need of a similar analysis in order to find its explanation, no real advance has been made. Therefore, the sufficient or ultimate reason must needs be outside of the sequence or series of these details of contingencies, however infinite they may be.

38. It is thus that the ultimate reason for things must be a necessary substance, in which the detail of the changes shall be present merely potentially, as in the fountain-head, and this substance we call God.

39. Now, since this substance is a sufficient reason for all the above mentioned details, which are linked together throughout, *there is but one God, and this God is sufficient*.

40. We may hold that the supreme substance, which is unique, universal and necessary with nothing independent outside of it, which is further a pure consequence of possible being, must be incapable of limitation and must contain as much reality as possible.

41. Whence it follows that God is absolutely perfect, perfection being understood as the magnitude of positive reality in the strict sense, when the limitations or the bounds of those things which have them are removed. There where there are no limits, that is to say, in God, perfection is absolutely infinite.

42. It follows also that created things derive their perfections through the influence of God, but their imperfections come from their own natures, which cannot exist without limits. It is in this latter that they are distinguished from God. An example of this original imperfection of created things is to be found in the natural inertia of bodies.

43. It is true, furthermore, that in God is found not only the source of existences, but also that of essences, in so far as they are real. In other words, he is the source of whatever there is real in the possible. This is because the Understanding of God is in the region of eternal truths or of the ideas upon which they depend, and because without him there would be nothing real in the possibilities of things,

and not only would nothing be existent, nothing would be even possible.

44. For it must needs be that if there is a reality in essences or in possibilities or indeed in the eternal truths, this reality is based upon something existent and actual, and, consequently, in the existence of the necessary Being in whom essence includes existence or in whom possibility is sufficient to produce actuality.

45. Therefore God alone (or the Necessary Being) has this prerogative that if he be possible he must necessarily exist, and, as nothing is able to prevent the possibility of that which involves no bounds, no negation, and consequently, no contradiction, this alone is sufficient to establish *a priori* his existence. We have, therefore, proved his existence through the reality of eternal truths. But a little while ago [36-39] we also proved it *a posteriori,* because contingent beings exist which can have their ultimate and sufficient reason only in the necessary being which, in turn, has the reason for existence in itself.

46. Yet we must not think that the eternal truths being dependent upon God are therefore arbitrary and depend upon his will, as Descartes seems to have held, and after him M. Poiret.[2] This is the case only with contingent truths which depend upon fitness or the choice of the greatest good; necessarily truths on the other hand depend solely upon his understanding and are the inner objects of it.

47. God alone is the ultimate unity or the original simple substance, of which all created or derivative monads are the products, and arise, so to speak, through the continual outflashings (fulgurations[3]) of the divinity from moment to moment, limited by the receptivity of the creature to whom limitation is an essential.

48. In God are present: power, which is the source of everything; knowledge, which contains the details of the ideas; and, finally, will, which changes or produces things in accordance with the principle of the greatest good. To these correspond, in the created monad, the subject or basis, the faculty of perception, and the faculty of appetition. In God these attributes are absolutely infinite or perfect, while in the created monads or in the entelechies *(perfectihabies,* as Hermolaus Barbarus translates this word[4]), they are imitations approaching him in proportion to the perfection.

2. Pierre Poiret (1646-1719), a Calvinist who attempted to reconcile Cartesian and Calvinist teachings. L.W.B.

3. A Stoic and mystical term referring to the creation of the world by emanation from the fire which represented the Godhead, L.W.B.

4. That is, a translation of the Aristotelian term *entelechy;* Barbarus (1454-1493) wished to make known Aristotle's "true teaching" in opposition to the scholastic interpretation of Aristotle. L.W.B.

49. A created thing is said to act outwardly in so far as it has perfection, and to be acted upon by another in so far as it is imperfect. Thus action is attributed to the monad in so far as it has distinct perceptions, and passion or passivity is attributed in so far as it has confused perceptions.

50. One created thing is more perfect than another when we find in the first that which gives an *a priori* reason for what occurs in the second. This why we say that one acts upon the other.

51. In the case of simple substances, the influence which one monad has upon another is only ideal. It can have its effect only through the mediation of God, in so far as in the ideas of God each monad can rightly demand that God, in regulating the others from the beginning of things,.should have regarded it also. For since one created monad cannot have a physical influence upon the inner being of another, it is only through the primal regulation that one can have dependence upon another.

52. It is thus that among created things action and passivity are reciprocal. For God, in comparing two simple substances, finds in each one reasons obliging him to adapt the other to it; and consequently what is active in certain respects is passive from another point of view, active in so far as what we distinctly know in it serves to give a reason for what occurs in another, and passive in so far as the reason for what occurs in it is found in what is distinctly known in another.

53. Now as there are an infinity of possible universes in the ideas of God, and but one of them can exist, there must be a sufficient reason for the choice of God which determines him to select one rather than another.

54. And this reason is to be found only in the fitness or in the degree of perfection which these worlds possess, each possible thing having the right to claim existence in proportion to the perfection which it involves.

55. This is the cause for the existence of the greatest good; namely, that the wisdom of God permits him to know it, his goodness causes him to choose it, and his power enables him to produce it.

56. Now this interconnection, relationship, or this adaptation of all things to each particular one, and of each one to all the rest, brings it about that every simple substance has relations which express all the others and that it is consequently a perpetual living mirror of the universe.

57. And as the same city regarded from different sides appears entirely different, and is, as it were multiplied respectively, so, because

of the infinite number of simple substances, there are a similar infinite number of universes which are, nevertheless, only the aspects of a single one as seen from the special point of view of each monad.

58. Through this means has been obtained the greatest possible variety, together with the greatest order that may be; that is to say, through this means has been obtained the greatest possible perfection.

59. This hypothesis, moreover, which I venture to call demonstrated, is the only one which fittingly gives proper prominence to the greatness of God. M. Bayle recognizes this when in his dictionary (article "Rorarius") he raised objections to it; indeed, he was inclined to believe that I attributed too much to God, and more than it is possible to attribute to him: But he was unable to bring forward any reason why this universal harmony which causes every substance to express exactly all others through the relation which it has with them is impossible.

60. Besides, in what has just been said can be seen the *a priori* reasons why things cannot be otherwise than they are. It is because God, in ordering the whole, has had regard to every part and in particular to each monad; and since the monad is by its very nature *representative,* nothing can limit it to represent merely a part of things. It is nevertheless true that this representation is, as regards the details of the whole universe, only a confused representation, and is distinct only as regards a small part of them, that is to say, as regards those things which are nearest or greatest in relation to each monad. If the representation were distinct as to the details of the entire universe, each monad would be a Deity. It is not in the object represented that the monads are limited, but in the modifications of their knowledge of the object. In a confused way they reach out to infinity or to the whole, but are limited and differentiated in the degree of their distinct perceptions.

61. In this respect composites are like simple substances, for all space is filled up; therefore, all matter is connected. And in a plenum or filled space every movement has an effect upon bodies in proportion to this distance, so that not only is every body affected by those which are in contact with it and responds in some way to whatever happens to them, but also by means of them the body responds to those bodies adjoining them, and their intercommunication reaches to any distance whatsoever. Consequently every body responds to all that happens in the universe, so that he who saw all could read in each one what is happening everywhere, and even what has happened and what will happen. He can discover in the present what is distant both as regards

space and as regards time; σύμπνοια πάντα,[5] as Hippocrates said. A soul can, however, read in itself only what is there represented distinctly. It cannot all at once open up all its folds, because they extend to infinity.

62. Thus although each created monad represents the whole universe, it represents more distinctly the body which specially pertains to it and of which it constitutes the entelechy. And as this body expresses all the universe through the interconnection of all matter in the plenum, the soul also represents the whole universe in representing this body, which belongs to it in a particular way.

63. The body belonging to a monad, which is its entelechy or soul, constitutes together with the entelechy what may be called a *living being,* and with a soul what is called an *animal.* Now this body of a living being or of an animal is always organic, because every monad is a mirror of the universe is regulated with perfect order there must needs be order also in what represents it, that is to say in the perceptions of the soul and consequently in the body through which the universe is represented in the soul.

64. Therefore every organic body of a living being is a kind of divine machine or natural automaton, infinitely surpassing all artificial automatons. Because a machine constructed by man's skill is not a machine in each of its parts; for instance, the teeth of a brass wheel have parts or bits which to us are not artificial products and contain nothing in themselves to show the use to which the wheel was destined in the machine. The machines of nature, however, that is to say, living bodies, are still machines in their smallest parts *ad infinitum.* Such is the difference between nature and art, that is to say, between divine art and ours.

65. The author of nature has been able to employ this divine and infinitely marvelous artifice, because each portion of matter is not only, as the ancients recognized, infinitely divisible, but also because it is really divided without end, every part into other parts, each one of which has its own proper motion. Otherwise it would be impossible for each portion of matter to express all the universe.

66. Whence we see that there is a world of created things, of living beings, of animals, of entelechies, of souls, in the minutest particle of matter.

67. Every portion of matter may be conceived as like a garden full of plants and like a pond full of fish. But every branch of a plant, every

---

5. "All things conspire" is what Leibniz means. [Montgomery]

member of an animal, and every drop of the fluids within it, is also
such a garden or such a pond.

68. And although the ground and air which lies between the plants
of the garden, and the water which is between the fish in the pond,
are not themselves plants or fish, yet they nevertheless contain these,
usually so small however as to be imperceptible to us.

69. There is, therefore, nothing uncultivated, or sterile or dead in
the universe, no chaos, no confusion, save in appearance; somewhat
as a pond would appear at a distance when we could see in it a confused movement, and so to speak, a swarming of the fish, without
however discerning the fish themselves.

70. It is evident, then, that every living body has a dominating
entelechy, which in animals is the soul. The parts, however, of this
living body are full of other living beings, plants and animals, which
in turn have each one its entelechy or dominating soul.

71. This does not mean, as some who have misunderstood my
thought have imagined, that each soul has a quantity or portion of
matter appropriated to it or attached to itself for ever, and that it
consequently owns other inferior living beings destined to serve it
always; because all bodies are in a state of perpetual flux like rivers,
and the parts are continually entering in or passing out.

72. The soul, therefore, changes its body only gradually and by
degrees, so that it is never deprived all at once of all its organs. There
is frequently a metamorphosis in animals, but never metempsychosis
or a transmigration of souls. Neither are there souls wholly separate
from bodies, nor bodiless spirits. God alone is without body.

73. This is also why there is never absolute generation or perfect
death in the strict sense, consisting in the separation of the soul from
the body. What we call generation is development and growth, and
what we call death is envelopment and diminution.

74. Philosophers have been much perplexed in accounting for the
origin of forms, entelechies, or souls. Today, however, when it has
been learned through careful investigations made in plant, insect and
animal life, that the organic bodies of nature are never the product
of chaos or putrefaction, but always come from seeds in which there
was without doubt some preformation, it has been decided that not
only is the organic body already present before conception, but also
a soul in this body, in a word, the animal itself; and it has been
decided that, by means of conception the animal is merely made ready
for a great transformation, so as to become an animal of another sort.
We can see cases somewhat similar outside of generation when grubs
become flies and caterpillars butterflies.

75. These little animals, some of which by conception become large animals, may be called spermatic. Those among them which remain in their species, that is to say, the greater part, are born, multiply, and are destroyed, like the larger animals. There are only a few chosen ones which come out upon a greater stage.

76. This, however, is only half the truth. I believe, therefore, that if the animal never actually commences by natural means, no more does it by natural means come to an end. Not only is there no generation, but also there is no entire destruction or absolute death. These reasonings, carried on a *posteriori* and drawn from experience, accord perfectly with the principles which I have above deduced *a priori*.

77. Therefore we may say that not only the soul (the mirror of the indestructible universe) is indestructible, but also the animal itself is, although its mechanism is frequently destroyed in parts and although it puts off and takes on organic coatings.

78. These principles have furnished me the means of explaining on natural grounds the union, or rather the conformity between the soul and the organic body. The soul follows its own laws, and the body likewise follows its own laws. They are fitted to each other in virtue of the preestablished harmony between all substances, since they are all representations of one and the same universe.

79. Souls act in accordance with the laws of final causes through their desires, ends and means. Bodies act in accordance with the laws of efficient causes or of motion. The two realms, that of efficient causes and that of final causes, are in harmony, each with the other.

80. Decartes saw that souls cannot at all impart force to bodies, because there is always the same quantity of force in matter. Yet he thought that the soul could change the direction of bodies. This was, however, because at that time the law of nature which affirms also that conservation of the same total direction in the motion of matter was not known. If he had known that law, he would have fallen upon my system of preestablished harmony.

81. According to this system bodies act as if (to suppose the impossible) there were no souls at all, and souls act as if there were no bodies, and yet both body and soul act as if the one were influencing the other.

82. Although I find that essentially the same thing is true of all living things and animals, which we have just said (namely, that animals and souls begin from the very commencement of the world and that they no more come to an end than does the world) nevertheless, rational animals have this peculiarity, that their little spermatic animals, as long as they remain such, have only ordinary or sensuous

souls, but those of them which are, so to speak, elected, attain by actual conception to human nature, and their sensuous souls are raised to the rank of reason and to the prerogative of spirits.

83. Among the differences that there are between ordinary souls and spirits, some of which I have already instanced, there is also this, that while souls in general are living mirrors or images of the universe of created things, spirits are also images of the Deity himself or of the author of nature. They are capable of knowing the system of the universe, and of imitating some features of it by means of artificial models, each spirit being like a small divinity in its own sphere.

84. Therefore, spirits are able to enter into a sort of social relationship with God, and with respect to them he is not only what an inventor is to his machine (as in his relation to the other created things), but he is also what a prince is to his subjects, and even what a father is to his children.

85. Whence it is easy to conclude that the totality of all spirits must compose the city of God, that is to say, the most perfect state that is possible under the most perfect monarch.

86. This city of God, this truly universal monarchy, is a moral world within the natural world. It is what is noblest and most divine among the works of God. And in it consists in reality the glory of God, because he would have no glory were not his greatness and goodness known and wondered at by spirits. It is also in relation to this divine city that God properly has goodness. His wisdom and his power are shown everywhere.

87. As we established above that there is a perfect harmony between the two natural realms of efficient and final causes, it will be in place here to point out another harmony which appears between the physical realm of nature and the moral realm of grace, that is to say, between God considered as the architect of the mechanism of the world and God considered as the monarch of the divine city of spirits.

88. This harmony brings it about that things progress of themselves toward grace along natural lines, and that this earth, for example, must be destroyed and restored by natural means at those times when the proper government of spirits demands it, for chastisement in the one case and for a reward in the other.

89. We can say also that God, the Architect, satisfies in all respects God the Law-Giver, that therefore sins will bring their own penalty with them through the order of nature, and because of the very structure of things, mechanical though it is. And in the same way the good actions will attain their rewards in mechanical way through their

relation to bodies, although this cannot and ought not always to take place without delay.

90. Finally, under this perfect government, there will be no good action unrewarded and no evil action unpunished; everything must turn out for the well-being of the good; that is to say, of those who are not disaffected in this great state, who, after having done their duty, trust in Providence and who love and imitate, as is meet, the Author of all Good, delighting in the contemplation of his perfections according to the nature of that genuine, pure love which finds pleasure in the happiness of those who are loved. It is for this reason that wise and virtuous persons work in behalf of everything which seems conformable to presumptive or antecedent will of God, and are, nevertheless, content with what God actually brings to pass through his secret, consequent and determining will, recognizing that if we were able to understand sufficiently well the order of the universe, we should find that it surpasses all the desires of the wisest of us, and that it is impossible to render it better than it is, not only for all in general, but also for each one of us in particular, provided that we have the proper attachment for the author of all, not only as the Architect and the efficient cause of our being, but also as our Lord and the Final Cause, who ought to be the whole goal of our will, and who alone can make us happy.

New Essays Concerning Human Understanding

Criticism of Locke's Denial of Innate Ideas[6]

Philalethes. Having examined the question of innate ideas, let us consider their nature and their differences. Is it not true that the *idea* is the object of thought?

Theophilus. I admit it, provided you add that it is an immediate internal object, and that this object is an expression of the nature or the qualities of things. If the idea were the *form* of thought, it would spring up and cease with the actual thought to which it corresponds; but being the *object* it may exist previous to and after the thoughts. External sensible objects are only *mediate* because they cannot act immediately upon the soul. God alone is the *external immediate* object. We might say that the soul itself is its own immediate *internal* object; but it is this in so far as it contains ideas, or what corresponds to things. For the soul is a little world, in which distinct ideas are a representation of God, and in which confused ideas are a representation of the universe.

Ph. We who suppose that at the beginning the soul is a *tabula rasa*, void of all characters and without an idea, ask how it comes to receive ideas, and by what means it acquires this prodigious quantity of them? To that question the reply in a word is: From experience.

Th. This *tabula rasa*, of which so much is said, is in my opinion only a fiction which nature does not admit, and which is based only upon the imperfect notions of philosophers, like the vacuum, atoms, and rest, absolute or relative, of two parts of a whole, or like the

---

6. From *New Essays Concerning Human Understanding*, Book II, Chapter i (which is Leibniz's criticism of the corresponding chapter in Locke's *Essay*, cf. above, p. 24). Theophilus represents Leibniz, Philalethes represents (and usually paraphrases) Locke. From A. G. Langley, trans., (La Salle, Illinois: The Open Court Publishing Company, 1949). Reprinted by permission.

primary matter which is conceived as without form. Uniform things and those which contain no variety are never anything but abstractions, like time, space, and the other entities of pure mathematics. There is no body whatever whose parts are at rest, and there is no substance whatever that has nothing by which to distinguish it from every other. Human souls differ, not only from other souls, but also among themselves, although the difference is not at all of the kind called specific. And, according to the proofs which I believe we have, every substantial thing, be it soul or body, has its own characteristic relation to every other; and the one must always differ from the other by *intrinsic connotations*. Not to mention the fact that those who speak so frequently of this *tabula rasa* after having taken away the ideas cannot say what remains, like the scholastic philosophers, who leave nothing in their primary matter. You may perhaps reply that this *tabula rasa* of the philosophers means that the soul has by nature and originally only bare faculties. But faculties without some act, in a word the pure powers of the school, are also only fictions, which nature knows not, and which are obtained only by the process of abstraction. For where in the world will you ever find a faculty which shuts itself up in the power alone without performing any act? There is always a particular disposition to action, and to one action rather than to another. And besides the disposition there is a tendency to action, of which tendencies there is always an infinity in each subject at once; and these tendencies are never without some effect. Experience is necessary, I admit, in order that the soul be determined to such or such thoughts, and in order that it take notice of the ideas which are in us; but by what means can experience and the senses give ideas? Has the soul windows, does it resemble tablets, is it like wax? It is plain that all who so regard the soul, represent it as at bottom corporeal. You oppose to me this axiom received by the philosophers, *that there is nothing in the soul which does not come from the senses.* But you must except the soul itself and its affections. *Nihil est in intellectu, quod non fuerit in sensu, excipe: nisi ipse intellectus.*[7] Now the soul comprises being, substance, unity, identity, cause, perception, reason, and many other notions which the senses cannot give. This view sufficiently agrees with your author of the Essay, who seeks the source of a good part of ideas in the spirit's reflection upon its own nature.

Ph. I hope, then, that you will agree with this skilful author that all ideas come through sensation or through reflection, that is to say,

---

7. "There is nothing in the intellect which was not first in the senses," to which Leibniz adds, "except the intellect itself."

from observations which we make either upon objects exterior and sensible or upon the inner workings of our soul.

Th. In order to avoid a discussion upon what has delayed us too long, I declare to you in advance, sir, that when you say that ideas come to us from one or the other of these causes, I understand the statement to mean their actual perception, for I think I have shown that they are in us before they are perceived so far as they have any distinct character.

Correspondence with Samuel Clarke

Criticism of Newton's Theory of Space[8]

3. These gentlemen [i.e., Newton and Clarke] maintain, that space is a real absolute being. But this involves them in great difficulties, for such a being must needs be eternal and infinite. Hence some have believed it to be God himself, or one of his attributes, his immensity. But since space consists of parts, it is not a thing which can belong to God.

4. As for my own opinion, I have said more than once that I hold space to be something merely relative, as time is; that I hold it to be an order of co-existences as time is an order of successions. For space denotes, in terms of possibility, an order of things which exist at the same time, considered as existing together, without inquiring into their particular manner of existing. And when many things are seen together, one perceives that order of things among themselves.

5. I have many demonstrations to confute the fancy of those who take space to be a substance or at least an absolute being. But I shall only use, at the present, one demonstration, which the author here gives me occasion to insist upon. I say, then, that if space was an absolute being, there would something happen for which it would be impossible there should be a sufficient reason. Which is against my axiom. And I can prove it thus. Space is something absolutely uniform, and, without the things placed in it, one point of space does not absolutely differ in any respect whatsoever from another point of space. Now from hence it follows (supposing space to be something in itself, besides the order of bodies among themselves) that 'tis impossible there should be a reason why God, preserving the same situations of bodies among themselves, should have placed them in space after one

---

8. From the third and fifth papers by Leibniz in the correspondence with Clarke. Reprinted from *Leibniz: Philosophical Papers and Letters*, Vol. II, trans. Leroy E. Loemker, by permission of the University of Chicago Press.

certain particular manner and not otherwise; why everything was not placed the quite contrary way, for instance, by changing east into west. But if space is nothing else but that order or relation, and is nothing at all without bodies but the possibility of placing them, then those two states, the one such as it now is, the other supposed to be the quite contrary way, would not at all differ from one another. Their difference therefore is only to be found in our chimerical supposition of the reality of space in itself. But in truth the one would exactly be the same thing as the other, they being absolutely indiscernible, and consequently there is no room to inquire after a reason of the preference of the one to the other.

6. The case is the same with respect to time. Supposing anyone should ask why God did not create everything a year sooner, and the same person should infer from thence that God has done something concerning which 'tis not possible there should be a reason why he did it so and not otherwise; the answer is that his inference would be right if time was anything distinct from things existing in time. For it would be impossible there should be any reason why things should be applied to such particular instants rather than to others, their succession continuing the same. But then the same argument proves that instants, considered without the things, are nothing at all and that they consist only in the successive order of things, which order remaining the same, one of the two states, viz., that of a supposed anticipation, would not at all differ, nor could be discerned from the other which now is.

47. I will here show how men come to form to themselves the notion of space. They consider that many things exist at once, and they observe in them a certain order of coexistence, according to which the relation of one thing to another is more or less simple. This order is their situation or distance. When it happens that one of those coexistent things changes its relation to a multitude of others which do not change their relations among themselves, and that another thing, newly come, acquires the same relation to the others as the former had, we then say it is come into the *place* of the former; and this change we call a *motion* in that body wherein is the immediate cause of the change. And though many, or even all, the coexistent things should change according to certain known rules of direction and swiftness, yet one may always determine the relation of situation which every coexistent acquires with respect to every other coexistent, and even that relation which any other coexistent would have to this, or which this would have to any other, if it had not changed or if it had changed any otherwise. And supposing or feigning

that among those coexistents there is a sufficient number of them which have undergone no change, then we may say that those which have such a relation to those fixed existents as others had to them before have now the same *place* which those others had. And that which comprehends all those places is called *space*. Which shows that in order to have an idea of place, and consequently of space, it is sufficient to consider these relations and the rules of their changes, without needing to fancy any absolute reality out of the things whose situation we consider; and to give a kind of definition, *place* is that which we say is the same to A and to B, when the relation of the coexistence of B, with C, E, F, G, etc., agrees perfectly with the relation of the coexistence which A had with the same C, E, F, G, etc., supposing there has been no cause of change in C, E, F, G, etc. It might be said also, without entering into any further particularity, that place is that which is the same in different moments to different existent things when their relations of coexistence with certain other existents which are supposed to continue fixed from one of those moments to the other agree entirely together. And *fixed existents* are those in which there has been no cause of any change of the order of their coexistence with others, or (which is the same thing) in which there has been no motion. Lastly, *space* is that which results from places taken together. And here it may not be amiss to consider the difference between place and the relation of situation which is in the body that fills up the place. For the place of A and B is the same, whereas the relation of A to fixed bodies is not precisely and individually the same as the relation which B (that comes into its place) will have to the same fixed bodies; but these relations agree only. For two different subjects, as A and B, cannot have precisely the same individual affection, it being impossible that the same individual accident should be in two subjects or pass from one subject to another. But the mind, not contented with an agreement, looks for an identity, for something that should be truly the same, and conceives it as being extrinsic to the subject; and this is what we here call *place* and *space*. But this can only be an ideal thing, containing a certain order, wherein the mind conceives the application of relations. In like manner as the mind can fancy to itself an order made up of genealogical lines whose bigness would consist only in the number of generations wherein every person would have his place; and if to this one should add the fiction of a metempsychosis and bring in the same human souls again, the persons in those lines might change place; he who was a father or a grandfather might become a son or a grandson, etc. And yet those genealogical places, lines, and spaces, though they should express real truths, would only be ideal things. I shall allege another example to show how the mind uses, upon occasion of accidents which are in subjects, to fancy to itself something answerable to those accidents out of the subjects. The ratio or proportion between two lines L and M may be conceived three several ways: as a ratio of the greater L to the lesser M, as a ratio of the lesser M to the greater L, and, lastly, as something abstracted from both, that is, the ratio between L and M without considering which is the antecedent or which the consequent, which the subject and which the object. And thus it is that proportions are considered in music. In the first way of considering them, L the greater, in the second, M the lesser, is the subject of that accident which philosophers call "relation." But which of them will be the subject in the third way of considering them? It cannot be said that both of them, L and M together, are the subject of such an accident; for, if so, we should have an accident in two subjects, with one leg in one and the other in the other, which is contrary to the notion of accidents. Therefore we must say that this relation, in this third way of considering it, is indeed out of the subjects; but, being neither a substance nor an accident, it must be a mere ideal thing, the consideration of which is nevertheless useful. To conclude, I have here done much like Euclid, who, not being able to make his readers well understand what *ratio* is absolutely in the sense of geometricians, defines what are the *same ratios*. Thus, in like manner, in order to explain what *place* is, I have been content to define what is the *same place*. Lastly, I observe that the traces of movable bodies, which they leave sometimes upon the immovable ones on which they are moved, have given men occasion to form in their imagination such an idea, as if some trace did still remain, even when there is nothing unmoved. But this is a mere ideal thing and imports only that *if there was any unmoved thing there, the trace might be marked out upon it*. And 'tis this analogy which makes men fancy places, traces, and spaces, though these things consist only in the truth of relations and not at all in any absolute reality. one from another. Hence I say, my present thoughts are clear.

WOLFF

CHRISTIAN WOLFF was born in Breslau in 1769 and started his career, with encouragement from Leibniz, as a mathematician. In 1706 he became professor of mathematics in the University of Halle, but was soon teaching in all branches of philosophy. His rationalism and commitment to the spirit of the Enlightenment offended the strong Pietistic faction in the University, who through intrigue in Berlin secured his banishment by Frederick William I in 1723. He took refuge in Marburg, where he taught until 1740, when Frederick the Great recalled him to his old position in Halle. He returned in triumph, but his influence was beginning to wane by the time of his death in 1754. For forty years however, he had been "the schoolmaster of Germany," and he had his epigones and imitators almost everywhere. His disciple Bilfinger coined the name, "the Leibniz-Wolffian philosophy" (to the displeasure of both men). It was the Leibniz-Wolffian philosophy against which the representatives of the second period of the German Enlightenment (cf. Introduction, p. 11) revolted, and it was in this philosophy that Kant was educated.

Wolff is indefatigably prolix; he is extravagant with definitions; he illustrates what needs no illustration; he prefers syllogisms to enthymemes, and proves what needs no proof—but when a proof is needed, he is often embarrassingly fallacious (cf. his attempt in §330 to prove the validity of induction). Yet his pedantry has at least the merit of clarity, systematic order, and encyclopedic coverage, and his influence upon the "professionalization" of philosophy in Germany should not be undervalued.

Our selection is from Chapter ii of his *Reasonable Thoughts on God, the World, the Soul of Man, and All Things in General*, first published in 1719 and commonly called *The German Metaphysics* to distinguish it from a similar, but even more scholastic, work he wrote in Latin during the period in Marburg.

These selections give a good picture of his theory of the relations betwee reason and experience and of his ideal of a demonstrative system of knowledg

The translation is my own. I have preserved something of his scholast style and his apparatus of proof through cross-references; but the reader mere selections can form little idea of the tedium of his work when re straight through, without omissions.

Reasonable Thoughts on GOD, the WORLD, the SOUL of MAN, and THINGS in GENERAL

On the First Principles of our Knowledge and of Things in General

194. . . . what we first perceive concerning our soul when we give attention to it is this: that we are conscious of many things as outside us. When this happens, we are *thinking*, and we call the alterations in our soul of which we are conscious *thoughts*. On the other hand, when we are not conscious of ourselves, as, for instance, in sleep, . . . we generally say we are not thinking.

196. We find a difference among our thoughts when we think of things within and without us. [We find the difference between our certainty of ourselves and our certainty of the axioms of geometry.]

197. Since I have said that there is this difference, it is necessary first of all to explain on what grounds we know something to be in us. [For we have already seen (45) that we know things outside us in as much as we know that they are different from us.] For since we are conscious of some things, e.g., we see houses or people, we know by the principle of contradiction that I, who am conscious of something, am not that thing of which I am conscious. Therefore I know it to be different from me. But since in myself I find only consciousness, i.e., my thoughts (194), so I ascribe to myself nothing more than thoughts, and whatever belongs to them I see as being in myself. Thus it was that the Cartesians thought that consciousness was the whole essence of the soul, and could not grant that there was anything in it of which we are not conscious. . . .

198. Some thoughts are so formed that we know very well what we think, and can distinguish them from others. Of them we say they are *clear*. For example, I now see buildings, people, and other things.

I am very aware of what I see, I recognize each and can distinguish one from another. Hence I say, my present thoughts are clear.

199. On the other hand, when we do not rightly know what to make of what we think, our thoughts are obscure. . . .

201. Clarity thus arises from noticing the differences among things; obscurity from failure to notice this.

206. Sometimes it happens that we can define the difference we think of, and if requested we can tell it to another person. In this case, our thoughts are *distinct*. For example, I think of a triangle and a square. I can define the difference, and if someone asks me how I distinguish these figures from each other and from all others, I can tell him the difference—namely, it is a question of the number of sides. In the triangle there are three, in the square, four. And therefore I know that the thought of a triangle is different from that of a square. Hence I know that the thoughts of the two figures are distinct. . . .

276. As soon as we have distinct thoughts or concepts of a thing, we understand it. Anything is understandable which we can know distinctly. In common life one usually says that one understands a thing when one has only a clear concept of it; but in the sciences it is necessary to distinguish mere knowledge of something from understanding it [and for the latter, distinct concepts are required].

277. The faculty of distinctly representing to ourselves what is possible is *understanding*. In this, the understanding differs from the senses and imagination; for the latter can at most give clear, not distinct ideas; but when understanding is added, the same ideas become distinct. . . .

278. As soon as we can represent a thing, we know it. And if the concepts are distinct, our knowledge is distinct. But if they are indistinct, our knowledge is indistinct. Distinct knowledge is the understanding of a thing (276).

279. The more distinctness there is in our knowledge, the better we understand a thing and the more we know to say about it (206). Thus the degree of knowledge is raised.

280. If someone conceives distinctly everything which can be known about a thing, he has attained the highest level of knowledge of this thing, and it is not possible to reach a higher level.

281. But where, on the contrary, indistinctness and obscurity remain, knowledge has not been brought to the highest level. . . . Thus the levels of imperfect knowledge are consequences of indistinctness and obscurity.

282. Because distinctness of knowledge belongs to understanding, while indistinctness belongs to the senses and imagination (277), under-

standing is separate from the senses and imagination when we have completely distinct knowledge. But it is united with them when there is indistinctness and obscurity in our knowledge. In the first case, understanding is called *pure*; in the second, *impure*.

283. Since we can now give a distinct difference between pure and impure understanding, a difference we find even in experience (282), they who hold pure understanding to be an empty fancy of the mathematicians have deceived themselves. They do so because they do not understand the difference between pure and impure understanding (276) or at least do not distinctly know it (278).

285. Our understanding is never pure . . . but there is in it, besides distinctness, much indistinctness and obscurity. Nonetheless one can ascribe to each faculty of the soul what [essentially] belongs to it and thus avoid giving occasion for misunderstandings through ambiguous expressions.

286. Understanding manifests itself in concepts by distinguishing what is found in one thing, as we represent it to ourselves, from what is found in another, and by separating what is found in one thing but not in the other so as to determine the differences between the things; by this we reach definitions and come to know the genus and species of things. Thus it is by understanding that we have universal concepts and universal knowledge.

329. Through experience we come to concepts and to judgments. . . . The art of experience and experiment is so rich in rules that one could make a particular branch of science of them. And it would not be without use if this were done, because we achieve much knowledge from experience. Not only among astronomers but also among some careful natural historians there are splendid experiments and tests by experience; and in studying them one could discover general rules which would occasion still further thoughts. My own attempts to open the path to a more fundamental observation of nature and art could serve this purpose, since with others I have undertaken to present things in such a manner that one can at the same time learn the kinds of useful experiments and ways of performing them.

330. But it is not my intention here to supply the lack of this art, though I must show the source of the certainty of experience. . . . Concepts are certain when we know their possibility. Since experience shows us that there are things of those kinds of which experience affords us a concept, we know from experience that they are possible. Judgments are certain, when that which we ascribe to a thing can or cannot pertain to it. When we reach a judgment through experience, we thereby know that this or that pertains to a thing, and thus it is

certainly clear that it *can* pertain to it. But since in judgments every
thing that is said of a thing is said only under certain conditions, i
is not certain that the same thing will happen again, except that th
same conditions occur again, i.e., except that there be similar cases
For example, I see that iron in the smithy begins to glow when it i
laid on glowing coals and the bellows is worked. Thence I judge
Iron begins to glow. But this judgment is not strictly true. For]
cannot hope that the iron will begin to glow if I do not put it into ;
hot fire.

331. Thus it is that those who look merely to experience wait fo
similar cases, and the expectation of similar cases is the basis of thei
action. But if they knew rightly how to distinguish cases, or at leas
had a clear concept of them, they would be certain in their anticipa
tions, for it is certain that the same thing happens in similar cases
But because the concept of similar cases is for the most part ver;
obscure, indeed often wrong, since often one defines it so as to includ
alien and not true circumstances, the outcome of an undertaking i
often very dubious, and those who are most certain are often mos
wrong. Of this there are daily examples in human life.

368. The art of inference [logic] shows that truths are connecte
with each other. . . . The insight we have into the connection of truths
or the faculty of seeing this connection, is called *reason*. . . . We say
for instance, that Sempronius has begun his business reasonably i
he has considered well what profits and losses might come from hi.
acts, and if he has arranged his acts so that he is not opposing himsel
but so that each act helps the others. What is here the reason h
shows? Nothing but this: the insight which he has into the connectio
of things, in the relations of his actions to each other and to things
For if one does not attend to these relations, one will do some thing.
to his advantage and some things to his hurt, and things will ru
against each other. Then one will not any more say: Semproniou
goes about his business rationally. Rather, everyone will say: Sem
pronius is acting unreasonably. One sees from this that the commo
notion of reason is nothing other than the insight into the connectio
between truths. If one says: "Someone has acted rationally," and i
asked, "Why?" one always answers: "Because he has procured som
advantage, or prevented some hurt, or the like—that is, because he saw
and took thought of what would come of his actions, and he thus gav
evidence of his insight into the connection of things."

369. Whatever is connected with known truths is said to be ir
conformity with reason; whatever is in conflict with them is said to
be against reason. Since one brings out by demonstration what is con

nected with known truths, whatever is demonstrated is in conformity with reason. Since, on the other side, without demonstration it is not seen whether something is connected with known truths or not, where there is no demonstration there it is uncertain whether something is connected with known truths or not, and hence it is not known whether something conforms to reason or not. If, finally, I can through demonstration from a given proposition bring out another which contradicts a known truth, I thereby show that the given proposition is against reason. In such manner do all truths of geometry conform to reason. . . . In the same manner it is seen that the teachings I present in my philosophy are reasonable, for I always show that the later ones depend upon the foregoing ones.

370. The more one sees the connection of truths, the more reason one has (see 368). Similarly, one has less reason the less one sees this connection. And if one does not at all see how things are connected, then one has no reason at all.

371. Because of that which one knows only by experience, one knows only that it *is* but does not see how it is connected with other truths, in knowledge from experience there is no reason (see 370). Hence experience is opposed to reason. Science, however, comes from reason (as we shall show below).

372. We have, then, two ways by which we can reach the knowledge of truth: experience and reason. The former is based on the senses, the latter on the understanding (see 277, 368). For example, that the sun will rise tomorrow is known to most men by experience, and they cannot say why it will happen. But an astronomer, who knows the causes of celestial movements and the relations between the earth and the heavens knows it by reason, and can demonstrate that, why, and when it will happen. . . .

374. The expectation of similar cases (see 331) [however] has some similarity to reason. For if we notice by repeated observation that something happens in certain circumstances, we can count on it that in the same circumstances the same thing will happen; this has the same worth as if we had an insight into the connection of things and knew how to deduce one thing from another. Thus our expectation is somewhat like reason (see 368).

375. This expectation not only takes the place of reason in the majority of human actions, but it can become equal in worth to reason and in perfect conformity with reason if one accurately determines the circumstances in which something occurs. For then one knows that the outcome is connected with the circumstance, even though one does not conceive how it happens and thus lacks a distinct insight (see 206).

376. Nevertheless, expectation of similar cases can occur without reason. For if we have only a clear but indistinct concept, or even have only an obscure concept, by which the case is defined, and if we then see these circumstances again, the imagination will present us with an image of what happened before, and memory will assure us that the two did occur together before; hence one will look for the same thing again.

381. Because reason is an insight into the connection of truths (see 368), and because truth is known when one understands the grounds on which this or that can be, it follows that reason shows us why this or that can be. And thus from reason there comes the knowledge of the philosophers . . . as well as the common knowledge which ordinarily comes from experience.

382. If one sees the connection of things in such manner that one can connect all truths with each other without taking any propositions from experience, reason is *pure;* if on the other hand one has to have assistance from propositions drawn from experience, reason and experience are mixed and we do not perfectly see the connection of one truth with another. For when we come to the proposition drawn from experience, we stop; reason can go no farther. We find sufficient cases in sciences to show that our reason is not always pure, especially in the knowledge of nature and of ourselves. And I hold it to be safest, to assume in the knowledge of nature nothing except what is founded in experience even though experience be deceptive. For those who want to claim more for reason than is meet have fallen upon fictional things and have thus wandered from truth to error. In arithmetic and geometry we have models of pure reason; for here all syllogisms proceed from distinct concepts and principles which are separate from the senses.

383. Science is the capacity to prove from indisputable grounds everything one asserts or, in a word, the capacity to demonstrate; and in demonstration truths are connected together; therefore through science one knows the connection of truths, and thus science comes from reason (see 368).

XIII

LESSING

GOTTHOLD EPHRAIM LESSING (1729-1781) was the most important literary figure of his time in Germany. He was noted as the playwright who freed German drama from sterile imitation of the French classics; his *Emilia Galotti, Miss Sarah Simpson,* and *Minna von Barnhelm* are still seen on the German stage. His writings about the drama and art (*The Hamburg Dramaturgy, The Laocoön*) made him the most important critic in Germany. His play, *Nathan the Wise,* inspired by his friend Moses Mendelssohn, is a plea for religious tolerance. Lessing was not a systematic dry-as-dust philosopher, but at the end of his life he confessed (a daring thing, at that time!) to being a Spinozist. Just what he meant by that, and whether he, in fact, said it, became one of the celebrated quarrels in Germany right after his death. But metaphysics aside, one can easily see Spinoza's influence (from the *Theological-Political Tractate*) on Lessing's interpretation of Biblical revelation.

Our selection, which is the whole of his *The Education of the Human Race,* is a fine example of the best thought of the German Enlightenment. The German Enlightenment did not, as we have seen, simply write off religion as an illusion or cry *Écrasez l'infame!,* as many French *philosophes* did. Yet it could not accept the Bible and religious tradition as literally true and morally decisive. The question that troubled many German thinkers was: How can I be Christian and enlightened at the same time? While some Germans, e.g., Hamann, were willing to give up reason in order to be Christian, and very few Germans (unike many Frenchmen) were willing to give up being Christian in order to be reasonable, Lessing wanted to be both. Lessing answered the question by arguing that revelation was a stage in the education of humanity, valid within limits, and leading towards reason, i.e., En-

223

lightenment. Inspired by Leibniz's doctrine that the world appears in various ways to each being and that none is wholly right or wholly wrong, and by Leibniz's theory of continuous development, Lessing was able to introduce a historical dimension into the religious conflicts of the time and to draw from the lessons of history a defense of toleration for both natural and revealed religion.

The EDUCATION of the HUMAN RACE[1]

1. What education is to the individual man, revelation is to the whole human race.

2. Education is revelation coming to the individual man; and revelation is education which has come, and is still coming, to the human race.

3. Whether it can be of any advantage to the science of instruction to consider education from this point of view I will not here inquire; but in theology it may unquestionably be of great advantage, and may remove many difficulties, if revelation be conceived of as an education of the human race.

4. Education gives man nothing which he could not also get from within himself; it gives him that which he could get from within himself, only quicker and more easily. In the same way too, revelation gives nothing to the human race which human reason could not arrive at on its own; only it has given, and still gives to it, the most important of these things sooner.

5. And just as in education, it is not a matter of indifference in what order the powers of a man are developed, as it cannot impart to a man everything at once; so also God had to maintain a certain order and a certain measure in his revelation.

6. Even though the first man was furnished at once with a conception of the One God; yet it was not possible that this conception, freely imparted and not won by experience, should subsist long in its clearness. As soon as human reason, left to itself, began to elaborate it, it broke up the one immeasurable into many measurables, and gave a distinguishing mark to every one of these parts.

7. Hence naturally arose polytheism and idolatry. And who can say for how many millions of years human reason would have been lost in these errors, even though at all places and times there were

1. G. E. Lessing: *Lessing's Theological Writings*—Selections in translation by Henry Chadwick, M. A., D. D., A. & C. Black Ltd.: London; and Stanford University Press. Reprinted by permission of the publishers.

individual men who recognized them *as* errors, had it not pleased God
to afford it a better direction by means of a new impulse?

8. But when he neither could, nor would, reveal himself any more
to *each* individual man, he selected an individual people for his special
education; and that the most rude and the most ferocious, in order to
begin with it from the very beginning.

9. This was the Hebrew people, about whom we do not even know
what kind of divine worship they had in Egypt. For so despised a race
of slaves could not have been permitted to take part in the worship of
the Egyptians; and the God of their fathers had become entirely unknown to them.

10. It is possible that the Egyptians had expressly prohibited the
Hebrews from having a god or gods, and having destroyed their faith
had brought them to the belief that they had no god or gods whatsoever; that to have a god or gods was the prerogative only of the
superior Egyptians; this perhaps in order to be able to tyrannize over
them with a greater show of fairness. Do Christians treat their slaves
much differently even now?

11. To this rude people God caused himself to be announced at first
simply as "the God of their fathers," in order to make them familiar
and at home with the idea of a God belonging to them too.

12. Following this, through the miracles with which he led them
out of Egypt and planted them in Canaan, he testified of himself to
them as a God mightier than any other god.

13. And as he continued demonstrating himself to be the mightiest
of all, which only one can be, he gradually accustomed them to the
idea of the One.

14. But how far was this conception of the One below the true
transcendental conception of the One, which reason, so late, teaches
us only to conclude with certainty out of the conception of the
infinite!

15. Although the best of the people were already more or less
approaching the true conception of the One, the people as a whole
could not for a long time elevate themselves to it. And this was the
sole reason why they so often abandoned their one God, and expected
to find the One, i.e. the mightiest, in some other god belonging to
another people.

16. But of what kind of moral education was a people so raw, so
incapable of abstract thoughts, and so entirely in their childhood
capable? Of none other but such as is adapted to the age of children,
an education by rewards and punishments addressed to the senses.

17. Here too, then, education and revelation come together. As yet

God could give to his people no other religion, no other law than one through obedience to which they might hope to be happy, or through disobedience to which they must fear to be unhappy. For as yet they envisaged nothing beyond this life. They knew of no immortality of the soul; they yearned after no life to come. But now to reveal these things, when their reason was so little prepared for them, what would it have been but the same fault in the divine rule as is committed by the vain schoolmaster who chooses to hurry his pupil too rapidly and boast of his progress, rather than thoroughly to ground him?

18. "But," it will be asked, "to what purpose was this education of so rude a people, a people with whom God had to begin so entirely from the beginning?" I reply: "In order that in the process of time he might all the better employ particular members of this nation as the teachers of all other peoples. He was bringing up in them the future teachers of the human race. These were Jews, these could only be Jews, only men from a people which had been educated in this way."

19. Then further. When the child by dint of blows and caresses had grown and was now come to years of understanding, the Father sent it of a sudden into foreign lands: and here it recognized at once the good which in its Father's house it had possessed, and had not been conscious of.

20. While God guided his chosen people through all the degrees of a child's education, the other nations of the earth had gone on by the light of reason. The most part had remained far behind the chosen people. Only a few had got in front of them. And this, too, takes place with children, who are allowed to grow up on their own; many remain quite raw; some educate themselves to an astonishing degree.

21. But as these more fortunate few prove nothing against the use and necessity of education, so the few heathen nations, who hitherto seemed to be ahead of the chosen people even in the knowledge of God, prove nothing against a revelation. The child of education begins with slow but sure footsteps; it is late in overtaking many a more happily placed child of nature; but it *does* overtake it; and thenceforth can never be overtaken by it again.

22. Similarly—putting aside the doctrine of the unity of God, which in a way is found, and in a way is not found, in the books of the Old Testament—the fact that the doctrine of immortality at least is not to be found in it, but is wholly foreign to it, and all the related doctrine of reward and punishment in a future life, proves just as little against the divine origin of these books. For let us suppose that these doctrines were not only wanting there, but even that they were not even true; let us suppose that for mankind all was over in this life; would the

being of God be for this reason less demonstrated? Would God on this account be less at liberty, would it less become him, to take immediate charge of the temporal fortunes of any people out of this perishable race? The miracles which he performed for the Jews, the prophecies which he caused to be recorded through them, were surely not for the few mortal Jews, in whose time they happened and were recorded: his intentions there concerned the whole Jewish people, the entire human race, who, perhaps, are destined to remain for ever here on earth, even though every individual Jew and every individual man dies and is gone for ever.

23. Once more, the absence of those doctrines in the writings of the Old Testament proves nothing against their divinity. Moses was sent from God even though the sanction of his law extended only to this life. For why should it extend further? He was surely sent only to the Israelitish people, to the Israelitish people *of that time*, and his commission was perfectly adapted to the knowledge, capacities, inclinations of the *then existing* Israelitish people, as well as to the destiny of the people that was to come. And this is sufficient.

24. So far ought Warburton[2] to have gone, and no further. But that learned man overdrew his bow. Not content that the absence of these doctrines did not *discredit* the divine mission of Moses, it must even be a *proof* to him of the divinity of the mission. If he had only sought this proof in the suitability of such a law for such a people!

But he took refuge in the hypothesis of a miraculous system continued in an unbroken line from Moses to Christ, according to which God had made every individual Jew just as happy or unhappy as his obedience or disobedience to the law deserved. This miraculous system, he said, had compensated for the lack of those doctrines [of eternal rewards and punishments] without which no state can subsist; and precisely this compensation proved what that lack at first sight appeared to deny.

25. How well it was that Warburton could by no argument prove or even make likely this continuous miracle, in which he placed the essence of the Israelitish theocracy! For could he have done so, then indeed, but not until then, he would have made the difficulty really insuperable, for me at least. For the truth which the divinity of Moses' mission was to restore, would, in fact, have been actually made doubtful by it: a truth which God, it is true, did not at that time want to reveal; but which, on the other hand, he certainly did not wish to make harder of attainment.

---

2. The English divine, William Warburton (1698-1779), in his *The Divine Legation of Moses* (1737-41). L.W.B.

26. I will illustrate by something that is a counterpart to the process of revelation. A primer for children may fairly pass over in silence this or that important piece of the science or art which it expounds, when the teacher considers that it is not yet suitable for the capabilities of the children for whom he was writing. But it must contain absolutely nothing which bars the way to the knowledge which is held back, or which misleads the children away from it. Rather, all the approaches towards it must be carefully left open; and to lead them away from even one of these approaches, or to cause them to enter it later than they need, would alone be enough to change the mere imperfection of the primer into an actual fault.

27. In the same way, in the writings of the Old Testament, those primers for the Israelitish people, rough, unpractised in thought as they are, the doctrines of the immortality of the soul, and future recompense, might be fairly left out: but they were bound to contain nothing which could even have delayed the progress of the people for whom they were written, in their way to this great truth. And what, to say the least, could have delayed them more than the promise of such a miraculous recompense in this life—promised by him who makes no promise that he does not keep?

28. For even if the strongest proof of the immortality of the soul and of a life to come were not to be alleged from the inequality of the distribution of the material rewards in this life, in which so little account appears to be taken of virtue and vice; yet it is at least certain that without this difficulty—to be resolved in the life to come—human reason would still be far from any better and firmer proofs, and perhaps even would never have reached them. For what was to impel it to seek for these better proofs? Mere curiosity?

29. An Israelite here and there, no doubt, might have extended to every individual member of the entire state those promises and threatenings which applied to it as a whole, and been firmly persuaded that whosoever is pious must also be happy, and that whoever was unhappy must be bearing the penalty of his wrong-doing, which penalty would at once change itself into blessing, as soon as he abandoned his sin. One like this appears to have written Job, for the plan of it is entirely in this spirit.

30. But it was impossible that daily experience should confirm this conviction, or else it would have been all over, for ever, with the people who had this experience, so far as all recognition and reception were concerned of the truth as yet unfamiliar to them. For if the pious man were absolutely happy, and it was also a necessary part of his happiness that his satisfaction should be broken by no uneasy thoughts

of death, and that he should die old and "full of days"[3]: how could he yearn for another life? and how could he reflect upon a thing for which he did not yearn? But if the pious did not reflect on it, who then should reflect? The transgressor? he who felt the punishment of his misdeeds, and if he cursed this life must have so gladly renounced that other existence?

31. It was of much less consequence that an Israelite here and there should directly and expressly have denied the immortality of the soul and future recompense, on the grounds that the law had no reference to it. The denial of an individual, had it even been a Solomon,[4] did not arrest the progress of the common reason, and was in itself, even, a proof that the nation had now taken a great step nearer to the truth. For individuals only deny what the many are thinking over; and to think over an idea about which before no one troubled himself in the least, is half-way to knowledge.

32. Let us also acknowledge that it is a heroic obedience to obey the laws of God simply because they are God's laws, and not because he has promised to reward those who obey them now and hereafter; to obey them even though there be an entire despair of future recompense, and uncertainty respecting a temporal one.

33. Must not a people educated in this heroic obedience towards God be destined, must they not be capable beyond all other of executing divine purposes of quite a special character? Let the soldier, who pays blind obedience to his leader, also become convinced of his leader's wisdom, and then say what that leader may not venture to do with his aid.

34. As yet the Jewish people had worshipped in their Jehovah rather the mightiest than the wisest of all gods; as yet they had rather feared him as a jealous God than loved him: this, too, is a proof that the conceptions which they had of their eternal One God were not exactly the right conceptions which we should have of God. However, now the time was come for these conceptions of theirs to be expanded, ennobled, rectified, to accomplish which God availed himself of a perfectly natural means, a better and more correct measure, by which they got the opportunity of appreciating him.

35. Instead of, as hitherto, appreciating him in contrast with the miserable idols of the small neighbouring peoples, with whom they lived in constant rivalry, they began, in captivity under the wise Persians, to measure him against the "Being of all Beings" such as a more disciplined reason recognized and worshipped.

---

3. Cf. Genesis xxv. 8; xxxv. 29.
4. Ecclesiastes iii. 19-21.

36. Revelation had guided their reason, and now, all at once, reason gave clearness to their revelation.

37. This was the first reciprocal influence which these two (reason and revelation) exercised on one another; and so far is such a mutual influence from being unbecoming to the author of them both, that without it either of them would have been useless.

38. The child, sent into foreign lands, saw other children who knew more, who lived more becomingly, and asked itself, in confusion, "Why do I not know that too? Why do I not live so too? Ought I not to have learnt and acquired all this in my Father's house?" Thereupon it again sought out its primer, which had long been thrown into a corner, in order to push the blame on to the primer. But behold, it discovers that the blame does not rest upon books, but the blame is solely its own, for not having long ago known this very thing, and lived in this very way.

39. Since the Jews, by this time, through the medium of the pure Persian doctrine, recognized in their Jehovah not simply the greatest of all national deities, but God; and since they could the more readily find him and show him to others in their sacred writings, inasmuch as he was really in them; and since they manifested as great an aversion for sensuous representations, or at all events were shown in these Scriptures as possessing an aversion as great as the Persians had always felt; it is not surprising that they found favour in the eyes of Cyrus with a divine worship which he recognized as being, no doubt, far below pure Sabeism, but yet far above the rude idolatries which in its stead had taken possession of the land of the Jews.

40. Thus enlightened respecting the treasures which they had possessed without knowing it, they returned, and became quite another people, whose first care it was to give permanence to this enlightenment amongst themselves. Soon apostasy and idolatry among them was out of the question. For it is possible to be faithless to a national deity, but never to God, after he has once been recognized.

41. The theologians have tried to explain this complete change in the Jewish people in different ways; and one, who has well demonstrated the insufficiency of these explanations, wanted finally to give, as the true reason—"the visible fulfilment of the prophecies which had been spoken and written respecting the Babylonian captivity and the restoration from it." But even this reason can only be true in so far as it presupposes the exalted ideas of God as they now are. The Jews must now, for the first time, have recognized that to do miracles and to predict the future belonged only to God, both of which powers they had formerly ascribed also to false idols; this precisely is the reason

why miracles and prophecies had hitherto made so weak and fleeting an impression upon them.

42. Doubtless the Jews became better acquainted with the doctrine of immortality among the Chaldeans and Persians. They became more familiar with it, too, in the schools of the Greek philosophers in Egypt.

43. However, as this doctrine did not correspond with their Scriptures in the same way that the doctrines of God's unity and attributes had done—since the former were entirely overlooked by that sensual people, while the latter would be sought for: and since too, for the former, previous exercising was necessary, and as yet there had been only *hints* and *allusions,* the faith in the immortality of the soul could naturally never be the faith of the entire people. It was and continued to be only the creed of a certain section of them.

44. An example of what I mean by "previous exercising" in the doctrines of immortality, is the divine threat of punishing the misdeeds of the father upon his children unto the third and fourth generation. This accustomed the fathers to live in thought with their remotest posterity, and to feel in advance the misfortunes which they had brought upon these innocents.

45. What I mean by an "allusion" is something which might merely excite curiosity, or call forth a question. As, for instance, the common figure of speech which describes death by "he was gathered to his fathers."

46. By a "hint" I mean something which contains some sort of germ, from which the truth which up to now has been held back, may be developed. Of this character was the inference of Christ from God's title as "the God of Abraham, Isaac, and Jacob."[5] This hint appears to me to be undoubtedly capable of development into a strong proof.

47. In such exercises, allusions, hints, consists the *positive* perfection of a primer; just as the above-mentioned quality of not putting difficulties or hindrances in the way to the truths that have been withheld, constitutes its *negative* perfection.

48. Add to all this the clothing and the style.

(1) The clothing of abstract truths which could scarcely be passed over, in allegories and instructive single circumstances, which were narrated as actual occurrences. Of this character are creation in the image of growing day; the origin of evil in the story of the forbidden tree; the source of the variety of languages in the story of the tower of Babel, etc.

49. (2) The style—sometimes plain and simple, sometimes poetical, throughout full of tautologies, but of such a call for a sharp wit, since

5. Matt. xxii. 32.

they sometimes appear to be saying something else, and yet say the same thing; sometimes seem to say the same thing over again, and yet to mean or to be capable of meaning, basically, something else:—

50. And there you have all the good qualities of a primer both for children and for a childlike people.

51. But every primer is only for a certain age. To delay the child, that has outgrown it, longer at it than was intended, is harmful. For to be able to do this in a way which is at all profitable, you must insert into it more than there is really in it, and extract from it more than it can contain. You must look for and make too much of allusions and hints; squeeze allegories too closely; interpret examples too circumstantially; press too much upon words. This gives the child a petty, crooked, .hairsplitting understanding: it makes him full of mysteries, superstitious, full of contempt for all that is comprehensible and easy.

52. The very way in which the Rabbis handled *their* sacred books! The very character which they thereby imparted to the spirit of their people!

53. A better instructor must come and tear the exhausted primer from the child's hands—Christ came!

54. That portion of the human race which God had wished to embrace in one plan of education, was ripe for the second great step. He had, however, only wished to embrace in such a plan that part of the human race which by language, habits, government, and other natural and political relationships, was already united in itself.

55. That is, this portion of the human race had come so far in the exercise of its reason, as to need, and to be able to make use of, nobler and worthier motives for moral action than temporal rewards and punishments, which had hitherto been its guides. The child has become a youth. Sweetmeats and toys have given place to an awakening desire to be as free, as honoured, and as happy as its elder brother.

56. For a long time, already, the best individuals of that portion of the human race had been accustomed to let themselves be ruled by the shadow of such nobler motives. The Greek and Roman did everything to live on after this life, even if it were only in the memories of their fellow-citizens.

57. It was time that another *true* life to be expected after this one should gain an influence over the youth's actions.

58. And so Christ was the first *reliable, practical* teacher of the immortality of the soul.

59. The first *reliable* teacher. Reliable, by reason of the prophecies which were fulfilled in him; reliable by reason of the miracles which he achieved; reliable by reason of his own revival after a death by which

he had put the seal to his teaching. Whether we can still *prove* this revival, these miracles, I put aside, as I leave on one side *who* the person of Christ was. All *that* may have been at that time of great importance for the first acceptance of his teaching, but it is now no longer of the same importance for the recognition of the *truth* of his teaching.

60. The first *practical* teacher. For it is one thing to conjecture, to wish, and to believe in the immortality of the soul, as a philosophic speculation: quite another thing to direct one's inner and outer actions in accordance with it.

61. And this at least Christ was the first to teach. For although, before him, the belief had already been introduced among many nations, that bad actions have yet to be punished in the life to come; yet they were only such actions as were injurious to civil society, and which had, therefore, already had their punishment in civil society too. To preach an inward purity of heart in reference to another life, was reserved for him alone.

62. His disciples have faithfully propagated this teaching: and even if they had had no other merit than that of having effected a more general publication among other nations of a truth which Christ had appeared to have destined for the Jews alone, yet if only on that account, they would have to be reckoned among the benefactors and fosterers of the human race.

63. If, however, they mixed up this one great truth together with other doctrines whose truth was less enlightening, whose usefulness was less considerable, how could it be otherwise? Let us not blame them for this, but rather seriously examine whether these very commingled doctrines have not become a new directing impulse for human reason.

64. At least, it is already clear from our experience that the New Testament Scriptures, in which these doctrines after some time were found preserved, have afforded, and still afford, the second, better primer for the race of man.

65. For seventeen hundred years past they have occupied human reason more than all other books, and enlightened it more, were it even only through the light which human reason itself put into them.

66. It would have been impossible for any other book to become so generally known among such different nations: and indisputably, the fact that modes of thought so completely diverse from each other have turned their attention to this same book, has assisted human reason on its way more than if every nation had had its *own* primer specially for itself.

67. It was also most necessary that each people should for a time consider this book as the *non plus ultra* of their knowledge. For the

youth must believe his primer to be the first of all books, so that his impatience to be finished with it may not hurry him on to things for which he has not yet laid the foundations.

68. And that is also of the greatest importance now. You who are cleverer than the rest, who wait fretting and impatient on the last page of the primer, take care! Take care that you do not let your weaker classmates notice what you are beginning to scent, or even see!

69. Until these weaker fellows of yours have caught up with you, it is better that you should return once more to this primer, and examine whether that which you take only for variations of method, for superfluous verbiage in the teaching, is not perhaps something more.

70. You have seen in the childhood of the human race, in the doctrine of the unity of God, that God makes immediate revelations of mere truths of reason, or has permitted and caused pure truths of reason to be taught, for a time, as truths of immediate revelation, in order to promulgate them the more rapidly, and ground them the more firmly.

71. You learn in the childhood of the human race the same thing, in the doctrine of the immortality of the soul. It is *preached* in the second, better primer as revelation, not *taught* as a result of human reason.

72. As we by this time can dispense with the Old Testament for the doctrine of the unity of God, and as we are gradually beginning also to be less dependent on the New Testament for the doctrine of the immortality of the soul: might there not be mirrored in this book also other truths of the same kind, which we are to gaze at in awe as revelations, just until reason learns to deduce them from its other demonstrated truths, and to connect them with them?

73. For instance, the doctrine of the Trinity. How if this doctrine should in the end, after countless waverings to one side or the other, merely bring human reason on the path to recognizing that God cannot possibly be One in the sense in which finite things are one, that even his unity must be a transcendental unity which does not exclude a sort of plurality? Must not God at least have the most perfect conception of himself, i.e. a conception which contains everything which is in him? But would everything be contained in it which is in him, if it contained merely a conception, merely the possibility even of his necessary reality, as well as of his other qualities? This possibility exhausts the being of his other qualities. Does it exhaust that of his necessary reality? I think not. Consequently either God can have no perfect conception of himself at all, or this perfect conception is just as necessarily real (i.e. actually existent) as he himself is. Admittedly

the image of myself in the mirror is nothing but an empty representation of me, because it only has that of me which is reflected by rays of light falling on its surface. If, however, this image contained everything, everything without exception, which is contained in me, would it then still be a mere empty representation, or not rather a true double of myself? When I believe that I recognize in God a similar reduplication, I perhaps do not so much err, as that my language is insufficient for my ideas: and so much at least remains for ever incontrovertible, that those who want to make the idea acceptable to the popular intelligence could scarcely have expressed themselves in a more apt and comprehensible form than by giving the name of a Son whom God begets from eternity.

74. And the doctrine of original sin. How if finally everything were to convince us that man, standing on the first and lowest step of his humanity, is by no means so much master of his actions that he is *able* to obey moral laws?

75. And the doctrine of the Son's satisfaction. How if everything finally compelled us to assume that God, in spite of that original incapacity of man, chose rather to give him moral laws, and forgive him all transgressions in consideration of his Son, i.e. in consideration of the living embodiment of all his own perfections, compared with which, and in which, all imperfections of the individual disappear, than *not* to give him those laws, and thus to exclude him from all moral bliss, which cannot be conceived of without moral laws?

76. Let it not be objected that speculations of this nature upon the mysteries of religion are forbidden. The word mystery signified, in the first age of Christianity, something quite different from what it means now: and the development of revealed truths into truths of reason, is absolutely necessary, if the human race is to be assisted by them. When they were revealed they were certainly not truths of reason, but they were revealed in order to become such. They were like the "facit" said to his boys by the mathematics master; he goes on ahead of them in order to indicate to some extent the lines they should follow in their sums. If the scholars were to be satisfied with the "facit," they would never learn to do sums, and would frustrate the intention with which their good master gave them a guiding clue in their work.

77. And why should not we too, by means of a religion whose historical truth, if you will, looks dubious, be led in a similar way to closer and better conceptions of the divine Being, of our own nature, of our relation to God, which human reason would never have reached on its own?

78. It is not true that speculations upon these things have ever done

harm or been injurious to civil society. Reproach is due, not to these speculations, but to the folly and tyranny which tried to keep them in bondage; a folly and tyranny which would not allow men to develop their own thoughts.

79. On the contrary, though they may in individual instances be found wanting, speculations of this sort are unquestionably the most fitting exercises of the human reason that exist, just as long as the human heart, as such, is capable to the highest degree of loving virtue for its eternal blessed consequences.

80. For this selfishness of the human heart, which wishes to exercise its understanding only on that which concerns our bodily needs, succeeds in blunting rather than in sharpening it. It is absolutely necessary for it to be exercised on spiritual objects, if it is to attain its perfect illumination, and bring out that purity of heart which makes us capable of loving virtue for its own sake alone.

81. Or is the human species never to arrive at this highest step of illumination and purity?—Never?

82. Never?—Let me not think this blasphemy, All Merciful! Education has its goal, in the race, no less than in the individual. That which is educated is educated for a purpose.

83. The flattering prospects which are opened to the youth, the honour and well-being which are held out to him, what are they more than means of educating him to become a man, who, when these prospects of honour and well-being have vanished, shall be able to do his *duty?*

84. This is the aim of *human* education, and does the divine education not extend as far? Is nature not to succeed with the whole, as art succeeded with the individual? Blasphemy! Blasphemy!

85. No! It will come! it will assuredly come! the time of the perfecting, when man, the more convinced his understanding feels about an even better future, will nevertheless not need to borrow motives for his actions from this future; for he will do right because it *is* right, not because arbitrary rewards are set upon it, which formerly were intended simply to fix and strengthen his unsteady gaze in recognizing the inner, better, rewards of well-doing.

86. It will assuredly come! the time of a new eternal gospel, which is promised us in the primers of the New Covenant itself![6]

87. Perhaps even some enthusiasts of the thirteenth and fourteenth centuries had caught a glimmer of this new eternal gospel, and only erred in that they predicted its arrival as so near to their own time.

88. Perhaps their "Three Ages of the World" were not so empty a

6. Revelation xiv. 6.

speculation after all, and assuredly they had no bad intentions when they taught that the new covenant must become as antiquated as the old has become. There remained with them the same economy of the same God. Ever, to put my own expression into their mouths, ever the selfsame plan of the education of the human race.

89. Only they were premature. They believed that they could make their contemporaries, who had scarcely outgrown their childhood, without enlightenment, without preparation, at one stroke men worthy of their *third age*.

90. And it was just this which made them enthusiasts. The enthusiast often casts true glances into the future, but for this future he cannot wait. He wants this future to come quickly, and to be made to come quickly through him. A thing over which nature takes thousands of years is to come to maturity just at the moment of his experience. For what part has he in it, if that which he recognizes as the best does not become the best in his lifetime? Does he come again? Does he expect to come again? It is strange that this enthusiasm is not more the fashion, if it were only among enthusiasts.

91. Go thine inscrutable way, Eternal Providence! Only let me not despair of thee because of this inscrutableness. Let me not despair of thee, even if thy steps appear to me to be going backward. It is not true that the shortest line is always straight.

92. Thou hast on thine eternal way so much that thou must concern thyself with, so much to attend to! And what if it were as good as proved that the great, slow wheel, which brings mankind nearer to its perfection, is only set in motion by smaller, faster wheels each of which contributes its own individual part to the whole?

93. It is so! Must every individual man—one sooner, another later— have travelled along the very same path by which the race reaches its perfection? Have travelled along it in one and the same life? Can he have been, in one and the selfsame life, a sensual Jew and a spiritual Christian? Can he in the selfsame life have overtaken both?

94. Surely not that! But why should not every individual man have been present more than once in this world?

95. Is this hypothesis so laughable merely because it is the oldest? Because human understanding, before the sophistries of the Schools had dissipated and weakened it, lighted upon it at once?

96. Why may not even I have already performed all those steps towards my perfection which merely temporal penalties and rewards can bring man to?

97. And, once more, why not all those steps, to perform which the prospects of eternal rewards so powerfully assist us?

98. Why should I not come back as often as I am capable of acquiring new knowledge, new skills? Do I bring away so much from one visit that it is perhaps not worth the trouble of coming again?

99. Is this a reason against it? Or, because I forget that I have been here already? Happy is it for me that I do forget. The recollection of my former condition would permit me to make only a bad use of the present. And that which I must forget *now*, is that necessarily forgotten for ever?

100. Or is it a reason against the hypothesis that so much time would have been lost to me? Lost?—And what then have I to lose?—Is not the whole of eternity mine?

XIV

KANT

IMMANUEL KANT (1724-1804) was awakened, he tells us, from his "dogmatic slumber" (i.e., the Leibniz-Wolffian philosophy) by his study of Hume. Kant's historic role was to mediate between the empiricist and rationalist traditions by showing precisely what contribution both experience and reason make to our knowledge. Where either is lacking, there is no knowledge. Hence empiricism, for which reason was only a manipulation of symbols, had, according to him, to end in skepticism; but also rationalism, which taught that experience is only confused thought, was unable to provide a satisfactory account of knowledge in the absence of sense experience. He criticized Leibniz for "intellectualizing appearances" and Locke for "sensualizing concepts." Neither reason nor sense can be reduced to the other; both are essential; the denial of the one makes real knowledge seem doubtful (as in Hume), and the denial of the other permits ignorance to parade as higher knowledge (as in Wolff). Metaphysics, properly, is only the study of the necessary features of experience; speculative metaphysics about the supersensible world is impossible, and our attitude to the things Leibniz and Wolff thought they *knew* can be only one of *faith*. Those who loved metaphysics thought Kant was "the Prussian Hume"; Mendelssohn called him "the great destroyer." But in his own eyes, he saved science from Hume, and religion and morality from their unwitting enemies such as Leibniz and Wolff.

All our selections are taken from Kant's greatest work, the *Critique of Pure Reason* (1781; Second Edition, 1787). The *Critique of Pure Reason* as a whole is a notoriously difficult book, but, fortunately, many of its parts are quite clear. I have selected some of its clearest and most important parts, and I shall now attempt to show how the selected parts fit together. I have supplied some of the section titles; each section is identified by its page number in the first edition (A) or second edition (B) or both. The translation used is that by Max Müller (New York, Macmillan, 1896), with a few emendations.

A. The first section is from the Introduction, and explains Kant's problem, viz., how reason and experience are related. He shows how this question can be made manageable by being formulated: "How are synthetic judgments a priori possible?"

B. "Transcendental Aesthetic" is devoted to determining what are the a priori forms of sense experience (intuition) in contrast to a priori concepts. He answers that there are two, space and time, and he contrasts his theory of space and time with those of Newton and Leibniz.

C. "Analytic of Concepts" is the third section. It is the part wherein Kant discovers what are the a priori concepts (categories) and then shows that these concepts are necessary for knowledge. This section is divided into two parts; the first, the "Metaphysical Deduction," shows what the categories are, and the second, parts of the "Transcendental Deduction," give his proof that they apply to experience.

D. From the next part of the *Critique*, the "Analytic of Principles," we have chosen three selections. The first argues that there are a priori principles as well as a priori concepts, and that these are the laws of experience. The second contains Kant's "Reply to Hume" on the law of causation. The third gives Kant's theory of possibility, actuality, and necessity, and explains the sense in which Kant believes that spatio-temporal objects really exist in the world.

E. These selections (with one minor exception) are taken from the "Transcendental Dialectic," Kant's attack on speculative metaphysics as a pretended "science of the super-sensible world." After a brief introduction, the selection entitled "Freedom of Will" commences with his "Third Antinomy" and then presents his effort to resolve the contradiction between freedom and causal necessity by assigning the former to the noumenal and the latter to the phenomenal world. The concluding selections from the "Transcendental Dialectic" give Kant's refutations of the classical theoretical arguments for the existence of God.

F. The last selection, "Knowledge and Faith," is taken from his Preface to the Second Edition. After summarizing his main conclusions, Kant describes the consequences in his famous statement (p. 300) which seemed to many to sound the knell of Enlightenment: "I had therefore to deny *knowledge* in order to make room for *faith*."

Critique of Pure Reason

A. Introduction

¶ OF THE DIFFERENCE BETWEEN
PURE AND EMPIRICAL KNOWLEDGE[1]

That all our knowledge begins with experience there can be no
doubt. For how should the faculty of knowledge be called into activity,
if not by objects which affect our senses, and which either produce
representations by themselves, or rouse the activity of our understanding to compare, to connect, or to separate them; and thus to convert
the raw material of our sensuous impressions into a knowledge of
objects, which we call experience? In respect of time, therefore, no
knowledge within us is antecedent to experience, but all knowledge
begins with it.

But although all our knowledge begins with experience, it does not
follow that it arises from experience. For it is quite possible that even
our empirical experience is a compound of that which we receive
through impressions, and of that which our own faculty of knowledge
(incited only by sensuous impressions), supplies from itself, a supple-
ment which we do not distinguish from that raw material, until long
practice has roused our attention and rendered us capable of separating
one from the other.

It is therefore a question which deserves at least closer investigation, and cannot be disposed of at first sight, whether there exists a
knowledge independent of experience, and even of all impressions of
the senses? Such *knowledge* is called *a priori*, and distinguished from
empirical knowledge, which has its sources *a posteriori*, that is, in
experience.

This term *a priori*, however, is not yet definite enough to indicate
the full meaning of our question. For people are wont to say, even with

---

1. B 1-2.

regard to knowledge derived from experience, that we have it, or might have it, *a priori*, because we derive it from experience, not *immediately*, but from a general rule, which, however, has itself been derived from experience. Thus one would say of a person who undermines the foundations of his house, that he might have known *a priori* that it would tumble down, that is, that he need not wait for the experience of its really tumbling down. But still he could not know this entirely *a priori*, because he had first to learn from experience that bodies are heavy, and will fall when their supports are taken away.

¶ WE ARE IN POSSESSION OF CERTAIN COGNITIONS A PRIORI, AND EVEN THE ORDINARY UNDERSTANDING IS NEVER WITHOUT THEM[2]

All depends here on a criterion, by which we may safely distinguish between pure and empirical knowledge. Now experience teaches us, no doubt, that something is so or so, but not that it cannot be different. *First,* then, if we have a proposition which is thought together with its necessity, we have a judgment *a priori;* and if, besides, it is not derived from any proposition, except such as is itself again considered as necessary, we have an absolutely *a priori* judgment. *Secondly,* experience never imparts to its judgments true or strict, but only assumed or relative universality (by means of induction), so that we ought always to say, so far as we have observed hitherto, there is no exception to this or that rule. If, therefore, a judgment is thought with strict universality, so that no exception is admitted as possible, it is not derived from experience, but valid absolutely *a priori*. Empirical universality, therefore, is only an arbitrary extension of a validity which applies to most cases, to one that applies to all: as, for instance, in the proposition, all bodies are heavy. If, on the contrary, strict universality is essential to a judgment, this always points to a special source of knowledge, namely, a faculty of knowledge *a priori*. Necessity, therefore, and strict universality are safe criteria of knowledge *a priori*, and are inseparable one from the other. As, however, in the use of these criteria, it is sometimes easier to show the contingency than the empirical limitation of judgments, and as it is sometimes more convincing to prove the unlimited universality which we attribute to a judgment than its necessity, it is advisable to use both criteria separately, each being by itself infallible.

That there really exist in our knowledge such necessary, and in the strictest sense universal, and therefore pure judgments *a priori*, is easy

2. B 3-6.

to show. If we want a scientific example, we have only to look to any of the propositions of mathematics; if we want one from the sphere of the ordinary understanding, such a proposition as that each change must have a cause, will answer the purpose; nay, in the latter case, even the concept of cause contains so clearly the concept of the necessity of its connection with an effect, and of the strict universality of the rule, that it would be destroyed altogether if we attempted to derive it, as Hume does, from the frequent concomitancy of that which happens with that which precedes, and from a habit arising thence (therefore from a purely subjective necessity), of connecting representations. It is possible even, without having recourse to such examples in proof of the reality of pure propositions *a priori* within our knowledge, to prove their indispensability for the possibility of experience itself, thus proving it *a priori*. For whence should experience take its certainty, if all the rules which it follows were always again and again empirical, and therefore contingent and hardly fit to serve as first principles? For the present, however, we may be satisfied for having shown the pure employment of the faculty of our knowledge as a matter of fact, with the criteria of it.

Not only in judgments, however, but even in certain concepts, can we show their origin *a priori*. Take away, for example, from the concept of a body, as supplied by experience, everything that is empirical, one by one; such as colour, hardness or softness, weight, and even impenetrability, and there still remains the space which the body (now entirely vanished) occupied: that you cannot take away. And in the same manner, if you remove from your empirical concept of any object, corporeal or incorporeal, all properties which experience has taught you, you cannot take away from it that property by which you conceive it as a substance, or inherent in a substance (although such a concept contains more determinations than that of an object in general). Convinced, therefore, by the necessity with which that concept forces itself upon you, you will have to admit that it has its seat in your faculty of knowledge *a priori*.

¶ Of the Distinction between
Analytical and Synthetical Judgments[3]

In all judgments in which there is a relation between subject and predicate (I speak of affirmative judgments only, the application to negative ones being easy), that relation can be of two kinds. Either the predicate B belongs to the subject A as something contained

3. A 6-10 = B 10-11, 13-14.

(though covertly) in the concept A; or B lies outside the sphere of the concept A, though somehow connected with it. In the former case I call the judgment analytical, in the latter synthetical. Analytical judgments (affirmative) are therefore those in which the connection of the predicate with the subject is conceived through identity, while others in which that connection is conceived without identity, may be called synthetical. The former might be called illustrating, the latter expanding judgments, because in the former nothing is added by the predicate to the concept of the subject, but the concept is only divided into its constituent concepts which were always conceived as existing within it, though confusedly; while the latter add to the concept of the subject a predicate not conceived as existing within it, and not to be extracted from it by any process of mere analysis. If I say, for instance, All bodies are extended, this is an analytical judgment. I need not go beyond the concept connected with the name of body, in order to find that extension is connected with it. I have only to analyse that concept and become conscious of the manifold elements always contained in it, in order to find that predicate. This is therefore an analytical judgment. But if I say, All bodies are heavy, the predicate is something quite different from what I think as the mere concept of body. The addition of such a predicate gives us a synthetical judgment.

It becomes clear from this,

1. That our knowledge is in no way extended by analytical judgments, but that all they effect is to put the concepts which we possess into better order and render them more intelligible.

2. That in synthetical judgments I must have besides the concept of the subject something else (x) on which the understanding relies in order to know that a predicate, not contained in the concept, nevertheless belongs to it.

In empirical judgments this causes no difficulty, because this x is here simply the complete experience of an object which I conceive by the concept A, that concept forming one part only of my experience. For though I do not include the predicate of weight in the general concept of body, that concept nevertheless indicates the complete experience through one of its parts, so that I may add other parts also of the same experience, all belonging to that concept. I may first, by an analytical process, realise the concept of body through the predicates of extension, impermeability, form, etc., all of which are contained in it. Afterwards I expand my knowledge, and looking back to the experience from which my concept of body was abstracted, I find weight always connected with the before-mentioned predicates. Experience therefore is the x which lies beyond the concept A, and on which rests the possibility of a synthesis of the predicate of weight B with the concept A.

In synthetical judgments *a priori*, however, that help is entirely wanting. If I want to go beyond the concept A in order to find another concept B connected with it, where is there anything on which I may rest and through which a synthesis might become possible, considering that I cannot have the advantage of looking about in the field of experience? Take the proposition that all which happens has its cause. In the concept of something that happens I no doubt conceive of something existing preceded by time, and from this certain analytical judgments may be deduced. But the concept of cause is entirely outside that concept, and indicates something different from that which happens, and is by no means contained in that representation. How can I venture then to predicate of that which happens something totally different from it, and to represent the concept of cause, though not contained in it, as belonging to it, and belonging to it by necessity? What is here the unknown *x*, on which the understanding may rest in order to find beyond the concept A a foreign predicate B, which nevertheless is believed to be connected with it? It cannot be experience, because the proposition that all which happens has its cause represents this second predicate as added to the subject not only with greater generality than experience can ever supply, but also with a character of necessity, and therefore purely *a priori*, and based on concepts. All our speculative knowledge *a priori* aims at and rests on such synthetical, i.e. expanding propositions, for the analytical are no doubt very important and necessary, yet only in order to arrive at that clearness of concepts which is requisite for a safe and wide synthesis, serving as a really new addition to what we possess already.

¶ IN ALL THEORETICAL SCIENCES OF REASON
SYNTHETICAL JUDGMENTS A PRIORI ARE
CONTAINED AS PRINCIPLES[4]

1. All mathematical judgments are synthetical. This proposition, though incontestably certain, and very important to us for the future, seems to have hitherto escaped the observation of those who are engaged in the anatomy of human reason: nay, to be directly opposed to all their conjectures. For as it was found that all mathematical conclusions proceed according to the principle of contradiction (which is required by the nature of all apodictic certainty), it was supposed that the fundamental principles of mathematics also rested on the

4. B 14-18.

authority of the same principle of contradiction. This, however, was a mistake: for though a synthetical proposition may be understood according to the principle of contradiction, this can only be if another synthetical proposition is presupposed, from which the latter is deduced, but never by itself. First of all, we ought to observe, that mathematical propositions, properly so called, are always judgments *a priori*, and not empirical, because they carry along with them necessity, which can never be deduced from experience. If people should object to this, I am quite willing to confine my statement to pure mathematics, the very concept of which implies that it does not contain empirical, but only pure knowledge *a priori*.

At first sight one might suppose indeed that the proposition $7 + 5 = 12$ is merely analytical, following, according to the principle of contradiction, from the concept of a sum of 7 and 5. But, if we look more closely, we shall find that the concept of the sum of 7 and 5 contains nothing beyond to union of both sums into one, whereby nothing is told us as to what this single number may be which combines both. We by no means arrive at a concept of Twelve, by thinking that union of Seven and Five; and we may analyse our concept of such a possible sum as long as we will, still we shall never discover in it the concept of Twelve. We must go beyond these concepts, and call in the assistance of the intuition corresponding to one of the two, for instance, our five fingers, or, as Segner does in his arithmetic, five points, and so by degrees add the units of the Five, given in intuition, to the concept of the Seven. For I first take the number 7, and taking the intuition of the fingers of my hand, in order to form with it the concept of the 5, I gradually add the units, which I before took together, to make up the number 5, by means of the image of my hand, to the number 7, and I thus see the number 12 arising before me. That 5 should be added to 7 was no doubt implied in my concept of a sum $7 + 5$, but not that that sum should be equal to 12. An arithmetical proposition is, therefore, always synthetical, which is seen more easily still by taking larger numbers, where we clearly perceive that, turn and twist our conceptions as we may, we could never, by means of the mere analysis of our concepts and without the help of intuition, arrive at the sum that is wanted.

Nor is any proposition of pure geometry analytical. That the straight line between two points is the shortest, is a synthetical proposition. For my concept of *straight* contains nothing of magnitude (quantity), but a quality only. The concept of the *shortest* is, therefore, purely adventitious, and cannot be deduced from the concept of the straight line by any analysis whatsoever. The aid of intuition, therefore, must be called in, by which alone the synthesis is possible.

It is true that some few propositions, presupposed by the geometrician, are really analytical, and depend on the principle of contradiction: but then they serve only, like identical propositions, to form the chain of the method, and not as principles. Such are the propositions, $a = a$, the whole is equal to itself, or $(a + b) > a$, that the whole is greater than its part. And even these, though they are valid according to mere concepts, are only admitted in mathematics, because they can be represented in intuition. What often makes us believe that the predicate of such apodictic judgments is contained in our concept, and the judgment therefore analytical, is merely the ambiguous character of the expression. We are told that we *ought* to join in thought a certain predicate to a given concept, and this necessity is inherent in the concepts themselves. But the question is not what we *ought* to join to the given concept, but what we *really think* in it, though confusedly only, and then it becomes clear that the predicate is no doubt inherent in those concepts by necessity, not, however, as though in the concept itself, by the means of an intuition, which must be added to the concept.

2. *Natural science (physica) contains synthetical judgments* a priori *as principles*. I shall adduce, as examples, a few propositions only, such as, that in all changes of the material world the quantity of matter always remains unchanged: or that in all communication of motion, action and reaction must always equal each other. It is clear not only that both convey necessity, and that, therefore, their origin is *a priori*, but also that they are synthetical propositions. For in the concept of matter I do not conceive its permanency, but only its presence in the space which it fills. I therefore go beyond the concept of matter in order to join something to it *a priori*, which I did not before conceive *in it*. The proposition is, therefore, not analytical, but synthetical, and yet *a priori*, and the same applies to the other propositions of the pure part of natural science.

3. *Metaphysic*, even if we look upon it as hitherto a tentative science only, which, however, is indispensable to us, owing to the very nature of human reason, is meant to *contain synthetical knowledge a priori*. Its object is not at all merely to analyse such concepts as we make to ourselves of things *a priori*, and thus to explain them analytically, but to expand our knowledge *a priori*. This we can only do by means of concepts which add something to a given concept that was not contained in it; nay, we even attempt, by means of synthetical judgments *a priori*, to go so far beyond a given concept that experience itself cannot follow us: as, for instance, in the proposition that the

world must have a first beginning. Thus, according at least to its intentions, metaphysic consists merely of synthetical propositions *a priori*.

¶ THE GENERAL PROBLEM OF PURE REASON[5]

Much is gained if we are able to bring a number of investigations under the formula of one single problem. For we thus not only facilitate our own work by defining it accurately, but enable also everybody else who likes to examine it to form a judgment, whether we have really done justice to our purpose or not. Now the real problem of pure reason is contained in the question, *How are synthetical judgments* a priori *possible?*

B. Transcendental Aesthetic

¶ DEFINITION OF INTUITION[6]

Whatever the process and the means may be by which knowledge reaches its objects, there is one that reaches them directly, and forms the ultimate material of all thought, viz. intuition. This is possible only when the object is given, and the object can be given only (to human beings at least) through a certain affection of the mind.

This faculty (receptivity) of receiving representations, according to the manner in which we are affected by objects, is called sensibility.

Objects therefore are given to us through our sensibility. Sensibility alone supplies us with intuitions. These intuitions become thought through the understanding, and hence arise conceptions. All thought therefore must, directly or indirectly, go back to intuitions, i.e. to our sensibility, because in no other way can objects be given to us.

The effect produced by an object upon the faculty of representation, so far as we are affected by it, is called sensation. An intuition of an object, by means of sensation, is called empirical. The undefined object of such an empirical intuition is called phenomenon.

In a phenomenon I call that which corresponds to the sensation its *matter*; but that which causes the manifold matter of the phenomenon to be perceived as arranged in a certain order, I call its *form*.

---

5. B 19.
6. A 19-21 = B 33-35.

Now it is clear that it cannot be sensation again through which sensations are arranged and placed in certain forms. The matter only of all phenomena is given us *a posteriori*; but their form must be ready for them in the mind *a priori*, and must therefore be capable of being considered as separate from all sensations.

I call all representations in which there is nothing that belongs to sensation, *pure* (in a transcendental sense). The pure form therefore of all sensuous intuitions, that form in which the manifold elements of the phenomena are seen in a certain order, must be found in the mind *a priori*. And this pure form of sensibility may be called the pure intuition.

Thus, if we deduct from the representation of a body what belongs to the thinking of the understanding, viz. substance, force, divisibility, etc., and likewise what belongs to sensation, viz. impermeability, hardness, colour, etc., there still remains something of that empirical intuition, viz. extension and form. These belong to pure intuition, which *a priori*, and even without a real object of the senses or of sensation, exists in the mind as a mere form of sensibility.

¶ Space[7]

a. Space does not represent any quality of objects by themselves, or objects in their relation to one another; i.e. space does not represent any determination which is inherent in the objects themselves, and would remain, even if all subjective conditions of intuition were removed. For no determinations of objects, whether belonging to them absolutely or in relation to others, can enter into our intuition before the actual existence of the objects themselves, that is to say, they can never be intuitions *a priori*.

b. Space is nothing but the form of all phenomena of the external senses; it is the subjective condition of our sensibility, without which no external intuition is possible for us. If then we consider that the receptivity of the subject, its capacity of being affected by objects, must necessarily precede all intuition of objects, we shall understand how the form of all phenomena may be given before all real perceptions, may be, in fact, *a priori* in the soul, and may, as a pure intuition, by which all objects must be determined, contain, prior to all experience, principles regulating their relations.

It is therefore from the human standpoint only that we can speak of space, extended objects, etc. If we drop the subjective condition under which alone we can gain external intuition, that is, so far as

7. A 26-27 = B 42-43.

we ourselves may be affected by objects, the representation of space means nothing. For this predicate is applied to objects only in so far as they appear to us, and are objects of our senses. The constant form of this receptivity, which we call sensibility, is a necessary condition of all relations in which objects, as without us, can be perceived; and, when abstraction is made of these objects, what remains is that pure intuition which we call space. As the peculiar conditions of our sensibility cannot be looked upon as conditions of the possibility of the objects themselves, but only of their appearance as phenomena to us, we may say indeed that space comprehends all things which may appear to us externally, but not all things by themselves, whether perceived by us or not, or by any subject whatsoever.

¶ TIME[8]

a. Time is not something existing by itself, or inherent in things as an objective determination of them, something therefore that might remain when abstraction is made of all subjective conditions of intuition. For in the former case it would be something real, without being a real object. In the latter it could not, as a determination or order inherent in things themselves, be antecedent to things as their condition, and be known and perceived by means of synthetical propositions *a priori*. All this is perfectly possible if time is nothing but a subjective condition under which alone intuitions take place within us. For in that case this form of internal intuition can be represented prior to the objects themselves, that is, *a priori*.

b. Time is nothing but the form of the internal sense, that is, of our intuition of ourselves, and of our internal state. Time cannot be a determination peculiar to external phenomena. It refers neither to their shape, nor their position, etc., it only determines the relation of representations in our internal state. And exactly because this internal intuition supplies no shape, we try to make good this deficiency by means of analogies, and represent to ourselves the succession of time by a line progressing to infinity, in which the manifold constitutes a series of one dimension only; and we conclude from the properties of this line as to all the properties of time, with one exception, i.e. that the parts of the former are simultaneous, those of the latter successive. From this it becomes clear also, that the representation of time is itself an intuition, because all its relations can be expressed by means of an external intuition.

c. Time is the formal condition, *a priori*, of all phenomena whatso-

8. A 33-35 = B 49-51.

ever. Space, as the pure form of all external intuition, is a condition, *a priori*, of external phenomena only. But, as all representations, whether they have for their objects external things or not, belong by themselves, as determinations of the mind, to our inner state, and as this inner state falls under the formal conditions of internal intuition, and therefore of time, time is a condition, *a priori*, of all phenomena whatsoever, and is so directly as a condition of internal phenomena (of our mind) and thereby indirectly of external phenomena also. If I am able to say, *a priori*, that all external phenomena are in space, and are determined, *a priori*, according to the relations of space, I can, according to the principle of the internal sense, make the general assertion that all phenomena, that is, all objects of the senses, are in time, and stand necessarily in relations of time.

If we drop our manner of looking at ourselves internally, and of comprehending by means of that intuition all external intuitions also within our power of representation, and thus take objects as they may be by themselves, then time is nothing. Time has objective validity with reference to phenomena only, because these are themselves things which we accept as objects of our senses; but time is no longer objective, if we remove the sensuous character of our intuitions, that is to say, that mode of representation which is peculiar to ourselves, and speak of things in general. Time is therefore simply a subjective condition of our (human) intuition (which is always sensuous, that is so far as we are affected by objects), but by itself, apart from the subject, nothing. Nevertheless, with respect to all phenomena, that is, all things which can come within our experience, time is necessarily objective.

C. Analytic of Concepts

¶ METAPHYSICAL DEDUCTION OF THE CATEGORIES[9]

General logic, as we have often said, takes no account of the contents of our knowledge, but expects that representations will come from elsewhere in order to be turned into concepts by an analytical process. Transcendental logic, on the contrary, has before it the manifold contents of sensibility *a priori*, supplied by transcendental æsthetic as the material for the concepts of the pure understanding, without which those concepts would be without any contents, therefore entirely empty. It is true that space and time contain what is manifold in the

9. A 76-81 = B 102-106.

pure intuition *a priori*, but they belong also to the conditions of the receptivity of our mind under which alone it can receive representations of objects, and which therefore must affect the concepts of them also. The spontaneity of our thought requires that what is manifold in the pure intuition should first be in a certain way examined, received, and connected, in order to produce a knowledge of it. This act I call *synthesis*.

In its most general sense, I understand by synthesis the act of arranging different representations together, and of comprehending what is manifold in them under one form of knowledge. Such a synthesis is pure, if the manifold is not given empirically, but *a priori* (as in time and space). Before we can proceed to an analysis of our representations, these must first be given, and, as far as their contents are concerned, no concepts can arise analytically. Knowledge is first produced by the synthesis of what is manifold (whether given empirically or *a priori*). That knowledge may at first be crude and confused and in need of analysis, but it is synthesis which really collects the elements of knowledge, and unites them to a certain extent. It is therefore the first thing which we have to consider, if we want to form an opinion on the first origin of our knowledge.

We shall see hereafter that synthesis in general is the mere result of what I call the faculty of imagination, a blind but indispensable function of the soul, without which we should have no knowledge whatsoever, but of the existence of which we are scarcely conscious. But to reduce this synthesis to concepts is a function that belongs to the understanding, and by which the understanding supplies us for the first time with knowledge properly so called.

Pure synthesis in its most general meaning gives us the pure concept of the understanding. By this pure synthesis I mean that which rests on the foundation of what I call synthetical unity *a priori*. Thus our counting (as we best perceive when dealing with higher numbers) is a synthesis according to concepts, because resting on a common ground of unity, as for instance, the decade. The unity of the synthesis of the manifold becomes necessary under this concept.

By means of analysis different representations are brought under one concept, a task treated of in general logic; but how to bring, not the representations, but the pure synthesis of representations, under concepts, that is what transcendental logic means to teach. The first that must be given us *a priori* for the sake of knowledge of all objects, is the manifold in pure intuition. The second is, the synthesis of the manifold by means of imagination. But this does not yet produce true knowledge. The concepts which impart unity to this pure synthesis and consist entirely in the representation of this necessary synthetical unity add the third contribution towards the knowledge of an object, and rest on the understanding.

The same function which imparts unity to various representations in one judgment imparts unity likewise to the mere synthesis of various representations in one intuition, which in a general way may be called the pure concept of the understanding. The same understanding, and by the same operations by which in concepts it achieves through analytical unity the logical form of a judgment, introduces also, through the synthetical unity of the manifold in intuition, a transcendental element into its representations. They are therefore called pure concepts of the understanding, and they refer *a priori* to objects, which would be quite impossible in general logic.

In this manner there arise exactly so many pure concepts of the understanding which refer *a priori* to objects of intuition in general, as there were in our table logical functions in all possible judgments, because those functions completely exhaust the understanding, and comprehend every one of its faculties.[10] Borrowing a term of Aristotle, we shall call these concepts *categories*, our intention being originally the same as his, though widely diverging from it in its practical application.

TABLE OF CATEGORIES

I

Of Quantity

Unity.
Plurality.
Totality.

II	III
Of Quality	*Of Relation*
Reality.	Of Inherence and Subsistence
Negation.	(*substantia et accidens*).
Limitation.	Of Causality and Dependence
	(cause and effect).
	Of Community (reciprocity
	between the active and the
	passive).

---

10. In a section omitted from this book (A 70 = B 95 in the *Critique*) Kant drew up a table of the logical forms of judgments (twelve forms divided into four groups). Since he is arguing here that the work of the understanding is to judge, it is not surprising that the table of categories (pure concepts or rules for the synthesis of representations which is judgment) should conform to the table of the logical forms of judgment. Kant's table of judgments has been much criticized, but it provided what he called "a clue" to the discovery of the categories. L.W.B.

IV

Of Modality

Possibility.	Impossibility.
Existence.	Non-existence.
Necessity.	Contingency.

This then is a list of all original pure concepts of synthesis, which belong to the understanding *a priori*, and for which alone it is called pure understanding; for it is by them alone that it can understand something in the manifold of intuition, that is, think an object in it.

¶ TRANSCENDENTAL DEDUCTION OF THE CATEGORIES[11]

Two ways only are possible in which synthetical representations and their objects can agree, can refer to each other with necessity, and so to say meet each other. Either it is the object alone that makes the representation possible, or it is the representation alone that makes the object possible. In the former case their relation is empirical only, and the representation therefore never possible *a priori*. This applies to phenomena with reference to whatever in them belongs to sensation. In the latter case, though representation by itself (for we do not speak here of its causality by means of the will) cannot produce its object so far as its existence is concerned, nevertheless the representation determines the object *a priori*, if through it alone it is possible to know anything as an object. To know a thing as an object is possible only under two conditions. First, there must be intuition by which the object is given us, though as a phenomenon only, secondly, there must be a concept by which an object is thought as corresponding to that intuition. From what we have said before it is clear that the first condition, namely, that under which alone objects can be seen, exists, so far as the form of intuition is concerned, in the soul *a priori*. All phenomena therefore must conform to that formal condition of sensibility, because it is through it alone that they appear, that is, that they are given and empirically seen.

Now the question arises whether there are not also antecedent concepts *a priori*, forming conditions under which alone something can be, if not seen, yet thought as an object in general; for in that case all empirical knowledge of objects would necessarily conform to

11. Working through the Transcendental Deduction has been compared (by H. J. Paton, one of the best commentators on Kant) to "crossing the Great Arabian Desert." I have selected two passages, regarded by Kant as "transitional" and "preliminary," which give a good over-all view of the Deduction. The first three paragraphs are A 92-94 = B 125-27; the remainder is from A 110-14 (omitted from second edition). L. W. B.

such concepts, it being impossible that anything should become an object of experience without them. All experience contains, besides the intuition of the senses by which something is given, a concept also of the object, which is given in intuition as a phenomenon. Such concepts of objects in general therefore must form conditions *a priori* of all knowledge produced by experience, and the objective validity of the categories, as being such concepts *a priori*, rests on this very fact that by them alone, so far as the form of thought is concerned, experience becomes possible. If by them only it is possible to think any object of experience, it follows that they refer by necessity and *a priori* to all objects of experience.

There is therefore a principle for the transcendental deduction of all concepts *a priori* which must guide the whole of our investigation, namely, that all must be recognised as conditions *a priori* of the possibility of experience, whether of intuition, which is found in it, or of thought. Concepts which supply the objective ground of the possibility of experience are for that very reason necessary. An analysis of the experience in which they are found would not be a deduction, but a mere illustration, because they would there have an accidental character only. Nay, without their original relation to all possible experience in which objects of knowledge occur, their relation to any single object would be quite incomprehensible. . . .

There is but one experience in which all perceptions are represented as in permanent and regular connection, as there is but one space and one time in which all forms of phenomena and all relations of being or not being take place. If we speak of different experiences, we only mean different perceptions so far as they belong to one and the same general experience. It is the permanent and synthetical unity of perceptions that constitutes the form of experience, and experience is nothing but the synthetical unity of phenomena according to concepts.

Unity of synthesis, according to empirical concepts, would be purely accidental, nay, unless these were founded on a transcendental ground of unity, a whole crowd of phenomena might rush into our soul, without ever forming real experience. All relation between our knowledge and its objects would be lost at the same time, because that knowledge would no longer be held together by general and necessary laws; it would therefore become thoughtless intuition, never knowledge, and would be to us the same as nothing.

The conditions *a priori* of any possible experience in general are at the same time conditions of the possibility of any objects of our experience. Now I maintain that the categories of which we are speaking are nothing but the conditions of thought which make experience possible, as much as space and time contain the conditions of that intuition which forms experience. These categories therefore are also fundamental concepts by which we think objects in general for the phenomena, and have therefore a *priori* objective validity. This is exactly what we wish to prove.

The possibility, nay the necessity of these categories rests on the relation between our whole sensibility, and therefore all possible phenomena, and that original apperception in which everything must be necessarily subject to the conditions of the permanent unity of self-consciousness, that is, must submit to the general functions of that synthesis which we call synthesis according to concepts, by which alone our apperception can prove its permanent and necessary identity a *priori*. Thus the concept of cause is nothing but a synthesis of that which follows in temporal succession, with other phenomena, but a synthesis according to concepts: and without such a unity which rests on a rule a *priori*, and subjects all phenomena to itself, no permanent and general, and therefore necessary, unity of consciousness would be formed in the manifold of our perceptions. Such perceptions would then belong to no experience at all, they would be without an object, a blind play of representations,—less even than a dream.

All attempts therefore at deriving those pure concepts of the understanding from experience, and ascribing to them a purely empirical origin, are perfectly vain and useless. I shall not dwell here on the fact that a concept of cause, for instance, contains an element of necessity, which no experience can ever supply, because experience, though it teaches us that after one phenomenon something else follows habitually, can never teach us that it follows necessarily, nor that we could a *priori*, and without any limitation, derive from it, as a condition, any conclusion as to what must follow. And thus I ask with reference to that empirical rule of association, which must always be admitted if we say that everything in the succession of events is so entirely subject to rules that nothing ever happens without something preceding it on which it always follows,—What does it rest on, if it is a law of nature, nay, how is that very association possible? You call the ground for the possibility of the association of the manifold, so far as it is contained in the objects themselves, the *affinity* of the manifold. I ask, therefore, how do you make that permanent affinity by which phenomena stand, nay, must stand, under permanent laws, conceivable to yourselves?

According to my principles it is easily conceivable. All possible phenomena belong, as representations, to the whole of our possible self-consciousness. From this, as a transcendental representation, numerical identity is inseparable and *a priori* certain, because nothing can become knowledge except by means of that original apperception. As this identity must necessarily enter into the synthesis of the whole of the manifold of phenomena, if that synthesis is to become empirical knowledge, it follows that the phenomena are subject to conditions *a priori* to which their synthesis (in apprehension) must always conform. The representation of a general condition according to which something manifold *can* be arranged (with uniformity) is called *a rule*, if it *must* be so arranged, *a law*. All phenomena therefore stand in a permanent connection according to necessary laws, and thus possess that transcendental affinity of which the empirical is a mere consequence.

It sounds no doubt very strange and absurd that nature should have to conform to our subjective ground of apperception, nay, be dependent on it, with respect to her laws. But if we consider that what we call nature is nothing but a whole of phenomena, not a thing by itself, but a number of representations in our soul, we shall no longer be surprised that we only see her through the fundamental faculty of all our knowledge, namely, the transcendental apperception, and in that unity without which it could not be called the object (or the whole) of all possible experience, that is, nature. We shall thus also understand why we can recognize this unity *a priori*, and therefore as necessary, which would be perfectly impossible if it were given by itself and independent of the first sources of our own thinking. In that case I could not tell whence we should take the synthetical propositions of such general unity of nature. They would have to be taken from the objects of nature themselves, and as this could be done empirically only, we could derive from it none but an accidental unity, which is very different from that necessary connection which we mean when speaking of nature.

D. Analytic of Principles

¶ OF THE HIGHEST PRINCIPLE OF
ALL SYNTHETICAL JUDGMENTS[12]

The explanation of the possibility of synthetical judgments is a subject of which general logic knows nothing, not even its name, while in a transcendental logic it is the most important task of all, nay, even the only one, when we have to consider the possibility of synthetical

12. A 154-58 = B 193-97.

judgments *a priori*, their conditions, and the extent of their validity. For when that task is accomplished, the object of transcendental logic, namely, to determine the extent and limits of the pure understanding, will have been fully attained.

In forming an analytical judgment I remain within a given concept, while predicating something of it. If what I predicate is affirmative, I only predicate of that concept what is already contained in it; if it is negative, I only exclude from it the opposite of it. In forming synthetical judgments, on the contrary, I have to go beyond a given concept, in order to bring something together with it, which is totally different from what is contained in it. Here we have neither the relation of identity nor of contradiction, and nothing in the judgment itself by which we can discover its truth or its falsehood.

Granted, therefore, that we must go beyond a given concept in order to compare it synthetically with another, something else is necessary in which, as in a third, the synthesis of two concepts becomes possible. What then, is that third? What is the medium of all synthetical judgments? It can only be that in which all our concepts are contained, namely, the internal sense and its *a priori* form, time. The synthesis of representations depends on imagination, but their synthetical unity, which is necessary for forming a judgment, depends on the unity of apperception. It is here therefore that the possibility of synthetical judgments, and (as all the three contain the sources of representations *a priori*) the possibility of pure synthetical judgments also, will have to be discovered; nay, they will on these grounds be necessary, if any knowledge of objects is to be obtained that rests entirely on a synthesis of representations.

If knowledge is to have any objective reality, that is to say, if it is to refer to an object, and receive by means of it any sense and meaning, the object must necessarily be given in some way or other. Without that all concepts are empty. We have thought in them, but we have not, by thus thinking, arrived at any knowledge. We have only played with representations. To give an object, if this it not meant again as mediate only, but if it means to represent something immediately in intuition, is nothing else but to refer the representation of the object to experience (real or possible). Even space and time, however pure these concepts may be of all that is empirical, and however certain it is that they are represented in the mind entirely *a priori*, would lack nevertheless all objective validity, all sense and meaning, if we could not show the necessity of their use with reference to all objects of experience. Nay, their representation is a pure schema, always referring to that reproductive imagination which calls up the objects of experience, without which objects would be meaningless. The same applies to all concepts without any distinction.

It is therefore the *possibility of experience* which alone gives objective reality to all our knowledge *a priori*. Experience, however, depends on the synthetical unity of phenomena, that is, on a synthesis according to concepts of the object of phenomena in general. Without it, it would not even be knowledge, but only a rhapsody of perceptions, which would never grow into a connected text according to the rules of an altogether coherent (possible) consciousness, nor into a transcendental and necessary unity of apperception. Experience depends therefore on *a priori* principles of its form, that is, on general rules of unity in the synthesis of phenomena, and the objective reality of these (rules) can always be shown by their being the necessary conditions in all experience; nay, even in the possibility of all experience. Without such a relation synthetical propositions *a priori* would be quite impossible, because they have no third medium, that is, no object in which the synthetical unity of their concepts could prove their objective reality.

Although we know therefore a great deal *a priori* in synthetical judgments with reference to space in general, or to the figures which productive imagination traces in it, without requiring for it any experience, this our knowledge would nevertheless be nothing but a playing with the cobwebs of our brain, if space were not to be considered as the condition of phenomena which supply the material for external experience. Those pure synthetical judgments therefore refer always, though mediately only, to possible experience, or rather to the possibility of experience, on which alone the objective validity of their synthesis is founded.

As therefore experience, being an empirical synthesis, is in its possibility the only kind of knowledge that imparts reality to every other synthesis, this other synthesis, as knowledge *a priori*, possesses truth (agreement with its object) on this condition only, that it contains nothing beyond what is necessary for the synthetical unity of experience in general.

The highest principle of all synthetical judgments is therefore this, that every object is subject to the necessary conditions of a synthetical unity of the manifold of intuition in a possible experience.

Thus synthetical judgments *a priori* are possible, if we refer the formal conditions of intuition *a priori*, the synthesis of imagination, and the necessary unity of it in a transcendental apperception, to possible empirical knowledge in general, and if we say that the conditions of the possibility of experience in general are at the same time conditions of the possibility of the objects of experience themselves, and thus possess objective validity in a synthetical judgment *a priori*.

¶ THE LAW OF CAUSATION[13]

Everything that happens (begins to be), presupposes something on which it follows according to a rule.

All changes take place according to the law of connection between cause and effect.

Proof

The apprehension of the manifold of phenomena is always successive. The representations of the parts follow one upon another. Whether they also follow one upon the other in the object is a second point for reflection, not contained in the former. We may indeed call everything, even every representation, so far as we are conscious of it, an object; but it requires a more profound investigation to discover what this word may mean with regard to phenomena, not in so far as they (as representations) are objects, but in so far as they only signify an object. So far as they, as representations only, are at the same time objects of consciousness, they cannot be distinguished from our apprehension, that is from their being received in the synthesis of our imagination, and we must therefore say, that the manifold of phenomena is always produced in the mind successively. If phenomena were things by themselves, the succession of the representations of their manifold would never enable us to judge how that manifold is connected in the object. We have always to deal with our representations only; how things may be by themselves (without reference to the representations by which they affect us) is completely beyond the sphere of our knowledge. Since, therefore, phenomena are not things by themselves, and are yet the only thing that can be given to us to know, I am asked to say what kind of connection in time belongs to the manifold of the phenomena itself, when the representation of it in our apprehension is always successive. Thus, for instance, the apprehension of the manifold in the phenomenal appearance of a house that stands before me, is successive. The question then arises, whether the manifold of the house itself be successive by itself, which of course no one would admit. Whenever I ask for the transcendental meaning of my concepts of an object, I find that a house is not a thing by itself, but a phenomenon only, that is, a representation the transcendental object of which is unknown. What then can be the meaning of the question, how the manifold in the phenomenon itself (which is not a thing by

13. From "The Second Analogy of Experience," A 189-95 = B 234-40; A 195-96 = B 240-41. The two sentences given before the *Proof* are, respectively, the formulations in the first and second editions.

itself) may be connected? Here that which is contained in our successive apprehension is considered as representation, and the given phenomenon, though it is nothing but the whole of those representations, as their object, with which my concept, drawn from the representations of my apprehension, is to accord. As the accord between knowledge and its object is truth, it is easily seen, that we can ask here only for the formal conditions of empirical truth, and that the phenomenon, in contradistinction to the representations of our apprehension, can only be represented as the object different from them, if it is subject to a rule distinguishing it from every other apprehension, and necessitating a certain kind of conjunction of the manifold. That which in the phenomenon contains the condition of this necessary rule of apprehension is *the object*.

Let us now proceed to our task. That something takes place, that is, that something, or some state, which did not exist before, begins to exist, cannot be perceived empirically, unless there exists antecedently a phenomenon which does not contain that state; for a reality, following on empty time, that is a beginning of existence, preceded by no state of things, can be apprehended as little as empty time itself. Every apprehension of an event is therefore a perception following on another peception. But as this applies to all synthesis of apprehension, as I showed before in the phenomenal appearance of a house, that apprehension would not thereby be different from any other. But I observe at the same time, that if in a phenomenon which contains an event I call the antecedent state of perception A, and the subsequent B, B can only follow A in my apprehension, while the perception A can never follow B, but can only precede it. I see, for instance, a ship gliding down a stream. My perception of its place below follows my perception of its place higher up in the course of the stream, and it is impossible in the apprehension of this phenomenon that the ship should be perceived first below and then higher up. We see therefore that the order in the succession of perceptions in our apprehension is here determined, and our apprehension regulated by that order. In the former example of a house my perceptions could begin in the apprehension at the roof and end in the basement, or begin below and end above: they could apprehend the manifold of the empirical intuition from right to left or from left to right. There was therefore no determined order in the succession of these perceptions, determining the point where I had to begin in apprehension, in order to connect the manifold empirically; while in the apprehension of an event there is always a rule, which makes the order of the successive perceptions (in the apprehension of this phenomenon) necessary.

In our case, therefore, we shall have to derive the subjective succession in our apprehension from the objective succession of the phenomena, because otherwise the former would be entirely undetermined, and unable to distinguish one phenomenon from another. The former alone proves nothing as to the connection of the manifold in the object, because it is quite arbitrary. The latter must therefore consist in the order of the manifold in a phenomenon, according to which the apprehension of what is happening follows upon the apprehension of what has happened, in conformity with a rule. Thus only can I be justified in saying, not only of my apprehension, but of the phenomenon itself, that there exists in it a succession, which is the same as to say that I cannot arrange the apprehension otherwise than in that very succession.

In conformity with this, there must exist in that which always precedes an event the condition of a rule, by which this event follows at all times, and necessarily; but I cannot go back from the event and determine by apprehension that which precedes. For no phenomenon goes back from the succeeding to the preceding point of time, though it is related to some preceding point of time, while the progress from a given time to a determined following time is necessary. Therefore, as there certainly is something that follows, I must necessarily refer it to something else which precedes, and upon which it follows by rule, that is, by necessity. So that the event, as being conditional, affords a safe indication of some kind of condition, while that condition itself determines the event.

If we supposed that nothing precedes an event upon which such event must follow according to rule, all succession of perception would then exist in apprehension only, that is, subjectively; but it would not thereby be determined objectively, what ought properly to be the antecedent and what the subsequent in perception. We should thus have a mere play of representations unconnected with any object, that is, no phenomenon would, by our perception, be distinguished in time from any other phenomenon, because the succession in apprehension would always be uniform, and there would be nothing in the phenomena to determine the succession, so as to render a certain sequence objectively necessary. I could not say therefore that two states follow each other in a phenomenon, but only that one apprehension follows another, which is purely subjective, and does not determine any object, and cannot be considered therefore as knowledge of anything (even of something purely phenomenal).

If therefore experience teaches us that something happens, we always presuppose that something precedes on which it follows by rule.

Otherwise I could not say of the object that it followed, because its following in my apprehension only, without being determined by rule in reference to what precedes, would not justify us in admitting an objective following. It is therefore always with reference to a rule by which phenomena as they follow, that is as they happen, are determined by an antecedent state, that I can give an objective character to my subjective synthesis (of apprehension); nay, it is under this supposition only that an experience of anything that happens becomes possible.

. . . It might seem indeed as if this were in contradiction to all that has been said on the procedure of the human understanding, it having been supposed that only by perception and comparison of many events following repeatedly in a uniform manner on preceding phenomena are we led to the discovery of a rule according to which certain events always follow on certain phenomena, and that thus only we were enabled to form to ourselves the concept of a cause. If this were so, that concept would be empirical only, and the rule which it supplies, that everything which happens must have a cause, would be as contingent as the experience on which it is based. The universality and necessity of that rule would then be fictitious only, and devoid of any true and universal validity; it would not be *a priori* but founded on induction only. The case is the same with other pure representations *a priori* (for instance, space and time), of which we are able to extract clear concepts from experience only because we have put them first into experience, and because experience is rendered possible only by them, it is true, no doubt, that the logical clearness of this representation of a rule determining the succession of events, as a concept of a cause, becomes possible only when we have used it in experience, but as the condition of the synthetical unity of phenomena in time, it was nevertheless the foundation of all experience, and consequently preceded it *a priori*.

¶ POSSIBILITY, REALITY, AND NECESSITY[14]

1. What agrees with the formal conditions of experience (in intuition and in concepts) is possible
2. What is connected with the material conditions of experience (sensation) is real
3. That which, in its connection with the real, is determined by universal conditions of experience, is (exists as) necessary

14. From "The Postulates of Empirical Thought in General," A 218, 225-30 = B 265, 267, 272-73, 278-82.

The postulate of the possibility of things demands that the concept of these should agree with the formal conditions of experience in general. This, the objective form of experience in general, contains all synthesis which is required for a knowledge of objects. A concept is to be considered as empty, and as referring to no object, if the synthesis which it contains does not belong to experience, whether as borrowed from it (in which case it is called an empirical concept), or as a synthesis on which, as a condition *a priori*, all experience (in its form) depends, in which case it is a pure concept, but yet belonging to experience, because its object can only be found in it. For whence could the character of the possibility of an object, which can be conceived by a synthetical concept *a priori*, be derived, except from the synthesis which constitutes the form of all empirical knowledge of objects? It is no doubt a necessary logical condition, that such a concept must contain nothing contradictory, but this is by no means sufficient to establish the objective reality of a concept, that is, the possibility of such an object, as is conceived by a concept. Thus in the concept of a figure to be enclosed between two straight lines, there is nothing contradictory, because the concepts of two straight lines and their meeting contain no negation of a figure. The impossibility depends, not on the concept itself, but on its construction in space, that is, the conditions of space and its determinations, and it is these that have objective reality, or apply to possible things, because they contain *a priori* in themselves the form of experience in general.

The postulate concerning our knowledge of the *reality* of things, requires *perception*, therefore sensation and consciousness of it, not indeed immediately of the object itself, the existence of which is to be known, but yet of a connection between it and some real perception, according to the analogies of experience which determine in general all real combinations in experience.

In the *mere concept* of a thing no sign of its existence can be discovered. For though the concept be ever so perfect, so that nothing should be wanting in it to enable us to conceive the thing with all its own determinations, existence has nothing to do with all this. It depends only on the question whether such a thing be given us, so that its perception may even precede its concept. A concept preceding experience implies its possibility only, while perception, which supplies the material of a concept, is the only indication of reality. It is possible, however, even before the perception of a thing, and therefore, in a certain sense, *a priori*, to know its existence, provided it hang together with some other perceptions, according to the principles of their empirical connection (analogies). For in that case the existence of a thing hangs together at least with our perceptions in a possible experience, and guided by our analogies we can, starting from our real experience, arrive at some other thing in the series of possible perceptions. Thus we know the existence of some magnetic matter pervading all bodies from the perception of the attracted iron fiings, though our organs are so constituted as to render an immediate perception of that matter impossible. According to the laws of sensibility and the texture of our perceptions, we ought in our experience to arrive at an immediate empirical intuition of that magnetic matter, if only our senses were more acute, for their acutal obtuseness does not concern the form of possible experience. Wherever, therefore, perception and its train can reach, according to empirical laws, there our knowledge also of the existence of things can reach. But if we do not begin with experience, or do not proceed according to the laws of the empirical connection of phenomena, we are only making a vain display, as if we could guess and discover the existence of anything.

With reference to the third postulate we find that it refers to the material necessity in existence, and not to the merely formal and logical necessity in the connection of concepts. As it is impossible that the existence of the objects of the senses should ever be known entirely *a priori*, though it may be known to a certain extent *a priori*, namely with reference to another already given existence, and as even in that case we can only arrive at such an existence as must somewhere be contained in the whole of the experience of which the given perception forms a part, it follows that the necessity of existence can never be known from concepts, but always from the connection only with what is actually perceived, according to general rules of experience. Now, there is no existence that can be known as necessary under the condition of other given phenomena, except the existence of effects from given causes, according to the laws of causality. It is not therefore the existence of things (substances), but the existence of their state, of which alone we can know the necessity, and this from other states only, which are given in perception, and according to the empirical laws of causality. Hence it follows that the criterion of necessity can only be found in the law of possible experience, viz. that everything that happens is determined *a priori* by its cause in phenomena. We therefore know in nature the necessity of those effects only of which the causes are given, and the character of necessity in existence never goes beyond the field of possible experience, and even there it does not apply to the existence of things, as substances, because such substances can never be looked upon as empirical effects or as something that happens and arises. Necessity, therefore, affects only the relations of phenomena according to the dynamical law of causality, and the possibility, dependent upon it, of concluding *a priori* from a given existence (of a cause) to another existence (that of an effect). Thus the principle that everything which happens is hypothetically necessary, subjects all the changes in the world to a law, that is, to a rule of necessary existence, without which there would not even be such a thing as nature. Hence the proposition that nothing happens by blind chance *(in mundo non datur casus)* is an *a priori* law of nature, and so is likewise the other, that no necessity in nature is a blind, but always a conditional and therefore an intelligible, necessity *(non datur fatum)*. Both these are laws by which the mere play of changes is rendered subject to a *nature of things* (as phenomena), or what is the same, to that unity of the understanding in which alone they can belong to experience, as the synthetical unity of phenomena.

E. Transcendental Dialectic

¶ INTRODUCTION[15]

We have now not only traversed the whole domain of the pure understanding, and carefully examined each part of it, but we have also measured its extent, and assigned to everything in it its proper place. This domain, however, is an island and enclosed by nature itself within limits that can never be changed. It is the country of truth (a very attractive name), but surrounded by a wide and stormy ocean, the true home of illusion, where many a fog bank and ice that soon melts away tempt us to believe in new lands, while constantly deceiving the adventurous mariner with vain hopes, and involving him in adventures which he can never leave, and yet can never bring to an end.

There exists a natural and inevitable Dialectic of pure reason, not one in which a mere bungler might get entangled from want of knowledge, or which a sophist might artificially devise to confuse rational people, but one that is inherent in, and inseparable from human reason, and which, even after its illusion has been exposed, will never cease to fascinate our reason, and to precipitate it into momentary errors, such as require to be removed again and again.

15. The first paragraph (A 235-36 = B 295-96) is not from the Dialectic proper, but serves as a good introduction to it; the second is from the Dialectic, A 298-99 = B 354-55.

¶ Freedom of the Will
The Third Antinomy[16]

If every collection of dogmatical doctrines is called *Thetic,* I ma
denote by *Antithetic,* not indeed dogmatical assertions of the opposit
but the conflict between different kinds of apparently dogmatica
knowledge *(thesis cum antithesis),* to none of which we can ascribe
superior claim to our assent. This antithetic, therefore, has nothing t
do with one-sided assertions, but considers general knowledge of reaso
with reference to the conflict only that goes on in it, and its causes. Th
transcendental antithetic is in fact an investigation of the antinomy o
pure reason, its causes and its results. If we apply our reason, not onl
to objects of experience, in order to make use of the principles of th
understanding, but venture to extend it beyond the limit of experienc
there arise rationalising or sophistical propositions, which can neithe
hope for confirmation nor need fear refutation from experience. Ever
one of them is not only in itself free from contradiction, but can poin
to conditions of its necessity in the nature of reason itself, only tha
unfortunately, its opposite can produce equally valid and necessar
grounds for its support.

Thesis

Causality, according to the laws of nature, is not the only causalit
from which all the phenomena of the world can be deduced. In order t
account for these phenomena is it necessary also to admit anothe
causality, that of freedom.

Proof

Let us assume that there is no other causality but that according
to the laws of nature. In that case everything that *takes place,* pre
supposes an anterior state, on which it follows inevitably according t
a rule. But that anterior state must itself be something which ha
taken place (which has come to be in time, and did not exist before)
because, if it had always existed, its effect too would not have onl
just arisen, but have existed always. The causality, therefore, of a
cause, through which something takes place, is itself an *event,* whicl
again, according to the law of nature, presupposes an anterior state and
its causality, and this again an anterior state, and so on. If, therefore
everything takes place according to mere laws of nature, there wil
always be a secondary only, but never a primary beginning, and there
fore no completeness of the series, on the side of successive causes
But the law of nature consists in this, that nothing takes place withou

16. A 420-21 = B 448-49; A 444-46 = B 472-74.

a cause sufficiently determined *a priori*. Therefore the proposition, that all causality is possible according to the laws of nature only, contradicts itself, if taken in unlimited generality, and it is impossible, therefore, to admit that causality as the only one.

We must therefore admit another causality, through which something takes place, without its cause being further determined according to necessary laws by a preceding cause, that is, an *absolute spontaneity* of causes, by which a series of phenomena, proceeding according to natural laws, begins by itself; we must consequently admit transcendental freedom, without which, even in the course of nature, the series of phenomena on the side of causes, can never be perfect.

Antithesis

There is no freedom, but everything in the world takes place entirely according to the laws of nature.

Proof

If we admit that there is *freedom*, in the transcendental sense, as a particular kind of causality, according to which the events in the world could take place, that is a faculty of absolutely originating a state, and with it a series of consequences, it would follow that not only a series would have its absolute beginning through this spontaneity, but the determination of that spontaneity itself to produce the series, that is, the causality, would have an absolute beginning, nothing preceding it by which this act is determined according to permanent laws. Every beginning of an act, however, presupposes a state in which the cause is not yet active, and a dynamically primary beginning of an act presupposes a state which has no casual connection with the preceding state of that cause, that is, in no wise follows from it. Transcendental freedom is therefore opposed to the law of causality, and represents such a connection of successive states of effective causes, that no unity of experience is possible with it. It is therefore an empty fiction of the mind, and not to be met with in any experience.

We have, therefore, nothing but *nature,* in which we must try to find the connection and order of cosmical events. Freedom (independence) from the laws of nature is no doubt a *deliverance* from restraint, but also from the *guidance* of all rules. For we cannot say that, instead of the laws of nature, laws of freedom may enter into the causality of the course of the world, because, if determined by laws, it would not be freedom, but nothing else but nature. Nature, therefore, and transcendental freedom differ from each other like legality and lawlessness. The former, no doubt, imposes upon the understanding the difficult task of looking higher and higher for the origin of events in the series of causes, because their causality is always conditioned. In return for this, however, it promises a complete and well-ordered unity of experience; while, on the other side, the fiction of freedom promises, no doubt, to the enquiring mind, rest in the chain of causes, leading him up to an unconditioned causality, which begins to act by itself, but which, as it is blind itself, tears the thread of rules by which alone a complete and coherent experience is possible.

¶ CRITICAL DECISION OF THE COSMOLOGICAL CONFLICT OF REASON WITH ITSELF[17]

The whole antinomy of pure reason rests on the dialectical argument that, if the conditioned is given, the whole series of conditions also is given. As therefore the objects of the senses are given us as conditioned, it follows, etc. Through this argument, the major of which seems so natural and self-evident, cosmological ideas[18] have been introduced corresponding in number to the difference of conditions (in the synthesis of phenomena) which constitute a series. These cosmological ideas postulate the absolute totality of those series, and thus place reason in inevitable contradiction with itself. Before, however, we show what is deceptive in this sophistical argument, we must prepare ourselves for it by correcting and defining certain concepts occurring in it.

First, the following proposition is clear and admits of no doubt, that if the conditioned is given, it imposes on us the regressus in the series of all conditions of it; for it follows from the very concept of the conditioned that through it something is referred to a condition, and, if that condition is again conditioned, to a more distant condition, and so on through all the members of the series. This proposition is really analytical, and need not fear any transcendental criticism. It is a logical postulate of reason to follow up through the understanding, as far as possible, that connection of a concept with its conditions, which is inherent in the concept itself.

Further, if the conditioned as well as its conditions are things by themselves, then, if the former be given, the regressus to the latter is not only *required,* but is really *given;* and as this applies to all the members of the series, the complete series of conditions and with it

---

17. A 497-502 = 525-30.

18. Kant uses the word "idea" to name a pure concept of reason, which is a necessary *a priori* concept for which no object can be found within experience. Hence it is (erroneously) thought by speculative metaphysicians that it has a super-sensible object. (That is why Kant uses the Platonic word "idea" when referring to a pure concept of reason; he is *not* using the word in Locke's sense.) L. W. B.

the unconditioned also is given, or rather it is presupposed that the conditioned, which was possible through that series only, is given. Here the synthesis of the conditioned with its conditon is a synthesis of the understanding only, which represents things *as they are*, without asking whether and how we can arrive at the knowledge of them. But if I have to deal with phenomena, which, as mere representations, are not given at all unless I attain to a knowledge of them (that is, to the phenomena themselves, for they are nothing but empirical knowledge), then I cannot say in the same sense that, if the conditioned is given, all its conditions (as phenomena) are also given, and can therefore by no means conclude the absolute totality of the series. For *phenomena* in their apprehension are themselves nothing but an empirical synthesis (in space and time), and are given therefore in *that* synthesis only. Now it follows by no means that, if the conditioned (as phenomenal) is given, the synthesis also that constitutes its empirical condition should thereby be given at the same time and presupposed; for this takes place in the regressus only, and never without it. What we may say in such a case is this, that a regressus to the conditions, that is, a continued empirical synthesis in that direction is required, and that conditions cannot be wanting that are given through that regressus.

Hence we see that the major of the cosmological argument takes the conditioned in the transcendental sense of a pure category, while the minor takes it in the empirical sense of a concept of the under-standing, referring to mere phenomena, so that it contains that dia-lectical deceit which is called *Sophisma figurae dictionis*. That deceit, however, is not artificial, but a perfectly natural illusion of our common reason. It is owing to it that, in the major, we presuppose the conditions and their series as it were *on trust*, if anything is given as conditioned, because this is no more than the logical postulate to assume complete premisses for any given conclusion. Nor does there exist in the con-nection of the conditioned with its condition any order of time, but they are presupposed in themselves as given *together*. It is equally natural also in the minor to look on phenomena as things by themselves, and as objects given to the understanding only in the same manner as in the major, as no account was taken of all the conditions of intuition under which alone objects can be given. But there is an important distinction between these concepts, which has been over-looked. The synthesis of the conditioned with its condition, and the whole series of conditions in the major, was in no way limited by time, and was free from any concept of succession. The empirical synthesis, on the contrary, and the series of conditions in phenomena, which was subsumed in the minor, is necessarily successive and given as such in time only. Therefore I had no right to assume the absolute *totality* of the synthesis and of the series represented by it in this case as well as in the former. For in the former all the members of the series are given by themselves (without determination in time), while here they are possible through the successive regressus only, which cannot exist unless it is actually carried out.

After convicting them of such a mistake in the argument adopted by both parties as the foundation of their cosmological assertions, both might justly be dismissed as not being able to produce any good title in support of their claims. But even thus their quarrel is not yet ended, as if it had been proved that both parties, or one of them, were wrong in the matter contended for (in the conclusion), though they had failed to support it by valid proof. Nothing seems clearer than that, if one maintains that the world has a beginning, and the other that it has no beginning, but exists from all eternity, one or the other must be right. But if this were so, as the arguments on both sides are equally clear, it would still remain impossible ever to find out on which side the truth lies, and the suit continues, although both parties have been ordered to keep the peace before the tribunal of reason. Nothing remains therefore in order to settle the quarrel once for all, and to the satisfaction of both parties, but to convince them that, though they can refute each other so eloquently, they are really quarrelling about nothing, and that a certain transcendental illusion has mocked them with a reality where no reality exists. We shall now enter upon this way of adjusting a dispute which cannot be adjudicated.

¶ SOLUTION OF THE COSMOLOGICAL IDEA WITH
REGARD TO THE TOTALITY OF THE DERIVATION
OF COSMICAL EVENTS FROM THEIR CAUSES[19]

We can conceive two kinds of causality only with reference to events, causality either of *nature* or of *freedom*. The former is the connection of one state in the world of sense with a preceding state, on which it follows according to a rule. As the *causality* of phenomena depends on conditions of time, and as the preceding state, if it had always existed, could not have produced an effect, which first takes place in time, it follows that the causality of the cause of that which happens or arises must, according to the principle of the understanding, have itself *arisen* and require a cause.

By freedom, on the contrary, in its cosmological meaning, I understand the faculty of beginning a state *spontaneously*. Its causality,

19. A 532-37 = B 560-65.

therefore, does not depend, according to the law of nature, on another cause, by which it is determined in time. In this sense freedom is a purely transcendental idea, which, first, contains nothing derived from *experience*, and, secondly, the object of which cannot be determined in any *experience;* because it is a general rule, even of the possibility of all *experience*, that everything which happens has a cause, and that therefore the causality also of the cause, which *itself has happened* or arisen, must again have a cause. In this manner the whole field of experience, however far it may extend, has been changed into one great whole of nature. As, however, it is impossible in this way to arrive at an absolute totality of the conditions in causal relations, reason creates for itself the idea of spontaneity, or the power of beginning by itself, without an antecedent cause determining it to action, according to the law of causal connection.

It is extremely remarkable, that the practical concept of freedom is founded on the *transcendental idea of freedom,* which constitutes indeed the real difficulty which at all times has surrounded the question of the possibility of freedom. *Freedom,* in its *practical sense,* is the independence of our (arbitrary) will from the *coercion* through sensuous impulses. Our (arbitrary) will is *sensuous,* so far as it is *affected pathologically* (by sensuous impulses); it is called animal *(arbitrium brutum),* if *necessitated* pathologically. The human will is certainly sensuous, an *arbitrium sensitivum,* but not *brutum,* but *liberum,* because sensuous impulses do not necessitate its action, but there is in man a faculty of determination, independent of the necessitation through sensuous impulses.

It can easily be seen that, if all causality in the world of sense belonged to nature, every event would be determined in time through another, according to necessary laws. As therefore the phenomena, in determining the will, would render every act necessary as their natural effect, the annihilation of transcendental freedom would at the same time destroy all practical freedom. Practical freedom presupposes that, although something has not happened, it *ought* to have happened, and that its cause therefore had not that determining force among phenomena, which could prevent the causality of our will from producing, independently of those natural causes, and even contrary to their force and influence, something determined in the order of time, according to empirical laws, and from originating *entirely by itself* a series of events.

What happens here is what happens generally in the conflict of reason venturing beyond the limits of possible experience, namely, that the problem is not *physiological,* but *transcendental.* Hence the question of the possibility of freedom concerns no doubt psychology; but its solution, as it depends on dialectical arguments of pure reason, belongs entirely to transcendental philosophy. In order to enable that philosophy to give a satisfactory answer, which it cannot decline to do, I must first try to determine more accurately its proper procedure in this task.

If phenomena were things by themselves, and therefore space and time forms of the existence of things by themselves, the conditions together with the conditioned would always belong, as members, to one and the same series, and thus in our case also, the antinomy which is common to all transcendental ideas would arise, namely, that that series is inevitably too large or too small for the understanding. The dynamical concepts of reason, however, which we have to discuss in this and the following section, have this peculiarity that, as they are not concerned with an object, considered as a quantity, but only with its *existence*, we need take no account of the quantity of the series of conditions. All depends here only on the dynamical relation of conditions to the conditioned, so that in the question on nature and freedom we at once meet with the difficulty, whether freedom is indeed possible, and whether, if it is possible, it can exist together with the universality of the natural law of causality. The question in fact arises, whether it is a proper disjunctive proposition to say, that every effect in the world must arise, *either* from nature, *or* from freedom, or whether *both* cannot coexist in the same event in different relations. The correctness of the principle of the unbroken connection of all events in the world of sense, according to unchangeable natural laws, is firmly established by the transcendental Analytic, and admits of no limitation. The question, therefore, can only be whether, in spite of it, freedom also can be found in the same effect which is determined by nature; or whether freedom is entirely excluded by that inviolable rule? Here the common but fallacious supposition of the *absolute reality* of phenomena shows at once its pernicious influence in embarrassing reason. For if phenomena are things by themselves, freedom cannot be saved. Nature in that case is the complete and sufficient cause determining every event, and its condition is always contained in that series of phenomena only which, together with their effect, are necessary under the law of nature. If, on the contrary, phenomena are taken for nothing except what they are in reality, namely, not things by themselves, but representations only, which are connected with each other according to empirical laws, they must themselves have causes which are not phenomenal. Such an intelligible cause, however, is not determined with reference to its causality by phenomena, although its effects become phenomenal, and can thus be determined by other phenomena. That intelligible cause, therefore, with its causality, is outside the series, though its effects are to be found in the series of empirical conditions. The effect therefore can, with reference to its intelligible cause, be considered as free, and yet at the same time, with reference to phenomena, as resulting from them according to the necessity of nature; a distinction which, if thus represented, in a general and entirely abstract form, may seem extremely subtle and obscure, but will become clear in its practical application. Here I only wished to remark that, as the unbroken *connection* of all phenomena in the context (woof) of nature, is an unalterable law, it would necessarily destroy all freedom, if we were to defend obstinately the reality of phenomena. Those, therefore, who follow the common opinion on this subject, have never been able to reconcile nature and freedom.

¶ POSSIBILITY OF A CAUSALITY THROUGH FREEDOM, IN HARMONY WITH THE UNIVERSAL LAW OF NATURAL NECESSITY[20]

Whatever in an object of the senses is not itself phenomenal, I call *intelligible*. If, therefore, what in the world of sense must be considered as phenomenal, possesses in itself a faculty which is not the object of sensuous intuition, but through which it can become the cause of phenomena, the *causality* of that being may be considered from *two sides*, as *intelligible* in its *action*, as the causality of a thing by itself, and as *sensible* in the *effects* of the action, as the causality of a phenomenon in the world of sense. Of the faculty of such a being we should have to form both an *empirical* and an *intellectual concept* of its causality, both of which consist together in one and the same effect. This twofold way of conceiving the faculty of an object of the senses does not contradict any of the concepts which we have to form of phenomena and of a possible experience. For as all phenomena, not being things by themselves, must have for their foundation a transcendental object, determining them as mere representations, there is nothing to prevent us from attributing to that transcendental object, besides the quality through which it becomes phenomenal, a *causality* also which is not phenomenal, although its *effect* appears in the phenomenon. Every efficient cause, however, must have a *character*, that is, a rule according to which it manifests its causality, and without which it would not be a cause. According to this we should have in every subject of the world of sense, first, an *empirical character*, through which its acts, as phenomena, stand with other phenomena in

20. A 538-41 = B 566-69.

an unbroken connection, according to permanent laws of nature, and could be derived from them as their conditions, and in connection with them form the links of one and the same series in the order of nature. Secondly, we should have to allow to it an *intelligible character* also, by which, it is true, it becomes the cause of the same acts as phenomena, but which itself is not subject to any conditions of sensibility, and never phenomenal. We might call the former the character of such a thing as a phenomenon, in the latter the character of the thing by itself.

According to its intelligible character, this active subject would not depend on conditions of time, for time is only the condition of phenomena, and not of things by themselves. In it no *act* would *arise* or *perish*, neither would it be subject therefore to the law of determination in time and of all that is changeable, namely, that everything *which happens* must have its cause in *the phenomena* (of the previous state). In one word its causality, so far as it is intelligible, would not have a place in the series of empirical conditions by which the event is rendered necessary in the world of sense. It is true that that intelligible character could never be known immediately, because we cannot perceive anything, except so far as it appears, but it would nevertheless have to be conceived, according to the empirical character, as we must always admit in thought a transcendental object, as the foundation of phenomena, though we know nothing of what it is by itself.

In its empirical character, therefore, that subject, as a phenomenon, would submit, according to all determining laws, to a causal nexus, and in that respect it would be nothing but a part of the world of sense, the effects of which, like every other phenomenon, would arise from nature without fail. As soon as external phenomena began to influence it, and as soon as its empirical character, that is the law of its causality, had been known through experience, all its actions ought to admit of explanation, according to the laws of nature, and all that is requisite for its complete and necessary determination would be found in a possible experience.

In its intelligible character, however (though we could only have a general concept of it), the same subject would have to be considered free from all influence of sensibility, and from all determination through phenomena: and as in it, so far as it is a *noumenon*, nothing *happens*, and no change which requires dynamical determination of time, and therefore no connection with phenomena as causes, can exist, that active being would so far be quite independent and free in its acts from all natural necessity, which can exist in the world of sense only. One might say of it with perfect truth that it originates its effects in the world of sense *by itself*, though the act does not begin *in itself*. And this would be perfectly true, though the effects in the world of sense need not therefore originate by themselves, because in it they are always determined previously through empirical conditions in the previous time, though only by means of the empirical character (which is the phenomenal appearance of the intelligible character), and therefore impossible, except as a continuation of the series of natural causes. In this way freedom and nature, each in its complete signification, might exist together and without any conflict in the same action, according as we refer it to its intelligible or to its sensible cause.

¶ EXPLANATION OF THE COSMOLOGICAL IDEA OF FREEDOM IN CONNECTION WITH THE GENERAL NECESSITY OF NATURE[21]

I thought it best to give first this sketch of the solution of our transcendental problem, so that the course which reason has to adopt in its solution might be more clearly surveyed. We shall now proceed to explain more fully the points on which the decision properly rests, and examine each by itself.

The law of nature, that everything which happens has a cause,— that the causality of that cause, that is, its *activity* (as it is anterior in time, and, with regard to an effect which has *arisen,* cannot itself have always existed, but must have *happened* at some time), must have its cause among the phenomena by which it is determined, and that therefore all events in the order of nature are empirically determined, this law, I say, through which alone phenomena become *nature* and objects of experience, is a law of the understanding which can on no account be surrendered, and from which no single phenomenon can be exempted; because in doing this we should place it outside all possible experience, separate from all objects of possible experience, and change it into a mere fiction of the mind or a cobweb of the brain.

But although this looks merely like a chain of causes, which in the regressus to its conditions admits of no *absolute totality*, this difficulty does not detain us in the least, because it has already been removed in the general criticism of the antinomy of reason when, starting from the series of phenomena, it aims at the unconditioned. Were we to yield to the illusion of transcendental realism, we should have neither nature nor freedom. The question therefore is, whether, if we recognise in the whole series of events nothing but natural

21. A 542-58 = B 570-86.

necessity, we may yet regard the same event which on one side is an effect of nature only, on the other side, as an effect of freedom; or whether there is a direct contradiction between these two kinds of causality?

There can certainly be nothing among phenomenal causes that could originate a series absolutely and by itself. Every action, as a phenomenon, so far as it produces an event, is itself an event, presupposing another state, in which its cause can be discovered; and thus everything that happens is only a continuation of the series, and no beginning, happening by itself, is possible in it. Actions of natural causes in the succession of time are therefore themselves effects, which likewise presuppose causes in the series of time. A *spontaneous* and original action by which something takes place, which did not exist before, cannot be expected from the causal nexus of phenomena.

But is it really necessary that, if effects are phenomena, the causality of their cause, which cause itself is phenomenal, could be nothing but empirical; or is it not possible, although for every phenomenal effect a connection with its cause, according to the laws of empirical causality, is certainly required, that empirical causality itself could nevertheless, without breaking in the least its connection with the natural causes, represent an effect of a non-empirical and intelligible causality, that is, of a caused action, original in respect to phenomena, and in so far not phenomenal; but, with respect to this faculty, intelligible, although, as a link in the chain of nature, to be regarded as entirely belonging to the world of sense?

We require the principle of the causality of phenomena among themselves, in order to be able to look for and to produce natural conditions, that is, phenomenal causes of natural events. If this is admitted and not weakened by any exceptions, the understanding, which in its empirical employment recognises in all events nothing but nature, and is quite justified in doing so, has really all that it can demand, and the explanations of physical phenomena may proceed without let or hindrance. The understanding would not be wronged in the least, if we assumed, though it be a mere fiction, that some among the natural causes have a faculty which is intelligible only, and whose determination to activity does not rest on empirical conditions, but on mere grounds of the intellect, if only the *phenomenal activity* of that cause is in accordance with all the laws of empirical causality. For in this way the active subject, as *causa phaenomenon*, would be joined with nature through the indissoluble dependence of all its actions, and the noumenon only of that subject (with all its phenomenal causality) would contain certain conditions which, if we want to ascend from the empirical to the transcendental object, would have to be considered as intelligible only. For, if only we follow the rule of nature in that which may be the cause among phenomena, it is indifferent to us what kind of ground of those phenomena, and of their connection, may be conceived to exist in the transcendental subject, which is empirically unknown to us. This intelligible ground does not touch the empirical questions, but concerns only, as it would seem, the thought in the pure understanding; and although the effects of that thought and action of the pure understanding may be discovered in the phenomena, these have nevertheless to be completely explained from their phenomenal cause, according to the laws of nature, by taking their empirical character as the highest ground of explanation, and passing by the intelligible character, which is the transcendental cause of the other, as entirely unknown, except so far as it is indicated by the empirical, as its sensuous sign. Let us apply this to experience. Man is one among the phenomena of the world of sense, and in so far one of the natural causes the causality of which must be subject to empirical laws. As such he must therefore have an empirical character, like all other objects of nature. We perceive it through the forces and faculties which he shows in his actions and effects. In the lifeless or merely animal nature we seen no ground for admitting any faculty, except as sensuously conditioned. Man, however, who knows all the rest of nature through his senses only, knows himself through mere apperception also, and this in actions and internal determinations, which he cannot ascribe to the impressions of the senses. Man is thus to himself partly a phenomenon, partly, however, namely with reference to certain faculties, a purely intelligible object, because the actions of these faculties cannot be ascribed to the receptivity of sensibility. We call these faculties understanding and reason. It is the latter, in particular, which is entirely distinguished from all empirically conditioned forces or faculties, because it weighs its objects according to ideas, and determines the understanding accordingly, which then makes an empirical use of its (by themselves, however pure) concepts.

That our reason possesses causality, or that we at least represent to ourselves such a causality in it, is clear from the *imperatives* which, in all practical matters, we impose as rules on our executive powers. The *ought* expresses a kind of necessity and connection with causes, which we do not find elsewhere in the whole of nature. The understanding can know in nature only what is present, past, or future. It is impossible that anything in it *ought to be* different from what it is in reality, in all these relations of time. Nay, if we only look at the course of nature, the ought has no meaning whatever. We cannot ask, what ought to be in nature, as little as we can ask, what qualities a circle ought to possess. We can only ask what happens in it, and what qualities that which happens has.

This ought expresses a possible action, the ground of which cannot be anything but a mere concept; while in every merely natural action the ground must always be a phenomenon. Now it is quite true that the action to which the ought applies must be possible under natural conditions, but these natural conditions do not affect the determination of the will itself, but only its effects and results among phenomena. There may be ever so many natural grounds which impel me to *will* and ever so many sensuous temptations, but they can never produce the *ought*, but only a willing which is always conditioned, but by no means necessary, and to which the ought, pronounced by reason, opposes measure, ay, prohibition and authority. Whether it be an object of the senses merely (pleasure), or of pure reason (the good), reason does not yield to the impulse that is given empirically, and does not follow the order of things, as they present themselves as phenomena, but frames for itself, with perfect spontaneity, a new order according to ideas to which it adapts the empirical conditions, and according to which it declares actions to be necessary, even though they *have not taken place*, and, maybe, never will take place. Yet it is presupposed that reason may have causality with respect to them, for otherwise no effects in experience could be expected to result from these ideas.

Now let us take our stand here and admit it at least as possible, that reason really possesses causality with reference to phenomena. In that case, reason though it be, it must show nevertheless an empirical character, because every cause presupposes a rule according to which certain phenomena follow as effects, and every rule requires in the effects a homogeneousness, on which the concept of cause (as a faculty) is founded. This, so far as it is derived from mere phenomena, may be called the empirical character, which is *permanent*, while the effects, according to a diversity of concomitant, and in part, restraining conditions, appear in *changeable* forms.

Every man therefore has an empirical character of his (arbitrary) will, which is nothing but a certain causality of his reason, exhibiting in its phenomenal actions and effects a rule, according to which one may infer the motives of reason and its actions, both in kind and in degree, and judge of the subjective principles of his will. As that empirical character itself must be derived from phenomena, as an effect, and from their rule which is supplied by experience, all the acts of a man, so far as they are phenomena, are determined from his empirical character and from the other concomitant causes, according to the order of nature; and if we could investigate all the manifestations of his will to the very bottom, there would be not a single human action which we could not predict with certainty and recognise from its preceding conditions as necessary. There is no freedom therefore with reference to this empirical character, and yet it is only with reference to it that we can consider man, when we are merely *observing*, and, as is the case in anthropology, trying to investigate the motive causes of his actions physiologically.

If, however, we consider the same actions with reference to reason, not with reference to speculative reason, in order to *explain* their origin, but solely so far as reason is the cause which *produces* them; in one word, if we compare actions with reason, with reference to *practical* purposes, we find a rule and order, totally different from the order of nature. For, from this point of view, everything, it may be, *ought not to have happened*, which according to the course of nature *has happened*, and according to its empirical grounds, was inevitable. And sometimes we find, or believe at least that we find, that the ideas of reason have really proved their causality with reference to human actions as phenomena, and that these actions have taken place, not because they were determined by empirical causes, but by the causes of reason.

Now supposing one could say that reason possesses causality in reference to phenomena, could the action of reason be called free in that case, as it is accurately determined by the empirical character (the disposition) and rendered necessary by it? That character again is determined in the intelligible character (way of thinking). The latter, however, we do not know, but signify only through phenomena, which in reality give us immediately a knowledge of the disposition (empirical character) only.[22] An action, so far as it is to be attributed to the way of thinking as its cause, does nevertheless not result from it according to empirical laws, that is, it is not *preceded* by the conditions of pure reason, but only by its effects in the phenomenal form of the internal sense. Pure reason, as a simple intelligible faculty, is not subject to the form of time, or to the conditions of the succession of time. The causality of reason in its intelligible character does *not arise* or begin at a certain time in order to produce an effect; for in

22. The true morality of actions (merit or guilt), even that of our own conduct, remains therefore entirely hidden. Our imputations can refer to the empirical character only. How much of that may be the pure effect of freedom, how much should be ascribed to nature only, and to the faults of temperament, for which man is not responsible, or its happy constitution (*merito fortunae*), no one can discover, and no one can judge with perfect justice. [Kant's note.]

that case it would be subject to the natural law of phenomena, which determines all causal series in time, and its causality would then be nature and not freedom. What, therefore, we can say is, that if reason can possess causality with reference to phenomena, it is a faculty *through which* the sensuous condition of an empirical series of effects first begins. For the condition that lies in reason is not sensuous, and therefore does itself not begin. Thus we get what we missed in all empirical series, namely, that the *condition* of a successive series of events should itself be empirically unconditioned. For here the condition is really *outside* the series of phenomena (in the intelligible), and therefore not subject to any sensuous condition, nor to any temporal determination through preceding causes.

Nevertheless the same cause belongs also, in another respect, to the series of phenomena. Man himself is a phenomenon. His will has an empirical character, which is the (empirical) cause of all his actions. There is no condition, determining man according to this character, that is not contained in the series of natural effects and subject to their law, according to which there can be no empirically unconditioned causality of anything that happens in time. No given action therefore (as it can be perceived as a phenomenon only) can begin absolutely by itself. Of pure reason, however, we cannot say that the state in which it determines the will is preceded by another in which that state itself is determined. For as reason itself is not a phenomenon, and not subject to any of the conditions of sensibility, there exists in it, even in reference to its causality, no succession of time, and the dynamical law of nature, which determines the succession of time according to rules, cannot be applied to it.

Reason is therefore the constant condition of all free actions by which man takes his place in the phenomenal world. Every one of them is determined beforehand in his empirical character, before it becomes actual. With regard to the intelligible character, however, of which the empirical is only the sensuous schema, there is neither *before* nor *after;* and every action, without regard to the temporal relation which connects it with other phenomena, is the immediate effect of the intelligible character of pure reason. That reason therefore acts freely, without being determined dynamically, in the chain of natural causes, by external or internal conditions, anterior in time. That freedom must then not only be regarded negatively, as independence of empirical conditions (for in that case the faculty of reason would cease to be a cause of phenomena), but should be determined positively also, as the faculty of beginning spontaneously a series of events. Hence nothing begins in reason itself, and being itself the unconditioned condition of every free action, reason admits of no condition antecedent in time above itself, while nevertheless its effect takes its beginning in the series of phenomena, though it can never constitute in that series an *absolute* first beginning.

In order to illustrate the regulative principle of reason by an example of its empirical application, not in order to confirm it (for such arguments are useless for transcendental propositions), let us take a voluntary action, for example, a malicious lie, by which a man has produced a certain confusion in society, and of which we first try to find out the motives, and afterwards try to determine how far it and its consequences may be imputed to the offender. With regard to the first point, one has first to follow up his empirical character to its very sources, which are to be found in wrong education, bad society, in part also in the viciousness of a natural disposition, and a nature insensible to shame, or ascribed to frivolity and heedlessness, not omitting the occasioning causes at the time. In all this the procedure is exactly the same as in the investigation of a series of determining causes of a given natural effect. But although one believes that the act was thus determined, one nevertheless blames the offender, and not on account of his unhappy natural disposition, not on account of influencing circumstances, not even on account of his former course of life, because one supposes one might leave entirely out of account what that course of life may have been, and consider the past series of conditions as having never existed, and the act itself as totally unconditioned by previous states, as if the offender had begun with it a new series of effects, quite by himself. This blame is founded on a law of reason, reason being considered as a cause which, independent of all before-mentioned empirical conditions, would and should have determined the behaviour of the man otherwise. Nay, we do not regard the causality of reason as a concurrent agency only, but as complete in itself, even though the sensuous motives did not favour, but even oppose it. The action is imputed to a man's intelligible character. At the moment when he tells the lie, the guilt is entirely his; that is, we regard reason, in spite of all empirical conditions of the act, as completely free, and the act has to be imputed entirely to a fault of reason.

Such an imputation clearly shows that we imagine that reason is not affected at all by the influences of the senses, and that it does not change (although its manifestations, that is the mode in which it shows itself by its effects, do change): that in it no state precedes as determining a following state, in fact, that reason does not belong to the series of sensuous conditions which render phenomena necessary, according to laws of nature. Reason, it is supposed, is present in all the actions of man, in all circumstances of time, and always the same; but it is itself never in time, never in a new state in which it was not before; it is *determining*, never *determined*. We cannot ask, therefore, why reason has not determined itself differently, but only why it has not differently determined the *phenomena* by its causality. And here no answer is really possible. For a different intelligible character would have given a different empirical character, and if we say that, in spite of the whole of his previous course of life, the offender could have avoided the lie, this only means that it was in the power of reason, and that reason, in its causality, is subject to no phenomenal and temporal conditions, and lastly, that the difference of time, though it makes a great difference in phenomena and their relation to each other, can, as these are neither things nor causes by themselves, produce no difference of action in reference to reason.

We thus see that, in judging of voluntary actions, we can, so far as their causality is concerned, get only so far as the intelligible cause, but not beyond. We can see that that cause is free, that it determines as independent of sensibility, and therefore is capable of being the sensuously unconditioned condition of phenomena. To explain why that intelligible character should, under present circumstances, give these phenomena and this empirical character, and no other, transcends all the powers of our reason, nay, all its rights of questioning, as if we were to ask why the transcendental object of our external sensuous intuition gives us intuition in *space* only and no other. But the problem which we have to solve does not require us to ask or to answer such questions. Our problem was, whether freedom is contradictory to natural necessity in one and the same action: and this we have sufficiently answered by showing that freedom may have relation to a very different kind of conditions from those of nature, so that the law of the latter does not affect the former, and both may exist independent of, and undisturbed by, each other.

It should be clearly understood that, in what we have said, we had no intention of establishing the *reality* of freedom, as one of the faculties which contain the cause of the phenomenal appearances in our world of sense. For not only would this have been no transcendental consideration at all, which is concerned with concepts only, but it could never have succeeded, because from experience we can never infer anything but what must be represented in thought according to the laws of experience. It was not even our intention to prove the *possibility* of freedom, for in this also we should not have succeeded, because from mere concepts *a priori* we can never know the possibility of any real ground or any causality. We have here treated freedom as a transcendental idea only, which makes reason imagine that it can absolutely begin the series of phenomenal conditions through what is sensuously unconditioned, but by which reason becomes involved in an antinomy with its own laws, which it had prescribed to the empirical use of the understanding. That this antinomy rests on a mere illusion, and that nature does *not contradict* the causality of freedom, that was the only thing which we could prove, and cared to prove.

Critique of Rational Theology[23]

There are only three kinds of proofs of the existence of God from speculative reason.

All the paths that can be followed to this end begin either from definite experience and the peculiar nature of the world of sense, known to us through experience, and ascend from it, according to the laws of causality, to the highest cause, existing outside the world; or they rest on indefinite experience only, that is, on any existence which is empirically given; or lastly, they leave all experience out of account, and conclude, entirely *a priori* from mere concepts, the existence of a supreme cause. The first proof is the *physico-theological*, the second the *cosmological*, the third the *ontological* proof. There are no more, and there can be no more.

I shall show that neither on the one path, the empirical, nor on the other, the transcendental, can reason achieve anything, and that it stretches its wings in vain, if it tries to soar beyond the world of sense by the mere power of speculation. With regard to the order in which these three arguments should be examined, it will be the opposite of that, followed by reason in its gradual development, in which we placed them also at first ourselves. For we shall be able to show that, although experience gives the first impulse, it is the transcendental concept only which guides reason in its endeavours, and fixes the last goal which reason wishes to retain. I shall therefore begin with the examination of the transcendental proof, and see afterwards how far it may be strengthened by the addition of empirical elements.

---

23. A 590-91 = B 618-19.

¶ OF THE IMPOSSIBILITY OF AN ONTOLOGICAL PROOF OF THE EXISTENCE OF GOD[24]

It is easily perceived, from what has been said before, that the concept of an absolutely necessary Being is a concept of pure reason, that is, a mere idea, the objective reality of which is by no means proved by the fact that reason requires it. That idea does no more than point to a certain but unattainable completeness, and serves rather to limit the understanding, than to extend its sphere. It seems strange and absurd, however, that a conclusion of an absolutely necessary existence from a given existence in general should seem urgent and correct, and that yet all the conditions under which the understanding can form a concept of such a necessity should be entirely against us.

People have at all times been talking of an *absolutely necessary* Being, but they have tried, not so much to understand whether and how a thing of that kind could even be conceived, as rather to prove its existence. No doubt a verbal definition of that concept is quite easy, if we say that it is something the non-existence of which is impossible. This, however, does not make us much wiser with reference to the conditions that make is necessary to consider the non-existence of a thing as absolutely inconceivable. It is these conditions which we want to know, and whether by that concept we are thinking anything or not. For to use the word *unconditioned*, in order to get rid of all the conditions which the understanding always requires when wishing to conceive something as necessary, does not render it clear to us in the least whether, after that, we are still thinking anything or perhaps nothing, by the concept of the unconditionally necessary.

Nay, more than this, people have imagined that by a number of examples they had explained this concept, at first risked as haphazard, and afterwards become quite familiar, and that therefore all further inquiry regarding its intelligibility were unnecessary. It was said that every proposition of geometry, such as, for instance, that a triangle has three angles, is absolutely necessary, and people began to talk of an object entirely outside the sphere of our understanding, as if they understood perfectly well what, by that concept, they wished to predicate of it.

But all these pretended examples are taken without exception from *judgments* only, not from *things*, and their existence. Now the unconditioned necessity of judgments is not the same thing as an absolute necessity of things. The absolute necessity of a judgment is only a conditioned necessity of the thing, or of the predicate in the judgment.

---

24. A 592-603 = B 620-31.

The above proposition did not say that three angles were absolutely necessary, but that under the condition of the existence of a triangle, three angles are given (in it) by necessity. Nevertheless, this pure logical necessity has exerted so powerful an illusion, that, after having formed of a thing a concept *a priori* so constituted that it seemed to include existence in its sphere, people thought they could conclude with certainty that, because existence necessarily belongs to the object of that concept, provided always that I accept the thing as given (existing), its existence also must necessarily be accepted (according to the rule of identity), and that the Being therefore must itself be absolutely necessary, because its existence is implied in a concept, which is accepted voluntarily only, and always under the condition that I accept the object of it as given.

If in an identical judgment I reject the predicate and retain the subject, there arises a contradiction, and hence, I say, that the former belongs to the latter necessarily. But if I reject the subject as well as the predicate, there is no contradiction, because there is nothing left that can be contradicted. To accept a triangle and yet to reject its three angles is contradictory, but there is no contradiction at all in admitting the non-existence of the triangle and of its three angles. The same applies to the concept of an absolutely necessary Being. Remove its existence, and you remove the thing itself, with all its predicates, so that a contradiction becomes impossible. There is nothing external to which the contradiction could apply, because the thing is not meant to be externally necessary; nor is there anything internal that could be contradicted, for in removing the thing out of existence, you have removed at the same time all its internal qualities. If you say, God is almighty, that is a necessary judgment, because almightiness cannot be removed, if you accept a deity, that is, an infinite Being, with the concept of which that other concept is identical. But if you say, God is not, then neither his almightiness, nor any other of his predicates is given; they are all, together with the subject, removed out of existence, and therefore there is not the slightest contradiction in that sentence.

We have seen therefore that, if I remove the predicate of a judgment together with its subject, there can never be an internal contradiction, whatever the predicate may be. The only way of evading this conclusion would be to say that there are subjects which cannot be removed out of existence, but must always remain. But this would be the same as to say that there exist absolutely necessary subjects, an assumption the correctness of which I have called in question, and the possibility of which you had undertaken to prove. For I cannot form to myself the smallest concept of a thing which, if it had been removed together with all its predicates, should leave behind a contradiction; and except contradiction, I have no other test of impossibility by pure concepts *a priori*. Against all these general arguments (which no one can object to) you challenge me with a case, which you represent as a proof by a fact, namely, that there is one, and this one concept only, in which the non-existence or the removal of its object would be self-contradictory, namely, the concept of the most real Being (*ens realissimum*). You say that it possesses all reality, and you are no doubt justified in accepting such a Being as possible. This for the present I may admit, though the absence of self-contradictoriness in a concept is far from proving the possibility of its object.[25] Now reality comprehends existence, and therefore existence is contained in the concept of a thing possible. If that thing is removed, the internal possibility of the thing would be removed, and this is self-contradictory.

I answer: Even in introducing into the concept of a thing, which you wish to think in its possibility only, the concept of its existence, under whatever disguise it may be, you have been guilty of a contradiction. If you were allowed to do this, you would apparently have carried your point; but in reality you have achieved nothing, but have only committed a tautology. I simply ask you, whether the proposition, that *this or that thing* (which, whatever it may be, I grant you as possible) *exists*, is an analytical or a synthetical proposition? If the former, then by its existence you add nothing to your thought of the thing; but in that case, either the thought within you would be the thing itself, or you have presupposed existence, as belonging to possibility, and have according to your own showing deduced existence from internal possibility, which is nothing but a miserable tautology. The mere word *reality*, which in the concept of a thing sounds different from existence in the concept of the predicate, can make no difference. For if you call all accepting or positing (without determining what it is) reality, you have placed a thing, with all its predicates, within the concept of the subject, and accepted it as real, and you do nothing but repeat it in the predicate. If, on the contrary, you admit, as every

---

25. A concept is always possible, if it is not self-contradictory. This is the logical characteristic of possibility, and by it the object of the concept is distinguished from the *nihil negativum*. But it may nevertheless be an empty concept, unless the objective reality of the synthesis, by which the concept is generated, has been distinctly shown. This, however, as shown above, must always rest on principles of possible experience, and not on the principle of analysis (the principle of contradiction). This is a warning against inferring at once from the possibility of concepts (logical) the possibility of things (real.) [Kant's note.]

sensible man must do, that every proposition involving existence is synthetical, how can you say that the predicate of existence does not admit of removal without contradiction, a distinguishing property which is peculiar to analytical propositions only, the very character of which depends on it?

I might have hoped to put an end to this subtle argumentation, without many words, and simply by an accurate definition of the concept of existence, if I had not seen that the illusion, in mistaking a logical predicate for a real one (that is the predicate which determines a thing), resists all correction. Everything can become a *logical predicate*, even the subject itself may be predicated of itself, because logic takes no account of any contents of concepts. *Determination*, however, is a predicate, added to the concept of the subject, and enlarging it, and it must not therefore be contained in it.

Being is evidently not a real predicate, or a concept of something that can be added to the concept of a thing. It is merely the admission of a thing, and of certain determinations in it. Logically, it is merely the copula of a judgment. The proposition, *God is almighty,* contains two concepts, each having its object, namely, God and almightiness. The small word *is*, is not an additional predicate, but only serves to put the predicate *in relation* to the subject. If, then, I take the subject (God) with all its predicates (including that of almightiness), and say, *God is*, or there is a God, I do not put a new predicate to the concept of God, but I only put the subject by itself, with all its predicates, in relation to my concept, as its object. Both must contain exactly the same kind of thing, and nothing can have been added to the concept, which expresses possibility only, by my thinking its object as simply given and saying, it is. And thus the real does not contain more than the possible. A hundred real dollars do not contain a penny more than a hundred possible dollars. For as the latter signify the concept, the former the object and its position by itself, it is clear that, in case the former contained more than the latter, my concept would not express the whole object, and would not therefore be its adequate concept. In my financial position no doubt there exists more by one hundred real dollars, than by their concept only (that is their possibility), because in reality the object is not just contained analytically in my concept, but is added to my concept (which is a determination of my state), synthetically; but the conceived hundred dollars are not in the least increased through the existence which is outside my concept.

By whatever and by however many predicates I may think a thing (even in completely determining it), nothing is really added to it, if

I add that the thing exists. Otherwise, it would not be the same that exists, but something more than was contained in the concept, and I could not say that the exact object of my concept existed. Nay, even if I were to think in a thing all reality, except one, that one missing reality would not be supplied by my saying that so defective a thing exists, but it would exist with the same defect with which I thought it; or what exists would be different from what I thought. If, then, I try to conceive a being, as the highest reality (without any defect), the question still remains, whether it exists or not. For though in my concept there may be wanting nothing of the possible real content of a thing in general, something is wanting in its relation to my whole state of thinking, namely, that the knowledge of that object should be possible *a posteriori* also. And here we perceive the cause of our difficulty. If we were concerned with an object of our senses, I could not mistake the existence of a thing for the mere concept of it; for by the concept the object is thought as only in harmony with the general conditions of a possible empirical knowledge, while by its existence it is thought as contained in the whole content of experience. Through this connection with the content of the whole experience, the concept of an object is not in the least increased; our thought has only received through it one more possible perception. If, however, we are thinking existence through the pure category alone, we need not wonder that we cannot find any characteristic to distinguish it from mere possibility.

Whatever, therefore, our concept of an object may contain, we must always step outside it, in order to attribute to it existence. With objects of the senses, this takes place through their connection with any one of my perceptions, according to empirical laws; with objects of pure thought, however, there is no means of knowing their existence, because it would have to be known entirely *a priori*, while our consciousness of every kind of existence, whether immediately by perception, or by conclusions which connect something with perception, belongs entirely to the unity of experience, and any existence outside that field, though it cannot be declared to be absolutely impossible, is a presupposition that cannot be justified by anything.

The concept of a Supreme Being is, in many respects, a very useful idea, but, being an idea only, it is quite incapable of increasing, by itself alone, our knowledge with regard to what exists. It cannot even do so much as to inform us any further as to its possibility. The analytical characteristic of possibility, which consists in the absence of contradiction in mere positions (realities), cannot be denied to it; but the connection of all real properties in one and the same thing is a synthesis the possibility of which we cannot judge *a priori* because these realities are not given to us as such, and because, even if this were so, no judgment whatever takes place, it being necessary to look for the characteristic of the possibility of synthetical knowledge in experience only, to which the object of an idea can never belong. Thus we see that the celebrated Leibniz is far from having achieved what he thought he had, namely, to understand *a priori* the possibility of so sublime an ideal Being.

Time and labour therefore are lost on the famous ontological (Cartesian) proof of the existence of a Supreme Being from mere concepts; and a man might as well imagine that he could become richer in knowledge by mere ideas, as a merchant in capital, if, in order to improve his position, he were to add a few noughts to his cash account.

¶ OF THE IMPOSSIBILITY OF A COSMOLOGICAL PROOF OF THE EXISTENCE OF GOD[26]

The *cosmological proof*, which we have now to examine, retains the connection of absolute necessity with the highest reality, but instead of concluding, like the former, from the highest reality necessity in existence, it concludes from the given unconditioned necessity of any being its unlimited reality. It thus brings everything at least into the groove of a natural, though I know not whether of a really or only apparently rational syllogism, which carries the greatest conviction, not only for the common, but also for the speculative understanding, and has evidently drawn the first outline of all proofs of natural theology, which have been followed at all times, and will be followed in future also, however much they may be hidden and disguised. We shall now proceed to exhibit and to examine this cosmological proof which Leibniz calls also the proof *a contingentia mundi*.

It runs as follows: If there exists anything, there must exist an absolutely necessary Being also. Now I, at least, exist; therefore there exists an absolutely necessary Being. The minor contains an experience, the major the conclusion from experience in general to the existence of the necessary.[27] This proof therefore begins with experience, and is not entirely *a priori*, or ontological; and, as the object of all

26. A 604-608 = B 632-36.
27. This conclusion is too well known to require detailed exposition. It rests on the apparently transcendental law of causality in nature, that everything *contingent* has its cause, which, if contingent again, must likewise have a cause, till the series of subordinate causes ends in an absolutely necessary cause, without which it could not be complete. [Kant's note.]

possible experience is called the world, this proof is called the *cosmological proof*. As it takes no account of any peculiar property of the objects of experience, by which this world of ours may differ from any other possible world, it is distinguished, in its name also, from the physico-theological proof, which employs as arguments, observations of the peculiar property of this our world of sense.

The proof then proceeds as follows: The necessary Being can be determined in one way only, that is, by one only of all possible opposite predicates; it must therefore be determined completely by its own concept. Now, there is only one concept of a thing possible, which *a priori* completely determines it, namely, that of the *ens realissimum*. It follows, therefore, that the concept of the *ens realissimum* is the only one by which a necessary Being can be thought, and therefore it is concluded that a highest Being exists by necessity.

There are so many sophistical propositions in this cosmological argument, that it really seems as if speculative reason had spent all her dialectical skill in order to produce the greatest possible transcendental illusion. Before examining it, we shall draw up a list of them, by which reason has put forward an old argument disguised as a new one, in order to appeal to the agreement of two witnesses, one supplied by pure reason, the other by experience, while in reality there is only one, namely, the first, who changes his dress and voice in order to be taken for a second. In order to have a secure foundation, this proof takes its stand on experience, and pretends to be different from the ontological proof, which places its whole confidence in pure concepts *a priori* only. The cosmological proof, however, uses that experience only in order to make one step, namely, to the existence of a necessary Being in general. What properties that Being may have, can never be learnt from the empirical argument, and for that purpose reason takes leave of it altogether, and tries to find out, from among concepts only, what properties an absolutely necessary Being ought to possess, i.e. which among all possible things contains in itself the requisite conditions (*requisita*) of absolute necessity. This requisite is believed by reason to exist in the concept of an *ens realissimum* only, and reason concludes at once that this must be the absolutely necessary Being. In this conclusion it is simply assumed that the concept of a being of the highest reality is perfectly adequate to the concept of absolute necessity in existence; so that the latter might be concluded from the former. This is the same proposition as that maintained in the ontological argument, and is simply taken over into the cosmological proof, nay, made its foundation, although the intention was to avoid it. For it is clear that absolute necessity is an existence from mere concepts. If, then, I say that the concept of the *ens realissimum* is such a concept, and is the only concept adequate to necessary existence, I am bound to admit that the latter may be deduced from the former. The whole conclusive strength of the so-called cosmological proof rests therefore in reality on the ontological proof from mere concepts, while the appeal to experience is quite superfluous, and, though it may lead us on to the concept of absolute necessity, it cannot demonstrate it with any definite object. For as soon as we intend to do this, we must at once abandon all experience, and try to find out which among the pure concepts may contain the conditions of the possibility of an absolutely necessary Being. But if in this way the possibility of such a Being has been perceived, its existence also has been proved: for what we are really saying is this, that under all possible things there is one which carries with it absolute necessity, or that this Being exists with absolute necessity.

¶ OF THE IMPOSSIBILITY OF THE PHYSICO-THEOLOGICAL PROOF[28]

If, then, neither the concept of things in general, nor the experience of any *existence in general,* can satisfy our demands, there still remains one way open, namely, to try whether any *definite experience,* and consequently that of things in the world as it is, their constitution and disposition, may not supply a proof which could give us the certain conviction of the existence of a Supreme Being. Such a proof we should call *physico-theological.* If that, however, should prove impossible too, then it is clear that no satisfactory proof whatever, from merely speculative reason, is possible, in support of the existence of a Being, corresponding to our transcendental idea.

After what has been said already, it will be easily understood that we may expect an easy and complete answer to this question. For how could there ever be an experience that should be adequate to an idea? It is the very nature of an idea that no experience can ever be adequate to it. The transcendental idea of a necessary and all-sufficient original Being is so overwhelming, so high above everything empirical, which is always conditioned, that we can never find in experience enough material to fill such a concept, and can only grope about among things conditioned, looking in vain for the unconditioned, of which no rule of any empirical synthesis can ever give us an example, or even show the way towards it.

If the highest Being should stand itself in that chain of conditions,

28. A 620-29 = B 649-58.

it would be a link in the series, and would, exactly like the lower links, above which it is placed, require further investigation with regard to its own still higher cause. If, on the contrary, we mean to separate it from that chain, and, as a purely intelligible Being, not comprehend it in the series of natural causes, what bridge is then open for reason to reach it, considering that all rules determining the transition from effect to 'cause, nay, all synthesis and extension of our knowledge in general, refer to nothing but possible experience, and therefore to the objects of the world of sense only, and are valid nowhere else?

This present world presents to us so immeasurable a stage of variety, order, fitness, and beauty, whether we follow it up in the infinity of space or in its unlimited division, that even with the little knowledge which our poor understanding has been able to gather, all language, with regard to so many and inconceivable wonders, loses its vigour, all numbers their power of measuring, and all our thoughts their necessary determination; so that our judgment of the whole is lost in a speechless, but all the more eloquent astonishment. Everywhere we see a chain of causes and effects, of means and ends, of order in birth and death, and as nothing has entered by itself into the state in which we find it, all points to another thing as its cause. As that cause necessitates the same further enquiry, the whole universe would thus be lost in the abyss of nothing, unless we admitted something which, existing by itself, original and independent, outside the chain of infinite contingencies, should support it, and, as the cause of its origin, secure to it at the same time its permanence. Looking at all the things in the world, what greatness shall we attribute to that highest cause? We do not know the whole contents of the world, still less can we measure its magnitude by a comparison with all that is possible. But, as with regard to causality, we cannot do without a last and highest Being, why should we not fix the degree of its perfection *beyond everything else that is possible*? This we can easily do, though only in the faint outline of an abstract concept, if we represent to ourselves all possible perfections united in it as in one substance. Such a concept would agree with the demand of our reason, which requires parsimony in the number of principles; it would have no contradictions in itself, would be favourable to the extension of the employment of reason in the midst of experience, by guiding it towards order and system, and lastly, would never be decidedly opposed to any experience.

This proof will always deserve to be treated with respect. It is the oldest, the clearest, and most in conformity with human reason. It gives life to the study of nature, deriving its own existence from it, and thus constantly acquiring new vigour.

It reveals aims and intention, where our own observation would not by itself have discovered them, and enlarges our knowledge of nature by leading us towards that peculiar unity the principle of which exists outside nature. This knowledge reacts again on its cause, namely, the transcendental idea, and thus increases the belief in a supreme Author to an irresistible conviction.

It would therefore be not only extremely sad, but utterly vain to attempt to diminish the authority of that proof. Reason, constantly strengthened by the powerful arguments that come to hand by themselves, though they are no doubt empirical only, cannot be discouraged by any doubts of subtle and abstract speculation. Roused from every inquisitive indecision, as from a dream, by one glance at the wonders of nature and the majesty of the cosmos, reason soars from height to height till it reaches the highest, from the conditioned to conditions, till it reaches the supreme and unconditioned Author of all.

But although we have nothing to say against the reasonableness and utility of this line of argument, but wish, on the contrary, to commend and encourage it, we cannot approve of the claims which this proof advances to apodictic certainty, and to an approval on its own merits, requiring no favour, and no help from any other quarter. It cannot injure the good cause, if the dogmatical language of the overweening sophist is toned down to the moderate and modest statements of a faith which does not require unconditioned submission, yet is sufficient to give rest and comfort. I therefore maintain that the physico-theological proof can never establish by itself alone the existence of a Supreme Being, but must always leave it to the ontological proof (to which it serves only as an introduction), to supply its deficiency; so that, after all, it is the ontological proof which contains the *only possible argument* (supposing always that any speculative proof is possible), and human reason can never do without it.

The principal points of the physico-theological proof are the following. 1st. There are everywhere in the world clear indications of an intentional arrangement carried out with great wisdom, and forming a whole indescribably varied in its contents and infinite in extent.

Secondly. The fitness of this arrangement is entirely foreign to the things existing in the world, and belongs to them contingently only; that is, the nature of different things could never spontaneously, by the combination of so many means, cooperate towards definite aims, if these means had not been selected and arranged on purpose by a rational disposing principle, according to certain fundamental ideas.

Thirdly. There exists, therefore, a sublime and wise cause (or many), which must be the cause of the world, not only as a blind and all-powerful nature, by means of unconscious *fecundity*, but as an intelligence, by *freedom*.

Fourthly. The unity of that cause may be inferred with certainty from the unity of the reciprocal relation of the parts of the world, as portions of a skilful edifice, so far as our experience reaches, and beyond it, with plausibility, according to the principles of analogy.

Without wishing to argue, for the sake of argument only, with natural reason, as to its conclusion in inferring from the analogy of certain products of nature with the works of human art, in which man does violence to nature, and forces it not to follow its own aims, but to adapt itself to ours (that is, from the similarity of certain products of nature with houses, ships, and watches), in inferring from this, I say, that a similar causality, namely, understanding and will, must be at the bottom of nature, and in deriving the internal possibility of a freely acting nature (which, it may be, renders all human art and even human reason possible) from another though superhuman art—a kind of reasoning, which probably could not stand the severest test of transcendental criticism; we are willing to admit, nevertheless, that if we have to name such a cause, we cannot do better than to follow the analogy of such products of human design, which are the only ones of which we know completely both cause and effect. There would be no excuse, if reason were to surrender a causality which it knows, and have recourse to obscure and indemonstrable principles of explanation, which it does not know.

According to this argument, the fitness and harmony existing in so many works of nature might prove the contingency of the form, but not of the matter, that is, the substance in the world, because, for the latter purpose, it would be necessary to prove in addition, that the things of the world were in themselves incapable of such order and harmony, according to general laws, unless there existed, even in their *substance*, the product of a supreme wisdom. For this purpose, very different arguments would be required from those derived from the analogy of human art. The utmost, therefore, that could be established by such a proof would be an *architect of the world*, always very much hampered by the quality of the material with which he has to work, not a *creator*, to whose idea everything is subject. This would by no means suffice for the purposed aim of proving an all-sufficient original Being. If we wished to prove the contingency of matter itself, we must have recourse to a transcendental argument, and this is the very thing which was to be avoided.

The inference, therefore, really proceeds from the order and design that can everywhere be observed in the world, as an entirely contingent arrangement, to the existence of a cause, *proportionate to it*. The concept of that cause must therefore teach us something quite *definite* about it, and can therefore be no other concept but that of a Being which possesses all might, wisdom, etc., in one word, all perfection of an all-sufficient Being. The predicates of a *very great*, of an astounding, of an immeasurable might and virtue give us no definite concept, and never tell us really what the thing is by itself. They are only relative representations of the magnitude of an object, which the observer (of the world) compares with himself and his own power of comprehension, and which would be equally grand, whether we magnify the object, or reduce the observing subject to smaller proportions in reference to it. Where we are concerned with the magnitude (of the perfection) of a thing in general, there exists no definite concept, except that which comprehends all possible perfection, and only the all (*omnitudo*) of reality is thoroughly determined in the concept.

Now I hope that no one would dare to comprehend the relation of that part of the world which he has observed (in its extent as well as in its contents) to omnipotence, the relation of the order of the world to the highest wisdom, and the relation of the unity of the world to the absolute unity of its author, etc. Physico-theology, therefore, can never give a definite concept of the highest cause of the world, and is insufficient, therefore, as a principle of theology, which is itself to form the basis of religion.

The step leading to absolute totality is entirely impossible on the empirical road. Nevertheless, that step is taken in the physico-theological proof. How then has this broad abyss been bridged over?

The fact is that, after having reached the stage of admiration of the greatness, the wisdom, the power, etc. of the Author of the world, and seeing no further advance possible, one suddenly leaves the argument carried on by empirical proofs, and lays hold of that contingency which, from the very first, was inferred from the order and design of the world. The next step from that contingency leads, by means of transcendental concepts only, to the existence of something absolutely necessary, and another step from the absolute necessity of the first cause to its completely determined or determining concept, namely, that of an all-embracing reality. Thus we see that the physico-theological proof, baffled in its own undertaking, takes suddenly refuge in the cosmological proof, and as this is only the ontological proof in disguise, it really carries out its original intention by means of pure reason only; though it so strongly disclaimed in the beginning all connection with it, and professed to base everything on clear proofs from experience. . . .

Thus we have seen that the physico-theological proof rests on the cosmological, and the cosmological on the ontological proof of the existence of one original Being as the Supreme Being; and, as besides these three, there is no other path open to speculative reason, the ontological proof, based exclusively on pure concepts of reason, is the only possible one, always supposing that any proof of a proposition, so far transcending the empirical use of the understanding, is possible at all.

F. Preface to Second Edition

¶ KNOWLEDGE AND FAITH[29]

We have established in the analytical part of our critique the following points:—First, that space and time are only forms of sensuous intuition, therefore conditions of the existence of things, as phenomena only; Secondly, that we have no concepts of the understanding, and therefore nothing whereby we can arrive at the knowledge of things, except in so far as an intuition corresponding to these concepts can be given, and consequently that we cannot have knowledge of any object, as a thing by itself, but only in so far as it is an object of sensuous intuition, that is, a phenomenon. This proves no doubt that all speculative knowledge of reason is limited to objects of *experience*; but it should be carefully borne in mind, that this leaves it perfectly open to us, to *think* the same objects as things by themselves, though we cannot *know* them.[30] For otherwise we should arrive at the absurd conclusion, that there is phenomenal appearance without something that appears. Let us suppose that the necessary distinction, established in our critique, between things as objects of experience and the same things by themselves, had not been made. In that case, the principle of causality, and with it the mechanism of nature, as determined by

---

29. B xxvi-xxxv (not in First Edition).

30. In order to *know* an object, I must be able to prove its possibility, either from its reality, as attested by experience, or *a priori* by means of reason. But I can *think* whatever I please, provided only I do not contradict myself, that is, provided my conception is a possible thought, though I may be unable to answer for the existence of a corresponding object in the sum total of all possibilities. Before I can attribute to such a concept objective reality (real possibility, as distinguished from the former, which is purely logical), something more is required. This something more, however, need not be sought for in the sources of theoretical knowledge, for it may be found in those of practical knowledge also. [Kant's note.]

it, would apply to all things in general, as efficient causes. I should then not be able to say of one and the same being, for instance the human soul, that its will is free, and, at the same time, subject to the necessity of nature, that is, not free, without involving myself in a palpable contradiction: and this because I had taken the soul, in both propositions, in *one and the same sense*, namely, as a thing in general (as something by itself), as, without previous criticism, I could not but take it. If, however, our criticism was true, in teaching us to take an object in two senses, namely, either as a phenomenon, or as a thing by itself, and if the deduction of our concepts of the understanding was correct, and the principle of causality applies to things only, if taken in the first sense, namely, so far as they are objects of experience, but not to things, if taken in their second sense, we can, without any contradiction, think the same will when phenomenal (in visible actions) as necessarily conforming to the law of nature, and so far, *not free*, and yet, on the other hand, when belonging to a thing by itself, as not subject to that law of nature, and therefore *free*. Now it is quite true that I may not *know* my soul, as a thing by itself, by means of speculative reason (still less through empirical observation), and consequently may not know freedom either, as the quality of a being· to which I attribute effects in the world of sense, because, in order to do this, I should have to know such a being as determined in its existence, and yet as not determined in time (which, as I cannot provide my concept with any intuition, is impossible). This, however, does not prevent me from *thinking* freedom; that is, my representation of it contains at least no contradiction within itself, if only our critical distinction of the two modes of representation (the sensible and the intelligible), and the consequent limitation of the concepts of the pure understanding, and of the principles based on them, has been properly carried out. If, then, morality necessarily presupposed freedom (in the strictest sense) as a property of our will, producing, as *a priori data* of it, practical principles, belonging originally to our reason, which, without freedom, would be absolutely impossible, while speculative reason had proved that such a freedom cannot even be thought, the former supposition, namely, the moral one, would necessarily have to yield to another, the opposite of which involves a palpable contradiction, so that *freedom,* and with it morality (for its opposite contains no contradiction, unless freedom is presupposed), would have to make room for the *mechanism* of nature. Now, however, as morality requires nothing but that freedom should only not contradict itself, and that, though unable to understand, we should at least be able to think it, there being no reason why freedom should interfere with the natural mechanism of the same act (if only taken in a different sense), the doctrine of morality may well hold its place, and the doctrine of nature may hold its place too, which would have been impossible, if our critique had not previously taught us our inevitable ignorance with regard to things by themselves, and limited everything, which we are able to *know* theoretically, to mere phenomena. The same discussion as to the positive advantage to be derived from the critical principles of pure reason might be repeated with regard to the concept of *God,* and of the *simple nature* of our *soul;* but, for the sake of brevity, I shall pass this by. I am not allowed therefore even to *assume,* for the sake of the necessary practical employment of my reason, *God, freedom,* and *immortality,* if I cannot *deprive* speculative reason of its pretensions to transcendent insights, because reason, in order to arrive at these, must use principles which are intended originally for objects of possible experience only, and which, if in spite of this, they are applied to what cannot be an object of experience, really changes this into a phenomenon, thus rendering all *practical extension* of pure reason impossible. I had therefore to deny *knowledge,* in order to make room for *faith.* For the dogmatism of metaphysic, that is, the presumption that it is possible to achieve anything in metaphysic without a previous criticism of pure reason, is the source of all that unbelief, which is always very dogmatical, and wars against all morality.

If, then, it may not be too difficult to leave a bequest to posterity, in the shape of a systematical metaphysic, carried out according to the critique of pure reason, such a bequest is not to be considered therefore as of little value, whether we regard the improvement which reason receives through the secure method of a science, in place of its groundless groping and uncritical vagaries, or whether we look to the better employment of the time of our enquiring youth, who, if brought up in the ordinary dogmatism, are early encouraged to indulge in easy speculations on things of which they know nothing, and of which they, as little as anybody else, will ever understand anything; neglecting the acquirement of sound knowledge, while bent on the discovery of new metaphysical thoughts and opinions. The greatest benefit however will be, that such a work will enable us to put an end for ever to all objections to morality and religion, according to the Socratic method, namely, by the clearest proof of the ignorance of our opponents. Some kind of metaphysic has always existed, and will always exist, and with it a dialectic of pure reason, as being natural to it. It is therefore the first and most important task of philosophy to deprive metaphysic, once for all, of its pernicious influence, by closing up the sources of its errors.

In spite of these important changes in the whole field of science, and of the *losses* which speculative reason must suffer in its fancied possessions, all general human interests, and all the advantages which the world hitherto derived from the teachings of pure reason, remain just the same as before. The loss, if any, affects only the *monopoly of the schools*, and by no means the *interests* of *humanity*. I appeal to the staunchest dogmatist, whether the proof of the continued existence of our soul after death, derived from the simplicity of the substance, or that of the freedom of the will, as opposed to the general mechanism of nature, derived from the subtle, but inefficient, distinction between subjective and objective practical necessity, or that of the existence of God, derived from the concept of an *Ens realissimum* (the contingency of the changeable, and the necessity of a prime mover), have ever, after they had been started by the schools, penetrated the public mind, or exercised the slightest influence on its convictions? If this has not been, and in fact could not be so, on account of the unfitness of the ordinary understanding for such subtle speculations; and if, on the contrary, with regard to the first point, the hope of a *future life* has chiefly rested on that peculiar character of human nature, never to be satisfied by what is merely temporal (and insufficient, therefore, for the character of its whole destination); if with regard to the second, the clear consciousness of *freedom* was produced only by the clear exhibition of duties in opposition to all the claims of sensuous desires; and if, lastly, with regard to the third, the belief in a great and wise *Author of the world* has been supported entirely by the wonderful beauty, order, and providence, everywhere displayed in nature, then this possession remains not only undisturbed, but acquires even greater authority, because the schools have now been taught, not to claim for themselves any higher or fuller insight on a point which concerns general human interests, than what is equally within the reach of the great mass of men, and to confine themselves to the elaboration of these universally comprehensible, and, for moral purposes, quite sufficient proofs. The change therefore affects the arrogant pretensions of the schools only, which would fain be considered as the only judges and depositaries of such truth (as they are, no doubt, with regard to many other subjects), allowing to the public its use only, and trying to keep the key to themselves, *quod mecum nescit, solus vult scire videri*. At the same time full satisfaction is given to the more moderate claims of speculative philosophers. They still remain the exclusive depositary of a science which benefits the masses without their knowing it, namely, the critique of reason. That critique can never become popular, nor does it need to be so, because, if on the one side the public has no understanding for the fine-drawn arguments in support of useful truths, it is not troubled on the other by the equally subtle objections. It is different with the schools which, in the same way as every man who has once risen to the height of speculation, must know both the pro's and the con's and are bound, by means of a careful investigation of the rights of speculative reason, to prevent, once for all, the scandal which, sooner or later, is sure to be caused even to the masses, by the quarrels in which metaphysicians (and as such, theologians also) become involved, if ignorant of our critique, and by which their doctrine becomes in the end entirely perverted. Thus, and thus alone, can the very root be cut off of *materialism, fatalism, atheism, free-thinking, unbelief, fanaticism,* and *superstition,* which may become universally injurious, and finally of *idealism* and *scepticism* also, which are dangerous rather to the schools, and can scarcely ever penetrate into the public. If governments think proper ever to interfere with the affairs of the learned, it would be far more consistent with their wise regard for science as well as for *society,* to favour the freedom of such a criticism by which alone the labours of reason can be established on a firm footing, than to support the ridiculous despotism of the schools, which raise a loud clamour of public danger, whenever the cobwebs are swept away of which the public has never taken the slightest notice, and the loss of which it can therefore never perceive.

BIBLIOGRAPHY

Since later parts of the Bibliography will contain references to works cited in its first section, General Works, the paragraphs of this section are numbered to permit easy reference. For example, "O'Connor (I, §2)" means: see the volume by O'Connor listed in the first section, second paragraph. Books followed by an asterisk are especially suitable for beginning study.

¶ I. GENERAL WORKS

§1. Almost every book on intellectual history and the history of philosophy must give a large amount of space to the eighteenth century, and competition among books is so keen that the level is, on the whole, very high. Among the many intellectual histories of Europe, the following are instructive and readily purchased: W. H. Coates, H. V. White, and J. S. Shapiro, *The Rise of Liberal Humanism* (New York, 1966), Ch. 7-13*; J. H. Randall, *The Making of the Modern Mind* (Boston, Revised Ed., 1940), Book III*; Crane Brinton, *A History of Western Morals* (New York, 1960), Ch. 11*; J. Bronowski and Bruce Mazlich, *The Western Intellectual Tradition* (New York, 1960), Part II*. A classical study which is still rewarding is W. E. H. Lecky, *History of the Rise and Influence of the Spirit of Rationalism in Europe* (New York, 1866, 2 vols.). Somewhat light and undependable, but exciting reading, is Egon Friedell, *Cultural History of the Modern Age* (New York, 1930-32, 3 vols.). Good materials on specific phases of eighteenth-century thought are: John Bury, *History of Freedom of Thought* (London, 1952) and *The Idea of Progress* (New York, 1932; reprint, 1955); G. H. Sabine, *A History of Political Theory* (New York, 1950), and T. I. Cook, *A History of Political Philosophy* (New York, 1957); William Cecil Dampier-Whetham, *A History of Science and its Relations with Philosophy and Religion* (New York, 1949); H. Butterfield, *The Origins of Modern Science* (London, 1949); W. P. D. Wightman, *The Growth of Scientific Ideas* (New Haven, 1933); Charles C. Gillispie, *The Edge of Objectivity* (Princeton, 1960), also on the history of science; Katherine Gilbert and H. Kuhn, *History of Esthetics* (New York, 1939).

§2. There are numerous comprehensive histories of philosophy which have lengthy studies of the eighteenth century. Each of the good ones has

its own distinctive merits. Though any selection from so rich a body of
writings is invidious, I mention three especially good works: Frederick J.
Copleston, *A History of Philosophy** (London, 1960, 1961), Vols. 5 and 6,
now available in paperback (New York, 1964), which is very comprehensive
and fair-minded but not uncritical, though the bibliographies are not without
serious blemishes; *Friedrich Uberwegs Grundriss der Geschichte der Philosophie*, Vol. 3 in the Twelfth Edition (Berlin, 1924), edited by M.
Frischeisen-Köhler and Willy Moog, which is the standard encyclopaedic
treatment of the history of philosophy, with indispensable bibliographies;
and D. J. O'Connor, ed., *A Critical History of Western Philosophy* (New
York, 1964), which includes scholarly and philosophically sophisticated
studies of most of the philosophers included in this book. Anyone interested
in the latest studies in the whole field of the history of philosophy, of course,
should make it his practice to follow the current philosophical journals,
especially the *Journal of the History of Philosophy, Journal of the History
of Ideas, Archiv für Geschichte der Philosophie*, and *Kant-Studien*. The
last two journals contain many articles in English.

§3. Intellectual histories which concentrate on the eighteenth century in
Europe are: Paul Hazard, *The European Mind 1680-1715* (London, 1953)
and *European Thought in the Eighteenth Century from Montesquieu to
Lessing* (New York, 1963), in paperback. The somewhat racy style of
these books should not obscure their depth and seriousness; Basil Willey,
The Eighteenth Century Background (Boston, 1961), in paperback, espe-
cially important to students of literature; Frank E. Manuel, *The Eighteenth
Century Confronts the Gods* (Cambridge, Mass., 1959); G. N. Newton,
Science and Social Welfare in the Age of Newton (Oxford, 1937); and
Carl Becker, *The Heavenly City of the Eighteenth Century Philosophers*
(New Haven, 1932; paperback, 1958). Becker's important study of the
Utopian and revolutionary ideals of the century has been extremely in-
fluential on all eighteenth-century scholarship. Cf. R. O. Rockwell ed., *Carl
Becker's Heavenly City Revisted* (Ithaca, 1958). Louis Kronenberger's *The
Republic of Letters* (New York, 1955) gives, in chapter ii, a good picture
of what I have called "the less seemly side" of eighteenth-century life and
thought.

§4. The principal histories of philosophy proper devoted to the eighteenth
century are: Ernst Cassirer, *The Philosophy of the Enlightenment* (Boston,
1955), in paperback, and J. G. Hibben, *The Philosophy of the Enlighten-
ment** (New York, 1910). Cassirer's book, though not restricted to Germany,
sees most of the philosophical movements in the light of their effect in
Germany. Hibben's book, though perhaps overly simple, is suitable for
beginning study; it contains a good chronological table of the principal
events of the period.

§5. The standard work on the history of British philosophy during the
period is: Sir Leslie Stephen, *English Thought in the Eighteenth Century**
(London, 1876, 2 vols.). This book is very comprehensive, and includes

much of the literary history too. L. A. Selby Bigge's *The British Moralists* (Oxford, 1897; reprint, New York, 1964) contains selections from the most important ethical works. W. R. Sorley's *History of English Philosophy** (Cambridge, 1920; reprint, 1961) and Leslie Paul's *The English Philosophers** (London, 1953) are recommended.

§6. The literature on the intellectual and strictly philosophical history of the eighteenth century in France is vast. There are two useful and inexpensive paperback anthologies in English: *French Philosophers from Descartes to Sartre*, ed. L. M. Marsak (New York, 1961), and *Les Philosophes*, ed. N. L. Torrey (New York, 1960). Strongly recommended for their comprehensiveness are: L. G. Crocker's *An Age of Crisis* and *Nature and Culture* (Baltimore, 1959 and 1963); G. R. Haven's, *The Age of Ideas** (New York, 1955; reprint, 1963); Kingsley Martin, *French Liberal Thought in the Eighteenth Century* (Boston, 1929); and J. S. Spink, *French Free Thought from Gassendi to Voltaire* (London, 1960). There is a brief but good study by Charles Frankel, *The Faith of Reason** (New York, 1948). A stimulating collection of essays by Peter Gay is *The Party of Humanity* (New York, 1963). A historical work of fundamental importance is J. P. Belin's *Le mouvement philosophique en France de 1748 à 1789* (Paris, 1913). Two generally neglected aspects of French thought are interestingly treated by R. R. Palmer, *Catholics and Unbelievers in Eighteenth-Century France* (Princeton, 1939), which gives the opponents of the *philosophes* their long-delayed day in court, and by Henry Vyvenberg, *Historical Pessimism in the French Enlightenment* (Cambridge, Mass., 1958), who corrects the exaggerated estimates of French optimism. The French materialists are considered by E. A. Gellner in O'Connor (I, §2)*.

§7. The German Enlightenment, unlike the French, has been somewhat neglected in English. W. H. Bruford, *Germany in the Eighteenth Century* (Cambridge, 1936) is the most comprehensive social and cultural history, but gives little attention to philosophical thinkers. Karl Hillebrand, *German Thought from the Seven Years' War to the Death of Goethe* (New York, 1880), though old and stuffy, is still useful. Frederick Hertz, *The Development of the German Public Mind* (London, 1962), Vol. 2, has some material of interest to the student of philosophy, but is more concerned with the development of German national self-consciousness. W. J. Bossenbrook, *The German Mind* (Detroit, 1961) is good, but somewhat brief on the Enlightenment. A. C. McGiffert, *Protestant Thought before Kant* (New York, 1911; reprint, New York, 1961) is good on the German sects and free-thinking. But the serious student of German philosophy must use the German histories, e.g., Cay von Brockdorff, *Die deutsche Aufklärungsphilosophie* (Munich, 1926) and the very detailed *Die deutsche Schulphilosophie im Zeitalter der Aufklärung* (Tübingen, 1945) by Max Wundt. H. M. Wolff, *Die Weltanschauung der deutschen Aufklärung* (Bern, 1949) is excellent on the interrelations of literature, philosophy, religion, and, to some extent, politics— matters largely untouched by von Brockdorff and Wundt. The most useful

BIBLIOGRAPHY

collections of sources are the many-volume series *Deutsche Literatur, Reihe Aufklärung,* ed. F. Brüggemann (Weimar and Leipzig, 1928 ff), *Die Aufklärung in ausgewählten Texten,* ed. Gerhard Funke (Stuttgart, 1963), and *Das Zeitalter der Aufklärung,* ed. Wolfgang Philipp (*Klassiker des Protestantismus,* Bd. 7, Bremen, 1963).

¶ II. Newton

The Mott translation of the *Principia,* from which our selection is taken, has been reprinted in many editions. The *Opticks* is now in the Dover paperback series. A good selection of texts is *Newton's Philosophy of Nature,* ed. H. S. Thayer (New York, 1953).

The best biography is L. T. More, *Isaac Newton* (New York, 1934). For beginners, E. N. Da C. Endrade, *Sir Isaac Newton** (London, 1954) is good, but perhaps too simple. Between them lies J. W. N. Sullivan's *Isaac Newton* (London, 1938). Newton's theories of space and time are examined by E. A. Burtt, *The Metaphysical Foundations of Modern Physical Science** (New York, 1927) Ch. 7; and by C. B. Garnett, *The Kantian Philosophy of Space* (New York, 1939), Ch. 2, 4. On Newton's influence, see G. Buchdahl, *The Image of Newton and Locke in the Age of Reason* (New York, 1961) and P. Brunet, *L'Introduction des théories de Newton en France au 18ᵉ siécle* (Paris, 1943).

¶ III. Locke

The *Essay Concerning Human Understanding* is readily available in two inexpensive sets: the Dover series of paperbacks, ed. A. C. Fraser, and the Everyman edition, ed. by John W. Yolton. There are good abridgments of the needlessly prolix *Essay* by A. S. Pringle-Pattison (Cambridge, 1915) and by Maurice Cranston (New York, Collier, 1964, in paperback). The most convenient edition of the political and religious writings is in Maurice Cranston's *Government, Liberty, and Reason* (New York, Collier, 1964, in paperback).

The best biography, using much new material, is also by Cranston: *Locke* (London, 1961). Yolton gives important material on Locke's predecessors and rivals in *John Locke and the Way of Ideas* (London, 1956). D. J. O'Connor has a good study* in O'Connor (I, §2). The best general studies are: R. I. Aaron, *Locke** (Oxford, 1937); James Gibson, *Locke's Theory of Knowledge and its Historical Connections** (Cambridge, 1917; new edition, 1960); and D. J. O'Connor, *Locke** (London, Pelican, 1952). Locke's influence is treated by Buchdahl (II); Kenneth MacLean, *John Locke and English Literature of the Eighteenth Century* (New Haven, 1936); S. G. Hefelbower, *The Relation of John Locke to English Deism* (Chicago, 1918); and, of course, Stephen (I, §5).

¶ IV. Berkeley

The standard edition is *The Works of George Berkeley*, ed. A. A. Luce and T. E. Jessop (London, 1948 ff., 9 vols.). There are scholarly editions of the *Principles*, the *Dialogues*, and all the works on vision by C. M. Turbayne (New York, Library of Liberal Arts, 1954-63, 3 vols.). Good one volume selections are by D. M. Armstrong (New York, Collier, 1964) and Mary W. Calkins (New York, 1928). T. E. Jessopp's *Bibliography of George Berkeley* (Oxford, 1934) has been brought up to date by C. M. Turbayne and Robert X. Ware, *Journal of Philosophy*, LX (1963), 93-112.

Biographies are by A. A. Luce, *The Life of George Berkeley* (London, 1949) and by J. M. Hone and M. M. Rossi, *Bishop Berkeley, His Life, Writings, and Philosophy* (New York, 1931). J. O. Wisdom, in *The Unconscious Origin of Berkeley's Philosophy* (London, 1953), attempts a psychoanalytic interpretation of Berkeley's immaterialism.

Sound studies of Berkeley's theory of knowledge and metaphysics are: G. Dawes Hicks, *Berkeley** (London, 1932); G. J. Warnock, *Berkeley** (London, Pelican, 1953); J. F. Thompson* in O'Connor (I, §2). D. M. Armstrong has given a penetrating study in *Berkeley's Theory of Vision* (Melbourne, 1960), which should be compared with the critical introduction by Turbayne to his edition of all of Berkeley's writings on vision. The English Berkeleian, A. A. Luce, has published three important studies in addition to the biography: *Berkeley's Immaterialism* (London, 1950), *Berkeley and Malebranche* (New York, 1934), and *The Dialectics of Immaterialism* (London, 1963). Turbayne's work, *The Myth of Metaphor* (New Haven, 1962) gives a radically new interpretation of Berkeley's work, approaching it from the standpoint of Berkeley's theory of language. John Wild's *George Berkeley* (Cambridge, Mass., 1936) is unique in the attention it gives to Berkeley's later works.

¶ V. Hume

Works of David Hume, ed. T. H. Greene and T. H. Grose (London, 1874-75, 4 vols.) is the standard edition, but has been largely superseded by the editions of the *Treatise* and *Enquiries* edited by L. A. Selby-Bigge (Oxford, 1888), often reprinted. Very good, inexpensive editions of the *Enquiry concerning Human Understanding* are by Charles W. Hendel (New York, Library of Liberal Arts, 1955) and by David C. Yalden-Thomson (Edinburgh, Nelson Philosophical Classics, 1951); of the *Enquiry Concerning the Principles of Morals* by Hendel (New York, Library of Liberal Arts, 1957) and Henry D. Aiken in *Hume's Moral and Political Philosophy* (New York, 1958); of the *Dialogues Concerning Natural Religion*, by Aiken (New York, 1948) and by Norman Kemp Smith (London, 1947; reprint, New York, Library of Liberal Arts, 1962), the last with a definitive introduction. The number of books of selections and abridgments in paperback is almost countless. The paperback volumes *Hume Selections*, ed. C. W. Hendel (New York, 1955) and *On Human Nature and Understanding*, ed. Antony Flew (New York, Collier, 1962) will be found useful. A new edition of the following useful book is needed: T. E. Jessop, *A Bibliography of David Hume and Scottish Philosophy* (London, 1938).

Biographies are J. Y. T. Greig, *David Hume* (New York, 1931); E. C. Mossner, *The Life of David Hume* (Austin, Texas, 1954); Mossner, *The Forgotten Hume* (New York, 1943).

The number of studies on Hume is immense; Hume is now the most thoroughly examined of all British philosophers. Whereas until about thirty years ago it was customary to see Hume primarily as an epistemologist who drew skeptical conclusions from Lockean beginnings (as Reid and Kant saw him), recently much more attention has been given to the positive aspects of his teaching. He has been treated more as a naturalist and humanist than as a skeptic. C. W. Hendel, *Studies in the Philosophy of David Hume** (Princeton, 1924; reprint, New York, 1962) anticipated this change in focus, and in the 1962 reprint of this book Professor Hendel gives a useful survey of the new Hume literature. Important books presenting this picture of Hume are: John Laird, *Hume's Philosophy of Human Nature** (New York, 1931), Norman Kemp Smith, *The Philosophy of David Hume** (London, 1941), John Passmore, *Hume's Intention* (Cambridge, 1952), Antony Flew, *Hume's Philosophy of Belief* (London, 1961), and Mary Shaw Kuyper, *Studies in the Eighteenth-Century Background of Hume's Empiricism* (Minneapolis, 1930). Flew also wrote the chapter on Hume* in O'Connor (I, §2). Perhaps the most instructive general introduction is by D. G. C. MacNabb, *David Hume, His Theory of Knowledge and Morality** (London, 1951). More advanced technical studies of his theory of knowledge will be found in R. W. Church, *Hume's Theory of the Understanding* (Ithaca, 1935); H. H. Price, *Hume's Theory of the External World* (Oxford, 1940); and F. Zabeeh, *Hume, Precursor of Modern Empiricism* (The Hague, 1960).

¶ VI. Reid

Works, ed. Sir William Hamilton (Edinburgh, 1895, 2 vols.). A good abridgment is by A. D. Woozley, *Reid's Essay on the Intellectual Powers of Man** (London, 1941). S. A. Grave, *The Scottish Philosophy of Common Sense* (Oxford, 1960) is a systematic, not strictly historical, presentation of the whole Scottish answer to Hume. Cf. also Andrew Seth Pringle-Pattison, *Scottish Philosophy: A Comparison of the Scottish and German Answers to Hume* (London and Edinburgh, 1885).

¶ VII. Rousseau

Oeuvres complètes, ed. B. Gagnebin and M. Raymond (Paris, 1959). *Political Writings* (in French), ed. C. E. Vaughan (Cambridge, 1915).

Translations are: *The Social Contract and Discourses* (New York, Everyman edition, 1950); *Confessions* (New York, Modern Library, n.d.); *Émile*, many editions and abridgments.

Biography using the latest materials: F. C. Green, *Jean-Jacques Rousseau, A Study of His Life and Writings** (Cambridge, 1955). Just what Rousseau stood for has been hotly debated for two centuries; the most recent controversy was begun by Irving Babbitt's *Rousseau and Romanticism* (New York and Boston, 1919). A very different picture of Rousseau from that of Babbitt was given by C. W. Hendel, *Jean-Jacques Rousseau, Moralist** (New York, 1934; paperback, New York, 1960), and Ernst Cassirer, *The Question of Jean-Jacques Rousseau** (New York, 1954; paperback, Bloomington, Indiana, 1960).

Well-balanced accounts are given also by E. H. Wright, *The Meaning of Rousseau** (London, 1929) and Harald Höffding, *Jean-Jacques Rousseau and his Philosophy** (New Haven, 1930). On Rousseau's relation to Kant, see Ernst Cassirer, *Rousseau, Kant, and Goethe** (Princeton, 1947; paperback, New York, 1963) and Klaus Reich, *Rousseau und Kant* (Tübingen, 1936). Rousseau's religious views are treated in an original way by Karl Barth, *Protestant Thought from Rousseau to Ritschl* (New York, 1959), Ch. ii.

¶ VIII. CONDILLAC

The complete works are being printed, in a splendid edition, in *Corpus general des philosophes francais* (Paris, 1947-   ). The only work in English is *Treatise on Sensations,* trans. Geraldine Carr (London, 1930).

G. Le Roy, *La psychologie de Condillac* (Paris, 1937) is a standard treatise. There is no full study of Condillac in English, but most books cited under I, §6 contain information on his work. Robert McRae, *The Problem of the Unity of Science* (Toronto, 1961), Ch. v; Charles Gillispie, *The Edge of Objectivity* (Princeton, 1960), Ch. v; and Charles Frankel, *The Faith of Reason* (New York, 1948), pp. 43-56, give good introductory studies of Condillac's theory of language, a subject that would repay careful and exhaustive study.

¶ IX. DIDEROT

Oeuvres, ed. A. Billy (Paris, 1957 ff.) is incomplete, but the most readily available edition. Much of Diderot's literary work has been translated several times, and there are three volumes of his strictly philosophical works in English: *Early Philosophical Works,* trans. M. Jourdain (Chicago, 1916); *Diderot, Interpreter of Nature,* trans. Jean Stewart and Jonathan Kemp (London and New York, 1937 and 1960, resp.); and L. G. Crocker, *Diderot, Selected Writings* (New York, Collier, 1964). The standard biography, now somewhat out of date, is by Viscount Morley, *Diderot and the Encyclopedists* (London, 1878; reprint 1923). More recent is L. G.

Crocker's *The Embattled Philosopher* (East Lansing, 1954; revised paper-back, New York, 1964). The best study of his philosophy is by Aram Vartanian, *Diderot and Descartes* (Princeton, 1953), which puts Diderot in the Descartes-Gassendi line instead of the Locke-Helvetius line of thought. A good French study is by I. K. Luppol, *Diderot, ses idées philosophiques* (Paris, 1936).

¶ X. D'HOLBACH

There is no uniform edition of his work, and little of his work is in English. *The System of Nature* (London, 1820) and *Good Sense* (New York, 1836) are both rare. A good life and survey of his work is W. H. Wickwar, *Baron de Holbach, A Prelude to the French Revolution* (London, 1935). Less interesting, but useful especially for its bibliographies, is M. P. Cushing, *Baron de Holbach* (New York, 1914). Most books cited under I, §6 contain sections on d'Holbach; Morley (IX) and Willey (I, §3) contain good chapters; also F. A. Lange's standard *History of Materialism* (London, 1957), Book I, Ch. iii. Vergil W. Topazio, *D'Holbach's Moral Philosophy* (Geneva, 1936) is excellent in contrasting d'Holbach with the other materialists, including Diderot, Helvetius, and La Mettrie.

¶ XI. VOLTAIRE

Ouevres complètes (Paris, 1877-1885, 52 vols.); *Works*, New York, 1901, 42 vols.). *Dictionaire philosophique*, a variorum edition by R. Naves (Paris, 1961) is the most useful publication of this work. There have been several translations of the *Dictionaire*, the latest being by Peter Gay (New York, 1962). *The Philosophical Letters*, translated by Ernest Dilworth (New York, 1961) is important for understanding the spread of English ideas in France. *Candide* and *Zadig* are in many editions, including Modern Library.

N. L. Torrey, *Voltaire and the English Deists* (New Haven, 1930) shows the decisive influence of the English deists on Voltaire, and W. H. Barber, *Leibniz in France* (Oxford, 1955) emphasizes Pope's and Leibniz's influence. Bernard N. Schilling, *Conservative England and the Case against Voltaire* (New York, 1950) is a revealing study of how English ideas, filtered through Voltaire, seemed dangerous at the end of the century in England. J. S. Spink is excellent on the whole Enlightenment in France, but especially complete on Voltaire.

¶ XII. LEIBNIZ

Philosophische Werke, ed. A. Buchenau and Ernst Cassirer (Leipzig, 1924-26, 4 vols.) is the most useful collected edition. The comprehensive and critical edition undertaken by the Berlin Academy was interrupted by the war and will probably not be completed. There are many volumes of

English translations, but unfortunately there is so much overlapping among them that only a small part of Leibniz' work is available in English. The most comprehensive selection of Leibniz' work is L. E. Loemker, *Leibniz. Philosophical Papers and Letters* (Chicago, 1955, 2 vols.). Also to be recommended are P. P. Wiener, *Leibniz Selections* (New York, 1951); Mary Morris, *Leibniz. Philosophical Writings* (New York, Everyman, 1934); G. R. Montgomery, *Leibniz, Basic Writings* (Chicago, 1902), in many reprints; Robert Latta, *The Monadology and Other Writings* (Oxford, 1898), in many reprints. Single works in English are *Theodicy*, trans. by E. M. Haggard (London, 1951); A. C. Langley, *New Essays Concerning Human Understanding* (Chicago, third edition, 1949), H. C. Alexander, *The Leibniz-Clarke Correspondence* (Manchester, 1953); H. W. Carr, *The Monadology* (Los Angeles, 1930); P. G. Lucas and Leslie Grint, *Discourse on Metaphysics* (Manchester, 1953; reprint, 1961).

There is no adequate biography in English. There is much biographical material, however, in J. T. Merz, *Leibniz** (1884; reprint, New York, 1948), and in Loemker, *op. cit.* R. W. Mayer, *Leibniz and the Seventeenth Century Revolution* (London, 1952) is interesting but unreliable in details. A full critical biography of Leibniz is very much needed.

Perhaps the most important book on Leibniz is Bertrand Russell's *A Critical Exposition of the Philosophy of Leibniz* (Oxford, 1900; reprint, 1958), which has been a source of many controversies. One of John Dewey's first works was a commentary, *Leibniz's New Essays Concerning Human Understanding** (1888; reprint, New York, 1961). Excellent introductory studies are by Emile Boutroux, *La philosophie allemande au 17ᵉ siècle* (Paris, 1948), Ruth L. Saw, *Leibniz** (London, Pelican, 1954) and also her essay in O'Connor* (I, §2); H. W. Carr, *Leibniz** (1929; New York, Dover reprint, 1962). More advanced are H. W. B. Joseph's *Lectures on the Philosophy of Leibniz* (Oxford, 1949), Gottfried Martin, *Leibniz. Logik und Metaphysik* (Cologne, 1960), and G. H. R. Parkinson, *Logic and Reality in Leibniz's Metaphysics* (Oxford, 1965). H. W. Barber's *Leibniz in France* (Oxford, 1955) is very instructive and interesting. On Leibniz' theory of space and his criticism of Newton most books give the basic information; especially recommended is C. B. Garnett, *The Kantian Philosophy of Space* (New York, 1939), Ch. iii, iv.

¶ XIII. WOLFF

There is no complete edition of Wolff; the critical edition, *Wolffs Deutsche und Lateinische Schriften* (Hildesheim, 1962-   ) is in its beginnings. The only Wolff available in English is *Preliminary Discourse on Philosophy in General,* trans. R. J. Blackwell (New York, Library of Liberal Arts, 1963). There is, indeed, very little on Wolff in English. There are good chapters on Wolff in E. Gilson and Thomas Langan, *History of Philosophy* (New York, 1963), and Copleston (I, §2), Vol 6. Most books cited under I, §7 have much Wolff material. W. H. Barber's *Leibniz in France* (XIII) deals with Wolff's influence on the French *philosophes,* an influence under-estimated until recently. The most complete study is probably that of Mariano Camp, *Christian Wolff e il razionalismo precritico* (Milan, 1939, 2 vols.). J. Baumann has edited a book of definitions drawn from Wolff's writings which is useful in studying the Wolffian philosophers and Kant, viz., *Wolffsche Begriffsbildungen* (Leibzig, n.d.).

¶ XIV. LESSING

Sämmtliche Schriften (Stuttgart, 1886-1924, 23 vols.) is the latest scholarly edition. Most of Lessing's dramatic works exist in several English transla-tions; *Laokoön* has recently been translated by E. A. McCormack (New York, 1962). *Lessing's Theological Works,* translated by H. Chadwick (Stanford, 1957) contains the most important philosophical works relating to religion.

Karl Aner, *Die Theologie der Lessingzeit* (Halle, 1929) is the standard treatment of Lessing and his opponents and disciples. H. B. Garland, *Lessing, the Founder of Modern German Literature* (London, 1937) is use-ful. E. Kretzschmar, *Lessing und die Aufklärung* (Leipzig, 1905) traces the development of Lessing's religious views, and comments extensively on *The Education of the Human Race.* There is a profound study of Lessing in Chapter iii of Karl Barth's *Protestant Thought from Rousseau to Ritschl* (New York, 1959). An unusually penetrating and brilliant re-creation of Lessing's character and work, by E. H. Gombrich, will be found in *Proceed-ings of the British Academy,* XLIII (1957), 133-56.

¶ XV. KANT

Gesammelte Schriften (Berlin, Akademie der Wissenschaften, 1902 ff, 23 vols.) is the standard edition. Other editions adequate for most purposes are by Ernst Cassirer (Berlin, 1914-23, 10 vols.); and Karl Vorländer (Leipzig, 1912 ff.), with several reprintings of single parts and various combinations of parts.

Most of Kant's works now exist in English translation; a uniform and complete edition is much to be desired. There are three translations of the *Critique of Pure Reason*: J. M. D. Meicklejohn (New York, Everyman edition); Max Müller (New York, 1896) now in paperback; Norman Kemp Smith (London and New York, 1929, often reprinted). The first is seriously inadequate; the Kemp Smith translation is the most accurate, but not so readable as the Max Müller, which is adequate for most purposes. (There is an abridgment of the Kemp Smith edition in the Everyman series.) There are three editions of the *Prolegomena* now in print: Paul Carus (Chicago, 1902), P. G. Lucas (Manchester, 1953), and L. W. Beck (New York, Library of Liberal Arts, 1951). Two translations of the *Critique of Practical Reason* are by T. K. Abbott (London, 1873), often reprinted, and L. W. Beck (Chicago, 1949; New York, Library of Liberal Arts, 1956).

Foundations of the Metaphysics of Morals is in the following translations: Abbott, *op. cit.*, Beck, *op. cit.*, and (New York, 1959), H. J. Paton (London, 1949). The *Critique of Judgment* has been translated by J. H. Barnard (London, 1892; New York, 1951) and by J. C. Meredith (Oxford, 1952). The *Inaugural Dissertation* is in translation by John Handyside (Chicago and Evanston, 1929). *Observations on the Feeling of the Beautiful and Sublime* is translated by T. Goldthwaite (Berkeley, 1960). *Religion within the Limits of Reason Alone* is translated by T. M. Greene and H. H. Hudson, with a fine introduction by John R. Silber (New York, 1963). Parts of the *Metaphysics of Morals* are translated by Mary Gregor (New York, 1964) and by James Ellington (New York, Library of Liberal Arts, 1964). *Perpetual Peace* is in innumerable editions. Kant's writings on natural science have been collected by William Hastie, *Kant's Cosmogony* (Glasgow, 1900); on his political theory by Hastie, *Kant's Theory of Politics* (Edinburgh, 1891); on his philosophy of history, by L. W. Beck, *Kant On History* (New York, Library of Liberal Arts, 1963). Kant's *Lectures on Ethics* and *Lectures on Education* have been translated respectively by Louis Infield (New York, 1963) and by Annette Churton (East Lansing, 1960). Selections for general use have been edited by T. M. Greene (New York, 1929) and by C. J. Friedrich (New York, Modern Library, 1949); the latter contains some minor works not easily found elsewhere, but the Introduction has some seriously misleading statements and must be used with care. R. B. Blackney's interesting effort to make Kant easily understandable by a mixture of paraphrase and translation, in *An Immanuel Kant Reader* (New York, 1960) cannot be considered successful.

There are four important reference books on Kant. Rudolf Eisler's *Kant-Lexikon* (Berlin, 1930) will remain indispensable until the new index, made on an electronic data processing machine, is issued by the Kant-Gesellschaft in Bonn. The first volume of this index, an index of names, is now available and is to be highly commended. Heinrich Ratke's *Systematisches Handlexikon zu Kants Kritik der reinen Vernunft** (Leipzig, 1929) is very useful even to those with little knowledge of German. Eric Adickes' great *Bibliography of Writings by and on Kant*, first published as supplements to *The Philosophical Review* (1893, ff.) though incomplete is essential for all studies of Kant's early influence.

There are only few biographies of Kant, perhaps because, in Heine's word. "Kant had no life." But Karl Vorländer, *Immanuel Kant der Mann und das Werk* (Leipzig, 1924, 2 vols.) should correct Heine's illusion; it is a magisterial biography. The only full biography in English is old, but still useful since not much new material has been turned up since it was published: J. H. W. Stuckenberg, *The Life of Immanuel Kant* (London, 1882).

Good introductory treatments of Kant are: S. Körner, *Kant** (Harmonasworth, Pelican, 1955), which relates Kant to modern analytic philosophy without distorting his teachings; A. D. Lindsay, *Kant** (Oxford, 1934) which is perhaps the best "traditional" interpretation; Friedrich Paulsen, *Immanuel Kant, His Life and Doctrine** (New York, 1902), also very

good but traditional. G. J. Warnock's essay* in O'Connor (I, §2) should
be consulted. Richard Kroner's *Kant's Weltanschauung** (Chicago, 1956)
defends a view of Kant which will be strange to most English readers, since
he presents the "Heidelberg" interpretation of Kant which makes his ethics
the central point of his system. It is highly recommended as a counterbalance
to other equally one-sided interpretations.

On the development of Kant's theory of knowledge and his relations
to his predecessors, there has been much good work. One should begin with
H. J. de Vleeschauwer's *The Development of Kantian Thought* (London,
1962) which recapitulates the results of his *La déduction transcendentale
dans l'oeuvre de Kant* (Amsterdam, 1934 ff, 3 vols.). The larger work
concerns almost all of Kant's writings, and the title is too restrictive. There
are two splendid studies in Italian: Mariano Campo, *La genesi del criticismo
kantiana* (Varese, 1953; 2 vols. published so far); and Giorgio Tonelli,
Elementi metodologici e metafisici in Kant dal 1745 al 1768 (Torino, 1959).
The number of "developmental" studies in German is staggering.

Commentaries and studies of the *Critique of Pure Reason* are: A. C.
Ewing, *A Short Commentary on the Critique of Pure Reason** (Chicago,
1950), which is best for beginning study; Hans Vaihinger, *Kommentar zu
Kants Kritik der reinen Vernunft* (Stuttgart, 1881, 2 vols.), which is a
monument of German thoroughness, covering only the first 57 pages of the
text!; Norman Kemp Smith, *A Commentary on Kant's Critique of Pure
Reason* (Second Edition, New York, 1950), which should be contrasted
with the strongly opposed commentary by H. J. Paton, *Kant's Metaphysic
of Experience* (New York, 1936, 2 vols.), both of which are in part suitable
for beginning study; T. D. Weldon, *Kant's Critique of Pure Reason* (Oxford,
1945; Second Edition, 1958), of which the first edition is perhaps the
better, since in the second edition the late Professor Weldon strained too
hard to deal with Kant from the point of view of linguistic philosophy;
H. W. Cassirer, *Kant's First Critique* (London and New York, 1954), which
is very uneven in quality; R. P. Wolff, *Kant's Theory of Mental Activity*
(Cambridge, Mass., 1962), a detailed study of the transcendental deduction
against the views of both Paton and Kemp Smith; Graham Bird, *Kant's
Theory of Knowledge* (London, 1962), which is in part a belated answer
to an older anti-Kantian book, H. W. Prichard's *Kant's Theory of Knowledge* (Oxford, 1909), an attack on Kant from the standpoint of English
naïve realism. In French, there is *L'Analytique transcendentale de Kant* by
A. de Coninck (Louvain and Paris, 1955) and in German, *Kommentar zur
Kritik der reinen Vernunft** by Hermann Cohen (3rd ed., Leipzig, 1920).

Against the common interpretation of Kant as the destroyer of metaphysics and hence as a precursor of positivism there has been a strong
reaction in recent German philosophy. The principal works presenting this
reaction are (besides the Kroner volume referred to above) Max Wundt,
Kant als Metaphysiker (Stuttgart, 1924); Gottfried Martin, *Kant's Metaphysics and Theory of Science* (Manchester, 1955); Martin Heidegger,
Kant and the Problem of Metaphysics (Bloomington, Indiana, 1962); and

Heinz Heimsoeth, *Studien zur Philosophie Kants* (Cologne, 1956). A radically different view is presented by Bella K. Milmed, *Kant and Current Philosophical Issues* (New York, 1961), which relates Kant to modern analytic and positivist thinkers (e.g., Reichenbach and Lewis).

Since this anthology contains writings by Kant only on theory of knowledge, it would not be appropriate to give an extensive bibliography on other phases of his philosophy. But the reader who wishes to understand Kant cannot neglect his other works entirely, and should consult some books on them. H. J. Paton's *The Categorical Imperative** (Chicago, 1948) is a commentary on the *Foundations of the Metaphysics of Morals*, and the best book on Kant's ethics. Commentaries on the other *Critiques* are: L. W. Beck, *A Commentary on Kant's Critique of Practical Reason* (Chicago, 1960), and H. W. Cassirer, *A Commentary on Kant's Critique of Judgment* (London, 1938). C. C. J. Webb and F. E. England have dealt with Kant's philosophy of religion in, respectively, *Kant's Philosophy of Religion** (Oxford, 1926) and *Kant's Conception of God* (London, 1929). C. J. Friedrich has dealt with Kant's theory of peace and war in *Inevitable Peace** (Cambridge, Mass., 1948). Mary J. Gregor has written a commentary on the *Metaphysics of Morals* under the title *The Laws of Freedom* (Oxford, 1963). Controversial works on Kant's theory of freedom, one of the central problems in his theory of knowledge and ethics, are: W. T. Jones, *Morality and Freedom in the Philosophy of Kant* (London, 1940) and A. R. C. Duncan, *Practical Reason and Morality* (Edinburgh, 1957)—the latter a commentary on the *Foundations of the Metaphysics of Morals*. Essays on various aspects of Kant's philosophy will be found in my *Studies in the Philosophy of Kant* (New York, 1965).

INDEX*

*The names of authors whose works are cited only in the Bibliography, pp. 303-15 are not included in this Index.